On the Persistence of Relationship Banking
within a Bank-Based Financial System

FINANCE, BANKING AND ACCOUNTING

Edited by Mark Mietzner

VOL. 1

PETER LANG

Katharina Sauter

On the Persistence of Relationship Banking within a Bank-Based Financial System

Post-Crisis Evidence from German SMEs

PETER LANG

Bibliographic Information published by the Deutsche Nationalbibliothek
The Deutsche Nationalbibliothek lists this publication in the Deutsche Nationalbibliografie; detailed bibliographic data is available online at http://dnb.d-nb.de.

Library of Congress Cataloging-in-Publication Data
A CIP catalog record for this book has been applied for at the Library of Congress.

Zugl.: Friedrichshafen, Zeppelin Univ., Diss., 2019

D 1141
ISSN 2698-637X
ISBN 978-3-631-80268-7 (Print)
E-ISBN 978-3-631-80477-3 (E-PDF)
E-ISBN 978-3-631-80478-0 (EPUB)
E-ISBN 978-3-631-80479-7 (MOBI)
DOI 10.3726/b16252

Peter Lang – Berlin · Bern · Bruxelles · New York · Oxford · Warszawa · Wien

This publication has been peer reviewed.

www.peterlang.com

Abstract The overall financial market environment has undergone a dramatic shift in the past few years as a result of the recent global financial crisis, associated regulatory changes, and new market participants. Against the backdrop of these changes and based on the fact that relationship lending remains an essential pillar of bank-based financial systems, an in-depth examination of this concept appears to be vital. This study undertook an online survey of 12,169 SMEs from all major sectors of the German economy between April and May 2016. We chose Germany for this study because it features a classic bank-based financial system with the traditional high significance of relationship lending. As a result, it offers a particularly strong example from which to explore changes in this relationship.

We collected a total of 576 completed and usable questionnaires. We extended our research on relationship lending by analyzing new evidence from the post-financial crisis period from a corporate perspective. The aim of this thesis is to explore the nature of lending relationships in light of the past financial crisis, the resultant structural changes, and the competition of new entrants into the financial system. We provide several important contributions. First, corporate customers wish to know how their peers are acting in the banking market and how important their bank relationships are. If banks know that relationship lending creates value from the corporate customer perspective, they may be more willing to invest in it to nurture their customer base. Second, relationship lending is essential for ensuring financial market stability. This study can offer insights into this concept for policymakers. Third, SMEs play a fundamental role in the German economy. This study can offer insights into how they differ from market-listed firms, both in their financial structure and in their financing needs. SMEs usually rely more heavily on bank financing than large companies because large firms tend to have a greater portfolio of financing options available to them such as the capital market.

Overview

Table of contents

List of figures

List of tables

List of abbreviations

AG	Corporation (Aktiengesellschaft)
AR	Argentina
BaFin	Federal Financial Supervisory Authority (Bundesanstalt für Finanzdienstleistungsaufsicht)
BCBS	Basel Committee on Banking Supervision
BIS	Bank for International Settlements
BLS	Bank lending survey by the European Central Bank
CDF	Cumulative distribution function
CEO	Chief executive officer
CH	Switzerland
CLRM	Classical linear regression model
Cov	Covariance
CZ	Czech Republic
DIP	Debtor in possession
EBA	European Banking Authority
ECB	European Central Bank
EU	European Union
EUR	EURO
GbR	Company constituted under civil law (Gesellschaft bürgerlichen Rechts)
GDP	Gross domestic product
GmbH	Limited liability company (Gesellschaft mit beschränkter Haftung)
GmbH & Co. KG	Limited partnership with a limited liability company as general partner
IRBA	Internal ratings-based approach
KfW	Kreditanstalt für Wiederaufbau
KG	Limited partnership (Kommanditgesellschaft)
KGaA	Joint-stock company (Kommanditgesellschaft auf Aktien)
KWG	German Banking Act (Kreditwesengesetz)
LPM	Linear probability model
M&A	Mergers and acquisitions
MaRisk	Minimum requirements for risk management
Max	Maximum
Min	Minimum

NSSBF	National Survey of Small Business Finances
OECD	Organisation for Economic Co-operation and Development
OHG	General partnership (Offene Handelsgesellschaft)
OLS	Ordinary least squares
PRF	Population regression function
ROE	Return on equity
SAFE	Survey on the Access to Finance of Enterprises by the European Central Bank
SD	Standard deviation
SIC	Standard industry classification
SME	Small and medium-sized enterprises
SME SF	SME supporting factor
SRF	Sample regression function
SSBF	Survey of Small Business Finances
TN	Trillions
U.K.	United Kingdom
U.S.	United States
U.S.$	United States dollar
Var	Variance
VIF	Variance inflation factor

1 Introduction

1.1 The importance and relevance of relationship banking

In recent years, the world has witnessed a rapid restructuring of the financial market and banking landscape, primarily due to the 2007-2009 worldwide financial crisis and the subsequent increase in competition. Banks are under pressure from declining profits, and many are struggling with high amounts of non-performing, or "distressed," loans. In some Southern European countries, the share of non-performing loans in certain bank portfolios is more than 45 %. Such distressed loans were one of the primary causes of the global financial crisis (Tauber 2017). Policymakers have ratcheted up the pressure on banks to reduce the number of distressed loans in their portfolios in an effort to prevent future crises. In addition to the regulatory consolidation through the Basel Accords, e.g., the implementation of leverage ratio requirements in 2013, banks are expected to take further action to reduce the risk of their day-to-day business activities (Bank for International Settlements 2014).

"In the aftermath of the recent financial crisis, many banks became either unwilling or unable to provide financing to companies. [...] This development is especially striking given the traditionally close financing relationships between German corporations and banks" (Mietzner, Schweizer, and Proelss 2018, p. 375). Moreover, corporations tried to reduce their need for bank loans in the post-crisis period (Davis and Stone 2004; Deutsche Bundesbank 2012; Nassr and Wehinger 2015). As a result of these developments, German financing methods underwent some radical shifts, particularly with respect to external financing, which was much more volatile than internal financing after the crisis.

Generally, the ratio between internal and external financing has varied sharply over time. While in the past banks were the main lenders, they have gradually lost some luster in favor of other creditors such as affiliated companies (Deutsche Bundesbank 2012; European Central Bank 2017a, 2017b). During economic downturns, companies typically resort to bank financing. Likewise, this change is also related to bank supply-side factors, such as stricter credit standards during economic downturns, and rising regulatory requirements, which have increased the relevance of alternative funding sources. The significance of bank loans, especially for small and medium-sized enterprises (SMEs), decreased. However, bank loans still represent the single most important source of external financing, despite the fact that their overall intermediation services through traditional credit business has declined (Deutsche Bundesbank 2012).

Empirical evidence shows that relationship lending, as one form of financial intermediation, created positive effects prior to the financial crisis, both for banks and firms. Personal relationships can benefit firms' credit terms and may also lead to an increase in financial flexibility. This can shield companies from financial shocks throughout macroeconomic downturns (Bolton, Freixas, Gambacorta, and Mistrulli 2016).

Karolyi (2018) finds that companies that engage in active relationship lending showed less constrained investment and were less likely to lay off employees. The author argues that, if companies had had weaker personal lending relationships during the crisis, they would have invested less. Therefore, personal lending relationships are a critical mechanism that allows companies to ease credit constraints and invest in profitable projects exactly when financing can be most difficult to attain (Karolyi 2018).

The notion of relationship lending was originally established within the context of asymmetric information between banks and borrowers. It was used in the theory of banking intermediation to justify the existence of banks. The literature also justifies the uniqueness of the bank, in contrast to other financial intermediaries, due to its capacity for reducing information asymmetries (see also Arbeitskreis Finanzierung 1988; Elsas 2001; Elsas and Krahnen 1998; Howorth and Moro 2012). Banks benefit from more intensive customer relationships as it allows them to evaluate the riskiness of their borrowers more precisely.

We note that more informationally opaque companies may gain an advantage from these relationships by obtaining better lending terms, as measured by amount, interest rate, and requests for collateral. During times of distress, they may also benefit from stronger support by their bank(s) due to their more intensive relationship with one or only a few banks. In this context, the literature highlighted an effort to define firm-bank relationship characteristics – the presence of which can actually qualify the activity of a bank as a relationship lender. Research has also explored the effects of a firm-bank relationship on collateral and on the cost and availability of credit.

Moreover, since the early 1990s the concept of relationship lending has expanded. It no longer means just being an exclusive source of financing. Instead, it is one of the key ways banks can conduct financial intermediation activities (Bolton et al. 2016; Bongini, Battista, and Nieri 2015).

Bank-related factors may also have contributed to the shift in the way companies finance themselves. For example, the temporary tightening of credit standards during the last two downturns, combined with greater regulatory requirements under the Basel Agreement, have prompted enterprises to turn to alternative forms of financing. Bongini et al. (2015) argue that the stringent rules introduced by the Basel Accords could potentially lead to a decrease in banks' incentives to invest in relationship lending. The new regulations value customer creditworthiness by means of strict rating systems. Thus, they leave no room for the consideration of soft information such as the assessment of trustworthy behavior.

At the same time, we find that the heightened intensity of global competition in the financial intermediation sector as well as the rise of FinTechs that offer alternative financing sources and services have likely aggravated the already high margin pressure in credit businesses. We posit this has prompted large, capital-market focused banks to extend their business activities in order to capture commission business and investment banking.

Finally, the reduced significance on bank loans is also evident in the maturity structure. The vast majority of funding during the 1990s was based on long-term bank loans. But the increase in loans from non-banks, notably those from other enterprises, was associated with shorter loan lives. Concurrently, we observe that, during economic downturns, cutbacks mainly seem to have affected short-term bank loans (Deutsche Bundesbank 2012).

Advancements in information and communication technology appear to have accelerated the transition from relationship-intensive services to more market- or transaction-oriented financial products. Accordingly, in the rapidly growing financial technology industry (the so-called FinTech industry) new services and business models, for instance, peer-to-peer platforms (e.g., crowdfunding, crowdlending, and block-chain applications) have emerged throughout the world, providing a variety of investment and financing opportunities to firms. These innovations have long been anticipated, but, in the aftermath of the financial crises, development accelerated.

FinTechs have been particularly adept at altering the way financial systems operate.[1] They are able to serve customer needs much more quickly, and they are

1 Dorfleitner and Hornuf (2016) point out that a general definition of the term FinTech is not possible, so it is often used to describe various market segments through a FinTech's characteristics or individual segments within the sector. The authors note further that FinTechs are generally companies that combine innovative technologies with financial services and aim to revolutionize the financial industry. Philippon (2016) writes that "Examples of innovations that are central to FinTech today include cryptocurrencies and the blockchain, new digital advisory and trading systems, artificial intelligence and machine learning, peer-to-peer lending, equity crowdfunding and mobile payment systems" (Philippon 2016, p. 2). FinTechs are active in different business segments, such as Lending & Financing, Retail Banking, Payments & Transfers, Financial Management,

not subject to the same strict regulatory frameworks, such as Basel II and Basel III, as traditional financial institutions. Furthermore, they may be attractive for opaque SMEs because they offer direct and convenient access to new funding sources.[2]

In line with Liberti and Petersen (2018), the advancements in information and communication technology have also promoted a reliance on hard rather than soft information.[3] However, the synergy between the two is fundamental to the realization of financial transactions. This is particularly true during times of distress, when a strict reliance on hard information may prevent short-term restructuring activities (see also Elsas and Krahnen 2002). These developments pose challenges to traditional banking operations such as relationship lending, which has long been the primary revenue model for savings and cooperative banks.[4]

One of the key elements of relationship lending is tacit knowledge (Howorth and Moro 2012), e.g., the establishment of trust in the bank-borrower relationship. But the changes have rendered communication between firms and banks more impersonal while also boosting the availability and facilitation of hard information. Consequently, the level of impersonality in the bank-borrower

---

Markets & Exchanges, and Insurance, with prominent companies such as "PayPal," "GObank," "Nutmeg," "Coinbase," "credible," "Even," "Moven," and "Oscar."

2 Dorfleitner and Hornuf (2016) study the FinTech sector in Germany. They collect data on the market volumes of companies for the 2007–2015 period. They identified a total of 433 FinTech companies with business activity in Germany, of which 346 were active. The remaining 87 were either not active prior to 2016 or had already discontinued their businesses. In 2015, the total market volume of FinTech companies operating in Germany in the finance and asset management segments amounted to EUR 2.2 billion. Very high growth rates have been observed in recent years in almost all FinTech segments. They thus have a growing relevance for the German banking market.

3 Petersen and Rajan (2002) showed as early as 2002 that geographical distance between small companies and their banks was increasing, which is also a critical factor in the increasing reliance on hard information.

4 The European Central Bank (ECB) provides the latest evidence on the importance of bank loans, which are at the foundation of relationship lending. The ECB conducted a Survey on the Access to Finance of Enterprises (SAFE) between March and April 2017 in the total euro area. Their sample size consisted of 11,724 enterprises. The results of the survey show that bank-related products continued to be the most relevant financing source for SMEs, compared to market-based instruments and other financing sources. From October 2016 to March 2017, 54 % of SMEs indicated bank overdrafts were their most important financing source, followed by 51 % that specified bank loans (European Central Bank 2017a). The following sections will discuss this in more detail.

relationship is increasing, putting pressure on traditional relationship lending and, therefore, on one of the most elementary forms of financing for SMEs.

Therefore, the bank-borrower relationship has been under stress and in transition beginning with the global financial crisis in 2007 (Bolton et al. 2016; Bongini et al. 2015). The importance of relationship lending and the status of bank-borrower relationships are both somewhat questionable today. Customers are more likely than ever to switch financing sources because of the increasing number of alternative methods available to them.

However, certain companies such as SMEs are particularly dependent on bank financing. SMEs tend to have distinct financial needs that stem from their small size and the nature of family ownership in general, which features a more concentrated structure. We seek here to establish the theoretical advantages of family firms. The rationale follows agency theory: Only when the interests of ownership and management are aligned as in the case with family-owned and -managed companies, will benefits be realized by the firm. When ownership and management are separate as in non-family firms, costs are necessarily borne by the firm as the two disparate parties pursue separate utility functions.

The expected advantages of family firms, however, may also carry some backlash, including inefficiency and the absence of professionalism. For the purposes of this study, we only refer to family-owned and -managed firms as family firms. Such companies have a family as their main shareholder. We examine their specific characteristics that are important to the housebank relationship and in this study we contrast them with non-family firms (Daily and Dollinger 1992). In addition, SMEs tend to have fewer resources available than larger firms to help them survive economic changes.

This study investigates relationship banking in the context of a country (Germany) with a bank-based economy. According to Antoniou, Guney, and Paudyal (2008), "the capital structure of a firm is heavily influenced by the economic environment and its institutions, corporate governance practices, tax systems, the borrower-lender relation, exposure to capital markets, and the level of investor protection in the country in which the firm operates" (Antoniou et al. 2008, p. 59). Germany has a bank-based financial system with widespread relationship lending and a solid tradition of SMEs as the backbone of the economy (Fohlin 2007).

As the engine of the economy, SMEs account for a significant proportion of gross national product. Their ability to acquire adequate funding is a critical factor in their performance, growth, and subsequent survival. Given their significant contributions to economic growth, a fuller understanding of their capital structure determinants is an important research question (Wu, Chua, and Chrisman 2007).

Firms began reevaluating their bank relationships after the financial crisis. In general, forming and maintaining strong lending relationships are not costly endeavors, but they can bring vital benefits. Firms often need to reconsider their costs and benefits during economic downturns, especially in light of the increasing number of alternative financing sources. During the crisis, many German banks needed to be recapitalized and were too overleveraged to provide external financing. SMEs faced enormous difficulties obtaining additional liquidity at the time they needed it the most (Berger, Goulding, and Rice 2014; Hochfellner, Montes, Schmalz, and Sosyura 2015; Nassr and Wehinger 2015). Hence, they began proactively exploring alternatives to financing their capital needs in order to end their reliance on bank loans as their primary source of capital.[5]

As a result and as noted earlier, the traditional perceptions of the corporate customer-bank relationship may no longer hold and the value firms assign to their bank relationships may have diminished over time. The aim of this study is to clarify the status quo of relationship lending in Germany and to investigate the economic costs and benefits of this relationship.

We use the German financial system in this study due to its historical development and institutional design. It is often described as a paradigm for a bank-based financial system where close lending relationships and intensive interactions between banks and firms (often defined as housebank relationships) have great significance. But bank loans account for the most important external financing source of non-financial corporations and for most of the external financing for households. The bank is the focus of the intermediation process between investors and borrowers, and corporate financing is primarily characterized by financing through bank loans rather than the capital market. This survey presents a useful tool for analyzing bank lending conditions in Germany. It complements current statistics on bank finance and bank lending rates with elsewise unobservable qualitative data on credit parameters in the German credit market. Moreover, since the 2007–2009 financial crisis the examination of bank lending parameters throughout Germany has gained growing attention

5 The desire by SMEs to substitute bank financing with non-bank alternatives after several banking crises is well documented for industrial countries (Davis and Stone 2004). Mietzner et al. (2018), for example, analyze whether the recently established market for mini-bonds can serve as an alternative source of financing for German SMEs.

to measure the dispersion and financial fragmentation of such conditions. In the years succeeding the financial crisis, the European Central Bank (ECB) presented an enhanced BLS (bank lending survey by the ECB) survey and a modified guide to facilitate the statistics of the developments after the crisis (Köhler-Ulbrich, Hempell, and Scopel 2016).[6]

This study analyzes a unique and comprehensive new dataset consisting of industry survey data. We use industry survey data rather than an evaluation of secondary databases because it allows us to focus on information directly related to a firm's decision-making processes concerning its financial needs. The customer's needs are critical, and this is the decisive factor that drives the banking market. Therefore, we examine the definition of relationship banking.

The literature focuses on six factors to determine housebank status: 1) whether the bank has a (relative to peer banks) large, often dominant share of the debt financing of the company, 2) whether the relationship is long-term in nature, 3) whether a special relationship of trust exists between the borrower and the bank, 4) whether the bank has an information advantage over competitive banks, 5) whether the bank performs most other financial services for the firm, and 6) whether the bank carries a special responsibility to the firm during times of financial distress. When these factors are observed, we expect to find a high probability of an existing housebank relationship (see also Elsas 2001; Boot 2000; Elsas and Krahnen 1998). We can confirm that these factors continue to hold today for the relationship between borrowers and banks.

"Given the asymmetric information between lenders and borrowers in credit markets, banks act as intermediaries to reduce the barriers to accessing credit. Thereby, they assume a key role in the financing of parts of the economy where information is opaque such as households and small firms" (Köhler-Ulbrich et al. 2016, p. 7). The prevalence of relationship banking in Germany suggests that housebanks might have greater enticements to accumulate data about borrowers that is usually proprietary in nature. They acquire information from repeated interactions with the borrower over the course of the relationship and/or across products (Greenbaum, Thakor, and Boot 2015). Moreover, bank loan contracts commonly include extensive information rights, debt covenants, and collateral requirements (Boot 2000). Hence, a widespread view is that housebanks engage in tighter creditor monitoring.

---

6 See also Deutsche Bundesbank (2009, 2011, 2012, 2014, 2015, 2016, 2017c, 2018a); Plankensteiner and Zimmermann (2009); Reize and Lo (2008); Schwartz (2016, 2017); Zimmermann (2017).

One way to reduce information asymmetries and the associated negative effects on funding terms is to send credible signals. However, signals are only credible and helpful if they lead to a separation equilibrium in the markets. It is generally more expensive (riskier) for non-creditworthy than for creditworthy firms to send such a signal (Janney and Folta 2006).

This study also takes information asymmetries into account by studying the number of bank relationships. The academic literature finds that bank-dependent borrowers are subject to the hold-up problem, which typically affects small firms. Usually, these firms are expected to have worse price conditions than non-bank-dependent borrowers. However, they are also expected to experience better non-price conditions in terms of credit availability (Stein 2014). By controlling for the number of bank relationships, the importance of the hold-up issue can be assessed.

Furthermore, ambiguous results exist about the duration of the firm-bank relationship. Kirschenmann (2016) argues that information asymmetries are resolved over the course of the firm-bank relationship. However, other authors, for instance, Elsas and Krahnen (1998) criticize the often simple assumption that the duration of a relationship reflects information intensity, and they have doubts that it results in reduced information asymmetries.

But, as Stein (2014) notes, valuable insights can result from controlling for the length of the relationship between the firm and its most important bank and how it impacts borrowing costs and credit availability. In this context, we also investigate the cross-selling aspect because we posit that a bank can learn more about its customers when they purchase other financial services from it. This aspect may be even more decisive than the length of the relationship.

Additional soft information, acquired through the personal interaction of loan officers with company managers, may be substantial in explaining the difference. In particular, this kind of information might have enabled banks to better assess company risk (D'Aurizio, Oliviero, and Romano 2015). Soft information collected by bank branches can play a pivotal role because it can be continuously updated by frequent contacts with the firm (Bolton et al. 2016). However, at the same time obtaining soft information may be costly as it requires that time and resources are spent on the relationship.

"Before the crisis, regulatory provisions played a role in shaping the optimal mix of hard and soft information for banks. The Basel II reform in 2004 recommended greater reliance on standardized criteria for gauging company default risk in order to increase cross-border banking transparency and comparability" (D'Aurizio et al. 2015, p. 287). For Italy, Albareto, Benvenuti, Mocetti, Pagnini, and Rossi (2008) show that almost all large Italian banks (as well as many others) have adopted hard information-based practices accordingly (D'Aurizio et al. 2015; Karolyi 2018). Overall, in the past years, hard information were increasingly critical in lending practices owing both to regulatory pressure and to the growth of information technology in the financial sector (D'Aurizio et al. 2015).

The problems of asymmetric information in firm-bank relationships tend to intensify banking shocks affecting some types of borrowers more than others (Bernanke and Mihov 1998). "Problems of moral hazard [...] and adverse selection [...] tend to discourage lenders from supplying credit to firms with high agency costs" (D'Aurizio et al. 2015, p. 279) (see also Holmström and Tirole 1997; Stiglitz and Weiss 1981). However, banks may acquire access to "inside" information, transmitted through repeated interactions between the loan officer and the firm's manager (Diamond 1989; Fama 1985; Petersen and Rajan 1994). Such information relates to the lending officer's subjective evaluation of the firm's creditworthiness and is commonly labeled soft (Berger and Udell 2002; Liberti and Petersen 2018). "Soft information is an important determinant of corporate lending, especially to small businesses" (D'Aurizio et al. 2015, p. 280).

Much research has also shown that soft information can mitigate the repercussions of aggregate credit contractions (De Mitri, Gobbi, and Sette 2010b; Jiangli, Unal, and Yom 2008). This is because hard information tells the loan officer about the company's past performance, and standardized risk measures help predict a company's risk profile, but soft information allows the loan officer to assess a firm's current results and future plans. Soft information allows the loan officer to be continuously updated and, thus, to better target the characteristics of the borrower in order to reduce uncertainty.

Our study further contributes to the debate over soft and hard information by examining whether moves to standardize and formalize the lending decision make soft information less valuable, e.g., the perception and role of trust. We also explore the relevance of a designated loan officer who functions as a counterpart and who balances hard and soft information in the lending decisions (Howorth and Moro 2012). In this way, we analyze whether a value-oriented strategy based on trust is of significance in lending relationships.

The aspect of having a designated loan officer in the lending relationship has long been neglected in the academic literature. In addition, due to the importance of soft information in banks' lending decisions, we study which types of companies benefit the most from an established banking relationship. To this end, we focus on heterogeneity in firms' ownership structure, namely, by contrasting family and non-family firms. Empirically, we examine whether the presence of a family mitigates credit parameters (D'Aurizio et al. 2015).

As Binks and Ennew (1997) note, credit availability is a very important element for SME development. The authors argue that more participative firms tend to receive much better quality with respect to charges and interest rates. In fact, banks may provide loans that are not profitable for the financial institution in the short run, but that could help build an advantageous long-term relationship (Boot 2000). Consequently, this relationship can lead to higher growth opportunities, which are so essential to SMEs. It is important to study the effects that impact the relationship (Di Giuli, Caselli, and Gatti 2011).

In this context, the small firm finance literature acknowledges the intermingling of firm and family resources. Research finds that many small firm owners fund their companies through their own personal savings, supplemented by family money (Zuiker, Lee, Olson, Danes, Van Guilder Dik, and Katras 2002). These financial commitments represent sacrifices not only of individual owners, but also their families. A major aspect of financial capital is the relationship between the firm and its lenders, a form of social capital. Larger banks impose indirect transaction costs on small firm borrowers because they are more likely to have loan officers with less longevity. Thus, it can be harder for small firms that depend on relationship lending to establish and maintain a deep relationship (Danes, Stafford, Haynes, and Amarapurkar 2009).

Family firms are the principal organizational structure around the world (Claessens, Djankov, Fan, and Lang 2002; Faccio and Lang 2002). From a theoretical perspective, family firms differ in several key ways from their non-family counterparts (Ampenberger, Schmid, Achleitner, and Kaserer 2013). Family firms may be perceived as more creditworthy because they are expected to have less incentive to default in the future, given their desire to pass the company on to descendants. "Therefore, even if the family status of firms is observable to all banks, only soft information gathered through personal contact with firms' managers can enable a loan officer to assess whether - for the same publicly available characteristics - a family firm is more creditworthy than a non-family one. In other words, soft information supplements hard information by revealing the possibly different objective functions of family and non-family firms" (D'Aurizio et al. 2015, p. 280).

Family firm characteristics have been regarded as a mechanism to reduce agency costs between the owners and managers of the firm (Jensen and Meckling 1976; Villalonga and Amit 2006).[7] Another perspective on the signal characteristics of family firms is control considerations. Many researchers argue that

7 Thus, one principal-agent conflict may be reduced, but others may arise. Many studies therefore focus on whether a family has a positive or a negative influence on the value

family ownership is linked with long-term commitment (Ampenberger et al. 2013; Casson 1999). At the same time, family firms avoid debt and choose higher equity ratios in an environment in which creditor monitoring is tight. But, if these firms want to grow, they may need to rely on other financing sources. Our analysis focuses on privately held family firms in Germany as they generally do not have direct market access and bank financing plays an even more important role for them.

The study asked whether family firms and their relationship management influence loan terms and banking conditions. We draw on recent attempts to identify the basis of family businesses' competitive advantage and investigate whether family-owned and -managed firms are better at building relationships with stakeholders. The academic literature finds that family firms embody incentives, authority patterns, and norms that lead to the creation of competitive advantages toward stakeholders such as banks. For our purposes, we define family firms as possessing core elements pertaining to ownership and control, family involvement in management, and the expectation or realization of family succession.

Overall, despite the dramatic changes in the financial environment that have affected the bank-borrower relationship, we expect relationship banking to exhibit a certain amount of persistence. We anticipate that the number of bank relationships, the level of trust in a firm's main bank, and the designated loan officer for the borrower play a crucial role in establishing a relationship that can significantly impact loan terms. In particular, we expect that trust and the variable loan officer will offer insights into the existence and importance of lending relationships even after the financial crisis. We posit that larger and older firms tend to obtain better credit terms and conditions, which is in line with expectations. However, especially for young start-up companies this may imply that an established banking relationship may not be as attractive, and they may need to look for more direct ways of funding.

At the same time, however, we anticipate that the most important determinants in the regression models may be the loan characteristics. Moreover, the distinction between family and non-family firms is expected to reveal interesting insights (Steijvers, Voordeckers, and Vanhoof 2010). The variable family firm is expected to generate measurable benefits that will be reflected in loan terms and conditions with housebanks. We believe it is worthwhile to study

of a company, and on whether family firms are more successful than non-family firms, which will be discussed in more detail in chapter 2.

lending relationships. On the one hand, it is economically important whether relationships can be established that will be useful for companies during uncertain times. On the other hand, banks with a relationship-oriented approach may be able to build upon this customer base by benefiting from further reduced information asymmetries.

1.2 Thesis structure

The thesis is divided into three main parts: The first (Chapter 2) provides a comprehensive literature review on relationship banking. The second (Chapter 3) describes the data and methodology including the presentation of the German-wide collected industry survey. The third (Chapter 4) presents the results of the descriptive statistics and the multivariate regression analyses.

The literature review in chapter 2 introduces the principal-agent theory in section 2.1 and places financial intermediation in the context of it in section 2.2. Section 2.3 highlights the characteristics of market- and bank-based financial systems, while the differences between relationship lending and arm's-length lending are described in section 2.4. Moreover, the German banking system and the ongoing tectonic shifts in the industry are discussed in section 2.5. Section 2.6 then explains why SMEs and family firms are such an appropriate investigation group when studying relationship banking. Finally, in section 2.7 we present our research model on relationship banking, analyze 177 articles in depth and contrast market- and bank-based financial systems, and finally derive the hypotheses based on the model in section 2.8.

Chapter 3 introduces the data and our methodology. Section 3.1 briefly outlines the different data collection methods, while section 3.2 describes the sample design, pretest, and data collection we use. Section 3.3 presents the survey design. Section 3.4 explains the endogenous variables, while section 3.5 portrays the exogenous variables. The overview of the analytical methods is drawn in section 3.6, followed by multiple robustness checks in section 3.7.

Chapter 4 then turns to the empirical evaluation. Section 4.1 discusses the findings of the descriptive statistics. The analysis includes the presentation of the firm characteristics and control variables, followed by the loan characteristics and endogenous variables. The relationship characteristics are also presented, and we draw our first indications of the differences between family and non-family firms.

Section 4.2 includes a comprehensive investigation of the endogenous variables consisting of the collateral requirements as well as collateral type, the cost of debt, and the availability of debt in the bank relationship. We also examine collateral, pricing, and the availability variables between family and non-family firms.

Chapter 5 summarizes the results of the empirical investigations. We discuss the main conclusions of the study, and the implications for entrepreneurs, the banking sector, policymakers, and scholars. In addition, the limitations of the empirical analyses as well as avenues for future research are presented.

2 Theoretical foundations

2.1 Principal-agent theory

"In the ideal world of frictionless and complete financial markets, both investors and borrowers would be able to diversify perfectly and obtain optimal risk sharing" (Freixas and Rochet 2008, pp. 15, 16). However, as soon as different levels of information arise between investors and borrowers, this ideal world is no longer attainable. If the information gap is too wide to overcome, investors may fear doing business with borrowers because of the risk of deception. This scenario suggests an intermediary may be needed to mitigate these issues and smooth transactions.

Financial intermediaries play an important role in facilitating the circulation of loanable funds between investors and borrowers (Freixas and Rochet 1997). In the following sections, we present the principal-agent relationship, describe the attendant conflicts of interest and information asymmetries, define the resulting risks, and discuss which instruments can reduce those risks as well as the importance of governance systems.

2.1.1 Principal-agent conflict

The principal-agent theory is part of the new institutional economics, which mainly goes back to the scientist Ronald Coase, who wrote about the theory of "incomplete contracts" (Coase 1937). The nature of the principal-agent conflict has been studied between shareholders and managers, (defined as principal-agent or type I) and between large and minority owners (defined as principal-principal or type II).

Jensen and Meckling (1976) present a theory of the ownership structure of a company that focuses on separation and control issues.[8] They define principal-agent theory as a contract "under which one or more persons (the principal(s)) engage another person (the agent) to perform some service on their behalf which involves delegating some decision-making authority to the agent" (Jensen and Meckling 1976, p. 308). Zeckhauser and Pratt (1991) define the agent and the principal as follows: "The individual taking the action is called the agent. The affected party is the principal" (Zeckenhauser and Pratt 1991, p. 2). The behavior of both actors is characterized by their utility maximization behavior (Zeckenhauser and Pratt 1991).

The separation of ownership and control then leads to control costs, the so-called agency costs, defined by Jensen and Meckling (1976) as the sum of: 1)

8 These sections follow Aguilera and Crespi-Cladera (2016) and Schmidt (2016).

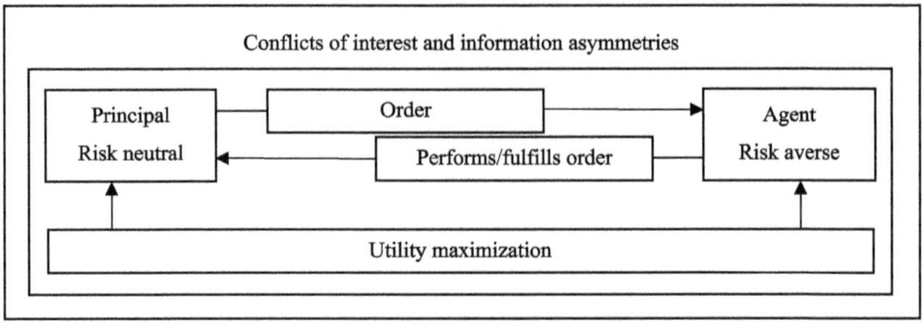

Figure 2-1: Basic model of the principal-agent relationship.

This figure shows the archetypal principal-agent relationship, with, e.g., the emerging conflicts of interest and information asymmetries, the utility maximization of both parties, and the different risk attitudes.[9]

the monitoring expenditures of the principal, 2) the expenditure costs of the agent, and 3) the residual costs. These costs reflect the ownership structure of an archetypal large, publicly traded U.S. corporation that is characterized by dispersed ownership structure and managerial decisions (Means 1991). Jensen and Meckling (1976) find that the level of agency costs depends on, among other things, statutory and common law.

If both parties, the principal and the agent, are utility maximizers, there is good reason to assume that the agent may not act on behalf of the principal, but may instead chase his own objectives. Consequently, the best possible firm performance may not be achieved. In addition, the principal-agent theory assumes different levels of risk between the principal and the agent. For example, the principal is usually classified as risk neutral, while the agent is classified as risk averse. Overall, this can result both in information asymmetries and in conflicts of interest (Alparslan 2007). Typically, the agent has an informational advantage in the decision-making process because the principal has imperfect knowledge about the agent and its characteristics. Both parties are pursuing the goal of high coverage of their personal needs. However, the principal cannot a priori assume the agent will perform the tasks assigned to him to his full satisfaction. Figure 2-1 presents a stylized illustration of the principal-agent relationship.

Note that information asymmetries, conflicts of interest, and different risk attitudes characterize the basic model of the principal-agent theory (Jost 2001). In order to reduce the loss of control, an attempt will be made to draft a contract

9 This figure follows Schmidt (2016).

that is as complete as possible. However, the complexity of everyday business operations cannot be captured in a contract, and imperfect contracts are frequently the result (Coase 1937). The principal faces the problem that, on the one hand, it is not possible to specify all the possible actions of the agent in a contract, while, on the other hand, it is not possible to fully observe the actions of the agent after the contract signing. Subsequently, risks - whether before the contract signing (adverse selection) or after the contract signing (moral hazard, hold-up) - will develop between the principal and the agent.

2.1.2 Conflicts of interest, information asymmetries, and the resulting risks

The principal wants the agent to fulfill his tasks and responsibilities as well as possible to achieve the highest possible profit. The principal wants to maximize his utility by minimizing the agent's compensation. Consequently, the agent may follow the objectives, but may try to maximize his compensation and minimize his effort (Jost 2001). To alleviate these conflicts of interest to some extent, the principal enters into a contractual relationship with the agent. The objective is to balance the competing interests and achieve compatibility (Jost 2001).

However, the risk that the principal will not know exactly what the agent has achieved or whether he has behaved in compliance with the contract yield information asymmetries (Eisenhardt 1989). Theoretically, an equal and complete information base for the principal and the agent is imaginable, but reality is far from this ideal state (Picot and Dietl 1993; Zeckhauser and Pratt 1991).

We distinguish among hidden characteristics, hidden information, hidden actions, and hidden intentions, depending on the date of origin of the information asymmetries. Hidden characteristics are "hidden properties" that exist between the principal and the agent before the conclusion of the contract (Küpper, Friedl, Hofmann, Hofmann, and Pedell 2013). Due to certain unobservable characteristics, the agent cannot be fully and accurately assessed by the principal. The resulting risk based on these information asymmetries is known as adverse selection.

In comparison, hidden information results in information asymmetries between the principal and the agent after the conclusion of the contract (Küpper 2013). At that time, both parties may have similar levels of information, but their levels may still change over time. The favor typically tilts toward the agent. Thus, in this way, the agent obtains an information advantage over the principal (Jost 2001; Küpper et al. 2013; Petersen 1989). And the level of information can change even more dramatically because the principal may not be able to gauge the exogenous factors that influence the agent's success (Alparslan 2007).

For example, there may be exogenous factors, such as private information in the context of the agent's task execution, that the principal is not aware of (Jost 2001). Due to the personal utility maximization of the agent, he will only forward information to the principal that is beneficial to himself. The resulting risk based on these information asymmetries is called moral hazard risk (Alchian and Woodward 1988; Arrow 1985; Kiener 2013; Küpper et al. 2013; Petersen 1989). Additionally, hidden actions are characterized by the fact that the principal can observe the results, but not necessarily the activities of the agent after the conclusion of the contract (Arrow 1984; Breid 1995; Picot 1991; Picot and Dietl 1993; Wenger and Terberger 1988; Wiemann 2011). In particular, the principal cannot estimate how much of the agent's efforts are due to exogenous influences. Therefore, the task execution cannot be clearly attributed to the behavior of the agent (Jost 2001).

The resulting risk based on these information asymmetries is also known as moral hazard risk. In addition, in the case of hidden intentions, the agent may follow "hidden" goals and objectives toward the principal. After signing the contract, for example, the principal cannot clearly know the agent's objectives over the course of the contractual relationship (Picot and Dietl 1993). Thus, the agent may exploit the situation and try to renegotiate (Goldberg 1980; Küpper et al. 2013).

Thus, the various types of information asymmetries can result in risks of adverse selection, moral hazard, or hold-up problems. Adverse selection refers to the selection of undesirable agents because the principal cannot observe the agent's below-average characteristics prior to the conclusion of the contract (Akerlof 1970; Küpper et al. 2013; Richter and Furubotn 2010).

In the case of adverse selection, a negative selection takes place. Akerlof (1970) uses the example of the used car market, where "good" and "bad" cars are traded. The buyer can only know the average quality of used cars, but the car salesman possesses much more detail. The buyer may decide on the price of a used car of average or poorer quality, and, as a result, providers of good used cars may withdraw from the market. Consequently, if lower-quality used cars prevail on the market, a quality loss will result (Kadan, Reny, and Swinkels 2017). Adverse selection is most commonly observed in the insurance market, the used car market, the labor market, and the banking market (Picot, Dietl, and Franck 2008).

In contrast to adverse selection, moral hazard occurs after contract signing. The properties of the agent either cannot be observed accurately by the principal, or the principal is not professionally qualified and, hence, unable to adequately judge the agent's properties (Holmström 1979; Mirrlees 1999; Picot et al. 2008). In addition, unobservable exogenous influences may impact the principal's judgment. The risk arises that the agent will try to take advantage of this leeway (Alparslan 2007; Kadan et al. 2017; Picot et al. 2008; Richter and Furubotn 2010).

The hold-up problem arises when a counterpart makes transaction-specific investments that he may later not be remunerated for because of their "sunk-cost" nature. The hold-up problem is closely linked to the incompleteness of contracts, which is due to the impossibility of writing a comprehensive contract for every feasible environmental condition (Bannier 2005; Klein, Crawford, and Alchian 1978). If the contracting parties observe opportunism with their counterparts, they will be unable to prevent it because of their dependent relationship (Picot et al. 2008). For example, the ability of a bank to observe proprietary information about a borrower creates a "lock-in" problem, because the borrower is unable to easily transfer to another lender due to switching or exit costs (Degryse and Van Cayseele 2000).

Degryse and Van Cayseele (2000) find that lock-in problems are greater for small firms, especially for more opaque borrowers and for those who have trouble finding financing alternatives (Adam and Streitz 2016). In addition, ending the bank-borrower relationship could convey a negative signal about the borrower's quality to other lenders. This implies that the main lender can use its market power over the firm to further reinforce the hold-up problem (Steijvers et al. 2010). Subsequently, the lender may even extend the lock-in effect to the full scope of the bank-borrower relationship, including all the products and services sold by the bank to the borrower. For example, through the scope of the relationship, the bank acquires better knowledge about the available assets that could be pledged as collateral (Degryse and Van Cayseele 2000). In a situation where hold-up is prevalent, the borrower may weigh the costs of changing banks carefully and may not wish to jeopardize a relationship that could be advantageous in financially difficult times (Adam and Streitz 2016).

2.1.3 Instruments to reduce risk and governance systems

There are different approaches to counteract the risks of information asymmetries. One way to minimize the risk of adverse selection within the principal-agent relationship is by trying to reduce the information gap between the two parties. With the help of signaling, a high-performing agent can try to set himself apart by convincing the principal that he has the desired features prior to contract signing (Picot et al. 2008). Moreover, the principal can try to reduce any perceived deficit by screening the characteristics of the agent prior to the conclusion of the contract (Alparslan 2007).

Screening can be done by quality reviews or performance tests (Alparslan 2007), for example, by checking the creditworthiness of the agent (Jost 2001; Picot et al. 2008; Richter and Furubotn 2010). The principal can also offer the agent various contract options (Alparslan 2007) and observe which one he chooses. According to Picot and Dietl (1993) and Alparslan (2007), the agent will select the contract of greatest benefit based on his quality characteristics. This is called self-selection, because the agent's characteristics are exposed to the principal via the contract selection. Furthermore, an incentive system could be established to compensate for the lack of assessability of the agent's work effort by the principal (Breid 1995; Picot and Dietl 1993). Generally, the higher the incentive for the agent, the greater will be his motivation to act in compliance with the principal's interests. This effectively lowers potential conflicts of interest (Alparslan 2007).

However, the use of incentive systems does not make control of the agent redundant. Effective control helps avoid wrong decisions and monitor the efficiency of an incentive system (Breid 1995). In this context, (Jensen 1986) points to the disciplinary role of debt within the scope of the free cash flow theory when trying to reduce principal-agent problems.

The free cash flow theory implies that managers with unused borrowing power and high free cash flows are more likely to undertake low-benefit or even value-destroying projects (Jensen 1986). The overinvestment is done with internal resources, meaning free cash flow, and in this way managers avoid having to raise money on the capital market.

In contrast, by issuing debt instead of equity, the shareholders/investors of a company obtain certain rights over it, because the discretionary resources under the managers' control become limited. Consequently, if managers do not act in the interest of the principal, managers can be disciplined. Therefore, debt, like dividend payments, may decrease the agency costs of free cash flow, because, according to Jensen (1986), debt is a substitute mechanism for dividends (Agrawal and Jayaraman 1994; Jensen 1986). Picot et al. (2008) emphasize that controls work best within a well-structured environment where stable, homogeneous, often identically repetitive tasks need to be fulfilled. In a dynamic environment, with a heterogeneous task situation, effective control becomes more difficult.

The design of corporate governance mechanisms typically emphasizes the mitigation and solution of the principal-agent conflict in the context of widely held companies. Shareholders of such companies typically prefer to leave monitoring activities to others, which is called the "free-rider" problem. In this context, (La Porta, Lopez-De-Silanes, Shleifer, and Vishny 1996, 1997) point to the differences in the nature and effectiveness of financial and governance systems across countries that are attributable to the differences in investor protections against expropriation by insiders, as demonstrated by legal rules and the quality of their execution.

Investor protections and their implementation vary critically and systematically around the world (La Porta et al. 1996, 1997). Because a strong legal environment protects potential financiers against expropriation by entrepreneurs, it increases their readiness to surrender funds in exchange for security, and, thus, increases the scope of financial markets. In addition, La Porta et al. (1997) find that public and private institutions are less effective in countries with low levels of trust among citizens. They conclude that broad underlying factors related to trust influence the development of laws and capital markets.

Rubach and Sebora (1998) classify the governance systems of the U.S., Germany, and Japan, and note how the systems in the U.S. and Japan differ with respect to investor protection. The U.S. system, for example, is defined by transparency, which enables investors to monitor corporations. Individual shareholders in the U.S. are considered dispersed, passive investors, with practically no control of corporate operations or aim of financial returns. The Japanese system, on the other hand, is defined by long-term relationships between investors and companies.

The cross-country differences in the ownership and control of companies are referred to as "insider" and "outsider" systems. Outsider systems are characterized by large, dispersed ownership structures; insider systems are characterized by concentrated ownership structures, where the controlling shareholders may be families, individuals, financial institutions, or other corporations. Thus, corporate governance conflicts may develop between 1) a controlling manager and "outside," widely dispersed shareholders, or 2) "inside" controlling shareholders and "outside" minority shareholders (Shleifer and Vishny, 1997). As Shleifer and Vishny (1997) conclude, "both the legal protection of investors and some form of concentrated ownership are essential elements of a good corporate governance system" (Shleifer and Vishny 1997, p. 769). Classification based on a country's legal minority investor protection differentiates between common law countries with greater legal protections and civil law countries with higher ownership concentration (La Porta, Lopez-de-Silanes, Shleifer, and Vishny 1998, 2000).

In companies with concentrated shareholding settings, the type of the agency problem is known as principal–principal (Young, Peng, Ahlstrom, Bruton, and Jiang 2008). Powerful shareholders have incentives to control and supervise managers appropriately. However, these actions can be detrimental for minority shareholders if the private benefits of control are greater than the losses. "This is when effective corporate governance mechanisms are needed to prevent actions of tunneling at the expense of the overall corporation's interests, including its minority shareholders towards the majority shareholders' interests. To control the misalignment of interests between the controlling and minority shareholders, regulators impose the fiduciary duty, and mandate an equal treatment among all shareholders" (Aguilera and Crespi-Cladera 2016, p. 53). Concentrated ownership is expected to demonstrate high long-term commitment levels, which take into account different shareholder types (e.g., families, banks, pension funds, individuals, industrial companies, etc.), exercise different interests, risk preferences, time horizons, and strategies (Aguilera and Jackson 2003, 2010). More recent literature differentiates between relational owners and transactional owners when studying the different effects on management decisions (Connelly, Tihanyi, Certo, and Hitt 2010; Desender, Aguilera, Crespi, and García-Cestona 2013; Desender, Aguilera, Lópezpuertas-Lamy, and Crespi 2016; Ma, Yiu, and Zhou 2014). Aguilera and Jackson (2003) find that relational owners are characterized by long-term performance goals. Typical relational owners are families. Transactional owners usually do not maintain a committed relationship with a firm in which they have ownership, except in the interest of gaining returns.

Several researchers have explored ownership by influential families (referred to as family firms) (Chrisman, Chua, Le Breton-Miller, Miller, and Steier 2018; Chrisman, Sharma, Steier, and Chua 2013; Schulze and Gedajlovic 2010). *The Economist* states that "family firms will remain an important feature of global capitalism for the foreseeable future" (The Economist Group Limited 2015). Such companies are largely or fully owned and managed by family member(s). They are thus relevant from both an insider and an outsider governance perspective. Accordingly, in family firms, the issue of the separation of ownership and control loses magnitude.

Nevertheless, the debate over the influence of family members is ambiguous. On the one hand, family firms display some poor social and economic outcomes when oligarchic families control large companies. But, on the other hand, family ownership and alignment with family values tends to mitigate to a certain extent the short-term perspective of the dispersed ownership of public firms (Gomez-Mejia, Cruz, Berrone, and De Castro 2011). Family firms typically pay more emphasis on long-term investments and have stronger incentives to monitor management. For example, Muñoz-Bullón and Sánchez-Bueno (2012) study data of family and non-family companies in the European Union and find that family involvement in ownership and control enhances performance (Chrisman et al. 2018).

Daily and Dollinger (1992) compare family-controlled and -managed companies with non-family firms. They document that family-controlled and -managed companies appear to have performance advantages as a result of the unification of ownership and control. According to Fama and Jensen (1983), family ownership is particularly effective at reducing agency costs. The fact that the principal-agent conflict, along with the expenditures for control, seem to arise to a lesser extent in family firms than in non-family firms generates positive performance effects (Chrisman, Chua, and Litz 2004; Gomez-Mejia, Larraza-Kintana, Moyano-Fuentes, and Firfiray 2018; Hess 2008). In addition, as family businesses are usually concentrated in the hands of a majority shareholder, these companies face a limited risk of the free-rider problem (Shleifer and Vishny 1997).[10]

Note that international corporate governance standards such as the 1999 OECD Principles of Corporate Governance (revised in 2004 and 2015) did not entirely cover the various corporate governance practices across countries, as they mainly focused on large publicly traded companies with dispersed ownership structures (OECD 1999, 2004, 2015, 2018). Global advancements in corporate governance systems are required to further improve practices. Such progress could also trigger the advancement of corporate governance systems of companies on a smaller scale. The 2015 G20/OECD Principles of Corporate Governance tried to expand beyond large publicly traded companies and to emphasize the importance of SMEs, among others, to shape corporate governance (Aguilera et al. 2016; OECD 2018). Following the theoretical foundations of the principal-agent conflict, the next sections will take a closer look at the importance of financial intermediaries.

2.2 Financial intermediation in the context of principal-agent theory

Because of the existing information asymmetries, a credit relationship is a complex contractual relationship. The debtor is better informed about his future earnings prospects than the creditor. Moreover, it is not easy for the creditor to assess how the borrower will use the provided capital. As a result, the creditor will try to become better informed about the creditworthiness of the debtor and to supervise him after the loan has been granted. Building on these considerations,

10 At this point, however, one should consider whether a company led by a founder is considered a family firm. This study leaves this question for future research. See section 2.6.2 for a discussion about the performance of family firms.

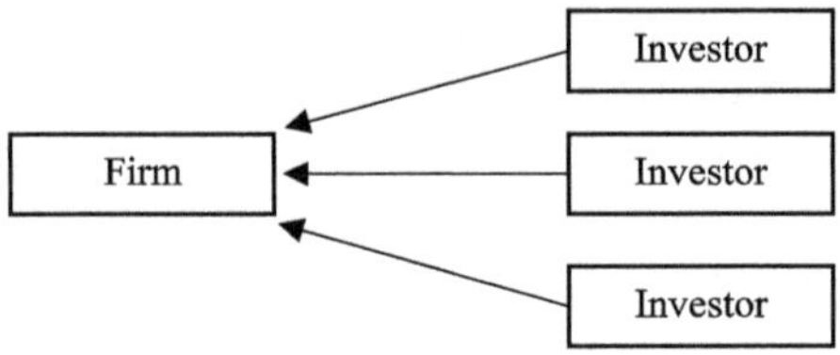

Figure 2-2: Direct finance - Each investor monitors the borrowing firm
This figure presents a stylized scenario in which each investor monitors the borrowing company without the use of a financial intermediary.

the aim of the theory of financial intermediation is to derive the existence of financial intermediaries from an asymmetric information perspective in the principal-agent relationship between investors and borrowers.

The following section explores the difficulties that can arise in bank-borrower lending (Klement 2007). We present the theory of financial intermediation first, followed by a description of the role of banks, and conclude with a discussion of the incentive problems in bank-borrower lending.

2.2.1 The theory of financial intermediation

Financial market imperfections have received a great deal of attention due to the asymmetries of information between borrowers and lenders and the incompleteness of their contracts. Banking theory assumes that information asymmetries will inhibit markets from being complete (Van Damme 1994). Diamond's (1984) theory is the basis for the explanation of financial intermediation, and it represents a fundamental contribution to the existence of banks in these markets. According to Diamond (1984), financial intermediation is "based on minimum cost production of information useful for resolving incentive problems" (Diamond 1984, p. 393). An intermediary (such as a bank) is assigned the costly monitoring of loan contracts with borrowing firms. There is a gross cost advantage for the intermediary in collecting this information, because the alternative would be either duplication, where each bank monitors the borrower directly, or the free-rider problem, where no bank monitors the borrower. Thus, financial intermediation is typically based on some cost advantages for the intermediary (Diamond 1984).

Figure 2-2 shows a stylized scenario in which each investor must monitor a borrowing firm and its investment projects without a financial intermediary (Freixas and Rochet 1997).

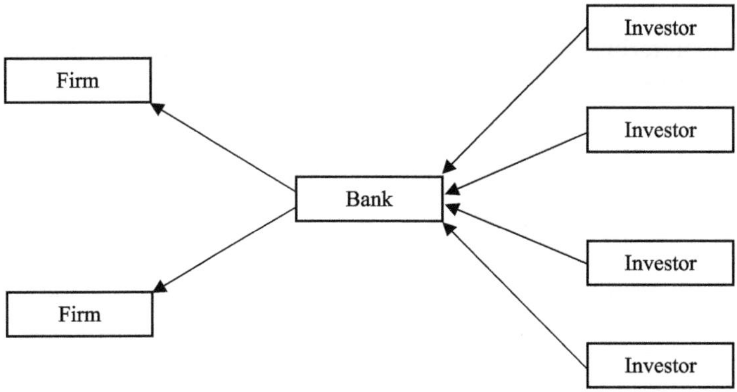

Figure 2-3: Intermediated finance - The bank monitors the borrowing firm
This figure presents a stylized scenario in which the bank performs the monitoring activities instead of individual investors.

The outcome of the investment project is not observable for the investor. Thus, divergence in information gives rise to a moral hazard problem. This problem can be approached by a financial intermediary, e.g., a bank, that is monitoring the borrowing firm and its investment projects (Freixas and Rochet 1997). Diamond (1984) states that banks as financial intermediaries have a comparative advantage in monitoring borrowers, because a bank can realize economies of scale as it usually manages many investments. This suggests that the costs for monitoring and controlling are lower than the surplus gained from the use of economies of scale in monitoring their borrowers' investment projects. Figure 2-3 shows a stylized scenario of intermediated finance, where the bank performs the monitoring activities instead of each investor.

The bank becomes, in effect, a delegate that conducts the monitoring activities of the borrowing firm in the interest of investors, hence avoiding the duplication of activities (Freixas and Rochet 1997). According to Diamond (1991), monitoring helps pinpoint borrowers who are worthy of funding. However, high-rated borrowers may not need monitoring, and low-rated borrowers have little to lose if they reveal bad news about themselves. Thus, there is no incentive for monitoring activities for low-rated borrowers.

Overall, mid-rated borrowers count on monitored bank loans because their ratings are too low for reputation effects to eliminate moral hazard, but they are high enough that monitoring can overcome it (Diamond 1991). Diamond (1991) also documents that a positive track record developed over the course of the bank loan contract will be valuable for forecasting future borrower actions without monitoring. Moreover, reputation effects may ultimately settle the moral hazard problem.

Nevertheless, the question arises as to who monitors the bank. According to Diamond (1984), the information production task delegated to the bank may lead to incentive problems, which are referred to as delegation costs. These costs may be so high that there is no net advantage for the investor to use an intermediary (Diamond 1984). The payments the bank receives from the borrowing firms are not observed by investors. Therefore, the bank could claim the payments were low, and pay out a smaller amount to investors than they should. One solution is a debt contract between the intermediary and the investor, so that the investor is promised a return. This contract provides incentives for the bank to make payments to investors.[11]

Hence, for financial intermediation to be feasible, certain conditions must be in place. First, the investor must obtain an expected return per unit deposited. Second, the intermediary, that is, the bank, must obtain an expected net return of monitoring costs and any deadweight penalties incurred, which is at least zero. In this context, diversification proves important to reduce delegation costs. Lastly, the borrowing firm must obtain an expected return that is at least as high as if it contracted directly with investors.

Financial intermediation is an advantage whenever the monitoring cost savings exceed the delegation costs of providing incentives. Thus, it is considered efficient whenever it dominates direct financing (Diamond 1984; Freixas and Rochet 1997). Cerasi and Daltung (1994) point out that, in reality, the loan officer is monitoring the firm, and thus the question arises who is monitoring the loan officer? This additional monitoring can become increasingly costly because internal delegation processes and costs increase with the size of the bank (Freixas and Rochet 1997). Nevertheless, the loan officer is usually monitored by the bank and must follow certain policies. Overall, banks are considered a means of mitigating information asymmetries between borrowers and investors (Davis 1994). The following section dissects the role of banks in more detail.

11 Calomiris and Kahn (1991) suggest that demand deposits are created. Thus, if something does not go as expected, the investor can withdraw his deposits, thereby disciplining loan officers. Holmström and Tirole (1993) propose the personal involvement of the bank in the investment projects of the borrowing firm (see also Freixas and Rochet 1997).

2.2.2 The role of banks

A bank is defined as an institution that grants loans and receives deposits. More precisely, the banking functions include access to a payment system, transfer of assets, management of risks, processing of information, and monitoring of borrowers. Nevertheless, each bank performs its activities in different ways. The combination of lending and borrowing is typical for banks. As such, they play a crucial role in resource and capital allocation (Freixas and Rochet 1997). Moreover, banks have a special role in managing the problems resulting from imperfect information by screening demands and monitoring the various investment projects. In line with Mayer (1988), the monitoring activity implies that banks and firms are building a long-term relationship in order to alleviate moral hazard problems (see also Freixas and Rochet 1997).

Gale (1992) states that the role of banks is as information gathering and information processing institutions. He uses a similar example to Akerlof (1970), whereby borrowers may face a "lemon" problem when they are trying to obtain bank credit. Some borrowers may exhibit good credit risk and know it, while others may carry bad risks they are trying to hide (Gale 1992).

Akerlof (1970) finds that "the difficulty of distinguishing good quality from bad is inherent in the business world" (Akerlof 1970, p. 500). The bank must employ information gathering and information processing methods in order to distinguish between good and bad credit risk (Gale 1992). The information produced by the intermediary may have two attributes: cross-sectional (across customers), and intertemporal (information used by means of time on a given customer) (Thakor 1995; Thakor and Wilson 1995). In addition, trust plays an important role in the business world and for facilitating transactions. Schumpeter (1934) considers bankers the doorkeepers of development and defines their role as examining possible innovators and issuing loans to the most promising ones (Van Damme 1994).

Through the lending relationship, the bank is able to obtain significant amounts of information about the borrower. With the initial screening of the borrower, and with the behavior of firm management during, for example, the repayment phase of a loan (duration), the bank is able to observe and study the borrower and acquire sensitive (proprietary) information (Degryse, Kim, and Ongena 2009; Van Damme 1994). Moreover, by the use of other services (scope), the bank's knowledge about the borrower increases, and may ultimately influence corporate (control) decision-making. The fact that banks have such broad access to confidential and proprietary information about borrowers prompted Fama (1985) to characterize them as "inside debt holders." However, the informational advantage of "inside" versus "outside" banks can impose considerable switching costs for companies once a firm decides to switch to an "outside" bank or a different lender (Degryse et al. 2009).

In this context, Bhattacharya and Thakor (1993) document that opaque firms are best served at banks because these intermediaries are most efficient at screening and monitoring potential borrowers. In addition, in Germany, smaller and less well-known firms often prefer bank financing due to the relatively high funding costs in the capital market (Bhattacharya and Thakor 1993). Such costs occur because, in order to issue outside debt, the organization must provide more public information, which is not required for inside debt (bank financing). As a result, information and contracting costs for these companies are typically lower for bank financing than for outside debt (capital market financing) (Fama 1985).

In this context, Fama (1985) highlights the difference between bank financing and capital market financing as follows: "There must be something special about bank loans that makes borrowers willing to pay higher interest rates than those on open-market securities (outside debt) of equivalent risk" (Fama 1985, p. 38). Since there is typically less competition in the banking market than in the capital market, and companies with bank financing are usually more rigid than companies with capital market financing, banks may offer higher loan pricing than they would in the capital market. Fama (1985) justifies these differences by noting that signals from short-term bank loans about an organization's creditworthiness can lower the information costs of other contracts. Thus, the renewal of short-term bank loans may provide a positive signal to market participants and other investors, who may consequently be eager to step in as well. Therefore, the bank provides a public good. If the benefits are sufficiently high, such signals are indeed optimal (Fama 1985; Van Damme 1994).

2.2.3 Incentive problems in bank lending

SMEs would rather finance business operations with bank loans than with capital market financing. Yet the information and disclosure practices of these companies sometimes make it difficult for banks to gauge their creditworthiness. With regard to adverse selection in lending, the borrower or entrepreneur knows the risks of the projects to be financed, but, because of the lack of available information, the lender may be unable to distinguish the quality of the various projects that could be carried out with the loan (hidden characteristics) prior to a contract. But the borrower now has an incentive to embellish his quality, so the lender may take this into account in his decision-making.

Because of such quality uncertainty, the lender may, for example, set the lending rate based on an average across all loans. The potential reaction of the borrower will be instructive. Borrowers with projects of above-average quality may not accept an overly expensive interest rate and will move on. Those with projects of below-average quality may accept the rate. Ex post, the lender may have initially calculated the loan rate too low. Consequently, this process of adverse selection could lead to a decline in the average quality of the projects to be financed. And, as such, the financial market becomes smaller, which can lead to complete market failure if only entrepreneurs with low quality projects remain as credit seekers (Akerlof 1970; Klement 2007).

With respect to moral hazard in lending, when the entrepreneur possesses private information after the loan granting, he has an incentive to exploit it opportunistically (hidden information). For example, the entrepreneur knows the share of the externally financed project success and the resulting project revenue. If this information is only available to the entrepreneur, he may simulate a project failure against the lender in order to claim the proceeds. If the lender correctly anticipates this behavior, he may refrain from further lending. However, if this behavior is not anticipated, the lender will need to spend money to obtain the necessary information for further projects. This is referred to as "Costly State Verification" (Attar and Campioni 2003; Gale and Hellwig 1985; Stiglitz 2000; Stiglitz and Weiss 1981).

In addition, after the loan granting, the entrepreneur may use that opportunity to influence the project's success in order to maximize his benefits at the expense of the lender's benefits (hidden actions). The lender observes the outcome, but not the actual behavior of the entrepreneur that led to the outcome. The entrepreneur may then change the probability distribution of project revenues to shift wealth in his favor (Burghof 1998; Klement 2007; Williamson 1986).

Regarding hold-up problems in lending, an additional incentive problem is based on the incompleteness of loan agreements between the lender and the borrower. It is virtually impossible for the parties to include all the eventualities of lending in a comprehensive contract (Hellwig 1991). The existence of incomplete contracts is mainly due to the extremely high costs that an all-inclusive contract would entail. Upon contract signing, the lender has decided to provide his resources to the borrower and knows that he depends on the borrower for the return of these resources. If the borrower's behavior is not in the interest of the lender, the desired behavior cannot be enforced with a contract. The entrepreneur may begin to maximize his own benefits by opportunistic behavior and may also pursue hidden goals and objectives (Henke 2002). The resulting

Table 2-1: Incentive problems in the principal-agent relationship

This table shows the problems, risks, and possible solutions to the principal-agent theory by comparison criteria.[12]

Comparison criterion	Hidden characteristics	Hidden information	Hidden actions	Hidden intentions
Date of origin	Before contract closing	After contract closing	After contract closing	After contract closing
Original cause	Ex ante hidden properties	Unobservable information level of the agent	Unobservable actions of the agent	Unobservable goals and objectives
Problem	Entering into a contractual relationship	Outcome assessment	Behavior and performance assessment	Irrevocable entering into a contractual relationship
Risk	Adverse selection	Moral hazard	Moral hazard	Hold-up
Solution	Signaling, screening, self-selection	Incentive systems and control systems	Incentive systems and control systems	Control systems

hold-up problem can again lead to a market failure, in which case no more capital by outside investors would be provided (Klement 2007).

Adam and Streitz (2016) find that hold-up issues are more likely to arise in long-term bank relationships, because they tend to develop from the information advantage that the bank acquires over the duration of the relationship. When the borrower is locked in and finds it difficult to change banks, the current bank with its improved knowledge may exploit the situation. For example, it may charge higher interest rates over the duration of the relationship (Degryse and Van Cayseele 2000). Table 2-1 presents the problems, risks, and possible solutions of the principal-agent theory with regard to hidden characteristics, information, actions, and intentions.

In the context of minimizing incentive problems, contract theory considers the optimal design of contracts between business entities. The main application of contract theory is in areas where asymmetric information creates incentive problems, for example, in the case of loan agreements (Bannier 2005). Compared to general equilibrium theory, contract theory primarily considers the strategic interactions of the decision-makers within the contract. It makes strong use of the theory of individual rationality, according to which economic subjects try

12 This table follows Schmidt (2016) and Küpper et al. (2013).

to maximize their own, but not necessarily the common, benefit. This distinction becomes particularly relevant when asymmetric information is present, because every decision-maker has a monopoly over his own information and will use it to gain an advantage. An optimal contract can address this issue by designing the contract to ensure behavioral control is achieved, leading to an optimal allocation of available resources and, under uncertainty, optimal risk sharing (Bannier 2005).

Due to the fact that it is not possible to include all exemptions and specifications in the contract, however, even basic contractual arrangements must give economic agents sufficient incentives to act in accordance with the objectives of the contract. In this context, pooling and separating equilibrium are of great importance (Bannier 2005).

According to Bannier (2005), the terms "pooling" and "separating" equilibrium refer to the behavior of the different "types" (agents). If the types differ, in that they choose different actions, this is called separating equilibrium. If it is not possible to conclude a certain type from an observed action, then pooling equilibrium is present. With respect to separating equilibrium, the less well-informed party (here: the bank) manages to oblige the agent (here: the borrower) into signaling private information truthfully. This allows the bank to differentiate between "good" and "bad" types, and to treat borrowers accordingly.

With respect to pooling equilibrium, borrowers with "bad" information can mimic other "types." Therefore, it is not possible for the bank to deduce the type of agent from a signal, and, thus, they must treat the two types the same. When the bank cannot distinguish the borrower type, they generally offer, for example, the same credit interest rate to all borrowers. In this situation, however, the "good" borrowers will not be adequately compensated, which reduces the likelihood that they will participate in the credit market, while increasing the proportion of "bad" borrowers available to the banks. It may even increase the pooling credit interest rate. Ultimately, it is possible that only "bad" borrowers will exist in the credit market.

Furthermore, during the screening process, the bank takes contractual and non-contractual approaches to reduce the information deficit regarding the properties of the borrower prior to the conclusion of the contract. This can be done by, e.g., checking the creditworthiness of the agent. In the case of self-selection, the bank first proposes a range of contracts and the borrower decides on his signal. Thus, the borrower responds to an already formulated contract design, without being able to influence it by his signal (see also Bannier 2005).

The next section discusses the characteristics of market- and bank-based financial systems first, and then contrasts the two.

2.3 Characteristics of market- and bank-based financial systems

There are two primary financial systems: market-based and bank-based. La Porta et al. (1998) differentiate between the two by applying a legal and financial view. The legal system is fundamental to forming a growth-promoting financial environment. The legal and financial view states that finance is a set of contracts, and these contracts are as effective as a country's legal system and enforcement mechanisms.

La Porta et al. (1998) also document that the differences in legal protections help clarify why companies are financed and owned in countries in different ways. They question why Germany, for example, has such a small stock market but very large and influential banks (La Porta et al. 1998; see also Edwards and Fischer 1994), as well as why ownership of large American and British companies is so broadly dispersed (Berle and Means 1932; La Porta et al. 1998).

La Porta et al. (1998) argue that the evaluation of legal rules in different countries may offer an answer to these questions. Legal rules derive from two broad traditions: common law, which comes from English law, and civil law, which originated in Roman law. Civil law countries include Germany, among others (La Porta et al. 1998). This consideration is intended to help understand why systems have developed in a certain way, and why the financing of companies around the world differs so significantly.

Empirical research on the virtues of market- and bank-based financial systems has tended to focus on the U.S. and the U.K. as market-based systems, and on Germany and Japan as bank-based systems (Elsas and Krahnen 2003; Levine 2002). The success of market-based systems in the U.S. and the U.K. has prompted some observers to stress their importance; others support bank-based systems because of their crucial role in German and Japanese industrialization (Chakraborty and Ray 2006). Overall, Demirgüç-Kunt and Levine (1999) document that banks, other financial intermediaries, and capital markets grow and become more active and efficient as nations become wealthier. This indicates that income growth and the development of the financial sector tend to develop in tandem.

2.3.1 Market-based financial systems

Financial systems tend to be more market-based in higher income countries, where stock markets are more active and efficient than banks. Additionally, financial systems tend to be more market-based, even after controlling for income, in countries with strong shareholder rights protection, good accounting standards, low levels of corruption, and no explicit deposit insurance (Demirgüç-Kunt and Levine 1999). The U.S. and the U.K. prefer equity trading and financing by the capital market, with the explanation being that traditionally they had more advanced accounting systems and more regulations in favor of shareholder rights (Allen and Gale 2000; Levine 2005).

As La Porta et al. (1998) put it, legal rules differ across countries due to differences in their legal origin. Civil laws traditionally provide investors with weaker legal rights than common laws. Common law countries provide shareholders and creditors, comparatively, with the strongest protections. French civil law countries tend to have the weakest protections, while German civil law countries and Scandinavian countries usually fall between the two. According to La Porta et al. (1998), Germany generally has the highest quality of legal enforcements, followed by common law countries such as the U.S. and the U.K. (La Porta et al. 1998).

One of the determinants of differences in legal protections is a high ownership structure. La Porta et al. (1998) note that some concentration of ownership of a company's shares is usually sufficient to give managers incentives to fulfill their responsibilities, because large investors are more efficient at controlling those managers (Jensen and Meckling 1976; Shleifer and Vishny 1986). Yet, some dispersion of ownership is important for risk diversification.

Shleifer and Vishny (1997) find that a very high ownership concentration may reflect poorer investor protection. The authors document a significant negative correlation between ownership concentration, as measured by the combined stake of the three largest shareholders, and the quality of investor legal protection. Their findings hence support the notion that legal systems are a key element for corporate governance systems, and that companies must adjust to the constraints of the legal environment in which they work (La Porta et al. 1998).

Thus, in the U.S. and the U.K., the capital markets are the focus, and observers stress that markets offer critical financial services, such as evaluating potential investment opportunities, exercising corporate control, facilitating risk management, increasing liquidity, and easing savings mobilization, while also stimulating innovation and long-run growth. In addition, markets usually alleviate the problems linked to extremely powerful banks (Demirgüç-Kunt and Levine 1999; Levine 2002).

Holmström and Tirole (1993) emphasize the growth-enhancing role of well-functioning markets in promoting greater incentives to research companies because it is easier to benefit from this data by trading in big liquid markets. Moreover, Jensen and Murphy (1990) highlight the enhanced corporate governance role by easing takeovers and tying managerial compensation to firm performance. Control occurs by the valuation of shares and by acquisitions (Metten 2010; Sachverständigenrat zur Begutachtung der Gesamtwirtschaftlichen Entwicklung 2005). Thus, U.S. studies often focus on the importance of market takeovers as corporate control devices (Jensen 1986). Furthermore, Levine (1991) and Obstfeld (1994) stress that liquid markets facilitate risk management.

Observers of market-based financial systems point to certain problems associated with banks, however. For example, powerful banks can slow down firm innovation by extracting informational rents and shielding companies with close firm-bank relationships from competition (Levine 2002; Rajan 1992). "In contrast, competitive capital markets play a positive role in aggregating diffuse information signals and effectively transmitting this information to investors, with beneficial implications for firm financing and economic performance" (Levine 2002, p. 400). In addition, in a market-based financial system, better adaptability may be possible due to increased competition (Metten 2010; Sachverständigenrat zur Begutachtung der Gesamtwirtschaftlichen Entwicklung 2005). Following this line of reasoning, advocates of these systems emphasize that capital markets can decrease the intrinsic inefficiencies associated with banks while increasing economic growth (Levine 2002).

Chakraborty and Ray (2006) state that more profitable companies depend more on market financing because they face a smaller information gap. However, if agency problems become severe, information inefficiencies may occur, and may lead to credit rationing due to information asymmetries between borrowers and lenders (Metten 2010; Sachverständigenrat zur Begutachtung der Gesamtwirtschaftlichen Entwicklung 2005). Overall, developed countries and higher-income countries are more likely than developing countries to feature market-based financial systems because the financial sophistication (financial literacy) of households and firms rises as economic development increases. This enriches demand for services linked to the capital market (Allen and Gale 2000; Levine 2005).

2.3.2 Bank-based financial systems

Financial systems are generally bank-based in countries such as Germany, Italy, and Japan, because banks play a larger role overall. Since the 19th century, many economists have claimed that bank-based financial systems are better at mobilizing savings, overseeing the investment decisions of corporate managers, recognizing good investment opportunities, and providing risk management vehicles, especially during the early stages of economic growth and in weak institutional settings (Demirgüç-Kunt and Levine 1999; Levine 2002). Proponents of bank-based systems emphasize the positive role of banks in obtaining information about the firm itself and the firm's managers, which can enhance capital allocation and corporate governance (Diamond 1984; Ramakrishnan and Thakor 1984). For example, banks can mobilize capital to benefit from economies of scale (Sirri and Tufano 1995). They are also better at managing cross-sectional, intertemporal, and liquidity risk, and, as a consequence, enhancing investment efficiency and economic growth (Allen and Gale 1999; Bencivenga and Smith 1991; Levine 2002).

Advocates of bank-based financial systems also point out some deficiencies of market-based systems. Stiglitz (1985), for example, states that well-developed markets rapidly and publicly disclose information, which decreases the motivation for individual investors to gather information. In this way, all kinds of information may enter the public, and may lead to diffuse information provision. Banks alleviate this problem by typically establishing long-term relationships with companies, collecting and evaluating information over time, and not disclosing information immediately in public markets (Boot, Greenbaum, and Thakor 1993). Boot and Thakor (1997) call banks coalitions of agents who coordinate their actions to improve monitoring of companies, thus reducing moral hazard (see also Boyd and Prescott 1986).

Moreover, proponents emphasize that liquid markets may lead to a short-sighted investor environment. This is because investors can easily sell their shares, so incentives are low to exercise thorough corporate control (Bhide 1993). Consequently, and in compliance with the bank-based view, systematic control may not be exercised well in market-based systems. Powerful banks, versus anonymous markets, can also better push firms to repay their debts, particularly in countries with deficient regulatory bodies. Therefore, in countries with weak financial institutions, external investors may be unwilling to finance, e.g., industrial development in the absence of banks that would typically control firm repayments (see also La Porta et al. 1998).

Bank-based financial systems operate under the assumption that banks can exploit economies of scale in information processing, resolve moral hazard through effective monitoring, and establish long-term relationships with companies to mitigate asymmetric information. In doing so, they enhance economic development and growth (Gerschenkron 1962; Rajan and Zingales 1998). Chakraborty and Hu (2006) find that bank-based systems are preferable to market-based systems because banks are better able to transform a traditional economy into a modern one. A key determinant of financing choices is a company's wealth and profitability. Less profitable companies usually have more incentives than more profitable ones to be self-serving. Banks can alleviate

Table 2-2: Structure of outstanding liabilities of non-financial corporations in Germany

This table shows the outstanding liabilities of non-financial corporations as of the end of selected years within the observation period.[13]

End-of-year levels	**1991**	**1995**	**2000**	**2005**	**2010**
Liabilities in € billions	2,042	2,519	3,891	3,944	4,718
	As a percentage of total liabilities				
Securities other than shares	1.8	2.3	1.4	2.7	3.1
Loans of these	38.1	35.5	29.3	30.3	31.8
From MFIs[14]	32.0	28.6	22.7	20.9	18.0
From non-MFIs	6.1	6.9	6.6	9.4	13.8
Insurance technical reserves	5.7	5.6	4.3	5.2	4.8
Other liabilities of these	24.4	21.2	17.0	17.6	17.8
Trade credits and advances	17.1	14.8	10.5	11.3	12.1
Shares[15] and other	30.0	35.6	48.0	44.1	42.6

such incentive problems by charging higher interest rates and establishing relationships to better monitor borrowers.

With respect to Germany and its historical development and institutional design, the German financial system is considered a typical bank-based system. It is therefore characterized by bank loans, rather than capital markets, as the primary means of corporate financing (Metten 2010). Hilferding (1910) found that the interaction between industrial companies and universal banks was of great importance to the industrialization of Germany in the 19th century. Edwards and Fischer (1994) note that the bank-based German financial system was considered a vital contributor to the post-World War II development of the German economy, which was quite successful. The fact that German banks are generally universal banks is reflected here. Universal banks conduct all the typical banking transactions, especially lending, securities, and deposit business.

The Deutsche Bundesbank, in its January 2012 monthly report, noted that Germany has a traditional bank-based financing system, but that alternative

13 The data come from Deutsche Bundesbank's January 2012 monthly report (Deutsche Bundesbank 2012).

14 Monetary financial institutions (MFIs) accept deposits from other entities to authorize loans or invest in securities. MFIs in the euro area primarily consist of central banks, credit institutions, electronic money institutions, and money market funds.

15 Securities, especially shares, are subject to valuation changes, which to some extent limit the comparability of percentages they provide to the overall understanding.

forms of funding had grown dramatically in recent years. Table 2-2 presents the outstanding liabilities of non-financial corporations at the end of various years (Deutsche Bundesbank 2012).

Among the various financing instruments, loans were the most important financing source, with an average 33 % of total liabilities. Most of those loans were granted by banks. However, during the sample period, the importance of bank loans declined gradually, while there was an increase in loans from non-MFIs (e.g., insurers). That percentage more than doubled, from about 6 % in 1991 to around 14 % at the end of 2010. It appears as if banks were to some degree substituted for by other creditors, particularly at the end of the observation period. Loans from non-banks seemed to be critical during times when external financing was reduced, such as the financial crisis periods of 2000–2004 (the dot-com bubble) and 2007–2009 (the subprime crisis) (Deutsche Bundesbank 2012).

Overall, external financing of non-financial corporations from 1991 to 2010 was dominated by loan financing in contrast to market-based financing. This is due to the corporate structure in Germany, because SMEs, which are characteristic of the German corporate landscape, are typically unable or unwilling to obtain capital market financing because of the high costs. According to the Deutsche Bundesbank, during the sample period, banks were eager to maintain long-term relationships with companies. This is because they aimed to cover the high cost of credit monitoring in order to generate positive income across a credit with long maturity in a competitive environment. Consequently, long-term bank relationships, often with just one bank, shaped the financing environment to an outsize degree during the observation period. Contrasting bank financing with capital market financing, banks often had information advantages that enabled them to more effectively assess a company's economic situation and growth potential. According to the Deutsche Bundesbank (2012), this also had a positive effect on the cost of financing for companies.

2.3.3 Key differences between market- and bank-based financial systems

By evaluating the key differences between market- and bank-based financial systems, La Porta et al. (1997) conclude that countries with poor investor protections tend to feature significantly smaller debt and equity markets. Good accounting standards and shareholder protection measures are linked to lower ownership concentration, which supports the idea that concentration reflects weak investor protection (La Porta et al. 1998). Despite changes in the last decades, La Porta et al.'s (1997, 1998) findings continue to facilitate understanding of the most important indicators for the establishment of these two systems.

At early stages of economic development, and in weak institutional environments, a bank-based financial system is more beneficial than a market-based one because it mobilizes savings, distributes capital, and better exercises corporate control (Levine 2002). Bank-based financial systems are also more beneficial for industrialization. Bank finance and market finance are typically differentiated based on their participation in investment projects. While banks are generally more involved in project selection, monitoring companies, and detecting promising companies, market finance is a type of "arm's-length" financing, with little participation in companies' investment projects (Chakraborty and Ray 2006).

With respect to the agency problem, borrowers may purposely decrease the success prospects of their investments in favor of their own benefits. The market, more specifically outside investors, are too dispersed to effectively control a borrower's activities (Chakraborty and Ray 2006; Holmström and Tirole 1997). Based on Diamond's (1984) theory, in bank-based financial systems, financial intermediaries act as delegated monitors by decreasing the costs of collecting and processing information about firms and management, thereby decreasing agency costs and to some extent resolving the agency problem (see also Chakraborty and Ray 2006; Holmström and Tirole 1997).

In this context, Holmström and Tirole (1997) differentiate between market- and bank-based financial systems by taking information content into account. Companies with lower marketable collateral and greater incentive problems borrow from banks because banks are better able to monitor these borrowers, which mitigates moral hazard problems. However, due to rapid technological developments, the classic function of banks as intermediaries is increasingly being questioned. In contrast, wealthier and more profitable firms, as well as companies with higher observable qualities, are able to pledge these as collateral. They thus rely more on unintermediated market finance, and, consequently, borrow from the capital market (see also Boot and Thakor 1997; Chakraborty and Ray 2006).

The Deutsche Bundesbank studied the changes in credit standards for lending to the private sector in its monthly report in January 2009. Its findings came from the Bank Lending Survey (BLS),[16] which aims to acquire qualitative

16 As of January 2003, the Euro system had conducted a quarterly bank lending survey (BLS) to increase its understanding about the role of lending in the monetary process, and to collect information for monetary policy studies. The survey currently includes twenty-three qualitative questions about past and expected future lending policies to the private non-financial sector and about loan demand.

information on the lending behavior of surveyed banks, paying particular attention to changes in credit standards for private sector lending. Regarding the changes in credit standards for loans to companies and households, banks indicated that, when the survey began in 2003, they had tightened their standards for all surveyed types of loans. From 2005 through mid-2007, there was a continuing easing of supply-side terms and conditions. However, since the beginning of the financial crisis, the surveyed banks say they have tightened their lending standards for companies (Deutsche Bundesbank 2009).

According to survey results for the most recent available quarters of the observation period, loan collateral had not played an increasing role as a constraining factor. The authors of Deutsche Bundesbank's 2009 monthly report found this striking. In line with the survey findings, over the 2005–2007 period, increasing competitive pressure in the German market contributed noticeably to an easing of credit standards. In general, the cumulative changes in credit standards by company size for Germany demonstrate a more accommodating lending policy by banks toward SMEs from mid-2004 onward. Moreover, the standards for loans to SMEs were eased markedly more (or have been tightened less) since mid-2007 compared to large companies. Overall, changes in credit standards play an important role in understanding the lending behavior of German banks (Deutsche Bundesbank 2009).

Proponents of market-based systems emphasize how market finance generates incentives for companies, because, as Scharfstein (1988) points out, capital markets discipline corporate governance by means of hostile takeovers of underperforming companies. In addition, Rajan and Zingales (2001) find that capital market financing can communicate price signals that may lead companies to undertake more worthwhile investments. In contrast, relationship-based bank financing may leave firms with underperforming cash flows and unwise investments.

Nevertheless, the academic literature acknowledges that relationship-based financing plays an important role in financial distress. Close relationships between lenders and borrowers are advantageous for firm financing because they alleviate information asymmetries and offer, for example, better credit availability. Edwards and Fischer (1994) note that banks tend to help firms in financial distress because they have better access to a firm's information (Elsas and Krahnen 1998). They can thus intervene more quickly when a firm is in financial distress (see also Li 2016). This support is often referred to as implicit insurance.

Levine (2002) states that a well-established and functioning legal system enables the actions of both markets and intermediaries and promotes the efficient allocation of resources and economic growth. He uses cross-country data to show that it is comparatively irrelevant whether overall financial growth originates from a market- or a bank-based financial system. What matters most is the efficiency of the country's financial and legal institutions (Levine 2002; see also Chakraborty and Ray 2006).

Chakraborty and Ray (2006) find that it is possible for two countries with different systems to generate similar rates of per capita GDP. In this context, Corbett and Jenkinson (1996) essentially challenge the renowned view that the U.S. and the U.K. are market-based, and that Japan and Germany are bank-based. The authors examine how physical investments have been financed in all four countries from 1970 to 1989. The data come from national income accounts and from company accounting data. They show that, during the sample period, only 11 % of total physical investment in Germany was funded by banks, which is noticeably less than in the other countries. Therefore, in the market-based systems of the U.S. and the U.K., banks actually funded a much higher amount of physical investment over the studied period than banks in Germany. The authors conclude that Germany is substantially more internally financed, and that Germany, the U.S., and the U.K. exhibit roughly equal proportions of bank financing. Yet, this proportion is higher in Japan. They find that, by the end of the sample period, Germany, the U.S., and the U.K. were becoming more alike (Corbett and Jenkinson 1996).

Terberger (2003) elaborates on the differences between the U.S. and Germany during the Glass-Steagall Act of 1933, which actually lasted until 1999. This Act regulated that banks in the U.S. could either be operated as investment or as commercial banks, in contrast to Germany, where universal banks were always permitted to exist. With regard to the structure of the regional presence of banks, there were significant differences between the U.S. and Germany. In the U.S., banks were not allowed to operate nationwide, and laws mandated that the number of branches in a region be within a certain geographic distance from the head office. In Germany, there were no similar restrictions since 1957, and banks were able to establish regional branches freely. Thus, in the U.S., stable capital markets came together with rather weak commercial banks, which was the opposite in Germany.

Terberger (2003) also documents key differences in the accounting systems. In the U.S., accounting systems developed to fulfill the informational needs of outside investors; in Germany, accounting systems are dedicated to securing the interests of creditors. Section 2.7.1 demonstrates in more detail how the concept of relationship lending plays a crucial role in bank- and market-based financial systems, and how it is fully consistent with both views. As Allen and Gale (1999) note, an ideal financial system depends on both financial markets and financial intermediaries. The next section will introduce the theoretical concepts of arm's-length lending and relationship lending.

2.4 Relationship lending versus arm's-length lending

Loan negotiations with small firms can vary dramatically from those with large firms, so banks need to know their customers well. However, banks may face some difficulties in properly assessing firm credit risk. Usually, balance sheet and income statement data will suffice. However, small companies carry greater informational opaqueness than larger companies, and are generally more difficult to assess. If balance sheet and income statement data are not fully available, as may be the case for smaller companies, banks must develop other methods to ensure they can obtain comprehensive information about a borrower.

Thus, examination of a borrower cannot only focus on hard data. Lenders may need to also build a relationship with a firm's owner/manager to accumulate needed information and broadly evaluate the creditworthiness of a borrower. Small local banks typically build close relationships with small companies, despite the fact that this can be resource-consuming, because relationship building is a vital part of the concept of relationship lending. Relationship lending, including building and nurturing a relationship and collecting proprietary information to evaluate a firm's credit risk, differs significantly from transactional lending, or arm's-length lending (Allen, DeLong, and Saunders 2004; Petersen 1999). This type of lending pools loans together and treats them as a homogeneous portfolio.

In this context, section 2.2.3 already discussed pooling and separating equilibrium, which come into effect here. With respect to separating equilibrium, the bank manages to oblige the borrower to signal private information truthfully. This allows the bank to differentiate between "good" and "bad" borrowers and treat them accordingly. With respect to pooling equilibrium, however, borrowers with "bad" information can imitate other borrowers. Therefore, it is not possible for banks to judge the borrower solely from the signal, and, thus, borrowers are generally treated the same. When the bank cannot distinguish the type of borrower, they will offer the same credit terms to all parties (Bannier 2005). Consequently, the bank will evaluate the overall risk of the entire portfolio, rather than evaluating the merits of an individual borrower, and this method is considered a transactional approach. Large banks often use this approach when dealing with loans to smaller companies, while smaller banks tend to concentrate on relationship lending (Allen et al. 2004; Berger and Udell 1995a; Petersen and Rajan 1994).

2.4.1 Arm's-length lending

Rajan (1992) defines arm's-length finance sources as less informed. Diamond (1991) states that companies try to build reputation by taking on costly bank-monitored debt. More reputable companies subsequently change to the arm's-length market in order to save on monitoring costs (Rajan 1992). Elsas (2005) defines arm's-length as a non-relational type of debt financing with a bank. He refers to the bank as an uninformed arm's-length lender. Arm's-length lending often involves banks providing financing on a one-time basis, with no further engagement (Fohlin 2016).

Agarwal and Hauswald (2008) find that soft private information is the main governing feature of relationship lending, while hard public information determines arm's-length lending (see also Hauswald and Marquez 2006; Rajan 1992). Public information characterizes transactional lending, while private information gathered by prior relationships characterizes relationship lending. Hence, the main difference between arm's-length and relationship lending is the information content that affects the availability and the pricing of credit (Agarwal and Hauswald 2008).

According to Rajan and Zingales (1998), a comprehensive law and enforcement structure is necessary for arm's-length lending to operate effectively. In an arm's-length system, contracts and associated prices govern the transactions that are undertaken. The capital market becomes the primary focus in defining the terms and conditions, and, consequently, lending relationships become less important. Moreover, in an arm's-length system, a company may be able to acquire more potential lenders, because more information is publicly available. If a loan is negotiated, it will be contracted for a definite period, and the interest rate will be competitive and will compensate the lender for the time and risk of the particular loan. Thus, in order to determine whether arm's-length transactions work, the adequacy of the contractual "infrastructure" must be determined, and the presence of property rights, laws, and institutions (such as auditors and regulators) must exist because they are necessary to facilitate transactions (Rajan and Zingales 1998).

Uzzi (1999) writes that arm's-length ties are defined by lean and sporadic contact between the lender and the borrower. There is no relationship building, and the lender does not get to know the customer well or acquire any proprietary information (Hirschman 1982). That type of information would arise more within a relationship lending context. Loans achieved by arm's-length ties also commonly show homogeneous structures because of the lack of a foundation of trust between the lender and borrower on which the lender can assess the firm's credit risks (Uzzi 1999).

However, relationships are costly to build and maintain because they are time consuming. Berger and Udell (1995b) find that small banks have a competitive advantage over larger banks in negotiating relationship loans. Relationships are usually costlier for large banks, because they have sufficient resources to negotiate large loans. Therefore, they do not need to engage in relationship building to comprehensively assess a firm's credit risk for the sake of a small loan. Spending time to nurture small accounts is basically not an efficient use of resources for a large bank, when the same effort can be put forth to negotiate a much larger loan.

Regardless of the costs, large banks have shown a willingness to lend to small companies in recent years. This is primarily attributable to the fact that large companies generally consider the capital markets as their first choice of financing. Hence, many of the most profitable customers are going directly to the capital market. In addition, and due to recent economic fluctuations, the attention of large banks toward smaller company loans has shifted to acquiring more reliable and consistent profits (Allen et al. 2004).

In contrast to relationship lending, transactional lending uses risk measurement tools such as credit scoring. Banks assess borrower risk and loan applications based on specific, quantifiable criteria. On the one hand, credit scores may be insufficient to fully assess informationally opaque small borrowers. On the other hand, banks that use credit scoring methods seem to be more productive and at lower costs. Longenecker, Moore, and Petty (1997) find that banks that implemented credit scoring appear to negotiate fewer bad loans. Feldman (1997) specifies the benefits of credit scoring. No face-to-face contact is needed, so geographic distance between the bank and the firm does not matter. And documentation is nominal, because only the credit history of the borrower is studied. The review of the loan application is, consequently, much quicker, and may, therefore, result in much lower costs.

In this context, Petersen and Rajan (2002) show that banks can offer loans to more distant borrowers, because hard information, like credit history, about them is more readily available. In addition, credit scoring methods offer benefits to borrowers, because competition between potential lenders is higher, and, thus, credit may be more easily attainable. As a result, companies in rural areas, for example, are no longer at the mercy of local banks. We posit that small banks may be hesitant to switch to the use of quantitative methods for small companies because they fear those companies will miss the personal contact of relationship lending. The singular relationship between a bank and its customers is naturally diminished or lost once lending is transformed into a transactional exercise (Allen et al. 2004).

According to Agarwal and Hauswald (2008), arm's-length loans are less readily available. However, these loans may be obtained at lower interest rates because equally informed banks compete on the basis of public information, which may bring down the price of the loan but also limit access. In relationship lending, more knowledgeable banks tactically employ their information advantage to capture borrowers that will pay higher rates but have easier access to credit.

In purely transactional credit markets, banks face symmetric adverse selection risks, so that, ceteris paribus, they can compete more aggressively for transactional borrowers who should be more likely to switch. Nevertheless, when transactional banks compete against a better informed inside bank, the risk of adverse selection is higher. In this context, less informed banks do business less aggressively, so relationship borrowers will be less likely to change banks (Agarwal and Hauswald 2008).

The duration and scope of a prior firm-bank relationship is expected to signal the presence of a lending relationship. Banks are occupied with thorough information collection done by the loan officers at a branch office. Hence, in-person applications and the subsequent interaction between the company and the loan officer characterizes relationship lending. For transactional lending, no such past evidence has been established. Nevertheless, in line with Agarwal and Hauswald (2008), the rise of online lending to small companies, which lacks any personal contact between the bank and the firm, enables researchers to detect purely transactional loans.

2.4.2 Relationship lending

The concept of relationship lending can be traced back to the traditionally close ties between banks and firms (Elsas and Krahnen 1998). In Germany, the concept of the "housebank" (or "main bank") is closely related to the theoretical idea of relationship lending. The fact that German banks are usually universal banks explains why the concept of housebanks does not exist in countries where a separation of commercial and investment banking formerly existed, such as in the U.S.[17] Germany is considered the prototype of the universal system (Fohlin 2016).

There are always references to close banking relationships when considering the concept of relationship lending. Petersen and Rajan (1994) provide the following information: "Through close and continued interaction, a firm may

17 The Gramm-Leach-Bliley Act (GLBA) of 1999, also known as the Financial Services Modernization Act, repealed part of the 1933 Glass-Steagall Act, which mandated the institutional separation of investment and commercial banking in the U.S.

provide a lender with sufficient information about, and a voice in, the firm's affairs so as to lower the cost and increase the availability of credit" (Petersen and Rajan 1994, p. 5). They define relationship banking by long-term relationships ("close and continued interaction"), as well as by a steady information supply, which is a critical factor ("sufficient information").

"Long-term relationships between banks and firms may be an important instrument for counteracting informational asymmetries" (Harhoff and Körting 1998, p. 1318). Especially for small firms, relationship banking is significant, because they can be informationally opaque. Relationship lending may mitigate asymmetric information problems between borrowers and lenders (Harhoff and Körting 1998; Hernández-Cánovas and Martínez-Solano 2010). As per Boot (2000), the access to information is by nature interconnected with the concept of relationship lending, and thus the relationship bank enjoys an information advantage over competitors (Elsas 2001).

Boot (2000) notes that relationship banking includes not only funding activities, but also other financial services, such as transaction services, cash management services, and pension plans. This notion is shared by Degryse and Van Cayseele (2000), who state that one source of information is related to the scope of a firm-bank relationship, which in turn relates to the breadth of a relationship or the amount of services a firm buys from a bank. Hence, the supply of other financial services may also be of value in lending relationships.

Ongena and Smith (2000a), for example, state that a greater scope of financial services may hold advantages for both the customer and the bank, while Santikian (2014) finds that a more intense relationship (i.e., more financial services) is associated with higher credit availability at more favorable terms. This view is in line with Cole (1998), who finds that pre-existing relationships, in which firms purchase other financial services from a prospective bank, are more important than length in increasing the likelihood that credit volume will be extended. This is because the bank may learn more about the payment behavior of customers, which reduces information asymmetries, and is consequently able to adapt contracts to better meet the financial needs of its customers. Specifically, for a firm that seeks to improve access to financing and reduce lending costs, the most important bank should contribute a large share of the firm's overall loan volume. As Elsas (2001) puts it, a relationship bank has a (relative to peer banks) large, often dominant, share of the credit financing of a firm, and performs most of the other financial services for the firm.

Aoki and Dinç (1997) define relationship banking as "a type of financing in which the financier is expected to make additional financing in a class of uncontractable states in the expectation of future rents over time" (Aoki and

Dinç 1997, p. 5). Petersen and Rajan (1994) further emphasize the aspect of funding availability. In this context, Boot (2000) refers to the benefits of relationship lending due to its contractual features. He notes that flexibility is one of the benefits of relationship banking. The relationship is usually less rigid than a capital market funding deal, meaning the renegotiation of terms is easier. This argumentation is empirically supported by Lehmann and Neuberger (2001), who show that housebanks provide services and loans to firms during times of financial distress. Elsas (2001) also finds that the relationship bank has a distinct responsibility to firms in crisis.

In accordance with Aoki and Dinç (1997), mutual expectations are central to the customer-bank relationship. The customer expects assistance during temporary financial difficulties. The bank, in turn, expects future earnings and follow-up financing. These expectations can be traced back to the commitment that is inherent to the definition of relationship lending, and that helps maintain these expectations over time.

Harhoff and Körting (1998) examine the mutual trust between the firm and bank and find it is characterized by high levels of trust. Hernández-Cánovas and Martínez-Solano (2010) find similar results for their sample of Spanish firms, while Ongena and Smith (2000a) recognize that the connection between a customer and a bank goes beyond the execution of simple, anonymous financial transactions. As Elsas (2001) writes, relationship banks are not only long-term in nature, but they also involve deep levels of trust.

For example, a firm in financial distress may be worth saving because of its economic value to society (see also Li 2016). However, in the short-term, the cost of funding that is offered by the transactional bank may exceed what a company is able to pay in such a situation, and, hence, the company may undertake unwise investment decisions. It may be encouraged to undertake riskier projects with negative net present values (Jensen and Meckling 1976).[18]

18 Much of the corporate finance literature has paid attention to the influence of stockholder/bondholder conflicts in corporate financing and to investment decisions. The main argument from this strain of research is that managers acting on behalf of equity holders may have incentives to both under- and overinvest. The agency costs generated from these incentives impact the cost of debt financing, and, therefore, the company's best combination of debt and equity. Thus, a risk-shifting problem may occur, where management may invest in unprofitable or overly risky projects or even reject positive net present value projects (Galai and Masulis 1976; Jensen 1986; Jensen and Meckling 1976; Leland 1998; Mauer and Sarkar 2005; Myers 1977; Stulz 1990).

Examining the more competitive arm's-length system, a bank may be afraid it will not be sufficiently compensated by the firm's projects in the long-term, and thus may be hesitant to provide short-term funding to a firm in financial distress. Consequently, companies may be less likely to receive financial support in this system.

Examining the relationship lending system, a bank may be certain enough about a company's projects and the strength of its relationship that the company will undertake wise investment projects despite the pressure of financial distress. In this situation, the bank can offer a below-market interest rate in the short-term, and then compensate for losses with an above-market interest rate in the long-term, when the company is out of distress. Overall, relationship banks may be regarded as intermediaries that have monopoly power. They use this power to charge above-market interest rates during normal times in return for implicit insurance to deliver below-market funding during times of distress, in contrast to transactional lending (Rajan and Zingales 1998).

Throughout this study, relationship lending is understood as a housebank relationship, which is a close relationship between a firm and its most important bank. The terms relationship lending, relationship banking, and housebank are generally interchangeable in this thesis.[19] Relationship lending appears long-term in nature, and to be characterized by a competitive advantage of the bank over its rivals in terms of information. Furthermore, the bank appears to hold a major, often dominant proportion of the credit financing of the firm relative to other banks, and carries out most of the financial services for the firm. The relationship is characterized by implicit trust, and the bank seems to have a particular responsibility to the firm during times of financial distress. According to Elsas (2001), the concept of relationship banking is typically an expression of the bank-based financial system. However, as noted in section 2.3.3, relationship lending can also occur in market-based financial systems.

Diamond's (1984) theory implies that lending relationships with banks and the availability of financing issued by banks have economic benefits because they generate economies of scale when screening and monitoring borrowers (Davis 1994; Diamond 1984). In addition, by loan diversification, banks can spread out the risks of their other investments (Mayer 1994). However, in recent years, and especially after the 2007–2009 financial crisis, financial markets have evolved. Current financial innovations are fostering changes in the banking system and

---

19 Elsas and Krahnen (1998) use the terms housebank relation and relationship lending interchangeably.

in the regulatory environment. Today, new financial innovators are offering services that banks used to provide exclusively (Freixas and Rochet 1997).

Since much of today's business is conducted via automated, anonymous actions, where relationship building is unnecessary, the status of the lending relationship is no longer clear. It seems the global trend toward deregulation has fostered this development and has amplified the transition from relationship-oriented to more transaction-oriented products. Considering these changes, it is questionable whether financial intermediaries and the associated concept of lending relationships can continue to resolve the described information asymmetries (Ongena and Smith 2000a) between lenders and borrowers to facilitate transactions (Boot 2000). Section 2.5 discusses this topic in more detail.

2.5 The German banking system and disruptive changes

Some companies consider obtaining adequate funding for investments and growth to be challenging, especially since the introduction of Basel II and Basel III. Studies show that traditional bank lending has become more expensive on average for SMEs due to the Basel regulations (Brackschulze, Mayer-Fiedrich, and Müller 2011; Dorfleitner, Hornuf, Schmitt, and Weber 2016; Schindele and Szczesny 2016). Moreover, firms' trust in the banking system deteriorated with the recent financial crisis, when many German banks needed to be recapitalized and were too leveraged to provide funding. This left some companies, particularly SMEs, which typically rely heavily on bank financing, facing real difficulties in obtaining additional liquidity (Berger et al. 2014; Hochfellner et al. 2015; Nassr and Wehinger 2015). As a result, firms began proactively exploring alternatives to financing their capital needs, and many do not rely solely on banks as their primary source of capital any longer.[20]

Technological progress and the increasing digitization of business processes among financial intermediaries is also dramatically changing the financial industry. One form of new funding comes from the rise of FinTechs, which potentially help companies seeking financing by using their innovative business models to reduce financing gaps. The automation of financial transactions has enabled FinTechs to offer services in a more transparent, cost-effective, and

20 The desire by SMEs to substitute bank financing with non-bank alternatives after the banking crisis is well documented for industrial countries (Davis and Stone 2004). Mietzner et al. (2018), for example, analyze whether the recently established market for mini-bonds can act as an alternative source of financing for German SMEs.

efficient manner than traditional financial institutions. They are thus a key alternative source of external finance for SMEs.

In this context, FinTechs increasingly compete with banks for financing, wealth management, and payment transaction processing. For financing in particular, this development may have far-reaching implications for countries with bank-based financial systems and for companies with characteristically high levels of debt, as is the case for Germany.

Traditional lending institutions remain the most important source of external financing for SMEs right now, but there is a clear trend that bank loans are systematically falling out of favor (Deutsche Bundesbank 2012, 2018a; European Central Bank 2017a; Schwartz 2017). Some reasons for the current shift in the banking system and corporate financing are the temporary tightening of credit standards during and following the financial crisis, and the increasing regulatory requirements under the Basel Agreement. At the same time, the intensity of competition for banks is likely to have further aggravated market transparency and the already high margin pressure in credit lending. This is affecting the value chain and the value proposition of banks (Deutsche Bundesbank 2012).

In light of these important changes, the significance and status quo of relationship lending for banks and borrowers is unclear. The traditional perception of the corporate customer-bank relationship may no longer hold, and the expected value firms assign to their bank relationships has likely diminished. The following section will explore these developments.

2.5.1 The current transformation of the German banking system

The financial crisis of 2007–2009 hit the German banking system hard and exposed the weaknesses of large banks from the private sector as well as those of banks with government participation. According to Behr and Schmidt (2015), the most notable aspect of the German banking system today is that it is still a three-pillar system, especially compared to other financial systems and despite the recent crisis. Three types of banks can be distinguished with respect to their institutional structures and business aims (Behr and Schmidt 2015).

The emergence of the German banking system has been mainly shaped by two developments, and both stem from industrialization in the nineteenth century. First, during industrialization, the German economy needed large volumes of capital, which were provided for the most part by banks. Second, during that time, profit-oriented commercial banks were founded, as well as two other bank types that were critical because they do not focus solely on profit maximization: savings banks and cooperative banks (Detzer, Dodig, Evans, Hein, Herr, and Prante 2017).

Overall, external funding for non-financial firms in Germany has been predominantly supplied by banks, and private bank financing was decisive in the development of the German railways in the 1830s and 1840s. Moreover, the establishment of joint stock banks in the 1850s was a fundamental development (Detzer et al. 2017; Tilly 1989). The first joint stock banks included the Disconto Gesellschaft (1851), the Darmstädter Bank (1853), and the Berliner Handelsgesellschaft (1853). These were followed in the 1870s by the Deutsche Bank (1870), the Commerz- und Disconto-Bank (1870), the Deutsche Nationalbank (1871), and the Dresdner Bank (1872). All played a significant part in the development of the industrial sector by investing their own capital in companies (Detzer et al. 2017; Feldenkirchen 1991). During that time, universal banks were also established, which marked the start of the provision of long-term bank lending to fund industrial growth (Detzer et al. 2017).

By that time, the business model of large banks focused primarily on the financing of large companies in sectors such as mining and metal production, mechanical engineering, chemicals, and electrical production. Besides funding, the banks tried to expand their influence by providing assistance when companies had financial problems. Feldenkirchen (1991) cites the company Krupp as an example. When Krupp encountered payment problems, a short-term loan was replaced with a long-term loan at a higher interest rate, and the company was required to place a bank representative on its board (Detzer et al. 2017). In addition, the strong focus of large banks on large industrial companies put other sectors, such as agriculture, housing, and the financing of small companies, in the background. Thus, savings banks and cooperative banks were the primary source of financing for those sectors (Detzer et al. 2017).

Savings banks were established by city and county governments. The first was founded in 1801, and they quickly grew in popularity. By 1900 there were 2,700 savings banks throughout Germany, and one-third of the German population had a savings account. Because these banks were obligated to restrict their lending activities to their local regions, it ensured lending was spread evenly through the country. Furthermore, Landesbanken were founded to promote regional economic development (Detzer et al. 2017). In the mid-nineteenth century, cooperative banks were then established primarily by self-employed craftsmen and small farmers because this group typically had trouble obtaining funding during industrialization.

The first urban cooperative bank (Volksbank) was founded in 1862 in Darmstadt, and the first rural cooperative bank (Raiffeisenbank) was founded in

1864. The expansion of the savings and cooperative bank sector, and their development of a broad network of branches, spurred the large private banks around 1890 to develop a network of branches as well. Fohlin (2007) documents that this attempt of large private banks was only somewhat fruitful, because joint stock banks comprised around 27 % of the financial system's assets by 1913, while savings banks comprised about 33 % (Detzer et al. 2017).

During the interwar period, the large private banks faced great challenges from foreign banks in the 1920s and from savings banks in the 1930s. Additionally, during that time, many mergers between large banks took place (Balderston 1991; Detzer et al. 2017). Meanwhile, the savings and cooperative banks reinforced their power. In 1909, the first clearing system was established by savings banks, and in 1918, the Deutsche Girozentrale Berlin was founded, connecting savings banks across all regions (Detzer et al. 2017). Yet, savings banks were also hit by a crisis in 1931, mainly due to non-performing loans to local authorities. After the crisis, the savings banks were granted legal autonomy, and the savings banks were able to quickly recover. Deposits to savings and cooperate banks in subsequent years increased much more rapidly than deposits to large private banks (Balderston 1991; Detzer et al. 2017).

After WWII, the three big private banks were split up into regional banks. However, following the "Big Bank Act" of March 1953, full reestablishment of the big banks was permitted from 1956 onward. The Deutsche Bank and the Dresdner Bank were restored as unified institutions in 1957, and the Commerzbank was reestablished in 1958 (Detzer et al. 2017; Tilly 1996). Yet the relative importance of the big banks in the German banking system deteriorated in the years after WWII, and by 1950, the big banks accounted for only 19 % of bank assets. By 1960, that number had decreased to around 10 %.

Nevertheless, large banks continued to play a crucial role in the corporate governance of companies because they often held company shares (Detzer et al. 2017). At the same time, savings banks granted loans to local companies and played a decisive role in the successful development of post-war West German SMEs. Landesbanken were able to increase their share of lending, and thus also presented competition for large private banks. The cooperative bank sector experienced an increase in their share of lending, and in 1974, the cooperative banks were allowed to do business with non-members. By 1976, the Deutsche Genossenschaftsbank, or DG Bank, expanded its business, and represented even more competition for large private banks (Deeg 1999; Detzer et al. 2017).

The large private banks faced a severe decline in the demand for lending from large manufacturing companies at the end of the post-WWII boom. This end led to a decrease in investments in West Germany, particularly in fixed physical assets, such as machinery, land, buildings, vehicles, and technology. In response to these developments, large banks tried to promote their businesses with SMEs, and they began competing with savings and cooperative banks for that sector. However, because they were less experienced in doing business with SMEs, they were not able to quickly grow their business models in that direction (Deeg 1999; Detzer et al. 2017). As a result, large private banks experienced an overall decline in their business operations.

On the one hand, there was a decline in the demand for lending from large companies, mainly manufacturing companies. On the other hand, large banks were not able to successfully establish business operations with SMEs. Thus, in the 1980s, the large private banks created the so-called "Finanzplatz Deutschland" to set up a financial center. One of the main goals of the initiative was to promote the growth of the securities market, because until then it was not well established. Large banks also hoped to generate income from investment banking activities. These actions were initiated to limit any further reliance on developments in traditional lending (Deeg 1999; Detzer et al. 2017; Vitols 2005).

In the years following, and through today, banking density in Germany has significantly declined. In 1990, the number of banks was approximately 4,700; today, that number has declined by more than half. Nevertheless, with around 1,888 banks as of the end of December 2016, according to the Deutsche Bundesbank (2017a), Germany still maintains a higher bank density than many other countries. Figure 2-4 illustrates the structure of the "three-pillar banking system."

Pillar I consists of credit institutions from the private sector, which includes 4 major banks, 189 regional banks and other financial institutions, and 188 foreign bank branch offices. Their primary aim is profit maximization, and these banks are typically owned by shareholders. The largest is the Deutsche Bank. Another major bank is Commerzbank, which took over Dresdner Bank in 2009, as well as the former Hypo-Vereinsbank, which now belongs to the Italian financial group UniCredit.

Pillar II encompasses the 403 savings banks and 9 Landesbanken. These banks aim to optimize their profits and promote local businesses, and they are owned by municipalities. Pillar III comprises the 976 cooperative banks. These banks seek to optimize their profits and encourage member businesses and are also owned by their members.

Figure 2-4 also lists special banks, which are usually not considered part of the "three-pillar system" because they only focus on special banking products and cannot comprehensively fund companies. Special banks include mortgage banks, building societies, banks with special functions, such as Kreditanstalt

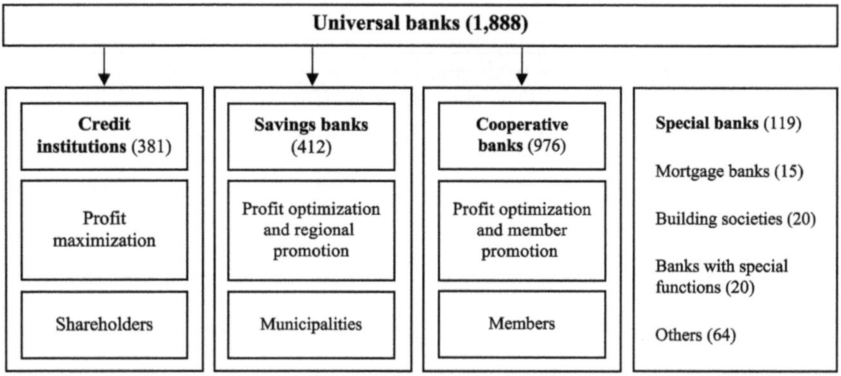

Figure 2-4: Germany's three-pillar banking system

This figure shows Germany's "three-pillar banking system," which consisted of 1,888 banks in total as of the end of December 2016. This breaks down to 381 credit institutions, 412 savings banks and Landesbanken, and 976 cooperative banks (as well as 119 "special" banks, which are not usually considered part of the three-pillar system). The figure lists the aim and the owners of each bank type (Deutsche Bundesbank 2017b).

für Wiederaufbau (KfW), and other special banks consisting of guarantee banks and housing companies with savings facilities (Deutsche Bundesbank 2017b).

The market share of the banking groups in Germany breaks down as follows: large private banks (18.5 %), savings banks (16.8 %), cooperative banks (12.1 %), Landesbanken (11.8 %), and branches of foreign banks and other credit institutions (40.8 %). At the end of 2016, total business volume was approximately EUR 6,999 billion (Statista 2017).[21] Table 2-3 shows the number of bank branches in Germany.

The number of bank branches decreased by a total of 1,939, from 34,260 in 2015 to 32,321 in 2016; this corresponds to a 5.66 % decrease. The trend in bank branch closures and consolidation continues today. The savings bank sector, with a total of 11,351 branches, including 412 head offices, remains the largest sector in Germany, followed by cooperative banks with 11,145 branches, including 976 head offices. As of December 31, 2016, the commercial bank sector had 9,825 branches, of which 381 were head offices (Deutsche Bundesbank 2017a). In addition, Table 2-4 shows the ten largest banks in Germany according to their

21 All figures presented are for year-end.

Table 2-3: Number of bank branches in Germany compared to the previous year

This table shows the number of bank branches including all legally independent credit institutions (head offices) for the 2016 reporting period (Deutsche Bundesbank 2017a).

	12/31/2015	**12/31/2016**	**Change absolute changes**	**Change in %**
Credit institutions	10,117	9,825	-292	-2.89
Savings banks	12,283	11,351	-932	-7.59
Cooperative banks	11,860	11,145	-715	-6.03

Table 2-4: Top 10 German banks by balance sheet total for the financial years 2015 and 2016

This figure presents the ten largest banks in Germany according to their balance sheet totals in the years 2015 and 2016 (Statista 2018).

	Balance sheet total 2016 (in million €)	**Balance sheet total 2015 (in million €)**
Deutsche Bank AG	1.590.546	1.629.130
DZ Bank AG	509.447	408.341
KfW	507.013	502.973
Commerzbank AG	480.450	532.701
UniCredit Bank AG	302.090	298.745
Landesbank Baden-Württemberg	243.620	234.015
Bayerische Landesbank	212.150	215.713
Landesbank Hessen-Thüringen	174.990	172.256
Norddeutsche Landesbank Girozentrale	174.797	180.998
ING-DiBa AG	157.553	143.977

balance sheet totals for the years 2015 and 2016. The Deutsche Bank takes first place in the ranking and includes the Postbank. The DZ Bank AG includes the merger with WGZ Bank (Statista 2018).

The next section discusses the developments of corporate financing of non-financial corporations. The financing conditions of non-financial companies have a significant influence on their investment behavior, which is of great significance for the economic development of the economy over both the short- and long-term (Deutsche Bundesbank 2018a).

2.5.2 Development of corporate financing of non-financial companies

Financing conditions have a significant effect on the investment behavior of companies and are a critical factor for both short- and long-term economic growth. Financing conditions are influenced by factors such as monetary policy. Thus, changes in monetary policy affect the overall financing climate. Changes in financing costs impact the demand for financing and the profitability of investments.

According to the Deutsche Bundesbank (2018a), the financing pattern of non-financial companies in the euro area has altered dramatically as a result of the financial crisis. The basis for the Deutsche Bundesbank study are the outcomes of the financial accounts. The sample periods are the first quarter of 2008 through the second quarter of 2011 and the third quarter of 2011 through the second quarter of 2017. The following changes are measurable: 1) a shift from funds raised externally to financing with internally generated sources and 2) a substitution of other forms of debt for bank loan financing, such as, for example, loans from non-banks and debt securities. This shift has primarily been triggered by temporary supply constraints at banks. The change to a higher share of internal and equity financing and a more diversified debt financing structure is expected to make companies less vulnerable to temporary financial constraints at banks (Deutsche Bundesbank 2018a).

Regarding the fundamentals of corporate financing, there are two competing theories: the pecking order theory, and the trade-off theory. The pecking order theory states that the cost of financing increases with asymmetric information. This theory documents that companies adhere to a hierarchy of financing sources, so firms prefer internal financing to borrowing, but borrowing is preferred to an increase in equity (equity would mean issuing shares, which indicate bringing external ownership into a company) (Myers 1984; Myers and Majluf 1984).

The trade-off theory of capital structure describes how much debt finance and how much equity finance firms use by balancing the costs and benefits. This theory derives from Kraus and Litzenberger (1973), who examine the balance between the deadweight costs of bankruptcy and the tax saving benefits of debt. This theory developed from the fact that companies are typically financed partly with debt and partly with equity in consideration of the marginal benefit, which is when debt increases, the marginal benefit of debt decreases. Consequently, a company that wants to improve its value will consider this trade-off when deciding how much debt and equity it uses to finance business operations (Bradley, Jarrell, and Kim 1984; Campbell and Kelly 1994; Hackbarth, Hennessy, and Leland 2007). Figure 2-5 presents an overview of the components of corporate financing, distinguishing between internal and external financing (Deutsche Bundesbank 2018a).

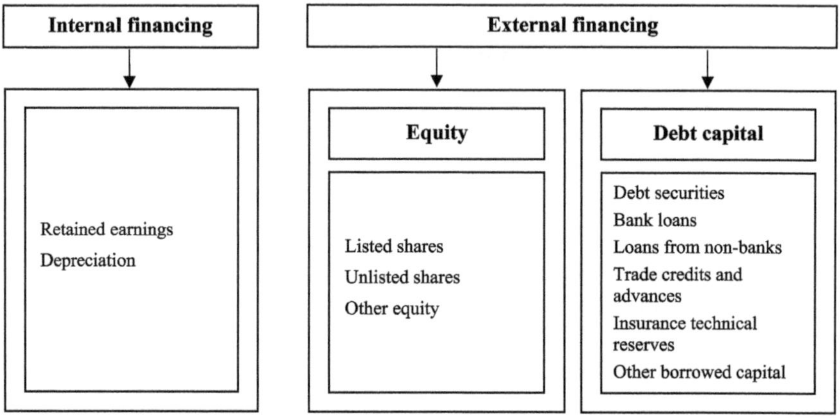

Figure 2-5: Components of corporate financing

This figure gives an overview of total financing, broken down between internal and external financing of non-financial corporations.[22]

Internal financing stems from a company's activities and comprises the sum of retained earnings and the equivalent of the depreciation of the capital stock. External financing is divided into borrowed capital and equity capital. Listed shares and debt securities are often also considered market financing instruments, while debt securities, bank loans, loans from non-banks, trade credits and advances, and insurance technical reserves are considered debt instruments (Deutsche Bundesbank 2018a).

We discuss the following current studies to present a market overview of corporate financing for the European and German markets: the "EBA Report on SMEs and SME supporting factor" by the EBA (European Banking Authority), monthly reports published by the Deutsche Bundesbank, the "Euro area bank lending survey" and the "Survey on the Access to Finance of Enterprises in the euro area" by the ECB, and the KFW SME panel.

The EBA issues a report on SMEs that evaluates the evolution of lending terms and conditions. The EBA (2016) study uses three different samples of the survey on the Access to Finance of Enterprises (SAFE). The study uses the available waves from April 2011 to March 2015, yielding a sample of up to 16,850 observations of companies that applied for bank financing in the eurozone. According to the EBA (2016) report, SMEs remain largely reliant on

22 This figure is closely aligned with the Deutsche Bundesbank (2018a).

bank-related lending (e.g., credit lines and bank loans) to finance their business operations. The EBA (2016) report documents that other sources of financing, such as equity finance, capital market debt, and securitization, although available, are not as widely used (European Banking Authority 2016).

Lending conditions for both SMEs and large companies have been impacted by the financial crisis, with a substantial credit contraction since 2008. Following the crisis, SME bank lending experienced a drop in volume. According to EBA (2016), regardless of growth, SME lending has continued to be below its pre-crisis level, and differences in SME bank lending exist across bank types. In contrast, bank lending to larger companies has now recovered to its pre-crisis level.

Lending conditions have been similarly affected by the financial crisis. Interest rates are commonly higher for SMEs than for large firms. Moreover, the EBA (2016) report documents that other lending terms, for example, charges, fees, and collateral requirements, were tightened in the post-crisis period, even though empirical results demonstrate there was no alteration over time in the volume of loans using collateral or guarantees (European Banking Authority 2016).

Moreover, EBA (2016) finds that, in recent years, access to finance has been of greater concern to SMEs than to large companies. The findings show that about 16 % of SMEs indicated some issue with bank loan financing (e.g., discouraged to apply, rejected, at too high a cost, or received only part of the loan), compared to 10 % of large companies. The financing difficulties vary by firm size, with micro and small companies most affected.

The report also shows that smaller and younger companies have a higher probability of experiencing credit constraints than larger and older companies. Firms with better credit histories and improved general economic outlooks are less likely to experience credit constraints. According to the EBA (2016) report, a company's legal status or ownership do not appear to impact the likelihood of obtaining bank financing (European Banking Authority 2016).

According to the Deutsche Bundesbank (2018a), "The external financing of non-financial corporations in the euro area weakened considerably following the onset of the financial and economic crisis [...]. While the inflows between 1999 and 2008 still averaged around 22 % of gross value added and were driven, above all, by dynamic (albeit unsustainable) bank loan growth, they dropped by roughly half following the onset of the financial and economic crisis. According to the pecking order theory, this development should have been due to the lower demand for external financing as a result of subdued investment and higher availability of internal financing" (Deutsche Bundesbank 2018a, p. 59). However, constrained access to bank financing may also have been a decisive factor and may in turn have led to weaker investment activity. Except for the second half of 2009, companies in Germany documented consistently positive developments in external financing, albeit lower than before the crisis. The reduced need for external financing is traceable to the growth in internal financing combined with moderate investment behavior, which, taken in isolation, reduced the demand for external financing (Deutsche Bundesbank 2018a).

Besides the EBA (2016) report and the monthly reports of the Deutsche Bundesbank (2018a), the ECB conducted the SAFE from March 2017 to April 2017, collecting data from 11,724 companies in the euro area. This survey provides evidence for the October 2016 to March 2017 period on the financial status quo, financing requirements, and access to external funding of SMEs, and contrasts those with the findings for large companies. This is the sixteenth round of the survey, and, similarly to the prior survey, finding customers was the main concern of euro area SMEs (26 %, compared with 25 % the previous year), followed by the availability of a skilled workforce (19 %, unchanged). Access to finance remained the least important concern.[23] The surveyed SMEs continued to document progress in their overall financial situations during the reference period, which indicates unchanged profits with differences across countries.[24]

The companies expressed progress in their debt situations by indicating ongoing deleveraging efforts, as shown by a net decline in their debt-to-total assets ratio. The need for external finance increased moderately during the reference period. 3 % of SMEs (compared to 1 % the previous year) stated an increase in their demand for bank loans, while 6 % (5 %) indicated a greater need for bank overdrafts. These results are in line with the results of the euro area bank lending survey (BLS) for the first quarter of 2017, which documented a continuing demand for loans as well (European Central Bank 2017b).

"For the fifth time in a row, SMEs confirmed, on balance, an increase in the availability of bank financing (loans and bank overdrafts) and the willingness of banks to provide credit at lower interest rates [...]" (European Central Bank 2017a, pp. 3, 4). These results are in line with findings from the euro area BLS for the first quarter of 2017, which showed a continued easing of bank lending credit terms (European Central Bank 2017b). Overall, "[...] SMEs reported that terms and conditions for bank loans had improved. SMEs continued to signal a net decline in interest rates, (...) while the available size and maturity of loans

23 Only SMEs in Greece were steadily concerned with poor access to finance, with 27 % expressing it as their main problem (24 % in the previous survey).

24 Greece reported a decline in turnover of -13 % (-4 %).

and overdrafts increased. By contrast, a positive net percentage of SMEs continued to indicate a tightening in the collateral and other requirements of banks, as well as in other costs of financing related, in particular, to charges, fees and commissions" (European Central Bank 2017a, p. 5).

SMEs stated that their firm-specific outlook, their capital situation, and their credit history all eased access to financing. However, they also indicated that the increase in their demand for external funding was lower than the improvement in their availability of external financing. Compared to the previous survey results, there was a rise in successful loan applications (74 %, versus 69 % in the previous survey) and a small decrease in those that were rejected (6 %, down from 7 %). Yet the overall indicator of financing obstacles[25] for successful loan applications was unchanged. Around 40 % of SMEs stated that they would like to keep their existing levels of debt, while 39 % preferred less debt and only 7 % desired to obtain more debt. 25 % named the ability to obtain more credit in the future as the most important factor, while, for 20 %, their credit rating was the most critical factor, followed by the risk of financial distress (16 %). The interest rate on new debt was the most critical factor for 13 % of the surveyed SMEs (European Central Bank 2017a).

In contrast, the status quo of large companies continued to show a better financial situation than that of SMEs. Around 39 % of large companies applied for a bank loan, and 86 % received a loan. The rejection rate was only 1 %, compared to SMEs with a success rate of 74 % and a rejection rate of 6 %. The average interest rate on credit lines for large companies was approximately 180 basis points lower than that charged to SMEs. These findings suggest that large companies profit more from easier access to finance than SMEs and larger companies expressed further progress in their external financing parameters. To conclude, the effects of the monetary policy measures that began in June 2014 continue to facilitate SMEs' access to bank financing (European Central Bank 2017a).

Besides the EBA (2016) report, the monthly reports of the Deutsche Bundesbank (2018a), the SAFE, and the BLS, the KfW also produces a written repeat survey of SMEs with a turnover of up to EUR 500 million per year, covering a database of up to 15,000 companies per year. This survey focuses solely

25 "The financing obstacles indicator is the sum of the percentages of SMEs reporting rejections of loan applications, loan applications for which only a limited amount was granted, and loan applications which resulted in an offer that was rejected by the SMEs owing to borrowing costs that were too high, as well as the percentage of SMEs which did not apply for a loan for fear of rejection" (European Central Bank 2017a, p. 5).

on Germany, and finds that, in 2016, two-thirds of SMEs used bank credit to finance an investment, while the loan financing of investments increased slightly. However, the strong desire for financial independence and concern about unfavorable financing conditions keep many SMEs from attempting credit negotiations, while a gap in the credit supply is small (Schwartz 2017).

That desire for financial independence is most often opposed to bank financing. This is especially true for SMEs: 44 % of small companies want to avoid (additional) borrowing. In addition, one-third of small companies are not seeking external financing (33 %). Larger SMEs are more open to bank financing, because the projects to be financed are larger. The possibilities of fully financing by their own resources is likely to be more limited for these companies. Financing is, therefore, more pronounced for larger companies, and, thus, the share of larger SMEs that generally do not seek debt financing is much lower at 21 %, compared to 33 % of small companies (Schwartz 2017).

SMEs are more concerned about facing unfavorable financing conditions or having to put too much effort into credit negotiations. For 29 % of small companies, high collateral requirements speak against bank financing. Small companies are typically required to provide private security when borrowing (for example, land, real estate, vehicles, life insurance). In addition, excessive disclosure and documentation requirements are also a barrier for many small companies (22 %). Skepticism over the financial and temporal effort of the application, and the length of time for processing and decision-making are clearly concerns as well (12 % and 11 %).

Larger SMEs are less discouraged by these aspects. It is likely that, with increasing company size, more specialized employees (or entire departments) exist (for example, in the areas of law, taxes, controlling) to handle loan applications. Overall, bank loans remain the second most important financing source, and, thus, SMEs continue to rely primarily on their own funds for investment financing (Schwartz 2017).

The findings of the different studies were presented in order to assess the lending environment for SMEs. The regulatory consequences that followed or were aggravated in the aftermath of the financial crisis will be described below.

2.5.3 Regulatory consequences of the 2007–2009 financial crisis

In response to the recent financial crisis, the concept of financial market regulation in science and politics has been omnipresent. After the financial crisis began in 2007, a picture emerged as to how risks, particularly systemic risks, arise and how they can be combated. The realization was that financial institutions must improve their risk management. This includes, among other things, enhancing lending policies and the management of credit risks.

Due to a series of bankruptcies in the 1970s, the need for a regulatory body became increasingly clear. Hence, the Basel Committee on Banking Supervision (BCBS), located at the Bank for International Settlements (BIS), was founded in 1974 by the central banks of the G10 countries. The BCBS develops supervisory standards for banking, with the aim of strengthening the cooperation between national supervisory authorities. The reason for the first regulation, Basel I, was the concern that the equity of the world's most important banks had fallen to dangerously low levels. As a result, in 1988, the BCBS set an internationally agreed upon equity standard for the international active banks of the G10 countries. Banks were required to hold minimum capital requirements of 8 % in relation to their risky assets. This was supposed to cover credit risks as well as other risks. Similarly, various risk classifications were identified, for example, 0 % for loans to government debtors (OECD countries), 20 % for loans to banks based in OECD countries, 50 % for mortgage-backed loans, and 100 % for loans to all other risk activities, e.g., corporate loans. Basel I quickly became a global supervisory standard and was applied in Europe by the implementation of EU directives (Basler Ausschuss für Bankenaufsicht 2004).[26]

However, in the meantime, it was heavily criticized for lacking adequate consideration of the actual default risk of borrowers, which is not observed in the case of uniform capital requirements. Such an undifferentiated rule structure could ultimately lead to cross-subsidization of "good" to "bad" credit ratings, and to a worsening of the risk structure. Thus, in June 1999 the Basel Committee published a first consultation paper on a new regulation of the capital requirements. After years of negotiations, Basel II was passed in June 2004.

The objective of Basel II is to create an appropriate balance between a bank's equity and its actual risk profile (Bundesanstalt für Finanzdienstleistungsaufsicht 2004).[27] Nevertheless, the global financial and economic crisis beginning in 2007 exposed the weaknesses of existing banking regulations and required further development. The financial crisis revealed that the global banking system did not provide enough high-quality equity capital. Therefore, Basel III focuses on the so-called core equity, the "common equity."

---

26 In Germany, Principle I, according to §§ 10 and 10a KWG, prevails (Deutsche Bundesbank 2018b).

27 On December 31, 2006, Basel II was finally implemented.

In November 2010, the G10 countries agreed on Basel III, and its reform package was published in December 2010. Basel III aims to ensure a stable financial system while preventing a credit crunch, as well as to limit and reduce the liability of public authorities and taxpayers. The new regulatory capital base and the new liquidity provisions include an increase in the quality of the equity ("common equity"), an increase in risk coverage, the introduction of a debt ceiling, an improvement in countercyclical buffers, and a reduction in systemic risks (Bundesministerium der Finanzen 2013; Tucker, Hall, and Pattani 2013). The German implementation of Basel III took place in 2013 by means of changes to the German Banking Act (KWG) and the CRD IV Implementation Act (Bundesministerium der Finanzen 2017). All credit institutions that operate deposit and lending businesses, as well as certain securities companies and other institutions that fall under the KWG, are required to implement Basel III (Bundesministerium der Finanzen 2013).

In addition to the Basel III regulations, the Federal Financial Supervisory Authority (BaFin) published a revised version of the MaRisk (Minimum Requirements for Risk Management), which became effective for all German credit institutions and financial services institutions in December 2012.[28] The MaRisk require adequate and effective risk management that takes into account risk-bearing capacity, including, specifically, the establishment of strategies and internal control procedures. These procedures establish a system and mandate internal auditing. The internal control system comprises regulations for the identification, assessment, control, monitoring, and communication of risks, as well as a compliance function (Bundesanstalt für Finanzdienstleistungsaufsicht 2017). In 2016, a fifth MaRisk amendment was announced that focuses on risk data aggregation and risk reporting, the risk culture in credit institutions, and the outsourcing of risk-controlling functions (Bundesanstalt für Finanzdienstle istungsaufsicht 2016).

It becomes clear that the regulatory changes triggered by the financial crisis have contributed to a rapid restructuring and continuously changing process in the financial market and for the banking landscape. This process has reached national banking markets such as Germany. The strict application of the Basel III regulations to those traditionally financing SMEs could potentially put at risk the stability of SME financing and, thus, economic recovery. This is because the

28 The Federal Financial Supervisory Authority published the first version of the MaRisk at the end of 2005. The MaRisk clarify the requirements of section § 25a (1a) and (2) KWG (Bundesanstalt für Finanzdienstleistungsaufsicht 2017).

other side of the far-reaching regulations on business activities triggered by the financial crisis may put credit lending to companies at risk, which would be detrimental for activities that are vital to national economies (Schwartz 2016).

SMEs tend to rely heavily on bank lending. With an annual turnover of about EUR 4,000 billion and 29.5 million employees in Germany in 2015, SMEs are the growth engine of the German economy (Schwartz 2016). Accordingly, the financing of these companies is critical, and must be assured. The providers of external financing for these companies tend to be regional banks, such as savings and cooperative banks, followed by bigger private banks, such as the Deutsche Bank and Commerzbank. Although savings and cooperative banks were not the primary trigger, Basel III includes them in its regulations as well. Thus, these regulations also affect smaller companies and may indirectly impede lending (Angelkort and Stuwe 2011).

SMEs are typically strongly bank-oriented, and bank loans with different maturities, credit lines, and leasing represent their most important sources of funding after internal financing (Zimmermann 2017). According to the results of the SAFE from October 2016 to March 2017, 54 % of SMEs reported that bank overdrafts are relevant, followed by 51 % that considered bank loans to be relevant (European Central Bank 2017a). Moreover, the results of the KfW panel show that, in 2016, two-thirds of all SMEs used bank credit to finance an investment, and the loan financing of investments increased slightly in 2016. Yet, the strong desire for financial independence and concern about unfavorable financing conditions continues to hinder SMEs from seeking credit (Schwartz 2017), partly because they tend to be more concerned about unfavorable financing conditions than large companies. And, as reported by the Deutsche Bundesbank during the financial and economic crisis including the European debt crisis, companies in the euro zone began substituting bank loans with other debt instruments and with equity (Deutsche Bundesbank 2018a).

In the context of SME lending, and given the greater regulatory burdens of the financial crisis, a capital discount factor, called the SME supporting factor (SME SF), was proposed by the EBA in January 2014 (European Banking Authority 2016). Article 501(1) of the Capital Requirements Regulation (CRR) introduces the SME SF, under which capital requirements for credit risk on exposures to SMEs are multiplied by a factor of 0.7619 (Amtsblatt der Europäischen Union 2013). This capital discount was introduced for all EU countries.[29]

29 Spain introduced the SME SF in September 2013 by national legislation (Mayordomo and Rodríguez-Moreno 2016).

The SME SF allows banks to decrease capital requirements for credit risk on exposures to firms with a turnover of below EUR 50 million. As detailed in the EBA (2016) report, the intention of this deduction is to allow banks to increase lending to SMEs following the crisis, and to ease regulatory changes that could have a disproportionate effect on SME lending. This ensures an adequate flow of credit to SMEs (European Banking Authority 2016; Mayordomo and Rodríguez-Moreno 2016).

Nevertheless, the concern persists that these regulations overall result in a depersonalization of the relationship between lenders and borrowers because they impose standardized processes on banks. This can severely restrict the personal character of the bank-borrower relationship that is distinctive in the concept of relationship lending. For example, since the introduction of Basel II and III, a rating has been mandatory for credit-taking companies.

The European Central Bank (2017a) found with the SAFE that SMEs felt that terms and conditions for bank loans had become better due to a net decline in interest rates. They also cited an increase in the available size and maturity of loans and overdrafts. However, a positive net percentage of SMEs continued to document a tightening in the collateral and other requirements of banks and in other financing costs. The SMEs surveyed indicated, "that the increase in their needs for external financing was less than the improvement in their access to external funds" (European Central Bank 2017a, p. 4).

In addition, in reference to the results of the KfW SME panel, the strong desire for financial independence and the concern about unfavorable financing conditions keeps many SMEs from seeking credit (Schwartz 2017). Brackschulze et al. (2011) point out that loans to companies with poor ratings have become significantly more expensive as a result of higher capital requirements for banks. Moreover, according to Schindele and Szczesny (2016), the introduction of the Basel regulation that banks use an internal rating system (IRBA approach) has significantly increased the cost of credit for SMEs. The study also shows that bank interest rates using the modified standardized approach have risen by 0.16 percentage points for loans to SMEs with a poor rating.

Instead of relying solely on mechanistic methods, regulations should also allow for and foster banking business models that include soft factors, such as trust and the strength of a relationship with firm management. This would encourage a more comprehensive assessment of companies (Ayadi, Arbak, and Pieter De Groen 2012; Ferri, Murro, and Rotondi 2014). At the same time, SMEs are reconsidering the costs and benefits associated with a bank relationship as more alternative financing options emerge. Consequently, firms must assess alternatives to classic bank lending.

2.5.4 New market entrants into the financial and banking system

The comprehensive regulations and new business models are altering the banking landscape and are thus shifting corporate financing. Financial transactions today are automated on anonymous markets, where little relationship building is needed. The impression is that advancements in information and communication technology appear to be accelerating the transition from relationship-intensive services to more market- or transaction-oriented financial products.

As Petersen and Rajan (2002) note, there is a continuing discussion about whether the effects of the advances in information technology produce improvements in productivity (see, e.g., Gordon 1999). Petersen and Rajan (2002) state that the advances in information technology are moving the financial sector to greater information availability and decreased processing expenses, and that these advances stand in line with improvements in bank productivity. Moreover, Ergungor (2005) relates the low performance of relationship bankers to the change in the competitive composition of the banking market. Although face-to-face relationships continue to be crucial for many borrowers, the barriers for other lenders to gain access to that segment of the banking market are falling. These developments are intensifying the competitive pressures on local banks. Ergungor (2005) concludes this pressure will lower the profitability of smaller local banks.

Accordingly, in the rapidly growing financial technology industry ("FinTech"), new services and business models such as peer-to-peer platforms (e.g., crowdfunding, crowdlending, block-chain applications) have emerged throughout the world, providing a variety of investment and financing opportunities to customers. These changes have been occurring for a long time, but the advancements since the financial crisis are striking. The technological progress and the continuing emergence of new FinTechs are especially attractive for more opaque SMEs because they offer direct and convenient access to new funding sources.

Jiménez, Salas, and Saurina (2009) find that banks and borrowers become more effective and efficient when technological improvements enable the use of transactional banking. Jiménez et al. (2009) expect that a more distinct specialization of banks in the future will emerge. They posit that local banks will focus mainly on opaque and informationally complex borrowers, while big national banks, with typically less distinct branch networks, will serve more transparent borrowers using transactional lending technologies.

FinTechs are one of the most prominent business sectors that have altered how financial systems operate. Philippon (2016) defines FinTechs as "digital innovations and technology-enabled business model innovations in the financial sector. Such innovations can disrupt existing industry structures and blur industry boundaries, facilitate strategic disintermediation, revolutionize how existing firms create and deliver products and services, provide new gateways for entrepreneurship, democratize access to financial services, but also create significant privacy, regulatory, and law enforcement challenges" (Philippon 2016, p. 2).[30]

Commissioned by the Federal Ministry of Finance, Dorfleitner et al. (2016) study the FinTech sector in Germany. They collect data on the market volumes of German FinTech companies for the 2007–2015 period. They identify a total of 433 companies with business activity in Germany. Of those, 346 had active business activity. The remaining 87 were either not active prior to 2016 or had already discontinued their businesses.

In 2015, the total market volume of FinTechs operating in Germany in the finance and asset management segments amounted to EUR 2.2 billion. Very high growth rates have been observed in recent years in almost all FinTech segments. Its relevance to the German banking segment is continuing to grow. FinTechs can serve customer needs much more quickly and are not as subject to new regulations (such as Basel II and Basel III) as banks.

Hainz and Wiegand (2013) find that, as the use of new information technologies has become more prevalent, credit risk models have concurrently gained in prominence. This has had a profound impact on information processing. The change makes itself felt most strongly in banking regulation, because it directs the focus to the use of these models, which are built on hard information (Hainz and Wiegand 2013). The Basel regulations foster a reliance on mechanistic

30 As reported by Dorfleitner et al. (2016), it is difficult to precisely define the term FinTech. Therefore, the definition is usually made by providing a general description of FinTechs' characteristics, as well as by a description of the individual segments that make up the FinTech sector. According to Dorfleitner et al. (2016), FinTechs are companies that combine innovative technologies with financial services and try to revolutionize the financial industry. Philippon (2016) writes: "Examples of innovations that are central to FinTech today include cryptocurrencies and the blockchain, new digital advisory and trading systems, artificial intelligence and machine learning, peer-to-peer lending, equity crowdfunding and mobile payment systems" (Philippon 2016, p. 2). FinTechs are active in various business segments, such as lending and financing, retail banking, payments and transfers, financial management, markets and exchanges, and insurance, with such prominent companies as Credible, Even, Moven, GObank, Nutmeg, Coinbase, and Oscar.

methods, while appropriate regulation should also incorporate banking business models that emphasize soft information.

Philippon (2016) describes the current financial system as somewhat inefficient. In order to reach significant welfare gains, especially in advanced economies, new players must enter the market. A total of 87 % of banks surveyed are currently cooperating with a FinTech company and are also striving to participate or cooperate with FinTech companies in the future. One of the key elements of relationship lending is tacit knowledge, for example, the acquisition of soft information and the establishment of trust in the bank-borrower relationship (see also Howorth and Moro 2012). But, due to the rapidly changing technological and financial environment, communication between firms and banks has become vastly more impersonal. Progress in information technology tends to boost the availability and facilitation of hard information. Thus, the level of impersonality in the bank-borrower relationship is only expected to increase.

In line with Liberti and Petersen (2018), technological progress has forced a reliance in financial transactions on hard information. Nevertheless, the synergy between hard and soft information is fundamental to the realization of financial transactions.[31] With a view to the future of FinTechs, these companies may find long-term survival challenging due to the growing share of very young companies and the difficulty of quickly building a large customer base. Because a banking license is fundamental to doing business, however, more collaborations and partnerships between FinTechs and traditional banks are being established. FinTechs can therefore gain access to market knowledge and funding, while simultaneously expanding their customer base and ideally ensuring their survival.

FinTechs offer arm's-length products and services, in contrast to relationship lending, which emphasizes building relationships over years and continuing to upsell products and services. Sette and Gobbi (2015) note again the critical aspect that, during financially difficult times, relationship banks support borrowers more than transactional lenders.

Overall, these developments have led to increased product transparency, as well as to ongoing pressure on the margins of a bank's products and services. At the same time, an ease in lending, a slight decline in bank lending due to improved internal financing, and a more diversified funding mix based on improved access to alternative funding sources, has permanently altered the capital structure of

31 Petersen and Rajan (2002) show that the distance between small companies and their banks is increasing, which is also a critical factor in the application of hard information.

non-financial corporations. Financing alternatives such as FinTechs are able to offer SMEs direct and convenient access to new sources of financing.

In this context, Li, Spigt, and Swinkels (2017) study 522 U.S. firms that engage in FinTech activities and find more complements between FinTechs and traditional banking than substitutions and disruptive innovations. They show that, despite the fact that FinTechs are growing quickly, they may still be too small to impact incumbent banks. Furthermore, it is difficult for consumers to adjust to some of the new developments, or to trust in their online and automatic services. Yet, successful FinTechs may ultimately attack banks' dominant position by enhancing the quality and efficiency of traditional services.

Banks have been responding to these developments by buying FinTech startups or by establishing their own FinTech associations (Li et al. 2017). In this respect, it is expected that financial institutions will interact even more with FinTechs in the future, because they may offer the potential to cut marginal costs, increase productivity, gain access to innovations, or provide services that banks do not. Dorfleitner and Hornuf (2016) report for the U.K. that, by 2015, 13.9 % of SMEs were already using FinTech financing. For the banks, this change means that, more than ever before, they will be forced to tailor their business models to the changing frameworks and needs of their customers.

2.6 SMEs and family firms

According to the EU Recommendation 2003/361/EG, companies with less than 250 employees or an annual turnover of less or equal to EUR 50 million, along with a balance sheet total of less or equal to EUR 43 million, are classified as SMEs (European Commission 2015).[32] SMEs are usually characterized by high economic and legal independence, as well as by integration of ownership and management. Most medium-sized companies are family businesses. Around 95 % of all companies in Germany are family-owned, and their specific way of operating - long-term, stable, with an aim of being independent - cannot be solely captured by a quantitative definition based on annual turnover or balance sheet total. Shareholder loyalty and capital

32 According to the IfM Bonn (2017), companies with less than 500 employees and an annual turnover of less than or equal to EUR 50 million are defined as family firms. This section follows in part an as yet unpublished paper, which is available upon request (Sauter 2014).

commitment also usually characterize these companies (Bundesverband der Deutschen Industrie e.V. 2015).

SMEs and, hence, family firms traditionally rely strongly on bank lending and bank loans with different maturities; in fact, credit lines and leasing contracts represent the most important sources of funding for these companies after internal financing (Zimmermann 2017). Zimmermann (2017) posits that bank loans will remain an important source of financing because 55 % of companies conducted credit negotiations in 2016. Long-term loans were most frequently in demand, with 56 % of companies conducting credit negotiations, followed by medium- (53 %) and short-term loans (37 %).

However, since the financial crisis, credit conditions have deteriorated, and the analysis of bank lending conditions across the euro area has received great attention in order to identify dispersion in funding conditions and financial fragmentation. This increasing attention is due to the fact that banks play a particularly important role for the European economy, and obviously for German SMEs because of their strong bank orientation. Banks undertake a key role in the financing of SMEs, where information can be more opaque. Given the asymmetric information between lenders and borrowers in debt markets, banks act as intermediaries to reduce the barriers to accessing credit (Köhler-Ulbrich et al. 2016).

Because bank lending is so critical for SMEs, this section explores the characteristics banks may favor when deciding on bank lending to SMEs. In this context, Bopaiah (1998) states that family ownership can proxy for firm characteristics that banks may favor, because family ownership typically stands for a long-term perspective, management cohesiveness, concern for company reputation, aspirations to be self-regulated, and personal interaction in lending relationships. Bopaiah (1998) writes that these factors may be referred to as the "character" of the family firm and may affect the loan decision.

Many studies examine the lending relationship from the perspective of the credit institution by investigating credit data files. This study considers the lending relationship from the firm's perspective, more precisely from the perspective of SMEs and, thus, family firms. In this context, the question arises: Why family firms? Family firms carry certain characteristics that can be captured by their investment and financing behavior and in dealing with stakeholders. Their relationship management differs from that of non-family firms. In the next section, different definitions of family firms and the definition used here are presented. In addition, characteristics of family firms, their investment and financing behavior, capital structure, as well as how they approach stakeholders are discussed.

2.6.1 Definition of family firms

Family firms, like other companies, differ widely, so a uniform definition is difficult to establish. How these companies operate can diverge dramatically as well (Miller, Le Breton-Miller, Lester, and Cannella 2007). The challenge of doing research on family firms without a consistent definition is even more difficult when international comparisons are drawn and cultural spaces compared. In this context, Lansberg, Perrow, and Rogolsky (1988) ask in the first edition of the Family Business Review: "What is a family business?" (Lansberg et al. 1988, p. 1). With regard to the need for a uniform definition, the authors write: "Until researchers agree on what a family business is, they will find it difficult to build on each other's work and to develop a usable knowledge base" (Lansberg et al. 1988, p. 2).

A typical family business is characterized as an organization under the control and leadership of one or several family members, and by the fact that it has been in the hands of one family for several generations (Miller et al. 2007). McConaughy, Walker, Henderson, and Mishra (1998) define a family enterprise as a company run by its founder or members of the founding family. Pérez-González (2006) concentrates on later generations with a genetic relationship to the founder, or a principal owner who acts as manager of the company. According to Villalonga and Amit (2006), a family business is a company whose founder, or whose member of the family by genetic relatedness or marriage, is the chief executive or owns at least 5 % of the company's capital. Klein, Astrachan, and Smyrnios (2005) analyze 1,166 firms from the German Hoppenstedt database in order to define family firms. They propose using a scale that measures the extent and quality of the influence of a family along three dimensions: power (ownership and property rights), experience (entrepreneurial experience of the generation), and culture (family affiliation with the company). These three dimensions are assigned values of between 0.0 and 1.0, which add up to the F-PEC scale (Family Influence on Power, Experience, and Culture). The F-PEC scale has been used in a series of studies and has contributed to theory development, especially with regard to the family influence on different resources and on the family as a source of a competitive advantage (Klein et al. 2005; Mietzner and Tyrell 2012).

Chua, Chrisman, and Sharma (1999) posit a distinction between theoretical and operational definitions. They believe a theoretical definition should describe the firm's character, because it distinguishes the family firm from other companies. In line with this reasoning, a definition should capture the essence of the firm's uniqueness. The authors analyze a sample of 453 family firms and test two structural equilibrium models. They document that definitions of family firms based on the components of ownership, governance, management, and succession are not sufficient because they do not capture character. Character comprises the vision for the company that is defined by the family, the intention to pursue this vision over generations, and the associated behavior (Chua et al. 1999).

Within the scope of this study, companies are defined as family firms when the majority ownership (> 50 %) is held by the family, and/or when one or more family members are active in the management of the company.[33]

2.6.2 Performance of family firms

Because family firms are the most common form of organization in the world, research has intensively focused on their characteristics over the past decade by drawing comparisons between family and non-family firms. La Porta, Lopez-de-Silanes, and Shleifer (1999) examined data on the ownership structure of large corporations in twenty-seven wealthy economies in order to identify the dominant shareholder. They find that most companies are owned by a shareholder which is a family (La Porta et al. 1999). Therefore, the focus of many studies is on whether a family has a positive or negative influence on the value of a company, and on whether family firms are more successful than non-family firms. Scholars have stated arguments both for and against the better performance of family firms. Family altruism and family nepotism proponents advise a negative influence of family firms on performance (Bloom and Van Reenen 2007; Pérez-González 2006), while advocates claiming a long-term orientation and lower owner-management agency costs suggest a positive influence (Audretsch, Hülsbeck, and Lehmann 2013; Miller and Le Breton-Miller 2005; Wagner, Block, Miller, Schwens, and Xi 2015). Since many studies put founder companies and successor family companies together, it is difficult to puzzle out the performance effects of family versus non-family firms.

Villalonga and Amit (2006) analyzed the Fortune 500 companies from 1994 to 2000 and show that a family business creates value when the founder acts as CEO or chairman, together with a non-family CEO. In contrast to this result, value in the company is diminished when a successor is appointed as CEO or chairman of the company. Thus, Villalonga and Amit (2006) show that the empirical relations among family ownership, control, or management and firm performance is entirely dependent on the definition of family firms being applied. The authors

33 The definition also includes family businesses that have not yet experienced the first generation transfer, i.e., founder-run firms.

note that this relation is not only decisive in the magnitude of the effects, but also in the signs, which change from positive to negative when founder-led companies are excluded from the definition (Amit and Villalonga 2014; Villalonga and Amit 2006).

Barontini and Caprio (2006) examined the relationship between ownership structure and corporate performance in Continental Europe with data from 675 listed companies from eleven countries. They show that company value and operational performance are higher in founder-controlled companies. If, however, a descendant holds the position of CEO, family-controlled companies are statistically indistinguishable from non-family companies in terms of value and operational performance. Ehrhardt, Nowak, and Weber (2006) investigated the development of the ownership structure, company control, and performance of family firms in Germany over a period of 100 years. Their sample consisted of German stock corporations that were established before WWI and still existed in 2003. The authors document that family firms in terms of operational performance exceed non-family firms, but this performance decreases over generations (Ehrhardt et al. 2006).

Miller et al. (2007) find that the superiority of family firms with respect to performance depends again on the definition of a family firm and the source of the data. They note the results are especially sensitive to the distinction between startups in which the family of the founder is not involved, and companies in which the founder controls the company, with other family members acting as owners or managers. While founder companies exhibit performance advantages over non-family firms, family firms that are run by successors do not. They examined the Fortune 1000 companies, and document that, as soon as individual founder companies are removed from the sample, there is no evidence for a superior market rating of family firms compared to other companies (Miller et al. 2007).

O'Boyle, Pollack, and Rutherford (2012) initiated a meta-analysis of the performance differences between family and non-family firms. Overall, they show a small and insignificantly positive effect of family involvement on firm performance. Wagner et al. (2015) conduct a meta-analysis including 380 primary studies from 41 countries and document a positive effect of family governance on financial performance in 61 % of the studies. The results of the meta-analysis show that this effect is statistically significant but economically relatively small. The authors note that the superior performance of family companies becomes stronger once an ownership definition is used (Chrisman et al. 2018; Fattoum-Guedri, Guedri, and Delmar 2018; Le Breton-Miller, Miller, and Lester 2011; Miller, Le Breton-Miller, and Lester 2013; Zellweger and Nason 2008). Yet, Sraer and Thesmar (2007) argue that, in France, family firms that are managed by successor generations tend to have higher performance.

Most studies find that companies run by a founder perform better and provide more value to a company than non-family firms, while successive generations cannot generate additional value for the company (Villalonga and Amit 2006). Furthermore, Bennedsen, Nielsen, Pérez-González, and Wolfenzon (2007) use a dataset from Denmark and investigate the influence of family characteristics in corporate decision-making. They explore how these decisions impact firm performance by concentrating on the decision to appoint either a family member or an external CEO. They show that family successions have a large negative effect on firm performance. Additionally, the authors find that family-CEO underperformance is predominantly higher in fast-growing industries, industries with a highly skilled labor force, and relatively large companies. The results show that professional, non-family CEOs offer extremely valuable services to the organizations they manage.

However, in this context, the question arises as to how the superior performance of founder-run firms can be explained (Hess 2008). The following subsections will shed light on this question by discussing several aspects of the investment and financing behavior, capital structure, and stakeholder relationships of these companies. Because most family firms fall in the SME sector, the results of current studies on SMEs will be presented, as they analyze the financing and investment behavior of these companies. The findings will then be placed in the context of family firms in more depth.

2.6.3 Financing of family firms

According to the Institut für Mittelstandsforschung (IfM) Bonn, around 3.7 million companies, or 99.6 % of all companies in the private sector in Germany, belong to the German Mittelstand. Most are family firms, and indeed around 95 % of all companies in Germany are family-owned (Bundesverband der Deutschen Industrie e.V. 2015). Family firms have special features or characteristics that will be outlined in the following. Lending conditions for both SMEs and large companies have been impacted noticeably by the financial crisis, with a substantial credit contraction since 2008 (European Banking Authority 2016). According to the EBA (2016) report, following the financial crisis, SME bank lending experienced a drop in volume, and, regardless of growth, SME lending continued to be below its pre-crisis level. Differences in SME bank lending exist across bank types (European Banking Authority 2016).

A review by the Deutsche Bundesbank (2011) of loans to non-financial corporations by bank type confirms these differences. Savings banks and cooperative banks made positive contributions to annual growth rates of loans to these companies from as early as mid-2006 throughout the reporting period until 2011. But from September 2009, the Landesbanken steadily cut back their contributions. Likewise, in 2009, branches of foreign banks were cutting back their contributions, and big banks followed suit. Thus, with a view to the crisis, savings banks and cooperative banks prolonged their lending activities during that time, while other bank types scaled back (Deutsche Bundesbank 2011).

In addition, as the EBA (2016) report documents, over recent years, access to finance has remained of greater concern to SMEs than to large companies. The survey results of the EBA (2016) report show that around 16 % of SMEs had trouble obtaining bank funding, due to such reasons as being discouraged to apply, rejection because of high costs, or receiving only a partial loan. This compares to 10 % of large companies that experienced these reasons when applying for bank lending. The difficulties of bank funding vary also by firm size within the SME sector, with micro and small firms being most affected (European Banking Authority 2016). According to the EBA (2016) report, interest rates are generally higher for SMEs than for large companies. In addition, collateral requirements were tightened in the post-crisis period. The Deutsche Bundesbank (2009) documents that the standards for SME loans were eased markedly more, or have been tightened less, since mid-2007 compared to large companies. In line with the survey results, collateral did not have an increasing impact on the credit standards in 2008 (Deutsche Bundesbank 2009). In the current SAFE by ECB, covering the October 2016–March 2017 period, a positive net percentage of SMEs continued to document a tightening in the collateral and other requirements of banks, as well as in other costs of financing (European Central Bank 2017a).

The study of the KfW Bankengruppe documents that the financing situation in SMEs relaxed considerably between 2004 and 2007. In 2004, 47 % of SMEs were affected by a bank rejection of their credit requests, but this share fell to 25 % by 2007. The number of companies that received a credit rejection fell over the same period, from 360,000 to 180,000. However, small businesses are still more affected by bank loan rejections than larger SMEs (Plankensteiner and Zimmermann 2009). With respect to the recent financial crisis, the study of the KfW Bankengruppe shows that in 2008 insufficient collateral was most frequently cited as the reason for credit rejections by responding companies (48 %). Next was the equity ratio as a key indicator of the creditworthiness of a company (42 %), followed by a change in the bank's business policy (33 %), and low profitability (29 %). Moreover, the reason for a credit rejection that the bank's business policy had changed rose significantly (+5 percentage points), while other reasons stagnated or declined slightly. This result is in line with the ECB's BLS of euro zone bank lending parameters for companies according to which credit institutions continued to tighten their credit standards in the euro zone after the financial crisis (Köhler-Ulbrich et al. 2016; Plankensteiner and Zimmermann 2009).

Overall, the newest KfW study and the EBA (2016) report confirm that SMEs are more concerned with facing unfavorable financing conditions or with putting too much effort into credit negotiations. For 29 % of small SMEs, high collateral requirements speak against bank financing (Schwartz 2017). It is particularly important for small businesses to strengthen their negotiating skills with credit institutions. This includes both intensive preparation for negotiations, as well as a transparent and comprehensible documentation of the business ideas and processes. In particular, companies must recognize their ratings and seek dialogue with their banks (Reize and Lo 2008).

Note next that family businesses, compared to non-family businesses, generally exhibit very different behavior. The behavior is reflected most strongly in a family's pursuit for independence and control, its planning horizon, and its risk exposure. In general, family firms are perceived as independent, long-term-oriented, and risk-averse, and these characteristics are also reflected in their financing behavior. In this context, the KfW SME panel shows that the strong desire for financial independence and concern about unfavorable financing conditions keeps many SMEs away from credit negotiations. Although family firms consider bank loans the most important external financing source, the desire for financial independence is most often opposed to bank financing. This is particularly true for SMEs: 44 % desire to avoid (additional) debt. In addition, 33 % are not seeking external financing (Schwartz 2017).

Family members often have a leading role in the strategic and operational management, and, thereby, have a strong influence on the business activities (Levin and Travis 1987; Schraml 2010). Moreover, they are usually very eager to preserve their privacy (Dreux 1990; Kets de Vries 1993). In this context, it is often argued that the absence of external influence on the family business operations and the power of the family may generate efficiency and flexibility in decision-making (Kets de Vries 1993). The family's control over the company is usually reflected in the limited distribution of company shares, which allows it to stay financially independent to a certain extent (Chrisman et al. 2003; Schraml 2010).

Brealey, Leland, and Pyle (1977) argue that a higher ownership stake may be an indicator of the value of a company's investments, which may hint at conservative investment choices of these companies and may improve the company's access to funding (see also Bopaiah 1998). However, at the same time, the desire for independence and control may bring potential negative consequences for family firms, because it may lead to stagnant or negative corporate development (Poutziouris 2001). Internal equity may not be sufficient, and, subsequently, external funding may be required. This appears to be particularly important for small and young family businesses. In this context, Hutchinson (1995) writes: "For most owner-managed small firms, there is an additional emphasis on the need to finance expansion through debt capital provided by banks because the use of equity in the early stages of development is limited to an individual and/or his family's contributions" (Hutchinson 1995, p. 233).

In this respect, the KfW study documents that larger SMEs are more open to financing by banks, as their investment projects are usually larger, and, thus, the possibilities of full financing by their own resources are likely to be more limited. The need for credit financing for larger companies is consequently more pronounced (Schwartz 2017).

With respect to the planning horizon of family firms, Ward (1997) finds that: "Family firms have a unique opportunity to be long-term oriented. [...] For a strong family, long-term value is much preferred to short-term results" (Ward 1997, p. 333). He emphasizes the unique advantage of a long-term orientation of these companies, in contrast to many other investors, who focus on short-term objectives.

James (1999) attributes the expanded planning horizon in family businesses to the fundamental desire of the family to pass the company to future generations. These companies focus on a long-term increase in company value (Krempel and Von Weizsäcker 2006). However, long-term orientation may also come with a certain risk aversion. With respect to investment decisions, this aversion may lead to reluctant behavior, reflected, e.g., in low research and development expenditures (Schraml 2010). Family firms are hesitant to diversify their assets because they want to preserve their influence.

Anderson and Reeb (2003) analyzed American companies, and document that family firms are less diversified than non-family firms. For the family, the company likely represents a long-term and little diversified investment, which, therefore, holds high unsystematic risk. This in turn suggests there may be a target conflict between the diversification of shares and the protection of the family's control over the firm. The long-term commitment of the family's financial resources in the company represents a risk factor. The family often invests large amounts of their own private assets in the company. When faced with a lack of financial diversification, a negative business development can have immediate effects on a family's assets, and may even lead to liquidity problems (Haynes, Walker, Rowe, and Hong 1999; Schraml 2010).

Moreover, long-term orientation is often seen as a competitive advantage of family businesses over non-family businesses. However, Block (2012) uses panel data from American family and non-family firms to assess whether and under what conditions family businesses are longer-term oriented than non-family businesses. He analyzes spending on research and development. The results show there is no evidence that family businesses are investing more resources in long-term projects than non-family businesses. However, the analysis of a sample of only family firms shows that family leadership has a positive effect on the level of R&D expenditures, while family ownership seems to have a negative effect (Block 2012).

In addition, Haynes et al. (1999) investigate 637 family firms to determine whether their financial resources are used to support the company or to finance family needs. They find that families tend to refer to financial resources to meet family needs, instead of contributing to the benefit of the company. The mix of entrepreneurial and family resources can make accountability more difficult and can lead to opportunism on the part of family members (Gibb Dyer 2006). Since control and management are both in the hands of the family, decisions may be adopted that primarily satisfy the family's preferences, while disregarding minority shareholders. Moreover, potential conflicts within the family may send negative signals to the outside, which could represent an increased risk for external investors.

Various studies have analyzed the capital structure of family firms and non-family firms. McConaughy et al. (2001) examined American family businesses and non-family businesses and find that family firms have higher equity ratios than non-family firms. In contrast, Anderson and Reeb (2003) analyze 319 S&P 500 firms from 1993 to 1999 and document no difference in the leverage of American family versus non-family firms. Gallo, Tàpies, and Cappuyns (2004) investigated Spanish family companies and non-family companies and find that family firms have a significantly lower degree of indebtedness than non-family firms. Studies on the financial structure of German family firms support these findings and show that family companies have a relatively healthy equity ratio. Redlefsen and Eiben (2006) also find an average equity ratio of around 36 % for family enterprises.[34]

---

34 Note, however, that the study by Redlefsen and Eiben (2006) was conducted before the recent financial crisis, and it can be assumed that the equity ratio level has changed since then.

The Deutsche Bundesbank (2009) documents that, overall, the favorable development of the equity base in 2007 continued. Among the various sectors of the economy, the manufacturing industry remained in the top position with 28.5 %, followed by the wholesale industry (25 %), business-related service providers (24 %), the transport industry (21 %), and the retail industry (18 %). The construction industry continued to rank at 11.5 %. At the same time, liabilities to banks lost their significance in the long-term, while those with short maturities managed to stabilize their positions (Deutsche Bundesbank 2009). The Deutsche Bundesbank (2014) evaluates that SMEs expanded their equity more sharply than their liabilities and provisions. However, at 25 %, the share of equity of SMEs is still below their pre-crisis level (Deutsche Bundesbank 2014). Additionally, the Deutsche Bundesbank (2015) documents that own funds as a share of non-financial companies' total assets was 29.5 % at the end of 2014. The long-term trend to strengthen the equity base thus continued. Differentiated by company size, SMEs slightly increased their equity ratio once again to 25.5 % (Deutsche Bundesbank 2015). In comparison with Redlefsen and Eiben (2006), the analyses show that the equity ratio decreased following the financial crisis starting in 2007 and picked up only slightly in the years afterward. Apart from that, the trend toward strengthening equity continued. Overall, this was significantly stronger than in the average of previous years (Deutsche Bundesbank 2016). According to the Deutsche Bundesbank (2017c), the services industry recorded a significant strengthening of the equity ratio to 35 %, particularly as a result of retained earnings. This is the highest aggregated value since the beginning of the survey in 2007 (Deutsche Bundesbank 2017c).

The KfW SME panel 2017 documents that the already high self-financing capacity of SMEs once again gained slightly. Stable revenues and returns increased the average equity ratio by 0.3 percentage points to 30 % for the first time in the past year (2015: 29.7 %), and the equity ratio of micro-enterprises rose sharply (22.5 %). Very large SMEs were able to increase their equity ratio again (33.6 %), despite the already very high level. According to the KfW study, in the past fifteen years, SMEs achieved massive improvements in their equity situation (2002: 18 %). The retention of profits and continued reluctance to invest contributed considerably. In 2016, only 30 % of SMEs had a relatively low equity base of less than 10 %. By contrast, almost half had relatively high equity ratios of at least 30 %. Again, the large SMEs showed the highest increase (+6 percentage points to 56 %).

Equally positive, only 10 % of SMEs still have a negative equity ratio. In contrast, the equity ratio of SMEs from the construction industry dropped sharply by 6 percentage points to 14 % (2015: 22 %). One driver of this is the increased borrowing in this segment due to booming residential construction (EUR 9 billion in 2016 compared to EUR 4 billion in 2015). Only 17 % of companies in this segment have a relatively high equity ratio of at least 30 % (2015: 36 %), and about 50 % of SMEs have a relatively low equity ratio of less than 10 % (2015: 38 %). Traditionally, the equity base of the construction industry has always been comparatively low. The KfW study also notes that the average equity ratio of companies has been fairly constant for three years, albeit at a high level. In the future, only small increases are expected (Schwartz 2017).

Due to the influence of the owner family on capital structure decisions, a preference for a healthy equity ratio can be assumed (Schraml 2010). Mishra and McConaughy (1999) find that family firms are afraid of a loss of control, and, as a result, they try to avoid indebtedness and to maintain a high equity ratio (see also Schraml 2010). In addition, a high debt ratio would increase the risk of insolvency, and, thus, the risk of losing the company (Jensen and Meckling 1976; Schraml 2010). However, a contradictory argument is also possible. The family's aim to maintain independence and control may allow these firms to avoid funding that implies a certain control over the management of the company. Exerting influence on a company's management by financing company activities may be the case for financing by banks, but it is mainly applicable to financing by external equity holders (Ellul 2008; Hutchinson 1995; Jensen and Meckling 1976; Myers and Majluf 1984; Poutziouris 2001; Schraml 2010).

In a lending relationship, a bank typically obtains non-public information, and may even gain a voice in the company's operations due to contractual arrangements or based on a seat on the control committee (Jensen 1986). Additionally, credit agreements may include covenants that can strengthen the control and co-decision-making rights of the relationship lender (Baker and Wruck 1989; Theilacker 2010). Although bank financing may imply it can exercise some control and co-decision-making rights, it does not result in any changes in ownership structure (in contrast to financing by external equity shareholders) (Schraml 2010). In line with this reasoning, family firms prefer bank financing because it allows the company a greater balance between independence and control by the owner family. Therefore, it is likely the family would prefer the influence of a bank over the far greater influence of an external equity investor.

Overall, Bopaiah (1998) documents that family ownership is probably not the only variable that influences the loan decision. Rather, the characteristics of family firms together stand for a more conservative approach to investments, which may have a positive influence on the bank's lending decision despite the financial crisis. A healthy equity ratio may also imply greater negotiating power toward banks, meaning a better starting position as well as a better renegotiation position. Bopaiah (1998) notes further that the more conservative approach of family firms could be an indicator of a limited moral hazard problem from the perspective of the bank. In general, the empirical findings seem to be somewhat mixed. However, the quest for financial independence, the long-term orientation, the degree of risk aversion, and the relatively high equity base appear to be generally agreed upon by scholars. These characteristics may finally lead to better credit availability and may outweigh any potentially negative characteristics that also come with family firms (Bopaiah 1998).

2.7 Deriving the research model on relationship banking

In order to measure the value of bank relationships, Figure 2-6 shows the graphical research model and the links among the determinants, characteristics, and impact of bank relationships. While today there are many different ways companies and banks can interact, in light of the theoretical argumentation, it is assumed that relationship banking remains a "key modus operandi" (Degryse et al. 2009, p. 58).

The next sections present evidence from global studies, followed by an outline of the differences between market- and bank-based financial systems. The empirical findings are then summarized. There is a great deal of literature that investigates whether and how relationship lending can benefit a borrower in a market- versus a bank-based financial system. This section studies the various characteristics of bank relationships with respect to loan, relationship, firm, and control characteristics. Research has focused primarily on these four categories of lending characteristics when studying banking relationships. Hence, the same classification has been adopted here. The research model in Figure 2-6 thus facilitates the derivation of the hypotheses in section 2.8.

2.7.1 Literature review on the economic costs and benefits of relationship banking

A total of 177 global studies have been analyzed in order to compare market- and bank-based financial systems. The effects of the various relationship lending characteristics, such as the number and duration of the bank relationships, on the variables collateral requirements, cost of debt, and credit availability, have all been studied. These three variables are investigated for the following reasons: Lending relationships can help solve potential information asymmetry problems between borrowers and lenders through repeated interactions, which

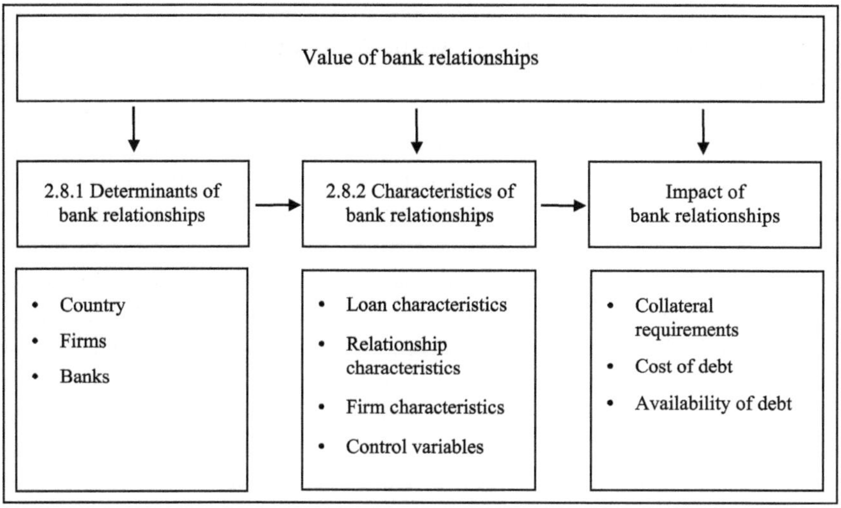

Figure 2-6: Research model

This figure shows the research model that is used throughout this study. It shows the composition of the value of bank relationships, which consists of their determinants, characteristics, and impact.[35]

lead to a certain transparency that can result in significant benefits and costs for borrowers.

The benefits are a lower probability of pledging collateral, lower interest spreads, and a greater availability of finance. EBA (2016) documents that access to finance has generally been of greater concern to SMEs than to large companies. The Deutsche Bundesbank shows that SMEs were often unable to raise funds on the capital market due to their size and legal form. In addition to the costs associated with an IPO, which can be a significant source of liquidity for SMEs, informational deficiencies contribute to a cautious funding supply (Deutsche Bundesbank 2012). The EBA (2016) highlights in its report that other sources of financing, for example, equity finance, capital market debt, and securitization, although available, are not as widely used (European Banking Authority 2016).

According to EBA (2016), SMEs remain largely reliant on bank-related lending (e.g., credit lines and banks loans) to finance company activities. Yet, especially during times of financial distress, scholars have found that companies

35 Illustration closely aligned with Degryse et al. (2009).

are more likely to obtain a loan with more favorable terms from a relationship bank (Bolton et al. 2016; Cotugno, Monferrà, and Sampagnaro 2013a; Jiangli et al. 2008).

However, these potential benefits also bring costs. Borrowers can get informationally captured, which may lead to hold-up costs. Borrowers may then face difficulties in obtaining credit from alternative lenders. In addition, banks may try to extract rents from the informationally captured borrowers. Because these three variables are the basis of each loan negotiation, the majority of empirical studies focuses on them when studying lending relationships. In order to ensure comparability with prior research, these variables are used in this study as well. The discussion will emphasize the differences between the market- and bank-based financial systems. Figure 2-7 shows the countries analyzed and how they are classified.[36]

Figure 2-7 shows the twelve countries with market-based systems and the fourteen countries with bank-based systems that were investigated here. Currently, no critical studies for Australia, Austria, Denmark, Greece, Hong Kong, Ireland, Israel, New Zealand, Portugal, or Singapore have been identified. However, two cross-country studies include Australia in their samples (Beck, Demirgüç-Kunt, and Pería 2011; La Porta et al. 1999; La Porta et al. 1997, 1998; Levine 2002; Qian and Strahan 2007). Each country studied is divided into a financial system according to whether it is shaped principally by market- or bank-based indicators. This classification was done to illustrate the potential differences between the two systems in the costs and benefits of relationship lending, and later to be able to classify the findings of this study accordingly. The classification into the two financial systems can be derived following La Porta et al. (1999), La Porta et al. (1997, 1998), and Levine (2002).

La Porta et al. (1998) study laws governing investor protection, the quality of enforcement of these laws, and ownership concentration in forty-nine countries. Countries with common law rules generally protect investors more strongly than those with civil law rules. The German civil law and the Scandinavian countries are somewhat in the middle regarding investor protections, while both had the highest quality of law enforcement. Traditionally, law enforcement was strong in common law countries as well, while it is weakest in French civil law countries.

One response to poor investor protection is ownership concentration. Moreover, good accounting standards and shareholder protection measures are related to a lower concentration of ownership, suggesting that concentration is

36 The classification of the countries in market- and bank-based systems stems from Demirgüç-Kunt and Levine (1999) and Levine (2002).

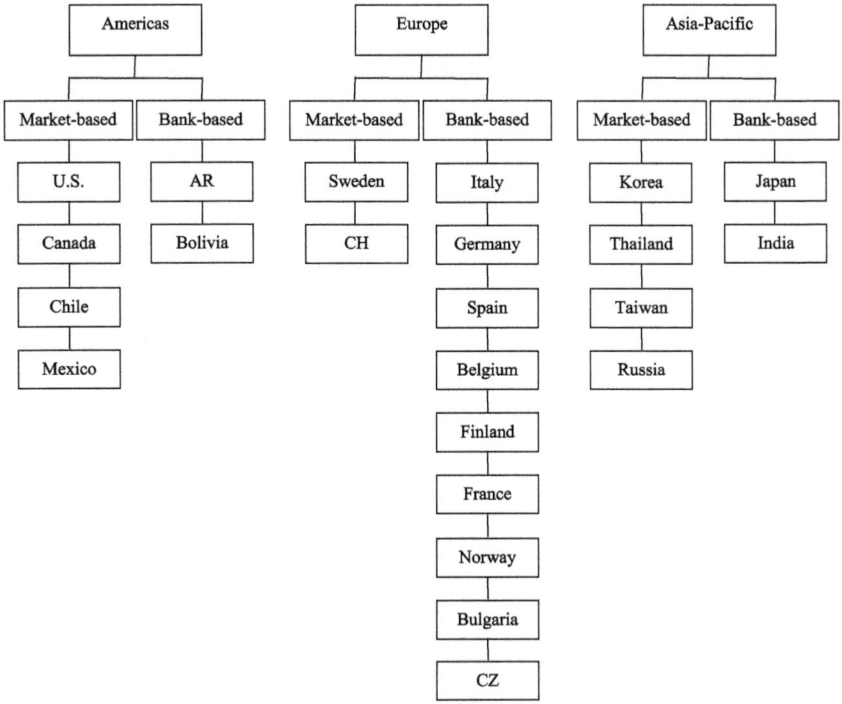

Figure 2-7: Global studies by geography

This figure shows the three main global regions: Americas, Europe, and Asia-Pacific. They are divided into market- and bank-based financial systems. AR for Argentina, CH for Switzerland, and CZ for Czech Republic.

a response to weak investor protection. La Porta et al. (1997) document that countries with weak investor protections have considerably smaller debt and equity markets. Overall, the findings offer a link from the legal system to the classification into market- or bank-based financial systems (La Porta et al. 1998).

La Porta et al. (1999) study data on the ownership structures of large companies in twenty-seven countries in order to determine the ultimate controlling shareholders.[37] They find that the good protection subsample is dominated by common law countries, while the bad protection subsample is dominated by civil law countries. The "strong" bank countries include, among others,

37 Equity control by financial institutions is far less common (La Porta et al. 1999).

Table 2-5: Distribution of studies

This table shows the seventy-one analyzed market-based studies and the ninety-four analyzed bank-based studies.

Market-based studies		**Bank-based studies**	
U.S.	47	Italy	31
U.K.	7	Germany	16
Korea	3	Japan	16
Thailand	3	Spain	8
Sweden	2	Belgium	5
Switzerland	2	Finland	5
Taiwan	2	Argentina	3
Chile	1	France	2
Canada	1	Bolivia	2
Brazil	1	Norway	2
Mexico	1	Bulgaria	1
Russia	1	Czech Republic	1
		India	1
		Portugal	1
Total	**71**	**Total**	**94**

Finland, France, Germany, Netherlands, and Spain. La Porta et al. (1999) define strong banks through lending as well as through less formal mechanisms of restricting banks' power as shareholders. Degryse and Ongena (2005) classify Belgium as a bank-based financial system (see also Levine 2002). Levine (2002) classifies Argentina, Italy, and Norway as bank-based systems. For the classification of Japan, see Weinstein and Yafeh (1998), as well as Morck and Nakamura (1999). Other studies have revealed significant concentration of ownership in Germany (Edwards and Fischer 1994; Gorton and Schmid 2000), Japan (Berglöf and Perotti 1994; Prowse 1992), and Italy (Barca 1995). Countries with "weak" banks include Canada, Sweden, the U.K. and the U.S. (La Porta et al. 1999). Levine (2002) classifies Switzerland as market-based. Table 2-5 shows the distribution of the analyzed studies across financial systems and countries.

In total, seventy-one studies with market-based structures and ninety-four with bank-based structures were considered relevant for this study and were examined. The U.S. and the U.K. contributed the highest number on market-based systems; Italy, Germany, and Japan contributed the highest number on bank-based systems. Twelve cross-country studies were also investigated.

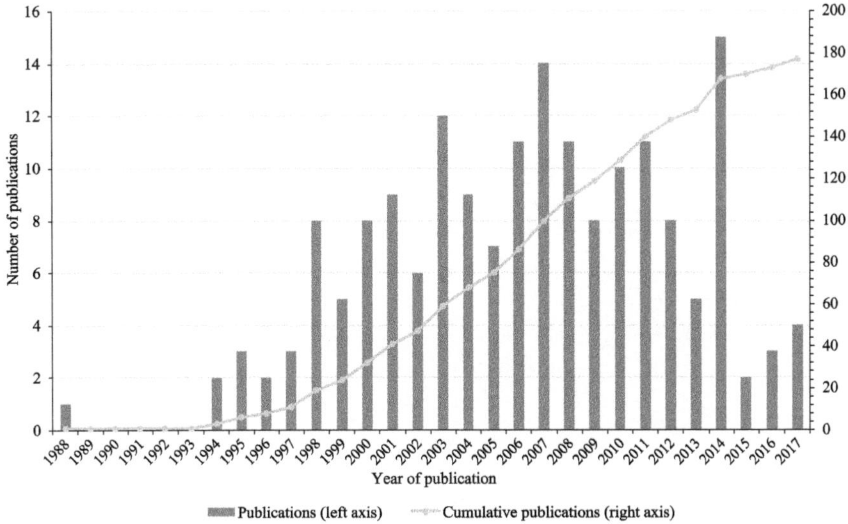

Figure 2-8: Year of publication

This figure shows the publications between 1988 and 2017 for the entire sample of 177 studies. Publications include published papers as well as accepted manuscripts, latest drafts, and working papers. The x-axis shows the year of publication. The left axis shows the number of publications in each year, and the right axis shows the cumulative publications over the years.

Figure 2-8 shows the development of the number of publications over the years. The first identified study began in 1988, and the final identified studies are from 2017. Four papers were already published in 2017 or are forthcoming. Moreover, the course of the cumulative publications highlights a growing interest in the topic of relationship banking.

The growing interest during the 1990s into the topic of relationship banking is probably attributable to Diamond's (1984, 1991) seminal papers. His research is the basis for many subsequent papers, especially in connection with the topic of agency costs by Jensen and Meckling (1976). There was another sharp increase in publications before and after the recent financial crisis, beginning in 2007. This demonstrates that, during financially difficult times, the behavior of banks toward borrowers, and vice versa, is especially important, because bank financing is often a critical economic factor for countries. Moreover, another rise in publications occurred around 2014, probably due to the disruptive changes in recent years and new market players entering the banking system as described in sections 2.5.3 and 2.5.4. These developments offer potential alternative sources of financing for borrowers and are altering banking power significantly.

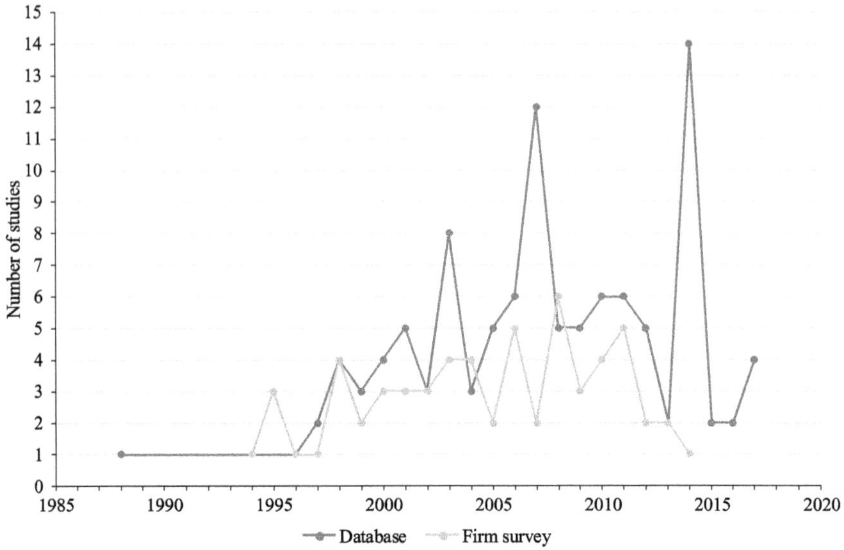

Figure 2-9: Distribution of third-party databases and firm surveys

This figure presents the year the studies were published from 1988 to 2017 for the sample of 170 studies. 109 third-party databases and 61 firm surveys are included. The x-axis shows the year of publication, and the y-axis shows the number of studies in a given year.

In addition, Figure 2-9 shows the data sources that were deployed by scholars and the distribution over the years. 109 third-party databases and 61 firm surveys present the most used data sources and, thus, these sources are shown in Figure 2-9. The rest of the studies use bank surveys, a combination of firm and bank manager surveys, and literature reviews. The data collection methods are analyzed further in section 3.1.

The figure shows a clear trend of studies in anticipation of and after the recent financial crisis. During a financial crisis, the so-called housebank can be particularly valuable. Scholars have found that companies are more likely to obtain a loan with favorable terms from a relationship bank (Bolton et al. 2016; Cotugno et al. 2013a; Jiangli et al. 2008). Elsas and Krahnen (1998) document that lenders can provide liquidity insurance for companies that suffer an unexpected decline in credit quality when they have a prior relationship. Moreover, Rosenfeld (2014) finds that companies that obtain a loan from a relationship lender in the six months prior to a situation of distress are more likely to emerge from distress. Thus, a lending relationship can be even more valuable at these times. Against this background of increased disruptive changes in recent years, the increased interest in relationship lending before and after the financial crisis can be better explained.

Regarding the evaluation period, the first identified sample year is 1855, followed by 1916 through 1947 (Bodenhorn 2003, 2007; Gan 2007; Sjögren 1994). Obviously, there is a time lag between the evaluation period and the year of publication. Note that the period between 1987 and 2005 is the most extensively analyzed, primarily because of the well-known Survey of Small Business Finances (SSBF)[38] conducted in the U.S. (see also Berger and Udell 1995a, 1995b; Cole 1998; Petersen and Rajan 1994, 1995, 2002). This survey was carried out for the first time in 1987, then in 1993, 1998, and 2003. The first survey was administered by the Federal Reserve Board and the Small Business Administration (SBA).

For Germany, one study conducted during this period and used multiple times by different scholars is the sample constructed by Elsas and Krahnen (1998). Their sample consists of records from five bank: Deutsche Bank, Dresdner Bank, HypoVereinsbank, DZ Bank, and WestLB (see also Machauer and Weber 1998; Elsas 2005). In addition, Lehmann and Neuberger (2001) conducted a bank survey for Germany with the participation of Deutsche Bank, Dresdner Bank, Commerzbank, and the merged Bayerische Vereinsbank, Bayerische Hypotheken, and Wechsel Bank, state-owned saving banks, and cooperative banks (see also Lehmann et al. 2004). The lack of examples demonstrates that this period is when the first large surveys were carried out, and the first big datasets were built on this subject. The following section will discuss the evidence of the costs and benefits of lending relationships in market- versus bank-based financial systems. This classification is necessary because it represents the basis for the latter empirical classification of the findings from this study.

38 The name of the survey was changed. It was called the National Survey of Small Business Finances (NSSBF) in 1987 and 1993, and the Survey of Small Business Finances (SSBF) in 1998 and 2003. The abbreviation SSBF was also used. The SSBF consists of information on companies with fewer than 500 employees in the U.S. The data were collected by telephone interviews with executives from 3,400 companies. Each interview consists of about 200 questions on governance, history, use of loans, relationship with credit institutions, balance sheet, and profit and loss accounts (Berger and Udell 1995a, 1995b; Board 2008).

2.7.2 Evidence from market-based financial systems

A great deal of literature investigates whether and how relationship lending benefits borrowers in market- versus bank-based systems. The U.S. and the U.K. are the most prominent market-based financial systems, which suggests that relationship lending plays a dominant role in these markets. The following explores the lending relationship across both systems in terms of four categories: loan, relationship, firm, and control characteristics. As mentioned earlier, the majority of researchers have focused on these lending characteristics. Therefore, the same classification has been adopted for this study.

These characteristics play a special role when lending relationships are analyzed because their effects can lead to both benefits and costs. Bharath, Dahiya, Saunders, and Srinivasan (2011) find that relationships are more important when firms exhibit low information transparency, because lending relationships provide significant benefits. Benefits can be a lower probability of pledging collateral, lower interest spreads, or a greater availability of finance. In addition, opaque firms are significantly more likely to obtain a future loan from a bank with which they have engaged in a lending relationship (Bharath, Dahiya, Saunders, and Srinivasan 2007).

Therefore, the aim of this section is to identify the effects of the loan, relationship, firm, and control characteristics on collateral requirements, cost of debt, and credit availability in order to establish the basis for a subsequent classification of the effects of the present study. The first part sheds some light on the loan characteristics, followed by the relationship and firm characteristics. The control variables are outlined later.

Because the relationship characteristics are the most prominent when studying lending relationships, these characteristics will be broken down further. Moreover, the characteristics and the associated effects in market-based financial systems will be outlined first, followed by those in bank-based financial systems. This approach is chosen to first establish a clear distinction. The differences will be outlined in section 2.7.4, followed by a summary of the effects in section 2.7.5.

2.7.2.1 Loan characteristics

Loan characteristics are useful for studying financing patterns. Firms with more debt are considered riskier from a financial point of view, and, consequently, are charged higher interest rates. The extent of the relationship is studied further by analyzing the number of products acquired from the bank. Greater debt and more products purchased provide increased opportunities for the bank to study the borrower.

Scope and finance share

A frequently studied variable in the literature on relationship lending is the number of financial products a firm has purchased from a bank, which is broadly defined as the scope of the relationship. Chakraborty and Hu (2006) document that a higher number of services decreases the collateral a firm must pledge for a non-credit line, while there is no effect on the credit line. Duarte and Gama (2011) study the U.K., and also find no effect of scope on collateral requirements. In addition, a higher number of loan services decreases the credit limit, while the number of non-loan services increases it (Chakraborty, Fernando, and Mallick 2010). No significant effect is detected on the cost of debt (see, e.g., Blackwell and Winters 1997; Duarte and Gama 2011; Petersen and Rajan 1994). The perception that relationship lending is only a function of credit decisions based on enhanced monitoring is not entirely correct. It is also a function of the potential synergies between a bank and a firm by which the bank has an opportunity to sell additional products and services (Santikian 2014).

Loan size is also frequently studied in the literature on relationship lending. Bharath, Dahiya, Saunders, and Srinivasan (2009) find a negative effect of loan volume on collateral requirements and the cost of debt (see also Bopaiah 1998; Cerqueiro, Degryse, and Ongena 2011; Duarte and Gama 2011). Loans from relationship banks are generally higher in amount than loans from non-relationship banks (Bharath et al. 2009). In this context, Gloy, Gunderson, and Ladue (2005) observe that, when loan volume increases, monitoring costs fall, and loan volume has a decreasing effect on the cost of debt (see also Bopaiah 1998). In the U.K., the level of collateral increases with the size of the loan and the firm's survival chances; this implies that better quality borrowers offer collateral because they are less likely to suffer financial distress. Smaller loans exhibit less collateralization, and larger loans exhibit more (see, e.g., Cressy 1996; Hanley 2002; Hanley and Crook 2005). However, the non-significant results seem to prevail overall.

2.7.2.2 Relationship characteristics

Relationship banking is often described as close and strong firm-bank relationships. With repeated interactions, potential information asymmetries between borrowers and lenders can be resolved because a certain degree of transparency is established. However, a closer interaction between borrowers and lenders may also be inevitable because the bank conducts stronger surveillance of the borrower due to a decreased credit rating.

With respect to the cost of debt, Petersen and Rajan (1994) note that lending relationships are beneficial, and are defined primarily by availability, not by price. In contrast, Blackwell and Winters (1997) find evidence that, overall, firms with close bank relationships pay lower interest rates. The opposite is the case if the bank monitors the firm frequently, because interest rates rise with higher monitoring frequency. Firms that have close bank relationships are also monitored less often. Dunkelberg, Leeds, and Scott (2004) show that, besides leading to a decrease in the firm's cost of debt, stronger bank relationships simultaneously lower the probability that the firm will need to search for other financing sources.

Petersen and Rajan (1994) also document that close ties between firms and financial institutions increase credit availability. There is a 42 % probability that a bank in a lending relationship will provide a future loan to a firm. That percent drops to 3 % for a bank that is not in a lending relationship (see also Bharath et al. 2007; Calomiris and Pornrojnangkool 2009). Lending relationships are also a crucial factor for obtaining higher credit limits (Chakraborty et al. 2010). Close ties between firms and financial institutions increase credit availability, because the company spends more time in the relationship. The firm increases its ties with the lender by expanding the number of financial services it buys and concentrating its borrowing with that lender. In addition, the relationship increases the lender's informational monopoly, so that cost reductions may not be passed on to the borrower. Furthermore, it may be easier for a loan officer to use his expertise to influence the loan amount and to examine whether the loan is granted at all, rather than the price (Petersen and Rajan 1994).

Companies with established lending relationships exhibited higher levels of leverage throughout the 2007–2009 financial crisis, obtaining new bank loans and eventually realizing greater profitability (Dewally and Shao 2014). In contrast, Ortiz-Molina and Penas (2008) study the loan maturity aspect in the lending relationship and find no evidence of a correlation between loan maturity and a strong lending relationship. For the U.K., Cowling (1999) finds that the closeness of the bank-borrower relationship, as measured by the company's assessment of how well the bank knows the company and its owner, tends to decrease loan collateralization.

Information asymmetries and trust and loan officers

The assessment of information is one of the main variables in lending relationships. Berger and Udell (1995a, 1995b) note that relationship lending produces crucial information about a borrower's credit quality. In this context,

Chakraborty and Hu (2006) show that firm-bank relationships can be a valuable source of private information, and a way that banks can acquire private information that is subject to the loan type. Private information lowers uncertainty in the loan process, and the duration of the firm-bank relationship can influence the decision.

According to Petersen and Rajan (2002), information about small businesses is believed to be "soft," and must be gathered by lenders over time through relationships with borrowers (see also Berger and Udell 1995a, 1995b; Petersen and Rajan 1994). By soft information, Petersen and Rajan (2002) refer to "tacit" information that is difficult to communicate to others or to capture in written documents. For example, the loan officer's thorough prior assessment of a firm manager helps him determine the appropriateness of a loan request (Polanyi 1958; Uzzi 1999). The duration of the relationship is a decisive factor when securing a credit line, because it also generates soft information by repeated interactions. Soft information overall is considered private, while hard information is considered public.

The duration of the relationship may be less important for non-recurring standardized non-lines of credit. Ortiz-Molina and Penas (2008) study credit line maturity, and find it is shorter for companies whose owners have weak past financial performance, are older, are less experienced, and for companies with greater information opaqueness. In contrast, relationships characterized by low asymmetric information tend to show longer loan maturities.

Cressy (1996) documents for the U.K. that observable firm characteristics are crucial in solving the moral hazard problem. Such characteristics are firm size, as measured by total assets, and publicly available information about a firm. In addition, Gama and Duarte (2015) find that personal collateral appears more effective as a sorting device than business collateral, because companies with good financial records are willing to pledge more collateral, particularly personal collateral. For the lender, personal collateral is more effective at obviating borrowers' risk incentives because a company owner, especially one who is active in management, will likely feel the consequences of any ex post managerial risk-taking (Gama and Duarte 2015).

Most of the opaque firms and most of the transparent firms show a lower likelihood of switching banks and they do usually switch from small to large banks (Gopalan, Udell, and Yerramilli 2007). Firms that change banks may require higher credit amounts, they may invest more in tangible assets, and they may exhibit higher leverage. These findings are in line with the graduation hypothesis, which posits that firms with rising credit needs are more likely to switch to larger banks (Gopalan et al. 2007). However, Dunkelberg et al. (2004) find that smaller and more informationally opaque companies face more uncertainty about loan terms, and these companies will look for other financing sources more frequently.

Hao (2004) examines banks' monitoring power and finds that those with greater monitoring power and higher risk, as measured by their capital asset ratio, extract higher rents from firms. Greater bank monitoring, measured by the level of a bank's labor resources engaged in monitoring, leads to longer loan maturities and higher costs of debt, as evidenced by higher yield spreads. These effects are especially strong for working capital loans and for companies with higher growth potential (Coleman, Esho, and Sharpe 2006). Sisli-Ciamarra (2012) also studies banks' monitoring power and shows that the presence of at least one bank executive on a company's board of directors has a monitoring effect. Schenone (2010) investigates banks' monopoly power with respect to information, and notes that relationship banks take advantage of this power by charging higher interest rates on loans, thereby increasing a firm's cost of debt.

Research has also focused on the impact of hard and soft information on lending relationships. Petersen and Rajan (2002) find that developments in technology have increased the accessibility and timeliness of hard information. While large banks use formal numbers-based documentation, such as, e.g., financial statements, in their loan process with small businesses, small banks still rely on information gleaned from certain borrower characteristics (Cole, Goldberg, and White 2004).

Cole et al. (2004) find that small banks face less severe agency problems and tend to have better quality firm information. This is because they have more private information about potential borrowers due to proximity and personal relationships between the loan officer and the firm. Therefore, small banks assess firms by using a "character" loan approach. Hence, small banks' lending decisions follow less strictly standardized numeric factors than those of large banks, which do business primarily with larger companies. They also generally operate at a greater distance, in a more impersonal manner, and engage in shorter and fewer relationships (Berger, Miller, Petersen, Rajan, and Stein 2005).

Scott (2004) notes that community financial institutions play a crucial role for small companies in the production of soft information, which enables them to access capital markets. Face-to-face interactions are still vital for many customers, but technological progress is decreasing entry barriers into relationship lending. This in turn leads to increased competitive pressure on community banks (Ergungor 2005).

Agarwal and Hauswald (2010) show that distance between the firm and the bank branch, both in miles and in driving distance, can somewhat deteriorate the quality of soft information. Proximity generally enhances the gathering of soft information, while more distant lenders communicate in more impersonal ways (Petersen and Rajan 2002). Advances in technology have only marginally overcome the limits created by distance thus far.

Cressy and Toivanen (2001) show for the U.K. that banks may be able to use qualitative information to better evaluate a company's business success. They are more likely than other institutions to use qualitative and quantitative information for loans with small companies. Petersen and Rajan (2002) conclude that transactions with banks show a greater probability of being achieved in person than transactions with non-banks,[39] and loans from banks are more relationship-based than loans from non-banks.

Public information drives the availability and price of credit in transactional lending, while private information drives decisions in relationship lending. Relationship banks rely on private information when available, and not on public information (Agarwal and Hauswald 2008). In contrast, Scott (2006) finds that the production of soft information and the availability of hard information are equally important.

The degree of trust and loan officer turnover in the lending relationship are two important proxies when studying the firm-bank relationship. Uzzi (1999) finds that firms embedding their economic transactions in social relations experience lower interest rates. Relational trust serves as a mediating factor between the strategy of a bank and the switching behavior of a company. Banks that are more customer-oriented tend to reduce companies' switching behavior (Saparito, Chen, and Sapienza 2004). In this context, Dunkelberg et al. (2004) document that companies with strong bank relationships, characterized by duration and a low turnover of the bank's contact person, will search for multiple financing sources less often. Moreover, lower bank officer turnover is related to decreased turndown rates, which are defined as the rejection of loans during the application process (Scott 2006).

Scott (2004) argues that loan officer turnover is a superior proxy for the strength of a relationship than duration, because the loan officer is the key element in the firm interaction. In this respect, Cerqueiro et al. (2011) study discretion, defined as the loan officer's idiosyncratic judgment, which is not independently confirmable. They show that the influence of discretion in the judgment of loan prices decreases with the volume of the loan, while it increases with the level of concentration in the banking market and the distance between

39 Non-banks include finance companies, insurance companies, brokerage firms, leasing companies, mortgage banks, and venture capitalists.

the company and the bank. As discussed above, there has been some research on trust in lending relationships in the U.S. and the U.K., but no significant empirical findings have emerged thus far.

Number of bank lending relationships

The number of bank relationships is one of the most important influencing factors in relationship banking. As Petersen and Rajan (1994) note, a higher number of relationships with creditors increases the cost of credit (see also Petersen and Rajan 1995, 2002; Hao 2004). Blackwell and Winters (1997) conclude that firms benefit by concentrating borrowing with one bank and fostering a long-term banking relationship. Lenders are also less likely to extend credit when a firm has multiple bank relationships, because the critical private information banks gain from relationships may lose some of its value (Cole 1998).

Houston and James (1996) find that, for companies with one bank relationship, a dependence on bank loans is negatively correlated with growth opportunities. For companies with multiple bank relationships, a dependence on bank loans is positively correlated with growth opportunities. The results, therefore, suggest that multiple bank relationships either alleviate hold-up problems, or indicate that bank information rents are considerably lower. Hold-up problems in this context arise from information monopolies associated with having a single bank relationship. Monopolies can lead to offsetting costs for even the largest companies (Houston and James 1996). Yet, most of the analyzed studies find no significant effect on credit availability from the number of bank relationships (Chakraborty and Mallick 2012; Park 2008; Petersen and Rajan 1994, 2002). Moreover, collateral requirements tend to decrease with an increasing number of bank relationships (Hübler, Menkhoff, and Suwanaporn 2008; Menkhoff, Neuberger, and Suwanaporn 2006).

Duration of lending relationship

Berger and Udell (1995a, 1995b) find that the duration of the bank relationship is also a crucial factor, because it can lower interest rates. Firms with longer banking relationships can also pledge collateral less often (Berger, Rosen, and Udell 2007; Berger and Udell 2002; Brick and Palia 2007; Chakraborty and Hu 2006; Scott and Dunkelberg 2003; Uzzi 1999). Bodenhorn (2003) documents that firms with extensive and durable bank relationships experience lower costs of credit, pledge fewer personal guarantees, and experience a greater likelihood of loan renegotiations during a financial crisis (Bodenhorn 2007; Chakraborty et al. 2010; Chakraborty and Hu 2006).

For the U.K., Cowling (1999) finds that small companies can mitigate any credit market difficulties they face by building long-term relationships with banks. Banks prefer borrowers with which they have a prior history (relationship). They rely heavily on this factor during the loan decision-making process (Hanley and Crook 2005). Long-term relationships also appear to be valuable for small firms that are comparatively opaque. In addition, a pre-existing deposit relationship has a significant positive effect during the loan process and makes the extension of credit more likely (see, e.g., Petersen and Rajan 1995; Cole 1998; Bodenhorn 2003, 2007; Chakraborty and Mallick 2012).

Conducting repeat business with the same lender further lowers the cost of debt for a firm, suggesting economies of scale are reflected in loan pricing. Empirical evidence shows that firms with multiple sources of financing obtain superior credit terms if they obtain a loan from a bank with which they have had a long-standing relationship (Bharath et al. 2011). In contrast, companies with shorter financial histories and weak financial statements face more credit constraints (Chakraborty and Mallick 2012).

Only one U.S. study, Gloy et al. (2005), shows that a longer lending relationship can increase the cost of debt while decreasing monitoring costs. For the U.K., Duarte and Gama (2011) also find that the duration of a lending relationship has an increasing effect on the cost of debt, suggesting that intertemporal rent shifting is likely to occur. The overall results with respect to duration imply there are benefits of longer lending relationships. But the empirical findings between duration and the cost of debt appear ambiguous.

Financial distress

Financial distress is another decisive variable when assessing the relationship between a bank and a firm. Agarwal and Hauswald (2008) find that firms in lending relationships benefit from intertemporal financing, i.e., these firms receive financial support at times when they would otherwise have trouble obtaining bank funding. Li and Srinivasan (2011) define distress by the default probability estimated by applying the Black-Scholes-Merton option pricing model. They observe[40] that, before a company is in distress, relationship banks offer more favorable loan terms by charging lower interest rates and requiring less collateral. In contrast, for companies that are already in distress, their

40 For each month the default probability is estimated, and if in six or more months of a certain year the default probability is equal to or higher than the 90th percentile, that year is defined as a distress year.

relationship bank acts like an outside bank: It requires collateral and fees that are comparable to what an outside bank would require. Nevertheless, companies that file for bankruptcy, defined as a dummy variable that equals 1 if the bankruptcy occurred in the given year, and 0 otherwise, have a higher probability of receiving debtor in possession (DIP) loans from their relationship bank.

Dewally and Shao (2014) conclude that, overall, companies with established lending relationships struggled less during the 2007–2009 financial crisis than those without such relationships. However, the results are ambiguous. Relationship banks appear to treat distressed companies differently than bankruptcy companies. Moreover, as the empirical findings show, studies from the market-based financial system primarily focus on the effect on credit availability, not the effects on collateral requirements or the cost of debt.

2.7.2.3 Firm characteristics

Different descriptive variables are also commonly studied to assess lending relationships. Company size and legal status have a negative effect on credit availability (Petersen and Rajan 1995; Uzzi 1999; Chakraborty and Mallick 2012). Credit from a relationship bank and credit from a non-relationship bank do not differ when a firm is large in terms of asset size, has rated public debt, and falls into the S&P 500 index (Bharath et al. 2011). In this context, Chakraborty and Mallick (2012) show that the credit gap differs across legal forms and industries. Corporations face larger credit gaps than partnerships, and manufacturing companies face larger credit gaps than wholesale or service industry companies. Furthermore, medium- and high-risk companies are charged higher interest rates (Gloy et al. 2005).[41]

For the U.K., Cowling (1999) finds that firm age can decrease loan collateralization. This characteristic is the most commonly used measure of risk in the bank-borrower relationship. Cowling (2010) also shows that a pledge of collateral is associated with high-risk borrowers[42] and asymmetric information. High-quality borrowers[43] accept high collateral requirements to obtain a lower

41 "Medium-risk borrowers are identified by the regulatory classifications of special mention, accruing substandard, or accruing doubtful. High-risk borrowers are defined as all non-accrual or loss borrowers. Borrowers in the highest risk category were at least ninety days past due on their interest and principal obligations for at least one loan, and many had experienced loan write-offs within the past year" (Gloy et al. 2005, p. 707).

42 Cowling (2010) finds that firm size is often a good proxy for firm risk, as is firm age.

43 According to Duarte and Gama (2011), these borrowers know ex ante their credit quality, but the banks do not know it.

interest rate (Duarte and Gama 2011). The decreasing effect of firm age on collateral requirements is also confirmed by studies from the U.S. (see, e.g., Berger and Udell 1995a, 1995b; Chakraborty and Hu 2006). In addition, firm age has a positive effect on credit availability (see, e.g., Petersen and Rajan 1995; Cole 1998; Bodenhorn 2003, 2007; Chakraborty and Mallick 2012).

2.7.2.4 Control variables

The concentration and competitiveness of the banking market are two common proxies for control variables that determine banking market structure. Petersen and Rajan (1995) show that banks smooth interest rates over the course of a relationship with a company in a concentrated financial market (a market in which a few banks dominate). Petersen and Rajan (1994) also find that companies in regions with fewer bank-like institutions are less likely to encounter rationing. This is in line with Mayer (1988) and Rajan (1992), who find that increased competition in financial markets decreases the value of relationships because it prevents a financial institution from gaining the rewards of supporting companies at an early stage. These companies may be better helped if banks can make their claims to the firm's future profits explicit (Petersen and Rajan 1994).

In addition, young companies in concentrated financial markets obtain more institutional credit than those in more competitive markets. However, the difference in winning institutional finance in concentrated, and competitive financial markets disappears by company age (Petersen and Rajan 1995). Park (2008) finds that commercial banks in concentrated financial markets offer lower loan amounts to small firms because credit applications may be more likely to be rejected. The total limit of lines of credit are lower in concentrated financial markets than in competitive ones.

Ogura (2010) determines that loan interest rates for younger companies in concentrated financial markets are lower when extended by an inside rather than an outside bank. Inside banks hold more than half of firms' total checking balances and have a relationship with a company for more than one year. The differences between inside and outside banks are not generally found in competitive financial markets, because competition discourages banks from accumulating private information about a firm. Inside banks charge lower interest rates than outside banks to capture a firm and extract future rents. In this context, Petersen and Rajan (2002) show that the availability of credit for small companies and the level of bank competition that small companies experience have increased over the years. In addition, Berger et al. (2007) find that a greater presence of large banks has a decreasing effect on the cost of credit in small firm lending. The probability that small firms will be granted a loan from a small or large bank is roughly proportional to the local market presence of that bank.

Depending on financial market competitiveness, access to bank and non-bank financing differs for small companies (Berger et al. 2007). Mitchell and Pearce (2011) document that small companies face difficulties obtaining bank non-lines of credit in very competitive financial markets. But it is usually easier for them to obtain bank lines of credit in very competitive markets. Moreover, companies in markets with low banking concentration and low transaction costs tend to seek other financing sources more often than companies in rural markets (Dunkelberg et al. 2004).

Ergungor (2005) documents that competition lowers the benefits of lending relationships, and Cerqueiro et al. (2011) conclude that a company's switching costs are a crucial indicator of the market power of a bank. In this context, Scott and Dunkelberg (2003) study mergers in banking markets, and find that mergers increase non-price loan terms and collateral requirements while decreasing service quality.

2.7.3 Evidence from bank-based financial systems

The most important bank-based financial systems are Italy, Germany, and Japan. Relationship lending thus plays a critical role in these markets, and most studies have focused on them. The lending relationship is divided among loan, relationship, firm characteristics, and control variables, and the effects of these variables on the firm-bank relationship are presented next. The first section presents the loan characteristics, followed by the relationship and firm characteristics, and the control variables. Since the relationship characteristics are the most dominant variables in bank-based financial systems, they are divided further into information, number, duration, trust and loan officer, bank type and distance, and financial distress.

2.7.3.1 Loan characteristics

The loan characteristics are analyzed first, in order to help determine borrower financing patterns. On the lender side, the bank is able to collect more information about the borrower.

Scope and finance share

With respect to loan characteristics, the variables finance share and scope are the key factors in German lending relationships, where scope represents the number of financial products a firm has purchased from a bank. Cosci and Meliciani (2002) study banking in Italy and find that banks may only want to finance a small amount of a firm's funding needs. This is attributable to risk sharing and to the aim of the bank to have as many customers as possible. However, concentrated borrowing is especially important for less profitable, highly leveraged, and less liquid companies, because companies with more concentrated borrowing are better shielded against loan supply shocks. Moreover, the growth of credit is greater when the relationship lender's share of credit volume is larger (Sette and Gobbi, 2015). In this context, Ferri and Messori (2000) find that the cost of debt also increases with the finance share.

Cross-selling is important at the beginning of a lending relationship, but it also increases the likelihood that a loan must be collateralized (Kano, Uchida, Udell, and Watanabe 2011). Firm bank account activity can be a predictor of a firm's default probability and is particularly valuable with respect to small companies. Early warning indicators from account activity and credit line usage can help considerably to predict future borrower defaults up to one year in advance and serve as a basis for banks' loan pricing (Norden and Weber 2010). In this context, Norden and Weber (2010) find that analyzing early warning signs can lead to higher credit spreads for firms.

2.7.3.2 Relationship characteristics

Agarwal and Hauswald (2010) find benefits as well as costs related to relationship lending. Their results suggest that banks may participate in rent-seeking activities. Bank-influenced firms are those in which a financial institution owns more than 25 % or 50 % of shares, where a bank is the majority shareholder, or where the chairman of the board is a banker. Agarwal and Elston (2001) find that bank-influenced firms have better access to capital, but also higher debt costs. Elsas and Krahnen (2003) find empirical evidence that banks perform some sort of corporate control through equity they hold in companies. Agarwal and Elston (2001) argue there is no evidence of greater profitability or faster growth with close bank relationships, however.

But close firm-bank relationships are likely to decline with the likelihood of sharp increases in interest rates and being credit rationed (Conigliani, Ferri, and Generale 1997; D'Auria, Foglia, and Reedtz 1999; Gambacorta and Mistrulli 2014). D'Auria et al. (1999) measure closeness by the bank's share of firm debt. Gambacorta and Mistrulli (2014) include duration when studying closeness and find that banks are more likely to support firms with more intense informational closeness.

For Italy, Ferri and Messori (2000) find that relationship lending may assist inefficiently run banks to survive. In contrast, Bongini et al. (2007) find that small banks can improve their performance by levering relationship banking, and Brancati (2015) shows that relationship banking can help overcome financial barriers to innovation. It tends to have a strong effect on the introduction of new products and processes. Malafronte, Monferrà, Porzio, and Sampagnaro (2014) conclude that, in Italy, there are beneficial effects from bank-borrower relationships.

For Japan, Yao and Ouyang (2007) document a dark side of relationship lending when the main bank has great power over the firm. Companies that are governed by a main bank borrow more from it, show higher investment expenditures, and demonstrate worse performance in the event of an economic shock (Yao and Ouyang 2007). In addition, the main bank as large debtholder may restrict firm growth (Weinstein and Yafeh 1998).

Gan (2007) shows that relationship lending plays a critical role, since it encompasses one-third of the lending portfolios of Japanese banks. Shin, Fraser, and Kolari (2003) note that a relationship with a main bank is valuable, however. The close relationship may be important during times of financial distress (Ono, Hasumi, and Hirata 2014). Transactional lenders may increase credit availability for firms during normal times. However, ultimately, this may have a bad impact on the relationship with the primary bank, because the primary lending attitude tends to deteriorate. This is referred to as the treatment effect. Thus, a company should always reassess its costs and benefits.

Information asymmetries, trust and loan officers

With respect to assessing variable information, Elsas and Krahnen (2003) find that housebanks establish an informationally strong relationship with companies. Such relationships are common for mid-sized companies. A bank's rapid liquidity provision for a firm depends on whether it has collected sufficient information in the past (Fischer 2000). Relationship banks show a lower probability of requiring more information from a firm during financial crises (Hainz and Wiegand 2013). In addition, bank relationships characterized by low asymmetric information exhibit longer maturities.

Kirschenmann and Norden (2012) find that small companies can use the advantage of reduced asymmetric information and their improved bargaining power to obtain better credit terms. In contrast, Hainz and Wiegand (2013) document that relationship lending has no significant effect on credit availability, which may be because banks use hard instead of soft information. Norden and

Weber (2010) also study the information aspect and find that the quality of hard information for big companies is generally higher than for small companies, due to financial reporting standards and disclosure requirements.

Sette and Gobbi (2015) show for Italy that firm support from a relationship lender is likely owed to the information advantage banks have acquired and would like to keep. Moreover, the beneficial effect of relationship lending is larger for smaller firms, because the information advantage for these firms is higher (Sette and Gobbi 2015). Bartoli, Ferri, Murro, and Rotondi (2012) study the UniCredit Group, and show that, at the peak of the recent financial crisis, the banking group reallocated its credit supply toward firms with more intense informational tightness. The tightness was proxied for by the length of the relationship and by share of total credit. The rating assigned to the company through the bank's internal rating system was also included. Measuring the influence of the rating is a critical control, because informational tightness between a bank and borrower may simply reflect the internal rating given to the company by the UniCredit Group. Thus, as soon as the internal rating is included, the relevance of the informational tightness disappears (Bartoli et al. 2012).

Cotugno et al. (2013a) and Cotugno, Stefanelli, and Torluccio (2013b) study soft information, and show that distance between the lender and the borrower, measured as the distance between the zip code of bank headquarters and the zip code of bank branches, is negatively correlated with the collection of soft information. Milani (2014) finds that soft information plays an important role in banks' lending decisions. The smaller the distance is between the bank and the firm, the higher are the chances that the bank will be able to generate soft information. The greater the distance between the firm and the bank, the greater the adverse selection problems and, consequently, the loan default rates because the bank has less private information.

Fiordelisi, Monferrà, and Sampagnaro (2014) show that the distance between the branch that granted the loan and the bank's headquarters has a positive effect on the company's default probability. This effect is stronger for smaller companies, suggesting that longer organizational distance makes the exchange of soft information even more difficult. Brancati (2015) notes that very small companies can experience disproportional benefits from banks' collection of soft information. However, hard information can alleviate adverse selection problems through technological advances, which lower the importance of lending relationships and the distance problem.

Horiuchi, Packer, and Fukuda (1988) also show for Japan that the main bank gathers a large amount of firm-specific information. Ono, Uesugi, and Yasuda (2013) find that, whenever loans are collateralized at the main bank, it tends to monitor the firm much more closely. With respect to soft information, Uchida, Udell, and Yamori (2012) show that a greater amount of soft information is produced by loan officers, who are frequently in contact with the firm and work at small banks.

With regard to the variable "trust," Harhoff and Körting (1998) state that trust between the firm and the bank decreases interest rates. Lehmann and Neuberger (2001) document that social interactions that may be defined by trust are beneficial to firms and banks. Howorth and Moro (2012) show for Italy that the level of trust, rather than the duration of the relationship, influences the lending decision. The level of trust has a decreasing effect on the interest rate. However, the relationship between the firm and the bank is characterized by a low level of trust when the firm is monitored more frequently. In addition, Guiso (2003) finds a positive effect on credit availability.

Loan officers play a critical role in the production of soft information and are likewise critical for lending relationships. However, there is no clear evidence why loan officers at large banks do not produce as much soft information as loan officers at small banks. Uchida et al. (2012) show that loan officers seem to have the same potential to engage in soft information production regardless of bank size.

Number of lending relationships

Firms concentrate their borrowing mainly with one or two banks. Smaller companies tend to have only one bank relationship. In many cases, one bank provides at least two-thirds of a firm's total credit volume (Harhoff and Körting 1998). Harhoff and Körting (1998) also document that concentrated debt financing is beneficial to firms, and that a growing number of bank relationships decreases credit availability. Note that there is no need for exclusivity in a firm's bank relationships for a housebank relationship to develop. For example, Elsas and Krahnen (1998) find that firms with a housebank relationship and normal bank relationships may even be better able to control for hold-up problems in housebank relationships. Hold-up problems can emerge through information monopolies that develop from borrowing from a single bank.

Moreover, the number of bank relationships increases the degree of collateralization (see, e.g., Harhoff and Körting 1998; Machauer and Weber 1998). Elsas (2005) shows that the status of a housebank is associated with a lower number of bank relationships, a higher share of loan financing, better information access, and greater bank influence on management. In addition, Neuberger and Räthke (2009) find that companies generally engage in two bank relationships on average. Firm size and age increase the number of bank relationships, which also increase when the firm requires a larger loan amount.

Neuberger and Räthke (2009) find that firms do not appear to increase the number of bank relationships to receive cheaper credit. Rather, they wish to obtain larger loans and to mitigate the likelihood of being credit rationed. For Italy, D'Auria et al. (1999) also point out that the likelihood of a firm facing a hold-up problem increases when the bank has an exclusive bank relationship. Firms may engage in multiple bank relationships to reduce this problem as well as the probability of being credit rationed (Tirri 2007). However, engaging in a smaller number of bank relationships decreases information asymmetries and agency issues, and these positive effects can compensate for hold-up issues.

Stein (2014) finds that bank-dependent companies (especially small companies) do not obtain reduced debt cost of. Higher costs for bank-dependent companies stem from the information advantage obtained by the bank, which enables it to hold up the company. Bank-dependent borrowers (typically small companies) face significant hold-up risk. Hainz and Wiegand (2013) also highlight that maintaining a second bank relationship may be beneficial because it resolves the hold-up problem.

For Italy, Conigliani et al. (1997) find that an increase in the number of bank relationships has a positive effect on interest rates. Companies with multiple bank relationships can ensure a continuous loan supply, and thereby reduce the probability that a project will not be financed by a single lender. Despite higher transaction costs, it may be useful to engage in multiple bank relationships whenever one bank does not provide enough funding to finance a firm's projects (Detragiache, Garella, and Guiso 2000). As the number of bank relationships increases, the return on assets and the return on equity decreases, because the interest expense over assets increases as well. This result is most noticeable for small companies. Therefore, Castelli, Dwyer, and Hasan (2006) document a negative link between engaging in multiple bank relationships and firm performance.

In addition, the number of bank relationships is a crucial factor in analyzing the probability that a company will experience milder effects of a financial crisis, which is proof that relationship lending helps mitigate information asymmetries. A limited number of banks has a positive effect on credit availability (Angelini, Di Salvo, and Ferri 1998).

Cotugno et al. (2013a) and Cotugno et al. (2013b) study firm-bank relationships between 2007 and 2009, and also find that companies with exclusive or few bank relationships experienced lower credit constraints than those with multiple bank relationships. Malafronte et al. (2014) document a positive effect of relationship exclusivity on credit availability. A larger concentration of bank relationships reduces the probability that companies will face financial distress, and the effect is greater for smaller companies, which may be because of their greater level of opaqueness (Fiordelisi et al. 2014).

According to Sette and Gobbi (2015), companies that borrow from a smaller number of banks and companies with more concentrated borrowing on average face a lower contraction in credit availability and a lower probability of credit constraints. However, the ability of a firm to replace a loan from a less-capitalized bank with a loan from another bank is limited and is almost impossible for firms that borrow from just a few banks (Albertazzi and Marchetti 2010).

For Japan, Sterken and Tokutsu (2003) show that companies that engage in a relationship with a top-equity holding bank tend to decrease their number of bank relationships. Companies that have a weak main bank, on the other hand, increase the number of their lending relationships (Ogawa, Sterken, and Tokutsu 2010). Moreover, companies with a higher debt share and less cash in the financial structure engage in more bank relationships (Sterken and Tokutsu 2003).

Ogawa et al. (2010) find that companies that engage in fewer bank relationships and disclose more of their private information exhibit a higher probability of pledging personal guarantees and face higher short-term interest rates. In contrast, engaging in more bank relationships can mitigate the hold-up problem and work against the extraction of monopoly rents (Ogawa et al. 2010). Especially for small firms, the co-existence of a main bank with other banks is important to reduce the likelihood of a credit constraint. Thus, building other bank relationships in addition to the main bank can help manage credit constraints. However, Shikimi (2013) shows that an increasing number of bank relationships has a positive effect on the cost of debt. Shikimi (2013) concludes that financially distressed companies engage in multiple bank relationships to improve access to finance, although this increases the general cost of credit.

Ultimately, it is not clear whether firms should ideally engage in concentrated borrowing with one main bank, or maintain multiple bank relationships, or both. While the main bank would have an incentive to offer lower interest rates due to information advantages, the other bank relationships could help mitigate possible hold-up problems (D'Auria et al. 1999).

Duration of lending relationship

Harhoff and Körting (1998) show that long-term firm-bank borrower relationships are beneficial to firms. In contrast, Lehmann and Neuberger (2001) find that the duration of the lending relationship has no effect on interest rates, while Stein (2014) finds that the cost of debt increases with the duration of the relationship (Bolton et al. 2016; D'Auria et al. 1999; Ewert, Schenk, and Szczesny 2000; Howorth and Moro 2012; Kano et al. 2011; Pozzolo 2004). However, Stein (2014) also documents that relationship strength, as measured by the bank's share in the firm's debt and the length of the relationship, has a different effect on the cost of debt. The cost of debt decreases with relationship strength, but it increases with the length of the lending relationship. The rise of the cost of debt over time is rather weak (Stein 2014).

Elsas (2005) argues that the duration of the lending relationship is not related to the status of a housebank. Therefore, housebanks are not defined by the length of a firm-bank relationship. Norden and Weber (2010) document that the quality of prediction about a borrower's credit quality (through assessing account activity and credit line usage) increases with the duration of the lending relationship and decreases with geographic distance between the company and the bank.

Ferri and Messori (2000) show for Italy that closer and longer-lasting firm-bank relationships are more common for smaller firms and smaller banks. With respect to credit availability, there is a positive effect of duration. Firms with long-term bank relationships experience an increase in credit granted, despite the fact that they may have multiple bank relationships (see, e.g., Angelini et al. 1998; Malafronte et al. 2014). In addition, longer bank relationships reduce the probability that companies will face financial distress, and this effect is larger for smaller companies. This may be attributable to their greater level of opaqueness (Fiordelisi et al. 2014). Sette and Gobbi (2015) find that longer bank relationships lead to greater growth of credit, while decreasing the cost of debt. Moreover, companies with longer bank relationships show a greater likelihood of being able to export into foreign markets (Bartoli, Ferri, Murro, and Rotondi 2014).

Ogawa et al. (2010) show for Japan that the duration of the main bank relationship has an increasing effect on the number of lending relationships. Firms with a long-term lending relationship face a greater probability of pledging collateral (Ogawa et al. 2010; Ono and Uesugi 2009; Pozzolo 2004). Kano et al. (2011) find that firms with longer bank relationships at small banks experience reduced costs of debt, as measured by decreases in the loan interest rate, and increased availability of credit. However, the reduction in the interest rate is not large and firms at small banks are likely to pledge more collateral when the bank relationship is long and the scope is large.

Bank type and distance

Italian studies also focus on the impact of bank type on the lending relationship. Firms that are members of a cooperative bank generally have lower interest rates and better credit availability than non-member firms (Angelini et al. 1998). In this context, Alessandrini, Presbitero, and Zazzaro (2008, 2009) find that banking consolidation has made access for informationally opaque companies in regional banking markets more difficult. There is also a persistent importance of regional banking markets for small companies and the regional economy. Moreover, foreign banks restrict lending more than domestic banks (Albertazzi and Bottero 2014). Bolton et al. (2016) show that, overall, banks with greater capital buffers are better at relationship banking. In addition, Albertazzi and Marchetti (2010) document that larger less-capitalized banks add to credit cyclicality.

Alessandrini et al. (2008) study functional distance in the lending relationship, which is the ratio of local branches weighted by physical, economic, and sociocultural distance to the total number of local branches. They show that an increase in functional distance has a positive effect on the likelihood of facing credit rationing, on the sensitivity of a company's investment cash flow, and on the amount of credit lines drawn. The effects of functional distance especially affect small companies and those in less developed areas. Cotugno et al. (2013a) find that the closer the distance between the company and the bank, the better the availability of credit. Milani (2014) notes that relationship lending should be favored when there is less distance, while transactional lending should be favored for relationships with greater distance. In addition, Sette and Gobbi (2015) find that credit availability is higher and the cost of debt is lower when distance is shorter between the borrower and the lender.

Financial distress

Harhoff and Körting (1998) show that firms' financial distress not only increases interest rates and decreases credit availability, but it also increases the probability of pledging collateral. Housebanks offer financial support during times of rating downgrades, because the bank's share of financing increases (Elsas and Krahnen 1998). Lehmann and Neuberger (2001) find similar empirical evidence, as they document that housebanks are significant sources of financing when companies are distressed. Within normal bank relationships, downgraded companies are more likely to experience a decrease in their credit volumes. In addition, housebanks show a greater probability during times of distress to help a company by engaging in workout activities (Elsas and Krahnen 2003). However, this support is not free, as there may be an increase in credit pricing in the long run. In contrast, normal bank relationships do not offer such implicit financial support.

Nevertheless, no additional financial support by a housebank is observed when a firm has a large rating decrease (Elsas and Krahnen 1998). Higher firm risk leads to higher interest rates (Ewert et al. 2000; Machauer and Weber 1998). Moreover, Elsas and Krahnen (1998) document that credit pricing depends on a firm's rating, and there is no difference between the pricing of housebanks and that of normal banks. Ewert et al. (2000) document that higher collateralization and the presence of covenants are significantly correlated with lower distress probabilities. Companies with established relationship lending are less likely to have their loan financing damaged by the financial crisis. Long-term relationships are especially value during crises (Hainz and Wiegand 2013).

Calcagnini, Farabullini, and Giombini (2012) show for Italy that the likelihood of a loan being collateralized increased during the recent financial crisis. Cotugno et al. (2013a) and Cotugno et al. (2013b) also show that banks prefer lending relationships over transactional relationships, which holds in a crisis situation (see also Malafronte et al. 2014). During financial difficulties, relationship banks tend to help firms more than transactional banks, although the loan terms of relationship lending borrowers deteriorate somewhat as well (Sette and Gobbi 2015). Gambacorta and Mistrulli (2014) show that banks with large capital buffers and banks that are primarily involved in traditional lending are better at protecting their customers from financial crises. Relationship lending lowers a company's default probability (Fiordelisi et al. 2014).

Bolton et al. (2016) study the real economic effects of a financial crisis and find that relationship banking can be crucial for alleviating the crisis. Relationship banks provide lending during difficult times to protect their investments. Hence, they smooth a credit crunch. Bolton et al. (2016) conclude that financial crises could be mitigated if more companies would maintain long-term relationships, and if more banks would keep larger capital buffers. However, Sette and Gobbi (2015) show that, in the case of the recent financial crisis, relationship banks that were more exposed to the crisis did not help weaker firms more than transactional banks.

For Japan, Yao and Ouyang (2007) find that the main bank's monopoly power during a shock may prompt it to issue financing to firms they can easily control in order to stabilize their situation. There is thus an observed commitment of the main bank toward their borrowing firms in distress (Horiuchi et al. 1988). In addition, Gan (2007) shows that companies cannot easily substitute bank lending with other sources of financing. They are thus also affected by a banking market shock, because their market valuation and investments decrease.

2.7.3.3 Firm characteristics

Riskier firms[44] face higher interest rates and depend more on bank financing (Machauer and Weber 1998). Such firms must disclose more information to a bank when engaging in loan negotiations (Fischer 2000). Moreover, there is a positive relation between a firm's risk and the maturity of a loan (Kirschenmann and Norden 2012). Partnerships and sole proprietorships must also pledge more collateral (Machauer and Weber 1998), while corporations can pledge less (Berger, Frame, and Ioannidou 2011; Lehmann and Neuberger 2001). Firm age further increases credit availability (see, e.g., Harhoff and Körting 1998; Angelini et al. 1998). Firms in East Germany and firms in city counties face higher interest rates and are more likely to be financially constrained than those in West Germany (Harhoff and Körting 1998). Lehmann, Neuberger, and Räthke (2004) document that East German firms tend to be rated lower than their West German counterparts, pay higher interest rates, and also must pledge more collateral. There is also a lending gap between firms in East and West Germany. Hommel and Schneider (2003) document that the access of German SMEs overall to bank loans is a crucial factor in the future growth of these companies.

Guiso (2003) shows for Italy that firms with higher equity exhibit a lower likelihood of having bank debt on their financial statements. Leverage has an increasing effect on the number of bank relationships (Cosci and Meliciani 2002). Firms that are larger, riskier, exhibit lower profitability, and have a higher degree of opaqueness prefer multiple bank relationships (Tirri 2007). Credit rationing in Italy does not appear widespread, but when it occurs, it is often due to a lack of size and equity (Guiso 2003).

Becchetti and Garcia (2011) show that collateralization is positively associated with borrowers' ex ante credit risk. Note that collateralized companies are riskier ex ante, but not ex post. Hence, the likelihood of loans being secured with collateral or personal guarantees rises with firm riskiness. In contrast, Calcagnini et al. (2012) document that pledging personal guarantees in combination with collateral is an indication of firm quality. Albertazzi and Marchetti (2010) find that larger less-capitalized banks have moved their financing away from riskier borrowers, while smaller less-capitalized banks have not. Uchida, Udell, and Watanabe (2008) find for Japan that larger companies are more likely to borrow from big banks, and smaller banks have closer borrower relationships. Ono, Sakai, and Uesugi (2012) and Ono and Uesugi (2009) study the impact of

44 Borrower risk is defined as the default risk of borrowers without taking collateral into account (Machauer and Weber 1998).

risk in the lending relationship, and document that firm riskiness[45] has no significant effect on the probability of pledging collateral.

2.7.3.4 Control variables

Fischer (2000) finds a positive relationship between bank concentration in a market and credit availability. Moreover, Elsas (2005) documents that relationship banking does not require the presence of monopoly market structures, although the probability of observing relationship banking increases with a rise in bank market concentration.

Tirri (2007) finds for Italy that the concentration of the local banking market and the concentration of bank relationships at a firm level have a decreasing effect on credit availability. Highly concentrated banking markets are related to a higher risk of company default (Fiordelisi et al. 2014). Firms with multiple bank relationships benefit from competition on the firm level because they therefore face a lower likelihood of being credit rationed (Tirri 2007). In contrast, Malafronte et al. (2014) document that the level of interbank competition and the presence of collateral have a negative effect on credit availability.

Relationships are more durable when interbank competition increases, the loan is secured by collateral, and the distance between the bank's branch and headquarter decreases. Sette and Gobbi (2015) find the opposite, as the effect of relationship lending is greater when the banking market is concentrated. This is because, in these markets, the rent of the relationship bank is larger, and companies have fewer opportunities to change their banks. Aggressive competition by transactional lenders may also undermine the access of relationship banking (Bolton et al. 2016).

Miarka (2000) shows for Japan that firm-bank relationships provide value regardless of competition. In contrast, Shin et al. (2003) document that the Mizuho merger (a merger of three large Japanese banks) had a negative impact on the share prices of borrowing companies. However, companies with one of the three banks as their main bank, or with a large credit volume at one of the banks, experienced fewer negative stock price reactions. Fraser, Rhee, and Shin (2012) find that greater capital market competition is related to a decrease in relationship banking, a decrease in long-term relationship loans, and an increase in short-term relationship loans. Fraser et al. (2012) conclude that great capital

45 A firm's observed riskiness is measured by means of its credit score (Ono et al. 2012; Ono and Uesugi 2009).

market competition leads banks to change their business from long- to short-term relationship banking.

2.7.4 Differences between market- and bank-based financial systems

This section summarizes the main empirical differences between the two financial systems of the 177 investigated studies. Sections 2.7.2 and 2.7.3 presented the effects of the most prominent market- and bank-based financial systems: the U.S. and the U.K. for market-based, and Italy, Germany, and Japan for bank-based. As a result, the precise sources of the potential value-added of relationship banking were pinpointed. In some cases, the empirical findings showed differing effects in one system. However, the prevailing effects from all studies are shown in Table 2-6. The classification of the evidence regarding the costs and benefits of lending relationships in market- and bank-based financial systems is needed in order to establish the basis for the later empirical classification of our findings.

Differences between the market- or bank-based systems exist with regard to the effect of the finance share on the three dependent variables. There is a decreasing effect of the variable finance share on the collateral requirements in the market-based financial system, and an increasing effect in the bank-based system. Moreover, a negative effect on the cost of debt can be observed in the market-based system, while an increasing finance share in the bank-based system leads to a higher cost of debt.

The variable finance share shows no effect on credit availability in the market-based financial system. However, a positive effect is noted in the bank-based system. Moreover, the scope of financial products purchased by the firm from the bank demonstrates no effect on the endogenous variables in the market-based financial system, but a positive effect on the likelihood of collateralized loans and on credit availability in the bank-based system. However, there is also no effect on the variable scope on the cost of debt in the bank-based financial system.

One measure of the closeness of a borrower to its banks is the concentration of a company's borrowing across lenders. Companies tend to concentrate their borrowing with one source, but this concentration typically decreases as company size increases. Thus, borrowing concentration could be one measure of how close a company is to its main bank (Petersen and Rajan 1994).

Regarding the number of bank relationships, while the variable number has a negative effect on the likelihood of collateralized loans in the market-based system, it has a positive effect in the bank-based system. In addition, the empirical results show no effect on the availability of credit in the market-based financial

Table 2-6: Panel A – Collateral requirements, Panel B – Cost of debt, Panel C – Credit availability

Panel A shows the correlations between the endogenous variable collateral requirements. Panel B shows the correlations between the endogenous variable cost of debt. Panel C shows the correlations between the endogenous variable credit availability. The exogenous variables carry one of the following signs: + positive effect, - negative effect, 0 no effect/not studied, e.g., an increase in the finance share leads to a positive effect on the collateral requirements in the bank-based financial system; no effect of the scope on the cost of debt in the bank-based system; and an increase in the number of bank relationships leads to a negative effect on credit availability in the bank-based system. The number of observations on which the effects are based vary because each of the studies evaluated examines a different number of effects.

	Panel A – Collateral requirements		**Panel B – Cost of debt**		**Panel C – Credit availability**	
Variables	**Market-based financial system**	**Bank-based financial system**	**Market-based financial system**	**Bank-based financial system**	**Market-based financial system**	**Bank-based financial system**
Finance share	–	+	–	+	/	+
Number	–	+	+	+	0	–
Duration	–	+	–	+	+	+
Trust	/	+	/	–	/	+
Scope	0	+	0	0	0	+
Firm age	–	0	0	0	+	+
Firm size	0	+	0	–	–	+
Legal form (Limited liability company)	0	–	0	–	–	0
Firm total assets	–	+	–	–	+	0
Firm sales	0	–	0	–	+	–
Sales growth	0	/	–	/	0	0
Financial distress	/	+	/	+	–	–
Family management structure	0	0	0	0	/	0
Family ownership structure	0	+	0	0	/	0

(continued on next page)

Table 2-6: Continued

Variables	Panel A – Collateral requirements		Panel B – Cost of debt		Panel C – Credit availability	
	Market-based financial system	Bank-based financial system	Market-based financial system	Bank-based financial system	Market-based financial system	Bank-based financial system
Construction industry	0	0	0	+	0	0
Manufacturing industry	0	–	0	0	0	/
Retail industry	0	0	0	0	0	–
Transport industry	0	0	0	+	0	0
Service industry	0	0	–	+	/	–
Agriculture industry	0	/	0	+	/	–
Energy industry	/	/	/	0	/	0

Table 2-7: Number of bank relationships in market- versus bank-based financial systems

For a total of eighty-three studies, this table shows the mean, median, standard deviation, minimum, and maximum of the number of bank relationships in both the market- and bank-based systems. The number of observations varies because not every study provided the number of bank relationships. Because complete datasets of the investigated studies are not available, the standard deviation was calculated from the mean and median values available.

	N	Mean	Median	SD (Mean)	SD (Median)	Min	Max
Market-based	31	2.82	2	1.41	0.99	1	6
Bank-based	52	4.37	3	3.06	2.39	1	16

system, but a negative effect on credit availability in bank-based. Nevertheless, both systems demonstrate a positive effect of the variable number on the cost of debt.

Table 2-7 shows that the median value of bank relationships in the bank-based systems is exactly one bank relationship higher, with three relationships compared to two. Another way of measuring concentration is the number of sources from which a firm borrows. Companies that borrow from multiple

Table 2-8: Duration of bank relationships in market- versus bank-based financial systems

For a total of ninety studies, this table shows the mean, median, standard deviation, minimum, and maximum of the duration of bank relationships in years in both the market- and bank-based systems. The number of observations varies because not every study provided the duration of the bank relationship. Because complete datasets of the investigated studies are not available, the standard deviation was calculated from the mean and median values available.

	N	Mean	Median	SD (Mean)	SD (Median)	Min	Max
Market-based	35	10.76	8	8.38	9.75	4	49
Bank-based	55	15.69	8	7.87	7.39	2	32

banks are charged higher rates. Multiple sourcing may therefore weaken lending relationships.

With respect to the duration of the bank relationship, the empirical findings in the market-based system show a negative effect of duration on collateral requirements and the cost of debt. In the bank-based financial system, the results show a positive effect of duration. Both systems demonstrate a positive effect of the length of the lending relationship on credit availability.

Table 2-8 shows the duration of the relationship in years and presents the same median value of eight years for both systems. However, the mean values exhibit a slight difference, with a length of around eleven years in the market-based system, and sixteen in the bank-based system. Thus, firms in bank-based financial systems appear to maintain longer relationships. The empirical evidence suggests that the availability of financing from banks increases when a company spends more time in a relationship, because it increases ties with a lender by expanding the number of financial services it buys. In that way, the company concentrates its borrowing with a lender even further.

With respect to the variable trust, there are no significant empirical findings in the market-based financial system. Trust leads to an increasing effect on collateral requirements and credit availability, and a decreasing effect on the cost of debt in the bank-based financial system. Researchers stress that high levels of trust encourage trustworthy behavior, which can be critical in reducing agency problems, moral hazard, adverse selection, and transaction costs (Nooteboom, Berger, and Noorderhaven 1997). It can also decrease the costs of monitoring and control (Lewicki, McAllister, and Bies 1998). Accordingly, a trusting relationship can benefit banks and SMEs alike by giving the loan manager access to more soft information. Because trust can increase the quantity of information a loan manager can access, it can promote loan managers' decision-making. The role of trust might also be more decisive for small companies that lack the capacity to provide the facts and figures required by banks (Moro and Fink 2013).

Moreover, with regard to the variable financial distress, which measures whether a firm has been in financial distress, the empirical findings show only a significant negative effect on credit availability in the market-based system, and no influence of this variable on collateral requirements or the cost of debt. In contrast, in the bank-based financial system, it demonstrates a positive effect on collateral requirements and the cost of debt, as well as a negative effect on credit availability. Firms in financial distress may need a bank-led "rescue operation." However, by engaging in a reorganization, a bank may suffer short-term losses because the company may not be capable of paying a higher debt or interest burden. If the company cannot commit itself to a long-term relationship with the bank, thereby allowing the lender to compensate for short-term losses in the long-term, then the lender may try to draw away. In addition, such situations may lead the bank to reassess a company's quality. Afterward, credit terms may deteriorate in price and non-price terms (Harhoff and Körting 1998).

Regarding firm characteristics, the empirical findings show that firm age has a negative effect on collateral requirements in the market-based financial system, although it has no effect in the bank-based system.[46] Furthermore, firm age has no effect on the cost of debt and an increasing effect on credit availability in both systems. Firm size, as measured by number of employees, demonstrates no effect on the likelihood of collateralized loans or the cost of debt in the market-based financial system, but a decreasing effect on credit availability. In contrast, in the bank-based system, there is a positive effect on the collateral requirements and on credit availability, while there is a negative effect on the cost of debt.

The total assets of a firm show a negative effect on collateral requirements and the cost of debt in the market-based system, and a negative effect only on total assets on the cost of debt can be found in the bank-based system. In addition, this variable shows a positive effect on credit availability in the market-based financial system, and no effect in the bank-based system, although a positive effect on collateral requirements in this system was documented. Furthermore, firms' sales showed no effect on collateral requirements or on the cost of debt in the market-based system, while, in the bank-based system, they showed a

46 When comparing the market- and bank-based datasets, they show similar characteristics with, for example, respect to firm age. The studied companies in the market-based datasets have a median value of fifteen years, while those in the bank-based datasets have a median value of fourteen.

negative effect on collateral requirements and the cost of debt. A positive effect on credit availability is seen in the market-based financial system, while a negative effect on this variable was documented in the bank-based financial system.

Furthermore, a firm's sales growth shows no effect on the likelihood of collateralized loans or on credit availability, and a negative effect on the cost of debt in the market-based financial system. In contrast, the influence of this variable on collateral requirements and the cost of debt has not been studied in the bank-based financial system. However, the effect of this variable on the availability of credit has been explored, but no significant effect documented.

In addition, the firm's legal status as a corporation shows no effect on collateral requirements or on the cost of debt, and a negative effect on credit availability in the market-based financial system. In contrast, this variable demonstrates a decreasing effect on collateral requirements and the cost of debt in the bank-based system, but no significant effect on credit availability.

Firms' ownership structure leads to a significant result as well. Family ownership shows an increasing effect on collateral requirements in the bank-based financial system. But, in another way, the ownership structure leads to no significant results or has not been examined thus far at all, suggesting a research avenue.

In addition, firms in the construction industry show an increasing effect on the cost of debt in the bank-based financial system. Firms in the manufacturing industry show a decreasing effect on collateral requirements in the market-based financial system. A negative effect of the service industry on the cost of debt in the market-based financial system is documented, while a positive effect on the cost of debt and a negative one on credit availability in the bank-based system was also found. A negative effect of the retail industry on credit availability in the bank-based system is noted. Furthermore, the transportation industry shows a positive effect on the cost of debt in the bank-based financial system. Finally, the agriculture industry exhibits a positive effect on the cost of debt, and a negative effect on the availability of credit in the bank-based financial system.

2.7.5 Summary of empirical findings

This section briefly presents the main drivers in the two financial systems. In the progressively competitive banking environment, differentiation between the distinct costs and benefits and empirical verification is key in order to predict the feasibility and scale of relationship banking in the future. Therefore, the advantages and disadvantages of the market-based systems (e.g., the U.S. and the U.K.) and the bank-based systems (e.g., Italy, Germany, and Japan) are disentangled, and the precise sources of potential value-added of relationship banking are measured.

According to most studies of the two systems, the likelihood of developing a series of repeated transactions, which is fundamental to the lending relationship, represents an approach to decreasing the cost of searching for and processing the information needed for the bank's screening activities. For, e.g., a one-period contract, this would be too onerous, and could lead to rejection of the loan. The duration of the relationship, therefore, allows for the use of information and access to more precise knowledge about the borrower and its related risk (Bongini et al. 2015).

Interestingly, in the bank-based context, lending terms with respect to collateral requirements and the cost of debt deteriorate with a longer duration. In the market-based system, decreasing collateral requirements and decreasing cost of debt are documented. Thus, this finding supports the hold-up problem hypothesis, which suggests that the hold-up problem is more prominent in bank-based financial systems. The literature is not decisive, but there are some explanations. For example, the banking sector in, e.g., Europe is still more consolidated, and fewer credit alternatives exist for borrowers than in market-based financial systems like the U.S. This phenomenon persists despite the disruptive changes and entrants of new market players that have led, to some extent to an increase in financing alternatives, as described in section 2.5.4 (Boot 2000). Yet, the capital market in, e.g., Germany, still poses an obstacle for most SMEs, as this form of financing is associated with more rules and regulations (e.g., high publication standards) than what they currently face.

One solution may be for firms to maintain multiple bank relationships. This can reduce the hold-up problem, but in turn can decrease credit availability. There is no significant effect of reduced credit availability in the market-based financial system. "A plausible explanation is that the presence of multiple relationships reduces the value of information acquisition to any one individual bank [...]. Alternatively, the presence of multiple lenders causes 'too much' competition ex post that can discourage lending to young firms" (Boot 2000, p. 21) (see also Petersen and Rajan, 1994). This effect is again more pronounced in bank-based than market-based systems.

Note that understanding the trust variable more fully could enhance the understanding of its effects on the nature of contracting. Especially in a small business lending context, the loan manager makes each loan decision based on trust as well as hard information. As the previous sections have demonstrated, too little attention has been paid thus far to trust, while much attention has been paid to it in bank-based financial systems. Trust increases credit availability and collateral requirements, and decreases the cost of debt (Tang, Deng, and Moro 2017). This shows its pivotal role in bank-based financial systems and appears to be the way to influence credit terms and improve access to finance. Thus, it represents a possibly competitive advantage for borrowers in bank-based financial systems.

2.8 Deriving the hypotheses based on the research model on relationship banking

The hypotheses are derived based on the presented empirical evidence and the following discussion of the determinants and characteristics of bank relationships. They are derived in the context of the relationship and firm characteristics, particularly with respect to family firms. Therefore, the outline of the determinants of bank relationships, including country, type of firms, and type of banks being analyzed are expected to facilitate the understanding of the overall setting of lending relationships in this study. The resulting impact of the determinants and characteristics of bank relationships on the collateral requirements, cost of debt, and credit availability will be presented in the regression analysis in section 4.2.

2.8.1 Determinants of bank relationships

This subsection presents a description of the structure of the bank-borrower relationships in the present thesis. We briefly outline the studied country, investigated type of firms, and banks.

Country

Kocka (1980) notes that it was probably the objective of German banks, during the development of the German economy in the years after WWII, to monopolize all the needs of industrial companies. When a bank was the unique lender of a company, it also meant it was able to observe a firm's outstanding debt and repayment behavior much better and was better able to assess the probability of default. Edwards and Fischer (1994) also document the major importance of banks in the development of the German financial system. The authors refer to the fact that German banks are usually universal banks and were considered crucial for the successful development of the German economy following WWII. The often strong involvement of German banks in companies is regarded as making them more willing to provide finance for long-term investments. The authors also find that German banks, as well as Japanese banks, take a long-term view ab initio. Hence, by their long-term involvement, they often gain strong knowledge of internal information systems.

Edwards and Fischer (1994) attribute the informational advantages that German banks enjoy to housebank relationships, which are relationships between particular banks and particular companies. These connections tend to be long-term, which enables the bank to know the company's business and personnel in much more depth, allowing for a better assessment of a firm's risk portfolio. In line with the authors, at least for the late nineteenth and early twentieth centuries, firms conducted all of their business with one housebank.

Mayer (1988) notes that, because banks were often the single lender to a company, they were more willing to support companies during times of financial distress (Edwards and Fischer 1994). This study, therefore, focuses on Germany, as housebank relationships are traditionally very strong.

Firms

The aim here is to analyze bank-oriented companies in order to describe the firm-bank relationship. According to the BDI (2015), the German middle class is strongly rooted regionally, and medium-sized companies primarily employ and invest at home. Yet, the proportion of companies with investments outside Germany increases significantly with the size of the company (Bundesverband der Deutschen Industrie e.V. 2015). In line with the European definition, only companies with fewer than 250 employees and either an annual turnover of up to EUR 50 million or a balance sheet total of EUR 43 million or less are considered SMEs. According to the Institut für Mittelstandsforschung (IfM) Bonn, approximately 3.7 million companies belong to the German Mittelstand, which equals 99.6 % of all companies in the German private sector. Companies with up to 500 employees generate 35.3 % of total sales in Germany. 15.7 million employees, or around 60 %, work in companies of this size. Many of these companies are family businesses (in Germany, about 95 % of all companies are family-owned (Bundesverband der Deutschen Industrie e.V. 2015).

Traditionally, German companies are heavily bank-oriented on external finance. However, according to the Deutsche Bundesbank (2018b), in recent years the following changes have been measurable: 1) a shift from funds raised externally (external financing) to financing with internally generated sources (internal financing), and 2) financing by bank loans being substituted for by other forms of debt, for example, loans from non-banks and debt securities. This shift has primarily been triggered by temporary supply constraints at banks. The change to a higher share of internal and equity financing, and a more diversified debt financing structure, are expected to make companies less vulnerable to temporary financial constraints at banks (Deutsche Bundesbank 2018b). Moreover, according to KfW survey results, in 2016, two-thirds of all SMEs used bank credit to finance an investment, and the loan financing of investments increased slightly. However, the strong desire for financial independence and the concern about unfavorable financing conditions discourage many SMEs from engaging in credit negotiations. At the same time, the gap in the credit supply is small (Schwartz 2017). The desire for financial independence is most often opposed to bank financing. This is particularly the case for SMEs (Schwartz 2017).

Access to bank credit and the terms and conditions under which it happens are decisive when raising external funds, because these aspects determine the "financing climate" of lending (Schwartz 2017; Zimmermann 2017). The environment for SME financing has changed fundamentally in recent years. Increased regulatory requirements and the consequences of the sovereign debt crisis in the eurozone make credit financing more difficult (BDI 2015).

Except for the second half of 2009, companies in Germany documented consistently positive developments in external financing, although lower than before the crisis. The reduced need for external financing is traceable to the growth in internal financing, combined with moderate investment behavior, which, taken in isolation, reduce the demand for external financing (Deutsche Bundesbank 2018b). These results are in line with the results of the euro area bank lending survey (BLS) for the first quarter of 2017, which documented a continuing demand for loans as well (European Central Bank 2017b). The SAFE and the BLS document a continued easing of bank lending credit terms (European Central Bank 2017b).

Overall, SMEs stated that terms and conditions for bank loans had become better. SMEs continued to document a net decline in interest rates. In addition, they expressed an increase in the available size and maturity of loans and overdrafts. In contrast, a positive net percentage of SMEs continued to document a tightening in the collateral and other requirements of banks, as well as in other costs of financing associated with charges, fees, and commissions (European Central Bank 2017a). According to the KfW SME panel, SMEs are more concerned with facing unfavorable financing conditions or having to put too much effort into credit negotiations. For 29 % of small companies, high collateral requirements speak against bank financing.

Overall, the financing situation is positive. The solid economy, the high self-financing power of companies, and the continued improvement in ratings provide a relatively stable financing environment. Bank loans remain the second most important financing source, and, thus, SMEs continue to primarily rely on their own funds for investment financing (Schwartz 2017). Due to the fact that most companies belong to the German Mittelstand, which continue to be primarily bank-oriented, these companies are considered a great source of learning about lending relationships.

Banks

The consolidation process in the German banking sector accelerated over the past year. The total number of credit institutions in Germany (including the legally independent building societies, "Bausparkassen") decreased by 72, or 3.7 %, from 1,960 in 2015 to 1,888 (compared to 2014: 1,990 institutions, 2006: 2,301 institutions, 2001: 2,896 institutes). While the number of banks declined sharply, especially in the 1990s and even in the first half of the subsequent decade, the consolidation process has been subdued since 2008. It has picked up again since 2013.

Bank density indicates how many inhabitants on average are customers of a bank office; rising values express a reduction in bank density. With 33,914 bank branches nationwide and a population of around 82.8 million,[47] the bank's reporting density for the 2016 reporting year was 2,441. This means that, in Germany, there is an average of one bank office per 2,441 inhabitants. As a result, the Deutsche Bundesbank (2017a) documents that the number of bank branches fell more sharply than in previous years.

Regarding sectoral distribution, the largest decrease, of 51 institutions, as well as in previous years was attributable to the cooperative sector. The number of cooperative institutions declined by 5.0 % during the year, from 1,027 to only 976 in 2016. Thus, the decrease was significantly stronger than in the previous year (24, or 2.4 %). The savings bank sector, with a total of 11,351 branches, including 412 head offices, remains the largest sector in Germany (Deutsche Bundesbank 2017a). The focus here is on assessing whether there are different measurable effects of lending relationships with respect to Germany's "three-pillar banking system."

2.8.2 Characteristics of bank relationships

This section describes the characteristics of bank relationships. This is obviously rather complex, so it will focus on loan, relationship, and firm characteristics. In addition, hypotheses are derived based on the theoretical argumentation. Before

47 As per a press release on January 27, 2017, about the population level at the end of 2016 in Germany (Destatis - Statistisches Bundesamt 2017).

turning to the role of relationship characteristics, it is important to control for the underlying loan characteristics.

Loan characteristics

Loan characteristics attempt to capture how close the working relationship is between the bank and the firm. With the disruptive developments, the distinction between companies and banks is perhaps not as clear as it once was. Eventually, firms reduce their dependence on banks, as SMEs continue to primarily rely on their own funds for investment financing (Schwartz 2017). This seems to suggest that companies follow a pecking order of borrowing over time, beginning with the closest sources. For example, family sources would be used first, progressing eventually to more arm's-length sources. One important process is the impact of loan characteristics on the availability or renewal of credit in the lending relationship (Petersen and Rajan 1994).

Bank-dependent borrowers (typically small companies in Germany) are especially likely to encounter substantial hold-up risk by the relationship bank. Bank-dependent borrowers may bear higher costs via the price impact of lending relationships. Nevertheless, they may profit to a greater degree than non-bank dependent borrowers from better non-price conditions, such as better access to credit. Yet, financial distress may prompt the bank to reevaluate company quality. Subsequently, loan terms may deteriorate, both in price and non-price terms (Harhoff and Körting 1998). However, banks can decide to "lean against the wind," and remain funding distressed but viable companies (Höwer 2016).

Fama (1985) refers to the importance of lending relationships by evaluating the public image of lending relationships. Due to the fact that there are often short-term bank loans, each time a bank renews the loan, it reassesses the ability of the company to meet its financial obligations. In accordance with Fama (1985), the renewal process involves two aspects: First, it allows other potential investors to rely on the evaluation process and avoid duplicating processes. Second, it reflects some type of accreditation for the public that the company is able to produce enough cash flows in the future. Thus, the renewal process is a very important aspect of the lending relationship.

In this context, James (1987) and Lummer and McConnell (1989) argue that bank loan announcements and renewals reflect the future value of a company. According to James (1987), loan announcements are associated with significant positive stock price reactions. This in turn supports Fama's (1985) observation that loan announcements reflect a company's accreditation to outside investors so that the company is able to generate future cash flows (Degryse et al. 2009).

Haubrich (1989) assumes that regular loan renewal and evaluation of repayment behavior make the cost to a bank of maintaining long-term relationships lower than repeated direct monitoring. Sharpe (1990), Rajan (1992), and Von Thadden (2004) suggest that close relationships develop in competitive markets due to information asymmetries. Sharpe (1990) states that long-term bank relationships develop because the incumbent bank wants to gain monopoly power by its informational advantage over competitors. This aspect, however, is already inherent in housebank relationships (Degryse et al. 2009).

Relationship characteristics

The information aspect of a relationship is very important, because the degree of information enables a firm to signal quality. Thus, the information advantage that banks can generate from a close relationship typically depends to a great degree on the company and how it is able to signal the quality of its business operations to outside investors. This study also includes the scope of the relationship, which measures the number of bank products the borrower acquired from the relationship lender. This is another defining factor of the lending relationship (Degryse et al. 2009).[48]

The number of bank relationships a firm maintains and the resulting concentration of borrowing are further key characteristics (Degryse et al. 2009). Berger et al. (2005) document that the number of branches influences a company's decision to stay with a bank, while bank size measured by assets has a negative impact on the length of a relationship. Engaging in several bank relationships may lower the holdup problem of relationship banking but may also give rise to coordination failure in the case of default. Moreover, banks may deduct higher profits from captured and locked-in (opaque) companies than from companies that have other financing sources already available. Changing banks may involve not only the observable direct (transactional) cost of closing an account with one and opening a new one with another, but also the unobservable, perhaps more significant, cost associated with the foregone capitalized value of the (previously established) long-term lending relationship. Note that switching costs may

---

48 Bank control is another factor in the bank relationship, because banks can own equity in a company. According to Mahrt-Smith (2006), banks may also hold seats on the board of directors (see also Degryse et al. 2009). However, at this point, note that none of the companies in this study have bankers on a company's board or have a bank holding stake. This may be due to the nature of the current dataset, which consists entirely of SMEs.

impose consequences, not only on the specific locked-in customers, but also on the overall efficient allocation of loans in the economy. In fact, switching costs may prevent substitution, a fundamental factor for the efficient functioning of the price system. As short-term loans represent an important source of financing for SMEs, the actual allocation of bank loans can have substantial real consequences for an economy (Degryse et al. 2009).

Bolton and Scharfstein (1996) find that only companies with the highest credit quality are likely to maintain several bank relationships. In contrast, Bris and Welch (2005) find that higher credit quality companies maintain relationships with a few banks in order to successfully signal their confidence.[49] Typically, older and larger companies maintain more bank relationships, and also less profitable, distressed, low cash flow, intangible, and leveraged firms have more bank relationships (Degryse et al. 2009).

This study aims to determine whether there are changes in the number of bank relationships through a company's lifecycle regarding firm age, size, and legal form (Degryse et al. 2009). Ongena and Smith (2000a, 2000b) examine the reasons for maintaining several bank relationships. They analyze a data set of 1,079 companies across 20 European countries. They identify large international differences in the number of bank relationships. Their results show that companies on average have more bank relationships in countries with inefficient legal systems and weaker creditor positions.

The academic literature usually states that firms borrowing from a lower number of banks tend to experience an increase in credit availability and a decrease in the cost of capital, because lenders have better information about the borrower. For SMEs, which are usually more opaque than larger firms, it is generally suggested that developing long-term relationships and obtaining most borrowing from a smaller number of banks is beneficial. Hence, especially for young firms, one exclusive relationship may be of benefit because a long track record does not exist.

Farinha and Santos (2002) explore why firms initiate more than one bank relationship. They study monthly reports of banks operating in Portugal between 1980 and 1996. The credit reports detail the debtor's identity, the amount it borrows from the bank over both the short- and long-term, and any overdue amounts. They find that the key reasons for changing from one

49 Demirgüç-Kunt and Detragiache (2009) and Detragiache et al. (2000) examine the bank's viewpoint, and document that multiple bank relationships are necessary to diversify liquidity risk.

relationship to more relationships are that the incumbent bank is hesitant to provide financing to a firm due to its poor performance in the past. These findings confirm the assumptions in this thesis. Considering the recent financial crises, firms faced credit constraints, and were looking for alternative funding sources. One alternative may be to establish new bank relationships and to therefore be less dependent on the main bank. Thus, it may actually be a defense strategy to fight financial constraints by establishing several bank relationships.

Cenni, Monferrà, Salotti, Sangiorgi, and Torluccio (2015) study Italian companies and the factors affecting credit rationing in a bank-based system. They find that several bank relationships increase the probability of rationing. For small businesses, carrying a debt concentration with a main bank is positive, but the opposite is true for large companies. Using a sample of German firms, Höwer (2016) shows that multiple relationships provide a cushion against financial shocks. Overall, it is assumed that more bank relationships will have a positive impact on credit terms. This leads to the first hypothesis:

Hypothesis 1: *Firms with more bank relationships receive better credit terms from their most important banks than firms with fewer bank relationships.*

But what is about small firms with just one bank relationship? Are there other ways to influence credit terms? With regard to Germany and its alleged close customer-bank relationships, the length of the lending relationship is a determining factor in housebank relationships. Whether a long-term relationship has a positive influence on credit conditions in the firm's most important bank relationship today is examined. Elsas and Krahnen (1998) doubt the reliability of duration as a suitable indicator for a strong firm-bank relationship, because duration does not adequately characterize intensity.

Nevertheless, Berger and Udell (1995a) use the duration of a bank relationship as a measure of its strength. They note that banks can accumulate increasing amounts of private information about the duration of a relationship. Furthermore, Degryse and Van Cayseele (2000) use two measures for relationship strength: 1) duration, and 2) scope, which is represented by the number of financial services between the firm and the bank. Although the findings are mixed, duration is expected to be a critical factor in a lending relationship, because repeated transactions between firms and their main banks create interactions and generate information. This facilitates the development of close ties. In this context, the second hypothesis is as follows:

Hypothesis 2: *Firms in long-term relationships with their most important banks experience increased credit availability and reduced lending costs.*

While many studies examine the number and duration of bank relationships, in regressing the cost and availability of debt, a few studies consider other measures to assess the intensity and strength of the lending relationship (Degryse et al. 2009). When trust is involved, the firm expects the bank to take on special responsibility if firms face financial distress (see also Arbeitskreis Finanzierung (1988); Elsas and Krahnen 1998). This argumentation is supported empirically by Lehmann and Neuberger (2001), who show that housebanks provide services and loans if a firm becomes financially distressed. Boot (2000) writes that, "A bank-borrower relationship is in many ways a mutual commitment based on trust and respect" (Boot 2000, pp. 13, 14). In this sense, the bank and the firm may recognize that their relationship produces value, and should, therefore, be nurtured.

In this context, Ongena and Smith (2000a) find that bankers perceive the creation of strong customer relationships as a core element when offering financial services. They describe as follows: "(…) the connection between a bank and customer that goes beyond the execution of simple, anonymous, financial transactions" (Ongena and Smith 2000a, p. 224). At the same time, a loyal customer will be more willing to obtain other financial services from the bank (Boot 2000; Ongena and Smith 2000a). According to Ongena and Smith (2000a), the benefits of such a relationship may be the transmission of confidential information on the part of firms, and the implicit commitment on the part of banks to continue doing business with the firm through financially difficult times. Howorth and Moro (2012) demonstrate that the assessment of the trustworthiness of SME owner-managers decreases interest rates, while Moro and Fink (2013) provide empirical evidence for a positive relation between trust and credit availability. In addition, Tang et al. (2017) show that trust in lending officers plays an important role in a firm's decision to apply for loans at the bank. This leads to the third hypothesis:

Hypothesis 3: *Credit availability and pricing are better for firms that have a trusting relationship with their most important banks.*

Firm characteristics

This study examines whether the state of being a family business influences credit conditions, because relationship management differs somewhat different from non-family firms. A family firm maintains relationships with different stakeholders, but the bank as one stakeholder will be described in this subsection.

For the family, the company not only represents an investment object, but it stands for the tradition and performance of the family (Le Breton-Miller and

Miller 2006; Schraml 2010). The personal and emotional attachments to the company can consequently be quite strong and can affect the quest for long-term preservation (Kets de Vries 1993). In this context, Kets de Vries (1993) note that family entrepreneurs have a different view of employees, customers, and other key stakeholders due to their general long-term perspective. This viewpoint has a positive effect on the quality of stakeholder relationships.

In many cases, the company and its relationships are a reflection of the family. For example, if the name of the owner appears on the building, this serves as a reminder of the position and reputation of the company in society. The family will rarely find it attractive to stand for short-term financial gains because this may tarnish the view of stakeholders. In addition, according to Kets de Vries (1993) the family spirit determines the prevailing attitudes, norms, and values of the company and are expressed by the family members. This helps create a sense of identification and engagement for employees. The assumption is that family firms show distinct behavior when engaging with their stakeholders that can differ dramatically from that of non-family firms (Mietzner and Tyrell 2012).

In this context, the concept of social capital is important to mention. Social capital is defined as the resources embedded in social networks and relationships that enhance the competitiveness of the firm, facilitate information exchange, collaboration (resource sharing), and knowledge transfer, and can lead to decreased transaction costs and improved financial performance (Burt 2003; Coleman 2000; Du, Guariglia, and Newman 2015; Florin, Lubatkin, and Schulze 2003; Hite 2005; Nahapiet and Ghoshal 1998).

Nahapiet and Ghoshal (1998) examine social relationships and the importance of social capital. In contrast to human capital, which focuses on individual attributes, social capital includes relationships between individuals or between organizations (often individual-based relationships). Social capital is the "sum of the actual and potential resources embedded within, available through, and derived from the network of relationships possessed by an individual or social unit" (Nahapiet and Ghoshal 1998, p. 243). Putnam (2001) describes social capital as the propensity of people to cooperate to produce socially efficient outcomes. It also emphasizes the norms of reciprocity and trustworthiness that emerge from connections among individuals (La Porta et al. 1996; Lins, Servaes, and Tamayo 2017). Social capital can encompass a number of key business activities, such as the exchange of resources and the creation of intellectual capital between individuals or organizations. As such, it represents a highly important company resource. According to Sirmon and Hitt (2003), social capital comprises three dimensions: structural, cognitive, and relational. The structural dimension is based on network connections, the cognitive dimension is based on a common language and on narratives, and the relational dimension is based on trust, norms, and duties. Each dimension is embedded in the family unit and connects the relationships that the family firm maintains with its stakeholders (Sirmon and Hitt 2003).

Financing choices are one of the most challenging and difficult decisions encountered by SMEs. Compared to larger companies, SMEs are often perceived as carrying higher levels of asymmetric information, which would result in higher agency costs (Norton 1991). This may be an obstacle to obtaining external funding and may result in being unable to finance company activities or chase market opportunities effectively. In the venture financing literature, inadequate access to financing has been shown to increase the likelihood of small business failure (Bridges and Guariglia 2008; Clarke, Cull, and Kisunko 2012; Cooper, Gimeno-Gascon, and Woo 1994; Huynh, Petrunia, and Voia 2010).

The lack of sufficient capital also affects the growth potential of new firms, with undercapitalized firms experiencing significantly lower levels of growth (Alsos, Isaksen, and Ljunggren 2006; Chandler and Hanks 1998; Du et al. 2015). As noted by Hutchinson (1995), owner-managed small firms may have additional needs to finance expansion through capital provided by banks due to the fact that other resources tend to be limited at early stages in a company's lifecycle. Thus, the need for credit financing exists (Schwartz 2017). For these reasons, it is crucial to understand the factors of SMEs' capital structures (Du et al. 2015).

Social capital is gathered through a process in which economic agents devote time and money to socialize with relevant persons and organizations (Bourdieu 1986). By engaging in relationships with others in their social networks, SMEs are able to access more financing mainly by promoting the transfer of information about their company both directly and indirectly. Network ties and reducing asymmetric information with potential capital providers also help in this endeavor (Chua, Chrisman, Kellermanns, and Wu 2011; Du et al. 2015). In line with Sirmon and Hitt (2003), the social capital of the family increases when effective relationships with stakeholders are in place (e.g., housebanks), because family firms can generate resources from their networks (e.g., knowledge, financial capital). In particular, interactions with financiers represent a key aspect of stable and sustainable funding of the company. They are thus an important factor in a company's relationship management (Schraml 2010). Lending relationships are about the connections between a company and its bank, and, therefore, about social relationships. Ongoing contact is vital to build such a relationship. This leads to the fourth hypothesis:

Hypothesis 4: *Family firms have more contact with their housebanks than non-family firms.*

Anderson and Reeb (2003) note that the long-term perspective of family firms promotes long-term investment projects. Mach (2007) finds from survey results about German family firms that the top objectives are long-term orientation and value orientation (Koeberle-Schmid, Fahrion, and Witt 2012; Mach 2007). However, long-term investment projects often involve long-term investment capital commitments, which may imply the current sacrifice of consumption in order to profit later (Krempel and Von Weizsäcker 2006).

At the same time, long-term orientation plays a key role in building sustainable relationships with stakeholders (e.g., borrowers, housebanks). It is important for the development of a positive reputation (Le Breton-Miller and Miller 2006). Stakeholders develop expectations about the risk of opportunistic behavior of a company based on past observed actions. Trusting behavior in the past tells stakeholders that the company will continue to be a reliable partner in the future. The company benefits from this reputation, and in light of a long-term vision, has fewer incentives to jeopardize reputation for short-term profits (Krempel and Von Weizsäcker 2006).

Le Breton-Miller and Miller (2006) believe that investments in stakeholders are especially high in family firms whose CEOs are planning to keep the business in the family for future generations. This gives these owners credibility, strength, and the incentive to raise the necessary resources. According to the authors, long-term relationships are more easily formed in family businesses whose CEOs are influential and have a long-term tenure. In these contexts, stakeholders assume that management is reliable because the name of the family is at stake. Therefore, family firms are attractive relationship partners and are usually in a good position to develop and nurture social capital. Le Breton-Miller and Miller (2006) conclude that family companies undertake higher investments in durable relations with stakeholders to gain superior stakeholder retention and stable partners. In this context, the fifth hypothesis is as follows:

> **Hypothesis 5**: *Family firms maintain longer relationships with their housebanks than non-family firms.*

Long-term goals require sustainable financing by a stable financing partner. Thus, long-term company development requires crisis-proof financing. In addition, the financial well-being of the company is mainly achieved by strong equity capital financing and by bank financing, because banks represent the most important external partner for privately held family firms in Germany (Sirmon and Hitt 2003; Schraml 2010). German companies are traditionally strongly bank-oriented. Bank loans with different maturities are the most important source of financing for SMEs, after financing by internal funds (Zimmermann 2017). In order to ensure sufficient financing, internal equity may not suffice, and external capital may therefore be required.

In general, external financing of non-financial corporations over the 1991–2010 period was strongly dominated by credit financing. Market-based financing was used to a lesser extent. The overall importance of credit-based financing was initially characterized by the traditionally high proportion of bank loans to total liabilities. Due to their size or legal form, SMEs often did not have the ability to raise funds via the capital market. In addition to the costs associated with an IPO, which can be a significant source of liquidity for SMEs, informational deficiencies contribute to a cautious supply of funding. But even banks themselves have shown a keen interest in a continuing business relationship with companies. In a competitive environment, they need to cover the high costs of credit checks over a long credit exposure to generate positive returns. For example, long-term credit relationships, which often consisted of only one bank - the so-called housebank - dominated in the past. As a result, unlike capital providers with less close business relationships with firms, banks in Germany often had privileged access to information that would enable them to adequately assess companies' economic situations and development potential. This also had a positive effect on the financing costs of companies (Deutsche Bundesbank 2012).

Overall, the KfW SME panel documents that larger SMEs are more open to bank financing because their business activities are typically larger, and, therefore, the options to fund such activities by their own resources are likely to be more limited (Schwartz 2017). Additionally, in reference to the pecking order theory, financing by a bank may imply that it can exercise some control and gain some co-decision-making rights. But funding by a bank does not lead intrinsically to any change in the ownership structure, as opposed to funding by external equity shareholders (Schraml 2010). Consequently, it is expected that family firms would rather fulfill their demands for financing with a close financier (e.g., the bank) than go to the capital market. This leads to the sixth hypothesis:

Hypothesis 6: *Family firms obtain the largest share of their external capital demands from their housebanks compared to non-family firms.*

Especially during financially difficult times, family firms are often more resilient, as they are willing to accumulate profits and provide them to the company. In this context, Sirmon and Hitt (2003) write about “Survivability Capital” and “Patient Capital.” “Survivability Capital” represents the unification of unique resources, for example, the free work that family members provide. “Patient Capital” represents the financial capital that can be invested in a company without the risk of liquidation (Sirmon and Hitt 2003). The long-term orientation allows projects to be pursued without the pressure to achieve short-term goals. According to Sirmon and Hitt (2003), "Patient Capital" is one of the most valuable assets of family firms (see also Schraml 2010).

Sharpe (1990) notes that the relationship between a borrower and its housebank is characterized by an implicit contract that results in long-term commitments and intertemporal pricing. In line with Azariadis (1975) and Azariadis and Stiglitz (1983), implicit contracts mean voluntary and self-enforcing long-term arrangements between two parties about the future exchange of goods or services. The credibility of an implicit contract depends on the valuation of future transactions and the behavior of the contracting parties (Sharpe 1990).

Petersen and Rajan (1994) document that implicit promises are important because a bank must be able to rely on the fact that it will receive future business from a company. Such promises are more credible in concentrated banking markets, because companies have fewer funding options. In this context, Allen and Gale (1999) explore how an implicit contract is enforceable, because it is unwritten, while an explicit contract is available in written form. Why should the borrower or the housebank believe that the other party will adhere to the conditions of the implicit contract?

In line with Allen and Gale (1999), it is possible that the value of a long-term relationship offers incentives for both parties, and this value causes them to comply with the contract. However, compliance is strongly determined by the status and value of the current relationship (Allen and Gale 1999). In addition, Boot (2000) writes that housebank relationships represent in many ways a mutual obligation that is based on trust and respect. The bank and the borrower realize that their relationship creates value, which would be unattainable by other means. As a result, the relationship should be encouraged.

Moreover, Neuberger (2005) documents that long-term lending relationships are a type of implicit contract, because the bank offers to support the borrower when it faces market risks in exchange for the right to make allocation decisions. Berg and Schrader (2009) mention the insurance function of the implicit contract and show that borrowers in this relationship receive implicit insurance whenever they are in distress. Research has found that, during a crisis, companies are more likely to obtain a loan with more favorable terms from a relationship bank (Bolton et al. 2016; Cotugno et al. 2013a; Jiangli et al. 2008).

Elsas and Krahnen (1998) document that lenders provide liquidity insurance for companies that suffer an unexpected decline in credit quality when they have a relationship with them. Moreover, Rosenfeld (2014) finds that companies that obtain a loan from a relationship lender in the six months prior to a situation of distress are more likely to emerge from it. Thus, the implicit contract is particularly valuable at these times, because it may lead to better credit terms, reflected in a smaller spread, greater availability of financing, and perhaps even to a lower probability of requiring collateral. The implicit contract is also expected to be more pronounced in a lending relationship between a family firm and a bank, as family firms tend to nurture lending relationships more than non-family firms. Overall, it is expected that companies that are owned and managed by a family will receive better price and non-price terms even when the firm has been in financial distress. In this context, the seventh hypothesis is as follows:

Hypothesis 7: *Family firms receive better pricing and non-pricing terms from their housebanks than non-family firms.*

Elsas and Krahnen (1998) state that the case of "relationship lending," or "housebank financing," is a specific implicit contractual agreement. Elsas and Krahnen (2002, 2003) and Elsas (2005) point out that housebank relationships are defined as long-term implicit contracts between a bank and its borrower. By means of information retrieval and repeated interaction with the borrower over time, the bank collects private information. This information privilege commits both parties and binds them together, thus creating a close relationship (Elsas and Krahnen 2002, 2003; Elsas 2005). Such commitments may create advantages, such as increased credit availability and support during financial difficulties (Elsas 2005). Nevertheless, in light of the developments outlined in section 2.5, the status of lending relationships between companies (in particular family firms) and banks is not clear. Therefore, in-depth analysis of the hypotheses is even more critical.

3 Data and methodology

This study aims to examine the status quo and the characteristics of the firm-bank relationship, as well as the factors that influence the costs and benefits of the credit parameters in this relationship. The data for this study come from a 2016 online survey of 576 German firms conducted from April 20–May 31. The dataset covers firms from all major sectors of the German economy.

This chapter first outlines the various data collection methods used in prior academic research, and describes the sample design, pretest, and data collection method we use here. We then explain the survey design in detail and present the endogenous and exogenous variables. Next, we illustrate the analytical methods used to analyze the variables. In this context, we introduce the probit regression and the ordinary least squares (OLS) regression. Last, we discuss the robustness of our data.

3.1 Data collection methods

This subchapter presents an overview of the data collection methods used to analyze relationship lending in prior empirical studies. It also briefly outlines the advantages and disadvantages of the various methods.

Kysucky and Norden (2016) examine relationship lending in a transnational context. The authors collected information from 101 studies in the U.S., Europe, Asia, and Latin America from 1970 to 2010, detailing multivariate empirical results on relationship lending and lending outcomes (loan terms). The data collection encompasses a sample of 2,979 effects gathered from 4.1 million company observations over 28 countries. The key characteristics include: relationship strength proxies, such as the duration of the lending relationship, age of the borrower, frequency of interactions, number of lending relationships, scope of financial services provision, and a dummy variable that indicates banking in person. The lending outcome proxies are price of credit, credit availability, and collateral requirements.

To identify the empirical studies, Kysucky and Norden (2016) use two search strategies. First, they searched for the terms "relationship lending" and "relationship banking" in six databases: ISI Web of Knowledge, Scopus, ScienceDirect, JSTOR, ABI/Inform, and SSRN. In particular, they looked for the following terms in the fields: "title," "abstract," and "keywords." Second, they looked up the references in the literature survey articles on relationship lending by Boot

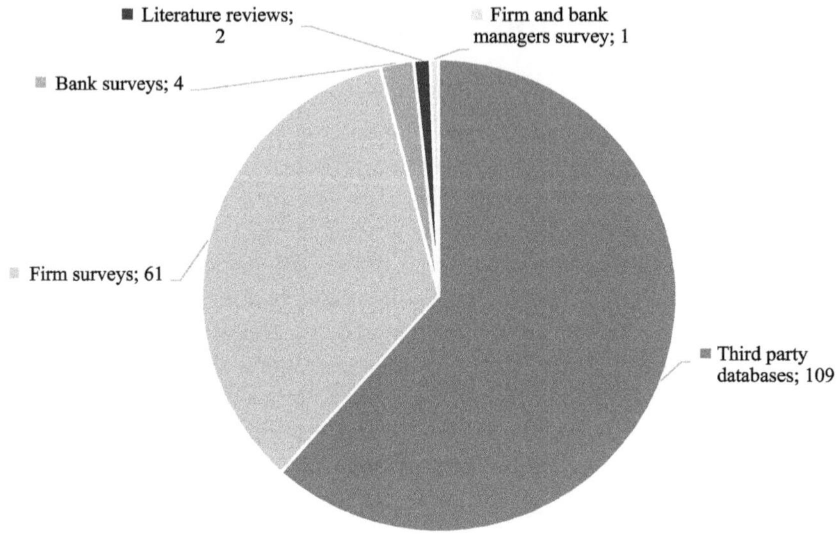

Figure 3-1: Data sources

This figure shows the data sources used in the 177 analyzed studies. The largest share is made up of third-party databases (109), followed by 61 firm surveys, 4 bank surveys, 2 literature reviews, and 1 combined firm and bank managers survey.

(2000), Elyasiani and Goldberg (2004), and Degryse and Ongena (2008). Of the 101 studies, Kysucky and Norden (2016) find that 46 used surveys and 23 used bank file data.[50] The remainder used either a combination of both or third-party databases. More than half the U.S. studies (20 of 35) used records from the NSSBF. Figure 3-1 shows the data sources for the 177 studies analyzed for this thesis.[51]

In total, 177 studies were analyzed, of which 109 studies used third-party datasets, such as central credit registers and bank records, along with 61 that used firm surveys. Of the 61 studies, 53 were conducted by third parties, and not

50 The advantages and disadvantages of the data collection methods, e.g., primary databases (surveys) versus secondary databases (bank file data), are explained at the end of this section.

51 The eleven cross-country studies that were investigated for this paper are also included in this figure.

by the authors themselves, while 20 used data from the NSSBF.[52] The remainder used, for example, a firm questionnaire by the World Bank, or datasets by service agencies or research institutes. In eight studies, the authors conducted the firm surveys themselves, in some cases (see, e.g., Hommel and Schneider 2003) in cooperation with the IHK. Four studies used bank surveys, and two (Kysucky and Norden 2016; Ongena and Smith 2000a) conducted literature reviews. In other words, they compare different datasets. Saparito et al. (2004) use firm and bank manager survey data to analyze lending relationships.

Because we use a firm survey here, we discuss in more detail studies in which the authors conducted surveys themselves in order to fully present the challenges. For example, Zineldin (1995) mailed 300 questionnaires to a random sample of companies in various cities in Sweden. Completed questionnaires were received from 179 firms (a response rate of 59.67 %). Angelini et al. (1998) derive data from a survey conducted in November 1995, addressed to a sample of 6,164 Italian non-financial companies. Of that, 1,811 could not be reached, 2,495 declined to participate or ended the interview before completion, and 1,824 companies eventually participated in the study (a response rate of 29.6 %).

Harhoff and Körting (1998) investigated the role of the most important bank relationship in a survey of SMEs in Germany in 1997. They conducted detailed person-to-person interviews using the help of a large professional surveying institute, which they forwarded a total of 9,699 addresses. However, 1,181 candidates refused the interview outright, 1,497 gave the topic of the survey as their main reason for not participating, and 165 gave other reasons for not participating. 14 interviews actually took place, but provided no usable information. A total of 1,509 interviews were ultimately conducted, but inconsistencies in 110 of them limited the sample to 1,399 usable interviews. Their response rate was 14.42 %.

Niskanen and Niskanen (2000) conducted a private survey, where they mailed questionnaires to 5,858 Finnish companies and 526 replied. The sample covered the four-year period from 1994–1997 (a response rate of 9 %). Ziane (2003) studied bank-firm relationships during 2001. He mailed surveys to a panel of 1,800 SMEs in the first quarter of 2002. The number of exploitable surveys, after eliminating those with significant missing values, was 244 (a response rate of 13.56 %).

52 NSSBF was the name of the survey in 1987 and 1993. For the 1998 and 2003 surveys, the name changed to Survey of Small Business Finances (SSBF). The surveys were conducted by the Federal Reserve Board and the Small Business Administration (SBA).

In 2002, Hommel and Schneider (2003) conducted a survey with the help of the IHKs (Chambers of Commerce) of Koblenz, Cologne, Saarland, and Wiesbaden, the Deutsche Sparkassen und Giroverband (Berlin), and PricewaterhouseCoopers Corporate Finance GmbH. The total sample consisted of 5,729 companies, of which 403 were received back. 10 were excluded because they were not filled out, and 17 were excluded because they exceeded the size criterion. Thus, their empirical analysis was based on a total of 376 observations (a response rate of 6.56 %).

De Bodt, Lobez, and Statnik (2005) used a database from the National Bank of Belgium, containing the annual accounts of all Belgian firms. They focused on small businesses in the French part of Belgium. In 2000, they sent out 4,932 questionnaires that asked for the firms' situations as of December 31, 1998. They received 473 back, of which only 296 were usable and contained complete information (for a response rate of 6 %).

Neuberger and Räthke (2009) studied microenterprises and collected data in 2002 from an online survey of 6,000 professionals in Germany. The addresses came from the yellow pages and from publicly available registers of chambers and industries. The authors received 230 completed surveys back (a response rate of 3.83 %). The authors explain the low response rate by the fact that the survey included some very personal questions as well as questions about financial issues, which respondents are typically more hesitant to answer. In addition, they find that, in Germany, people are chronically concerned about Internet safety, and thus with the confidentiality of online surveys. Older generations are also generally more reluctant to use this medium.

Several key studies, however, have highlighted that surveys are used quite frequently when investigating relationship lending. Thus, research can be gathered from both primary and secondary data collection methods, although they differ in how they are conducted and in how they are analyzed. Each method offers certain advantages and disadvantages. In this study, we use an online survey to gather data instead of a secondary database.

Examples of a primary database are company or bank surveys. Using primary databases allows researchers to better align the research with their specific goals and purposes, eliminating wasted resources. The course of study can be modified as necessary, and the most appropriate platform for observation chosen more easily. However, primary research may require more expense than secondary research, and it may be more time-consuming. Thus, it generally uses greater resources overall.

Online surveys are typically less expensive to administer, as they offer lower-cost implementation and more rapid data collection than, for example, large-scale personal interviews. Nevertheless, the outcome from primary data collection methods may not always be as clear-cut as expected. Additionally, there is the risk of a lack of representativeness due to selection bias.

A selection bias can emerge when the selection of data for analysis occurs in such a way that appropriate randomization is not realized. As a result, the sample obtained is not representative of the population being studied. For example, certain banks may be more willing to participate in a survey if the aim is close to the structure of their portfolios; banks that are critical of the aim of the survey may not be willing to participate. Accordingly, the data collected may not be representative of the full population, which would obviously impact the empirical findings. The conclusions may not apply to the real world, because the observed effect may be exaggerated. Or, it may not be possible to determine any effect for those not included in the study. Hence, selection bias must be considered in order to derive suitable conclusions from a study. Nevertheless, especially in recent years, surveys have gained increasing importance (Bieber and Bytzek 2012).

Using secondary data involves using information that someone has already researched, prepared, and analyzed. Examples include company annual reports and online databases. This data collection method is usually quite cost-effective, offers readily usable observations, and requires less time be spent on gathering information (Ghauri and Grønhaug 2005). It also typically provides statistically reliable data and, therefore, less expertise from researchers is needed.

However, there are several drawbacks. The information provided may be inappropriate for the research question, and the data may lack sufficient details while simultaneously providing a vast amount of information (Denscombe 2014). As a result, the data may need to be customized, and may require intensive examination in order to judge its validity. Researchers may also face a lack of control over data quality. Government and other official institutions usually present a guarantee of data quality, but this may not be the case when using data from other institutions (Bryman and Bell 2015). Thus, a selection bias may occur as well, albeit in a weakened form.

In this study, we use a cross-sectional design, meaning the data for the survey was collected once, and thus only represents one particular moment in time. However, the study uses industry survey data rather than an evaluation of different databases, as this allows for a more direct focus on information related to firms' banking decisions. Hence, the methodology provides a clear measure of the value of the bank relationship as perceived by the firm. Note the importance of this last point. Without such a direct measure of firms' perspectives on bank relationships, it would be impossible to focus the analysis on which factors impact value at the firm level.

3.2 Sample design, pretest, and data collection

To conduct the survey, we exported firms' email addresses from the Dafne company database, which is managed by Bureau van Dyck. In order to filter for the target companies, we chose only solvent firms, those with available email addresses, and those with a given name of someone with an executive function in treasury, controlling, or accounting. This person then became the contact person in the email forwarding. Moreover, we excluded the following legal forms: foundations, cooperatives, and public institutions. We also excluded banks and financial institutions, insurance companies, hedge funds, venture capital firms, pension and investment funds, research institutes, government agencies, states, and governments. Prior to emailing the survey, we ensured that firms from all sixteen federal states in Germany were included evenly in the email database.

To improve the overall questionnaire design, we conducted a pretest of the survey from November 26, 2015, through April 19, 2016. A random sample was produced by industry and firm size for purposes of the pretest. In addition, twenty academics and non-professionals were asked to participate. Pretest participants had the opportunity to provide comments on each question. The pretest ensured the questions were understood and that the duration was tested. Hence, we were able to verify that the defined categories were relevant and appropriate. Within this period, we also incorporated the comments of the pretest participants in the survey design. We then conducted technical tests. Overall, the pretest showed that the survey took approximately fifteen minutes to answer.

The questionnaire was sent via email to the selected companies throughout Germany, running from April 20–May 31, 2016. A total of 12,169 firms were contacted. After removing observations with insufficient data on the key variables, we were left with 834 responses. Of those 834, we use 576 that were completely filled out in this study (a response rate of 6.85 %). This is in line with the 3.8 % which are reported by Neuberger and Räthke (2009), the 6 % reported by De Bodt et al. (2005), and the 6.56 % reported by Hommel and Schneider (2003).[53] We incentivized study participants by offering them a summary of the results and the opportunity to participate in a lottery. A total of 445 participants left their email addresses for the summary and/or lottery participation.

---

53 The low response rate is likely attributable to the fact that the survey included some sensitive questions and questions about financial matters, which respondents are generally more reluctant to answer online, as noted earlier by Neuberger and Räthke (2009).

3.3 Survey design

At the beginning of the survey, participants were intentionally not provided with a set definition of the most important bank, as it was our objective to assess how participants viewed various banking characteristics. Respondents were only told that the survey was about their most important bank relationship, and they were asked to answer all questions in relation to that particular bank.

Section 2.4.2 presents the characteristics that commonly define the most important banking relationship, such as 1) the bank provides (relative to peer banks) a large, often dominant share of the credit financing to the firm, 2) they are typically long-term, 3) they involve a "special relationship of trust" between the bank and the firm, 4) the bank has an information advantage over competitive banks, 5) the bank performs most other financial services for the company, and 6) the bank has a "special responsibility" to the firm during situations of financial distress (Elsas 2001).

Overall, the survey contained forty-four questions and the online survey was administered by the online software SoSci Survey (Leiner 2014). Each company was invited by an individual cover letter sent via email to potential participants. The cover letter included a short description of the study and a request to have the person in charge of the firm's bank relationships fill it out. It was directed to the person in treasury, controlling, or accounting whenever those names were provided in Dafne. The survey was made available to participants via a link. The cover letter also included the researchers' contact details in case of questions. The cover letter described the strictly confidential treatment of the data and guaranteed the study would not allow conclusions with regard to the participants' companies.[54] Participants were also asked to leave their email addresses at the end of the questionnaire, in order to send the summary results or the lottery offer.

At the beginning of the survey, participants were once again assured the survey was in accordance with applicable privacy policies, that it is performed anonymously, and that the data are used and evaluated solely for scientific research. Participants were asked to answer all questions with regard to their most important bank relationship, even if the firm had business relationships with several banks.

Particular emphasis was placed on completeness of answers, which is of the utmost importance to study success. When information to a question was not

54 See Appendix Figure A - 1 for the cover letter.

available in detail, participants were asked to give estimates.[55] Furthermore, if participants closed their browser before completing the survey, it would begin again.

Regarding the order of the questions, at the beginning, the questionnaire asked about relatively neutral facts, instead of formative opinions. In this way, participants were offered an easy entry to the questionnaire.[56] The survey was then subdivided into two sections: The first collected general information on firm characteristics, for example, the year it was founded, the number of employees, industry sector, and legal form. This part also asked whether firms had been in financial distress prior to the survey. The second included qualitative and quantitative questions about the firm's relationship with its most important bank, and collected information on firms' financing patterns, including loan characteristics. Questions included, for example, the number of bank relationships and the duration of the relationship with the most important bank, moving on to questions about collateral requirements, interest rates, and credit availability.

The survey questions were scaled according to the following four measurement methods: metric, ordinal, nominal, and dichotomous. Moreover, for some questions, participants were required to enter numbers, e.g., the firm's year of founding and the year the relationship between the firm and its bank was established. Ordinal scaled variables were requested on a five-point Likert-type scale. This technique serves to measure attitudes (Likert 1932). Respondents were asked to agree more or less strongly with questions and statements on a given multi-level response scale.

Likert scales are particularly useful for performing multivariate analysis, and are thus used frequently in research, where they are applied in various forms (e.g., four, five, seven, or more stages). For the purpose of this study, the five-point Likert scale seems most suitable, as it has also been applied by other authors studying relationship lending. See, for example, Lehmann and Neuberger (2001), who examine the perception of the relationship between the bank and the firm on a five-point Likert-type scale.

Questions without Likert scales require an explicit specification of key figures, for example, the equity ratio and sales growth, or involve the choice between different response categories, for example, industry sector. Moreover, three

---

55 Participants also confirmed that the duration of the survey was approximately fifteen minutes.

56 The survey can be found in Appendix Figure A - 2. The questions are based on the previously developed and presented hypotheses in section 2.8.2.

questions included the response option “not specified”.[57] Note that all questions were obligatory, meaning that, in order to proceed to the next page, all questions must be answered. This was done to ensure the completeness of the data, and, hence, to increase the usability of the data for the empirical analyses.

The questionnaire also included two filter questions with regard to participants' answers. The first question was about the generation that manages the firm. This question only came up when respondents indicated the firm is a family business. The second question was about whether the firm plans to change its most important bank relationship in the near future. If so, the following question asked why. The questionnaire also contained one question where multiple answers were possible: the respondent's position in the company. Because it is possible to hold more than one position at the same time (for example, someone may be a firm's manager and owner), multiple answers to this question were permitted. Particularly in smaller firms, one person may hold more than one position.

The next section presents the endogenous and exogenous variables created for the survey on the basis of the literature review in sections 2.7 and 2.8.

3.4 Endogenous variables

In order to ensure comparability of our regression results with evidence from prior studies, we operationalize the dependent and independent variables in line with those in other academic publications, as presented in sections 2.7 and 2.8.[58] The endogenous and exogenous variables we use here are summarized in Table 3-1.

To determine the significance of relationship banking for German SMEs and to test our hypothesis, our focus is on the three following variables: *Collateral Requirements*, *Cost of Credit*, and *Credit Availability*. We take these as endogenous variables because they allow comparability with prior research especially well. In addition, Kysucky and Norden (2016) conduct a meta-analysis using information from 101 studies from the U.S., Europe, Asia, and Latin America from 1970 to 2010. The basis of the selected studies is made up of 4.1 million

57 These questions were the respondent's years of experience, the firm's financial distress, and whether the bank owns shares in the firm. All were considered sensitive by the pretest participants.

58 See, for example, studies by Petersen and Rajan (1994), Berger and Udell (1995a), Harhoff and Körting (1998), Elsas and Krahnen (1998), Degryse and Van Cayseele (2000), Hernández-Cánovas and Martínez-Solano (2010), Kano et al. (2011), Howorth and Moro (2012), and Moro and Fink (2013).

company observations, and the authors show that all the studies build upon these same three variables. Moreover, there is uniform opinion about the suitability of applying credit lines to analyze the bank-firm relationship and to determine any potential added value.

We note that lines of credit are especially revealing, because relationships are more likely to matter in this context than for other types of loans (e.g., mortgages, equipment loans, spot loans) (Berger and Udell 1995a). These types of loans are typically one-time loans for non-recurring credit needs, and, therefore, they tend to be more transaction-driven and less relationship-driven. Hence, the effect of relationship lending when analyzing these loans in a sample may have been diluted (Berger and Udell 1995a).

Berger and Udell (1995a) note that lines of credit can be especially suitable for studying firm-bank relationships because they are an important instrument to resolve information asymmetries between firms and banks, especially for small-firm financing. Following the authors, a bank's line of credit "is a particularly important part of relationship lending because it represents a forward commitment to provide working capital financing under prespecified terms" (Berger and Udell 1995a, p. 355). The authors also justify the use of credit lines by finding that they tend to be secured by accounts receivable and inventory, which are the riskiest forms of working capital financing. The authors expected the requirements and the related effects to be higher for this type of credit.

One of the aims of this thesis is to explore whether there is any benefit for an SME to maintain a close relationship with a bank. Relationship banking theory finds a positive correlation among the strength of the relationship, the level of soft information generated, and the level of potential benefits with respect to credit availability and pricing. Because the amount of soft information that is collected cannot be observed directly, we only obtain empirical evidence by examining the connections among the relationship variables, credit terms, and credit availability variables. These variables are presented in more detail next (Kano et al. 2011).

Collateral Requirements

The variable *Collateral Requirements* indicates whether collateral or a guarantee was required for obtaining the most important line of credit. Bester (1985) states that collateral may be a response to adverse selection. He notes that the use of collateral in general is costly, and, hence, its use is inefficient in a credit market under perfect information. However, because credit markets under perfect information are hypothetical, collateral requirements can be described as a response to imperfect information. Collateral may serve to reveal information about the default risk of loan applicants. Bester (1985) argues that the bank may require collateral in order to enable the institution to put borrowers into risk categories.

Bester (1985) also finds that low-risk firms tend to provide a sufficient amount of collateral in order to distinguish themselves from high-risk firms. Following this, borrowers will not be denied credit if companies use collateral as a signaling mechanism. Thus, different collateral requirements in loan contracts may become a self-selection mechanism and signaling mechanisms may eliminate credit rationing in a competitive equilibrium.

Collateral may also be necessary to obtain credit in the first place, and assets presented as collateral may influence credit availability. Hence, banks may be more willing to provide financing to borrowers from which they hold a substantial amount of collateral. In this context, Berger and Udell (1995a) recognize that it may be challenging to obtain information about a firm's cost of debt, because it may be hesitant to reveal whether personal assets were pledged as collateral to obtain financing.

The variable *Collateral Requirements* asks for the percentage of credit line volume to be collateralized, using the following categories: 0 %; more than 0 % to less than 25 %; 25 % to less than 50 %; 50 % to less than 75 %; 75 % to less than 100 %; and 100 %. For the purpose of the multivariate analysis, we define a dummy variable that equals 1 when the response exceeds the median sample responses, and 0 otherwise. The variable is derived from Harhoff and Körting (1998), who study the incidence of collateral requirements for the firm's most important line of credit. The binary dummy variable also equals 1 if some form of collateral or guarantee was required to receive the line of credit, and 0 otherwise.

Niskanen and Niskanen (2000) likewise study collateral requirements. They classify the dummy variable as 1 if collateral was pledged, and 0 otherwise. De Bodt et al. (2005) ask for the proportion of firm financial debt that was required to be guaranteed. They also specify categories, including: less than 25 %; between 25 % and 50 %; between 50 % and 100 %; and more than 100 %. Hernández-Cánovas and Martínez-Solano (2010) obtain a similar variable on a five-point Likert-type scale by asking on a scale from 1 (totally disagree) to 5 (totally agree) for an opinion on the following statement: "Financial institutions grant you loans and credit on the basis of collateral." They also transform the variable into a dummy variable in a similar fashion by assigning 1 when the response exceeds the median, and 0 otherwise.

Moreover, Howorth and Moro (2012) asked whether collateral was pledged and included a dummy variable that equals 1 if collateral was pledged as security on the overdraft, and 0 otherwise. Kano et al. (2011) establish a dummy variable that equals 1 if the SME pledges collateral to the main bank. Hence, the benefit of a lending relationship should be reflected in a lower probability of pledging collateral.

Harhoff and Körting (1998) do not distinguish between different types of collateral. However, our approach here follows Berger and Udell (1995a), and distinguishes between firm assets pledged as collateral, and personal guarantees deposited as collateral. For this purpose, we ask for the *Collateral Type* pledged to obtain the credit line and define the following categories: 1) collateral on the assets of the company was pledged, 2) personal guarantees were pledged, 3) collateral on the assets of the company and personal guarantees were pledged, and 4) no collateral or guarantees were pledged. This variable is in accordance with De Bodt et al. (2005), who examine the main types of guarantees pledged for financial debts. Hernández-Cánovas and Martínez-Solano (2010) also analyze the type of collateral pledged for the granting of loans and credit. Their variable determines whether a majority of a firm's assets or personal guarantees was required as security for the most important credit line.

Accordingly, our study follows a proven approach that allows us to answer the research question empirically. For this reason, we operationalize the variable *Collateral Requirements* as a dummy variable. In addition, it is highly useful to inquire about collateral type. This question is particularly interesting in the context of SMEs, because a company that must deposit personal securities may again feel a different responsibility than a company that deposits only business collateral. We expect to obtain further insights from this query. We also find that several recent studies have used questions about this variable (see, e.g., Hernández-Cánovas and Martínez-Solano 2010).

Cost of Debt

The second endogenous variable is *Cost of Debt*, defined as the interest rate on the most important credit line with the reference day January 1, 2015. Empirical studies on small business lending are often consistent with the importance of strong relationships (Berger and Udell 2002). Stronger relationships, measured in various ways as described in sections 2.7 and 2.8, are empirically linked with lower loan interest rates (e.g., Berger and Udell 1995a; Degryse and Van Cayseele 2000; Harhoff and Körting 1998; Scott and Dunkelberg 1999). Thus, cost savings generated, e.g., by trust may be passed onto companies by lower provision costs (lower interest rates). In contrast, Greenbaum, Kanatas, and Venezia (1989), Sharpe (1990), and Wilson (1993) find that loan rates increase with the duration of a bank-borrower relationship. The authors argue that the bank's enhanced knowledge locks the borrower into the relationship, enabling it to charge above-market interest rates as the relationship continues. In general, empirical studies find that the investigation of credit interest rates is appropriate, because, by means of a strong relationship, the bank will give something back to the customer via the lending rate.

The variable *Cost of Debt* is a metric variable, and the focus of the analyses is again on credit lines, because that type of credit is generally more revealing. The variable follows Harhoff and Körting's (1998) approach, which studies the interest rate on the most important line of credit as well, using the reference day January 1, 1997. Their variable is also a metric variable.

Petersen and Rajan (1994) and Berger and Udell (1995a) also examine the effect of relationship lending on a firm's cost of debt by studying interest rates. However, they analyze the interest rate by exploring the difference between it and the prime rate. They study interest rates on the firm's most recent loan, but do not necessarily focus on lines of credit. They therefore only find a small effect of relationships on the prices charged by lenders. With respect to Petersen and Rajan's (1994) results, Berger and Udell (1995a) write: "That is, they included a number of different types of loans for which reputation and relationship effects may be substantially less important than those associated with the forward commitment embodied in an L/C" (Berger and Udell 1995a, p. 356).

Berger and Udell (1995a) use the same dataset as Petersen and Rajan (1994), but they focus their analysis of collateral requirements and interest rates on credit lines and find more significant results. They find that regression results may be less clear when combining different types of loans than when concentrating on one particular type of loan, such as credit lines. Because results can be blurred, there must be special features about credit lines.

There is a range of empirical literature on "bank uniqueness," which often discusses lines of credit. For example, James (1987) finds evidence of the uniqueness of bank loans when studying bank loan agreements with a focus on lines of credit. He finds a positive stock price response to the announcement of new bank credit agreements that is larger than that related to announcements of private placements or public straight debt offerings.

Hernández-Cánovas and Martínez-Solano (2010) measure the interest rate as well by defining the variable as the ratio of financing charges to liabilities: [financing charges/(long-term liabilities + short-term liabilities)]. Kano et al. (2011) measure the loan interest rate as the highest annual short-term borrowing rate on loans from the main bank with a maturity of less than one year (Kano et al. 2011). Howorth and Moro (2012) use the interest rate paid by each

SME on their overdraft as a dependent variable, as documented by the bank lending manager.

This thesis aims to investigate the effect of relationship lending on the cost of credit. We thus ask participants for the interest rates on their credit lines. These are generally easier to assess than interest rates on other types of loans, because those typically depend on the maturity of the loan. Furthermore, Sette and Gobbi (2015) find that credit lines represent a crucial source of financing for companies, especially during financial crises (see also Acharya, Almeida, Ippolito, and Perez 2014).

Thus, this thesis follows a proven approach to measuring the cost of the relationship over the lending rate, and the procedure makes it easy to obtain a metric variable that would otherwise be very difficult to capture in a company survey. It is usually more difficult for participants in a company survey to indicate a ratio such as financing charges to liabilities, because it must be calculated. It is not as easily accessible as, for example, the equity ratio, which most entrepreneurs would probably know.

In addition, the pretest shows that it is especially important not to make questions about financing types too complicated, because participants may leave the survey without answering the question. However, this approach has already shown by metric scaling that, for example, an OLS regression can be performed, which is very fitting for the question about costs in a lending relationship.

Credit Availability

This study focuses on the ease with which a firm can renew its short-term loans. Overall, bank relationships are more important in the context of short-term loans than other types. Transaction loans, for example, can be easily replicated by other banks, are collateralized, and, therefore, do not require an intense informational exchange (Ergungor 2005). When a firm applies for additional financing to realize a project, the bank will most likely evaluate the specific risk of potential borrowers each time before making a decision. Because this type of loan is typically required multiple times, the bank continuously revisits the state of its relationship with the firm.

In this context, we posit that loan officers play a crucial role, because they ultimately decide whether to grant a loan, based on the available information, and they subsequently evaluate a borrower's creditworthiness (Kano et al. 2011). Automatic renewal of short-term debt on maturity implies that a firm can renew its access to short-term credit more easily, which in turn can indicate reduced information asymmetries.

According to Hernández-Cánovas and Martínez-Solano (2010), studying the availability of loans and credit can be challenging. One reason is the lack of precision inherent in the process. For example, because the debt ratio is simultaneously determined by the supply of and demand for financing, using it as an estimate of the demand for debt does not tell the full story. Consequently, changes in the debt ratio depend on changes in the demand from firms and on changes in the supply offered by banks.

Moreover, the effect of relationship lending potentially differs among short- and long-term debt. On the one hand, there are long-term loans, which may be one-off loans to finance a particular project. In this case, the bank evaluates one moment in time and the specific risk of the firm at that time. This type of loan is thus considered transaction-driven. On the other hand, there are short-term loans, which may be needed, for example, to finance firms' production cycles. Because this type of loan is usually requested multiple times, the bank reconsiders the state of its relationship with the firm each time a request is made. That is why short-term loans in general are more revealing about the current state of the firm-bank relationship.

In this study, the dependent variable, *Credit Availability*, documents whether short-term debt with the most important bank is renewed automatically upon maturity. Following Hernández-Cánovas and Martínez-Solano (2010), we use a five-point Likert-type scale that ranges from 1 (does not apply) to 5 (strongly applies). The variable is then transformed into a dummy variable that equals 1 when the response exceeds the median of the sample responses, and 0 otherwise. Hernández-Cánovas and Martínez-Solano (2010) also transform the responses into a dummy variable.

Harhoff and Körting (1998) measure credit availability by the ratio of trade credit with fast payment discounts actually taken to trade credit with discounts offered. The authors follow Petersen and Rajan (1994) and use a measure of trade credit usage (Harhoff and Körting 1998). For another measure of credit availability, Kano et al. (2011) use a dummy variable that equals 1 if a participant responds "a refusal" or "a reduction in amount" when answering the question, "What has been the most common response by your main bank to your loan applications in the past 1 year?" (Kano et al. 2011, p. 939).

Shikimi (2013) measures credit availability by observing the amount of bank credit requested by a firm, the maximum amount of credit available to the firm, and the realized amount of bank credit. Malafronte et al. (2014) measure credit availability as the change in the amount of credit granted between 2008 and 2010 by the bank to the firm. In addition, Kirschenmann (2016) examines the factors that influence the degree of credit rationing by observing the ratio of the granted to requested loan amount.

Basically, all approaches assess credit availability by examining short-term loans. This thesis follows the line of reasoning that short-term loans are a valuable source for the study of credit availability, particularly with respect to the re-evaluation aspect. Moreover, this type of survey question seems more appealing in purely theoretical terms, because it allows for the aggregation of soft information that is crucial to relationship lending through the continued interactions that come with the request for a short-term loan. This question was also rated as very fitting in the pretest, and thus it also offers a solid basis for the company survey.

3.5 Exogenous variables

Capturing a full picture of the firm-bank relationship requires a variety of variables. We divide the explanatory variables into four categories: loan characteristics, relationship characteristics, firm characteristics, and control variables. Some of these variables will be evaluated in the descriptive analyses of our dataset; others will be included in the regression analyses.

Loan characteristics

The second set of variables describes the firm's loan characteristics and financing patterns. The variable *Finance Share* captures the share of total debt financing of the firm financed by the most important bank. This is calculated by the following formula: (bank loans provided by the most important bank)/(debt). This variable is a critical determinant of housebank status. We expect that the higher a bank's share of a company's total debt financing, the more likely it is the primary relationship lender. The bank's crucial lending position might create access to distinct sources of information, and the continuous nature of the relationship may decrease competitive pressure from other banks. At the same time, from the perspective of the bank, this measure may provide some bargaining power for the relationship lender (Elsas 2005).

The variable is in line with Petersen and Rajan (1994), who also investigate the percentage of debt a firm borrows from financial institutions. De Bodt et al. (2005) and Elsas (2005) likewise explore the proportion of each firm's debt financed by the main bank. According to these authors, housebank status is systematically related to debt financing share.

Furthermore, the repeated use of certain types of financing, such as credit lines, can create economies of scale on the part of the lender, and further consolidate contact between the bank and the borrower. Hence, one of the questionnaire sections asks participants to indicate, on a scale of 1 (never) to 5 (always), the extent to which they use short- versus long-term bank debt.

The variables *Short-term Bank Debt* and *Long-term Bank Debt* follow the approach of Hernández-Cánovas and Martínez-Solano (2010). They ask respondents to indicate, on a scale of 1 (never) to 5 (always), how often they use bank financing with terms of less than and longer than one year. Particularly, the variable *Credit Lines* describes the extent that a firm uses credit lines from the most important bank to finance their business operations. This variable also follows Hernández-Cánovas and Martínez-Solano (2010), who ask managers how often they finance operations with lines of credit.

These variables further help determine firms' financing patterns and assess the relevance of certain types of corporate finance.[59] Moreover, including these variables in the multivariate regression analyses helps control for heterogeneity in the use of short- and long-term bank debt and credit lines among the sample companies.

Relationship characteristics

The relationship characteristics are elements used to further assess the bank-borrower relationship. They provide revealing insights into the impact of soft information. The variable *Number of Banks* is defined as the number of banks the firm works with and is defined in accordance with Harhoff and Körting (1998). Hommel and Schneider (2003) also examine the average number of banking relationships, and Hernández-Cánovas and Martínez-Solano (2010) study the concentration of the market by calculating the natural logarithm of the number of banks with which the firm works.

The variable *Duration* is included to document the length of the firm-bank relationship. Hernández-Cánovas and Martínez-Solano (2010) also study length by calculating the logarithm of the number of years the firm has worked with its oldest bank. Beck, Degryse, De Haas, and Van Horen (2017) investigate length

---

59 In addition, the variable *Credit Line Volume* captures the amount financed by the most important bank. This variable is in line with Harhoff and Körting (1998), who study credit line volume by calculating the natural logarithm of the volume of the most important credit line. This variable is included to measure whether the probability that the firm's most important line of credit had to be collateralized is a function of credit line volume. However, this variable was too similar to *Finance Share*, and, therefore, was evidence of multicollinearity.

by the number of months from the time the bank first sold a credit product to the company. This variable measures the ability of the bank to study the firm through repeat interactions over time.

The literature review shows that the variable *Duration* can be somewhat controversial. Elsas and Krahnen (1998) criticize the often simple acceptance that the duration of a relationship reflects information intensity. They posit that duration reflects only length, not intensity. In contrast, Berger and Udell (1995a) use duration as a measure of the strength of the relationship. They argue that, based on their empirical results, banks collect increasing amounts of private information over the duration of the relationship.

Harhoff and Körting (1998) use duration as an indicator of quality. Degryse and Van Cayseele (2000) use two dimensions for relationship strength: duration, and scope[60], which is represented by the number of existing financial services between the firm and the bank. Malafronte et al. (2014), among others, document that the duration of a relationship is positively related to credit availability.

As noted, the duration proxy is controversial in the literature. However, we follow Berger and Udell (1995a), Harhoff and Körting (1998), Hernández-Cánovas and Martínez-Solano (2010), Moro and Fink (2013), and Beck et al. (2017), and use duration, defined as the length of the main bank relationship, to investigate whether the time aspect has a significant effect on the dependent variables. Moreover, by matching *Duration* with the variable *Age*, we can assess whether the relationship is relatively new or an established long-term relationship.

A great deal of research has focused on trust and small business lending from the bank's perspective (i.e., the loan manager's trust in the firm manager). But the other side of this relationship is explored here. We examine the firm's perspective in order to shed more light on the role that trust plays in lending relationships today.

In the literature review, it is claimed that relationship banking is characterized by trust between the firm and the bank, as well as by an expectation by the firm that the bank carries a special responsibility toward it during times of financial distress. In order to examine this statement, we create the variable *Trust* to capture overall trustworthiness. This variable documents whether the firm-bank relationship is characterized by great levels of trust from the respondent's perspective. It follows the strategy of Harhoff and Körting (1998), who study mutual

60 We follow Degryse and Van Cayseele (2000) by putting the variable *Scope* in the category of relationship characteristics.

trust between the bank and the firm by creating a dummy variable to indicate the degree to which respondents believe their firms and their most important institutions trust each other.

Hernández-Cánovas and Martínez-Solano (2010) also study trust by asking managers whether financial institutions consider trust in the firm's managers when making financing decisions. Meanwhile, Howorth and Moro (2012) and Moro and Fink (2013) analyze trust by asking for the bank loan officer's assessment of the SME's manager's trustworthiness. Perceived trust is a vital condition for sharing and truthfully providing information, and for pursuing a strong bank relationship (see also Tang et al. 2017).

Studies find that high levels of trust facilitate trustworthy behavior, and that trust can play a critical role in decreasing agency problems such as moral hazard and adverse selection (Howorth and Moro 2012; Nooteboom 2002). Trustworthiness impacts the reliability of firm information provided for lending decisions, and any possible moral hazards (Howorth and Moro 2012). According to Moro and Fink (2013), trust is even more essential in risky circumstances, where the potential harm is greater than the potential advantage. Thus, a prior engagement with a borrower and an evaluation of the borrower's behavior is required.

Overall, trust depends on both the observation of past behavior and on information collected independently of the relationship (Fink and Kessler 2010; Moro and Fink 2013). To some extent, trust may "reimburse" loan officers for information asymmetries and help determine a company's creditworthiness. Therefore, a trusting relationship can help banks and SMEs by giving the loan officer access to more soft information (Moro and Fink 2013).

Uchida et al. (2012) and Scott (2006) also show that trust can increase the amount of soft information loan managers are able to access, thus helping them make better lending decisions. The literature review suggests that trust may provide a positive influence on credit conditions. However, after the 2007–2009 worldwide financial crisis, it is very questionable whether this is still the case.[61]

According to Moro and Fink (2013), trust as a variable is far too vital to be disregarded. Bromiley and Harris (2006) state that excluding trust from relationship models partially decreases their quality. The trust variable seems to capture information that is not measurable in other explanatory variables. Harhoff and

61 The variable *Bank Behavior* is also defined and explores whether the firm expects the bank will have a special responsibility to it during times of financial distress. However, this variable does not lead to significant results with respect to the dependent variables.

Körting (1998) mention the examples of relationship duration and company age. Moreover, trust between lenders and borrowers is a key component in the definition of housebanks. These relationships are characterized by considerable trust between partners (Harhoff and Körting 1998).

It is clear that there is more to the evaluation of trust than simply the passing of time (i.e., duration) or the extent of competition (number of lenders) (Howorth and Moro 2012). However, in this thesis, we do not measure the determinants of the evolution of trust in the bank-borrower relationship. This is because the question is not how to build trust, but rather whether it exists in this relationship, and how it impacts credit conditions. In addition, the development of trust does not usually lead to any direct conclusions from the situation to the trusting behavior. In contrast, the status quo regarding trust can be tested or indicated directly by the person. Trust is a personal trait. Therefore, any measurement must (ultimately) rely on people, so trust in business relations can only be measured by the individual.

Earlier studies found it difficult to differentiate empirically between components of trust, especially benevolence and integrity. It has been argued that observations of trustworthiness depend somewhat on the situation (Nooteboom et al. 1997). Additionally, evaluations of trustworthiness are also impacted by the trustor's propensity to trust (Howorth and Moro 2012).

For example, Howorth and Moro (2012) capture different factors of trust and use principal components analysis to reduce the factors into one component. In this way, they combine different factors into a vector and create one variable. Because trust is such an intangible asset, and each survey participant may perceive it slightly differently, questions about various factors could be misleading. Furthermore, the pretest helped determine that capturing trust in this way is probably the most precise way for our purposes. At this point, we also note that trust may be problematic, because it may be determined endogenously. This issue is acknowledged. However, the empirical results using this variable nevertheless offer worthwhile insights (Harhoff and Körting 1998).

Following the approach of Howorth and Moro (2012), we include the variable *Meeting Frequency*, measured as the number of meetings held per year. This is an indicator for engagement level in the lending relationship.[62] Note that *Meeting Frequency* may lead to different assumptions for distressed or non-distressed

62 The variable *Information Sharing* documents whether a large amount of information is exchanged between the firm and the most important bank. However, this variable did not lead to significant results.

firms. For example, firms may voluntarily share more information with banks, or they may be required to provide more information, particularly in the case of distressed firms. The analysis will shed light on these assumptions.

In addition, the variable *Scope* describes whether the most important bank provides most of the other banking services to the firm besides loan provision. This variable is in line with Ongena et al. (2011), who study the scope of the relationship between the firm and the bank by analyzing the bank services the company uses. If the bank does provide most of the other bank services, we would assume that more information is being shared between the firm and the bank. This would also suggest a higher level of interaction.

In this context, we created the variable *Loan Officer*, which shows whether the firm is assigned to a designated loan officer at the most important bank. An important argument can be made that the most important relationship in relationship banking is that with the loan officer. The loan officer usually has the most personal contact with the company's managers and owners and is thus the person in the bank with the greatest access to the soft information about the borrower, owner, and community. The loan officer is also likely to live in the local community and may have contacts with other local companies and individuals from which he may acquire relevant information about the company and the financing environment in the local market. These associations help examine and verify the company's financial conditions more deeply, as well as its actions on explicit and implicit contracts with the bank and with others.

The loan officer also typically has the best understanding of the hard information in the loan data file and is thus best positioned to combine the soft and hard information (Berger and Udell 2002). Kirschenmann (2016) finds it is important to study whether the loan officer has changed during the previous loan duration. If the information gathered by the loan officer cannot be fully transmitted within the bank, which is likely for qualitative soft information, important data can be lost when a loan officer change takes place (Berger and Udell 2002; Liberti and Mian 2009; Stein 2002; Uchida et al. 2012). In addition, prior literature suggests that the potential for information-related agency problems between the borrower and lender is higher for relationships with a multitude of loan officers, or a relatively frequent replacement of lending managers. The reasoning here is that a single relationship manager over the course of a long-lasting lending relationship can better accumulate and monitor customer information.

Thus, a designated loan officer may be better at extensively assessing the firm's riskiness and trustworthiness than loan officers with high turnover frequencies (Howorth and Moro 2012). The fact that a designated loan officer exists may be an indicator of how close or intimate the relationship between a bank and a borrower is.

In addition, we define the variable *Relevance* to denote the general importance of this particular bank in the overall financing structure of the company. The variable follows Elsas and Krahnen's (2002) approach. They study, from a bank's perspective, the relative importance of a bank in the borrower's debt financing by calculating the ratio of debt provided by the bank to the total debt financing according to the annual report of the borrower. The variable is, therefore, a proxy for the relative importance of the bank.

To study the differences between banking groups, we further examine the bank type of the most important bank. Thus, the variable *Bank Type* describes whether the firm's most important banking relationship is with a savings, cooperative, or private bank. The variable follows Lehmann and Neuberger's (2001) strategy of attempting to capture whether there are significant differences between the various banking types. Because Germany has a three-pillar banking system, with considerable differences between the three pillars, we expect this variable to reveal more insights. Note that savings and cooperative banks are typically smaller than private banks, and predominantly operate in local banking markets, which is why they tend to serve SMEs (Hochfellner et al. 2015).

Firm characteristics

We include various firm characteristics in the survey in order to gain knowledge about each sample firm's riskiness. In particular, we use two firm-specific variables to determine composition: *Age* and *Size*. *Age* is the firm's age in years. This variable follows the approach of Hernández-Cánovas and Martínez-Solano (2010), who also ask for the years since the firm's founding. *Size* is measured by the average number of employees as of 2015. This variable is in line with the strategy of Harhoff and Körting (1998), who also analyze firm size by asking for the number of employees.

Hernández-Cánovas and Martínez-Solano (2010) investigate firm size as well, but they calculate it by using the natural logarithm of net turnover. Both variables are used in this study because they are proxies for the level of information availability. Jiménez et al. (2009) use firm age as a measure of information transparency, and Degryse and Van Cayseele (2000) apply firm age as a measure of the availability of public information.

The variable *Legal Form* captures the legal form of the company and determines whether the firms' owners have limited or unlimited liability. This is particularly noteworthy in the context of SMEs, as these companies frequently have the legal form of limited liability. This variable is in accordance with Harhoff and Körting (1998), who create two legal form dummy variables, one indicating whether the firm is a limited liability company, GmbH, or stock company AG, and the other indicating whether the firm is an unlimited liability company, KG, OHG, or GbR.

Lehmann and Neuberger (2001) investigate the firm's legal form by creating a dummy variable that indicates whether the firm is incorporated (limited liability company, GmbH, or stock corporation AG) or not (KG, OHG, GbR). Additionally, it is expected that more insights will be gained by including the legal form because the publication requirements for corporations are higher than they are for partnerships. This translates into an indicator for the level of publicly available hard information for the bank (e.g., audited balance sheets and income statements, etc.).

We create different financial indicators to assess firms' financial stability and growth. The variable *Equity Ratio* measures the firm's leverage in line with Harhoff and Körting (1998), who examine the leverage ratio by analyzing the firm's debt divided by its assets.[63] The equity ratio is thus a direct measure of a firm's riskiness and an important hard fact for the bank's credit decision. The variables *Sales* and *Sales Growth* are also included in the survey. Sales was required for the year 2015, according to the 2015 annual results, and sales growth was calculated by using the following formula: [(present value of the year 2015) - (past value of the year 2014)/(past value of the year 2014)] x 100 %.

Montoriol-Garriga (2006) also study sales growth as an indicator of firm performance. In addition, the variable *Financial Distress* was used to determine whether the firm experienced any significant financial distress since the last financial crisis, which began in 2007. Financial distress is defined generally as a situation where firms require liquidity on short notice, and are unable to fulfill their current obligations, such as, for example, bank loans. This variable follows the strategy of Harhoff and Körting (1998), who also define a dummy variable indicating whether a firm was in financial distress within the last five years of their survey.

According to Elsas and Krahnen (2003), banks in a housebank relationship are considered primary financiers, because they usually have more relevant and timely information than other banks, and they are deemed to accept special responsibility if a firm faces financial distress. Elsas and Krahnen (2003) note further that the housebank notion implicitly underlies the supposed advantages of bank-firm relationships.

63 The authors do not specify debt or assets in more detail.

Regarding firms' ownership and management structures, respondents were asked to give an overall assessment of the firm. The variable *Assessment* determines whether the respondent considers the firm a family business. We also created the dummy variable *Family Firm* in order to better investigate the ownership and management structure. This variable follows the approach of the IfM Bonn (2016), which defines a firm as a family business when one or more members of the family hold at least 50 % of the shares of a firm. These family members must also be active in the firm's management. The variable also follows Harhoff and Körting (1998) who use a "Dummy variable indicating whether more than 50 % of shares are owned by persons related to each other" (Harhoff and Körting 1998), p. 1329) and another "indicating whether at least one of the (up to) four top managers is shareholder and engaged in management" (Harhoff and Körting 1998), p. 1329). In addition, the variable *Generation* was created to assess the generation of the family that manages the company.[64]

Control variables

For robustness checks, control variables are also included in the regression. The variable *Industry* reflects the firm's sector or industry in the dataset. This variable defines the most important firm activity with regard to its products and/or services. The categorization of industries follows the approach of the Statistisches Bundesamt (2016). The set of different industry dummy variables describes the distribution of the industries in the dataset.

In the regression analysis, we include *Construction Industry, Trade, Hospitality and Tourism, Traffic and Transportation*, and *Service Industry* versus *Manufacturing Industry*, due to the fact that including all the industry variables would have led to issues of multicollinearity. For example, Harhoff and Körting (1998) study a set of dummy variables that indicate to which industry each company examined belongs. Lehmann and Neuberger (2001) also include a set of dummy variables that indicate firms' industries, which are manufacturing and production, trade, service, building and construction, and others. Hernández-Cánovas and Martínez-Solano (2010) likewise examine the sector of activity by creating a dummy variable that equals 1 when a firm belongs to one of the three

64 The variable *Managers* is defined as the number of managers in the firm's top management team. This variable is in line with Harhoff and Körting (1998), who define top managers as those who take part in the central decisions of the firm in order to capture the scope and timing of the decision-making processes. This variable did not lead to any significant results.

following sectors: industry, construction, or services. Ongena, Tümer-Alkan, and Vermeer (2011) also control for industry effects in their sample.

The variable *Headquarters* captures the geographic location of firms' headquarters. This variable indicates whether the headquarters is located in an urban area in West Germany (reference case: urban area in East Germany) or in a rural area in West Germany (reference case: rural area in East Germany). Lehmann and Neuberger (2001) also include a dummy variable that determines whether the firm is located in West Germany. Howorth and Moro (2012) determine firm region as well. Thus, these two variables will help assess potential industry or geographic effects.[65]

In addition, regional dummies may reflect differences in the proximity between the bank and the borrower. In a rural area, the loan officer is more likely to live in the local community and have contacts with other local companies and individuals. Therefore, he may obtain relevant information about the company and about the financing conditions in the local market. By means of these contacts, the loan officer may be better able to assess the company's financial conditions and its actions.

Furthermore, the variable *Subsidiary* was included in the dataset to capture whether the firm is a subsidiary of another firm. Subsidiaries are defined as firms in which other firms hold 50 % or more of the firm's shares. This variable follows the approach of De Bodt et al. (2005), who also study this characteristic. The scientific literature documents many reasons why subsidiaries should be excluded from datasets when analyzing the relationships between firms and banks. For example, it is argued they convey no information about creditworthiness. Banks may request so-called letters of comfort ("Patronatserklärung"), which describe the liabilities of the parent company. But, in the case of insolvency, any liability is usually passed on to the parent company (Harhoff and Körting 1998; Harhoff, Stahl, and Woywode 1995). Therefore, we include the variable *Subsidiary* to control for a potential explanatory effect in the multivariate analyses.

65 Variables examining the supervisory and advisory board ("Beirat") and any shares the bank holds in the firm provided no results. Hence, they have no explanatory power for the dependent variables. The variables *Counterpart*, *Change*, and *Reason* are descriptive variables that offer further insights into the dataset and were not applied in the regression analyses. The variables *Change* and *Reason* follow the approach of De Bodt et al. (2005), who asked whether the firm plans to change their main bank in the near future, and if so, why.

We also include the variable *Stock Market* to assess whether the firm is market-listed. The latter variable occurs in three places in the dataset, but it does not provide any explanatory power in the regression analyses.[66] The endogenous and exogenous variables are summarized in Table 3-1.

3.6 Analytical methods

We conduct several multivariate analyses in order to investigate the characteristics of the most important bank relationship and the question of whether and to what extent the variables influence the firm-bank relationship. The anticipated added value of this study is empirical in nature. We aim to examine whether the correlations, as assumed from the literature review, and the hypotheses on bank relationships can also be proven empirically. Consequently, we include the loan characteristics, relationship variables, firm characteristics, and control variables in the empirical models.

Because of the conceptual nature of this thesis, the results of the multivariate regression facilitate the hypotheses. Overall, the choice of the analytical method is based on the research questions, the associated hypotheses, and the scaling of the endogenous variables. For the empirical evaluation of the data, we calculate 1) probit regressions, and 2) ordinary least squares (OLS) regressions.

Probit and OLS regressions are appropriate within the scope of this research, because they are also commonly used in the academic publications discussed in the literature review. Berger and Udell (1995a) examine the interest rate with an OLS regression and the probability tests on collateral for lines of credit with a logit regression. Harhoff and Körting (1998) use a probit regression to investigate the incidence of collateral requirements for line of credit. They also use an OLS regression to analyze the costs of external financing, which is defined as the line of credit interest rate.

Degryse and Van Cayseele (2000) investigate the interest rate with an OLS regression and explore whether the strength of the bank-firm relationship influences the probability of pledging collateral with a logit regression. Lehmann and Neuberger (2001) also analyze the interest rate with an OLS regression. They further use a probit regression to examine credit approval. De Bodt et al. (2005) use a logit regression to model the probability of rationing. Neuberger

66 The companies were initially filtered with no stock market listing. However, this shows that the Dafne database is not always up to date.

Table 3-1: Definition of endogenous and exogenous variables

This table gives the variables used throughout the descriptive and multivariate analyses, including variable name, definition, and scale.

	Variable	Definition	Scale
Endogenous variables			
	Collateral Requirements	Variable indicating the proportion of collateral or guarantees required to obtain the most important credit line.	Nominal scale
	Collateral Type	Variable indicating whether the main kind of collateral that was pledged to obtain the most important credit line was collateral on the company's assets, personal guarantees of the firm's owners' assets, or both.	Nominal scale
	Cost of Debt	Interest rate on the most important credit line with the reference day January 1, 2015.	Metric input in %
	Credit Availability	Respondent indicates whether short-term debt with the main bank is renewed automatically upon maturity.	Ordinal scale: five-point Likert-type scale: 1 (does not apply at all) to 5 (strongly applies)
Exogenous variables			
Loan characteristics	*Finance Share*	Overall share of total debt financing of the firm that is financed by the most important bank.[67]	Metric input in %
	Short-Term Bank Debt	Respondent indicates the frequency the firm uses bank financing of smaller than 1 year.	Ordinal scale: five-point Likert-type scale: 1 (never) to 5 (always)
	Long-Term Bank Debt	Respondent indicates the frequency with which the firm uses bank financing that is longer than one year.	Ordinal scale: five-point Likert-type scale: 1 (never) to 5 (always)
	Credit Lines	Respondent indicates the frequency with which the firm finances the business with lines of credit.	Ordinal scale: five-point Likert-type scale: 1 (never) to 5 (always)

(*continued on next page*)

67 The variable *Credit Line Volume* indicates the volume of the most important credit line that was used in the year 2015. The input was measured in EUR on a metric scale.

Table 3-1: Continued

	Variable	Definition	Scale
Relationship characteristics	*Number*	Number of banks the firm works with.	Metric input in integral numbers
	Duration	Number of years the firm has worked with the most important bank.	Metric input in years
	Trust	Respondent indicates whether great trust exists between the firm and the bank.[68]	Ordinal scale: five-point Likert-type scale: 1 (does not apply at all) to 5 (strongly applies)
	Meeting Frequency	Variable indicating how often physical as well as non-physical meetings between the firm and the bank occur each year on average.[69]	Metric input in integral numbers
	Scope	Variable indicating whether the bank provides most of the other bank services for the firm besides debt financing.	Ordinal scale: five-point Likert-type scale: 1 (does not apply at all) to 5 (strongly applies)
	Loan Officer	Variable indicating whether the firm has a permanent relationship manager assigned at the bank.	Nominal scale
	Relevance	Importance of the bank in corporate finance.	Ordinal scale: five-point Likert-type scale: 1 (not important at all) to 5 (very important)
	Bank Type	Variable indicating whether the bank belongs to the savings, the co-operative, or the private banks.	Nominal scale
Firm characteristics	*Age*	Number of years since the firm's founding as recorded in the survey.	Metric input
	Size	Firm size measured by average number of employees in the year 2015.	Metric input
	Legal Form	Variable indicating the legal form of the firm (GmbH, AG, KGaA, GmbH & Co. KG, KG, OHG, or GbR).	Nominal scale

68 The variable *Bank Behavior* indicates whether a respondent believes the bank has a special responsibility to the firm in the case of financial distress. It was measured on a five-point Likert-type scale from 1 (does not apply at all) to 5 (strongly applies).

69 The variable *Information Sharing* measures whether a large amount of information is exchanged between the firm and its most important bank. It was measured on a five-point Likert-type scale from 1 (does not apply at all) to 5 (strongly applies).

Table 3-1: Continued

	Variable	Definition	Scale
	Equity Ratio	Solvency of the firm measured by the firm's equity ratio in the year 2015 according to the 2015 annual results.	Metric input in %
	Sales	Firm's sales in the year 2015 according to the 2015 annual results.	Nominal scale
	Sales Growth	Firm's sales growth in the year 2015 according to the 2015 annual results.	Metric input in %
	Financial Distress	Dummy variable indicating whether the firm had been in any financial distress since 2007.	Dichotomous scale
	Assessment	Dummy variable indicating whether respondent considers the firm a family business.	Dichotomous scale
	Family Ownership	Dummy variable indicating whether more than 50 % of shares are owned by persons related to each other.	Dichotomous scale
	Family Management	Dummy variable indicating whether persons related to each other are active in firm management.	Dichotomous scale
	Family Firm	Dummy variable indicating whether more than 50 % of shares are owned by persons related to each other, and whether these persons are active in firm management.	Dichotomous scale
	Generation	Variable indicating which generation of family members manages the firm (founder and buyer are considered first generation).	Nominal scale
Control variables	*Industry*	Set of variables indicating the industry to which the firm belongs.	Nominal scale
	Headquarters	Set of variables indicating whether the firm is located in West or East Germany and whether the firm is located in an urban or a rural county.	Nominal scale
	Subsidiary	Variable indicating whether the firm is a subsidiary of another firm.	Dummy variable
	Stock Market	Variable indicating whether the firm is market-listed.	Dummy variable

and Räthke (2009) investigate the dependent variable measured as the logarithm of the number of bank relationships using an OLS regression.

Hernández-Cánovas and Martínez-Solano (2010) investigate the dependent variables *Credit Availability* and *Collateralization* with a probit regression, and the dependent variable *Cost of Debt*, defined as the ratio of financing charges to liabilities, with an OLS regression. Howorth and Moro (2012) examine *Cost of Debt*, measured as the interest rate charged on the line of credit with an OLS regression. Furthermore, Moro and Fink (2013) use an OLS regression to analyze *Credit Availability*. Beck et al. (2017) use an OLS regression to analyze *Collateralization* in lending relationships, and a probit regression to study *Credit Availability*.

Overall, most of the studies analyzed in the context of the literature review use a probit regression to analyze *Collateral Requirements* and *Credit Availability*, and an OLS regression to study *Cost of Debt*. Our choice here for an analytical approach is based on the scaling of the endogenous variables. An overview of the analytical methods we use here is in Table 3-2.

In the following section, we present the analytical models used to analyze the effects of the relationship, loan, and firm characteristics on *Collateral Requirements*, *Collateral Type*, *Credit Availability*, and *Cost of Debt*.[70]

3.6.1 Ordinary least squares

There are two commonly used methods of estimation: 1) ordinary least squares (OLS), and 2) maximum likelihood (ML). OLS is most widely applied in regression analysis. OLS can be traced back to Carl Friedrich Gauss, a German mathematician. OLS regression analyses find applications in a variety of scientific contexts (Stone and Brooks 1990). OLS is one of the most common techniques for performing multivariate regressions (Dismuke and Lindrooth 2006).

Stone and Brooks (1990) document how a linear model is an adequate representation of the truth. OLS regression is a generalized linear modeling technique that is applied to model a response variable measured on at least an interval scale. This technique may be applied to a single or multiple explanatory variables (Hutcheson 2011).

Under certain assumptions, OLS has some properties that have made it one of the most powerful and popular methods of regression analysis. Consider a two-variable population regression function (PRF) as follows (Gujarati 2004):

---

70 The following sections presenting the OLS and the logit and probit models are closely aligned with Gujarati (2004).

Table 3-2: Overview of analytical methods

This table shows the endogenous variables studied in the multivariate analyses. It presents the name, definition, and scale of the variables, as well as the analytical methods.

Endogenous variables	Definition	Scale	Analytical method
Collateral Requirements	Variable indicating whether collateral or guarantees were required to obtain the most important credit line. The responses are measured on a five-point Likert-type scale ranging from 5 = "does not apply at all" to 1 = "strongly applies." For the purpose of the multivariate analysis, a dummy variable is then defined that equals 1 when the response exceeds the median sample responses, and 0 otherwise.	Dichotomous scale	Probit regression
Collateral Type	Variable indicating whether the main type of collateral pledged to obtain the most important credit line were personal guarantees on the firm's owners' assets.	Dichotomous scale	Probit regression
Credit Availability	Respondent indicates whether short-term debt with the main bank is renewed automatically upon maturity. The responses were measured on a five-point Likert-type scale ranging from 5 = "does not apply at all" to 1 = "strongly applies." For the purpose of the multivariate analysis, a dummy variable was defined that equals 1 when the response exceeds the median sample responses, and 0 otherwise.	Metric input in %	Probit regression
Cost of Debt	Interest rate on the most important credit line with the reference day January 1, 2015.	Metric input in %	OLS regression

$$Y_i = \beta_1 + \beta_2 X_i + u_i \tag{1}$$

The PRF is not directly observable, but it can be estimated from the sample regression function (SRF):

$$Y_i = \hat{\beta}_1 + \hat{\beta}_2 X_i + \hat{u}_i \tag{2}$$

$$= Y_i + \hat{u}_i \tag{3}$$

where $\hat{Y}_i$ is the estimated (conditional mean) value of Y_i. Formula (3) is first expressed as follows:

$$\hat{u}_i = Y_i - \hat{Y}_i \tag{4}$$

$$= Y_i - \hat{\beta}_1 - \hat{\beta}_2 X_i$$

which shows that the $\hat{u}_i$ (the residuals) are the differences between the actual and estimated Y values. Assuming n pairs of observations on Y and X, the SRF is calculated so that it is as close as possible to actual Y. Hence, the SRF is chosen so that the sum of the residuals $\sum \hat{u}_i = \sum (Y_i - \hat{Y}_i)$ is as small as possible. However, this is a subpar criterion. Minimizing $\sum \hat{u}_i$ implies that, for example, the residuals $\hat{u}_2$ and $\hat{u}_3$, as well as $\hat{u}_1$ and $\hat{u}_4$, are given the same weight in the sum $(\hat{u}_1 + \hat{u}_2 + \hat{u}_3 + \hat{u}_4)$, even though the first two residuals may be much closer to the SRF than the latter two.

In other words, this means that all the residuals have equal importance regardless of how close or how broadly scattered the individual observations are from the SRF. As a result, it may be possible that the algebraic sum of the $\hat{u}_i$ is small (even zero), although the $\hat{u}_i$ are broadly scattered about the SRF. This problem can be circumvented by applying the least squares criterion, which states that the SRF can be fixed so that:

$$\sum \hat{u}_i^2 = \sum (Y_i - \hat{Y}_i)^2 = \sum (Y_i - \hat{\beta}_1 - \hat{\beta}_2 X_i)^2 \quad (5)$$

is as small as possible, and where $\hat{u}_i^2$ are the squared residuals. By squaring $\hat{u}_i$, this method gives more weight to, for example, residuals such as $\hat{u}_1$ and $\hat{u}_4$ than to $\hat{u}_2$ and $\hat{u}_3$. As described above, under the minimum $\sum \hat{u}_i$ criterion, the sum of the residuals can be small despite the $\hat{u}_i$ being broadly scattered about the SRF. This is not possible when the least squares approach is applied, because the greater the $\hat{u}_i$ (in absolute value), the larger the $\sum \hat{u}_i^2$.

Further reasoning for the least squares approach is given by the fact that the estimators obtained by it have desirable statistical properties. It is obvious from (5) that:

$$\sum \hat{u}_i^2 = \sum f(\hat{\beta}_1, \hat{\beta}_2) \quad (6)$$

where the sum of the squared residuals is some function of the estimators $\hat{\beta}_1$ and $\hat{\beta}_2$. For any given set of data, choosing different values for $\hat{\beta}_1$ and $\hat{\beta}_2$ will give different $\hat{u}s$,and hence different values of $\sum \hat{u}_i^2$. The least squares approach chooses $\hat{\beta}_1$ and $\hat{\beta}_2$ so that, for a given sample, $\sum \hat{u}_i^2$ is as small as possible. The process of differential calculus provides the following equations for estimating $\hat{\beta}_1$ and $\hat{\beta}_2$:

$$\sum Y_i = n\hat{\beta}_1 + \hat{\beta}_2 \sum X_i \quad (7)$$

$$\sum Y_i X_i = \hat{\beta}_1 \sum X_i + \hat{\beta}_2 \sum X_i^2 \quad (8)$$

where n is the size of the sample. These simultaneous equations are known as the normal equations. By solving the normal equations simultaneously, we obtain the following:

$$\hat{\beta}_2 = \frac{n\sum X_iY_i - \sum X_i \sum Y_i}{n\sum X_i^2 - \left(\sum X_i\right)^2} = \frac{\sum (X_i - \bar{X})(Y_i - \bar{Y})}{\sum (X_i - \bar{X})^2} = \frac{\sum x_i y_i}{\sum x_i^2} \tag{9}$$

where $\hat{X}$ and $\hat{Y}$ are the sample means of X and Y, and $x_i = \left(X_i - \hat{X}\right)$ and $y_i = \left(Y_i - \hat{Y}\right)$. Moreover, we use the convention of letting the lowercase letters denote deviations from mean values:

$$\hat{\beta}_1 = \frac{\sum X_i^2 \sum Y_i - \sum X_i \sum X_iY_i}{n\sum X_i^2 - \left(\sum X_i\right)^2} = \bar{Y} - \hat{\beta}_2\bar{X} \tag{10}$$

Formula (9) for calculating β_2 can be presented alternatively as:

$$\hat{\beta}_2 = \frac{\sum x_i y_i}{\sum x_i^2} = \frac{\sum x_i Y_i}{\sum X_i^2 - n\bar{X}^2} = \frac{\sum X_i y_i}{\sum X_i^2 - n\bar{X}^2} \tag{11}$$

OLS estimators have statistical properties "that hold only under certain assumptions about the way the data were generated" (Davidson and MacKinnon 1993, p. 3).

3.6.2 The assumptions underlying the least squares method

In regression analysis, the aim is not only to obtain $\hat{\beta}_1$ and $\hat{\beta}_2$, but also to form conclusions about true β_1 and β_2, meaning how close $\hat{\beta}_1$ and $\hat{\beta}_2$ are to their counterparts in the population, or how close $\hat{Y}_i$ is to the true $E(Y \quad X_i)$. Besides the specification of the functional form of the model, as in (1), certain assumptions about the way Y_i is generated must also be made. Consider the PRF: $Y_i = \beta_1 + \beta_2 X_i + u_i$, which shows that Y_i depends on both X_i and u_i. Hence, without being specific about how X_i and u_i are generated, there is no way to draw any statistical inferences about Y_i, β_1, or β_2. Consequently, the assumptions drawn about the X_i variable(s) and the error term are fundamental to a valid interpretation of the regression estimates.

The Gaussian, standard, or classical linear regression model (CLRM), which is the basis of most econometric theory, makes ten assumptions. These assumptions are presented in the context of the two-variable regression model, but they can also be extended to multiple regression models, meaning models with more than one regressor.

Assumption 1: The regression model is linear in the parameters as presented in the following:

$$Y_i = \beta_1 + \beta_2 X_i + u_i \tag{12}$$

Assumption 2: Values taken by regressor X are considered fixed in repeated samples, and X is expected to be non-stochastic.

Assumption 3: Given the value of X, the mean value of the random disturbance term u_i is 0, as shown in the following formula:

$$E\left(u_i X_i\right) = 0 \tag{13}$$

Assumption 4: Homoskedasticity, or equal variance of u_i, is assumed. Given the value of X, the variance of u_i is the same for all observations, as presented in the following formula:[71]

$$\begin{aligned} var\left(u_i|X_i\right) &= E[u_i - E\left(u_i|X_i\right)]^2 \\ &= E\left(u_i^2|X_i\right) \text{ because of assumption 3} \\ &= \sigma^2 \end{aligned} \tag{14}$$

Assumption 5: No autocorrelation between the disturbances is assumed. Given any two X values, X_i and $X_j\ (i \neq j)$, the correlation between any two u_i and $u_j\ (i \neq j)$ is 0, as shown in the following formula:[72]

$$\begin{aligned} cov\left(u_i, u_j|X_i, X_j\right) &= E\left\{\left[u_i - E\left(u_i\right)\right]|X_i\right\}\left\{\left[u_j - E\left(u_j\right)\right]|X_j\right\} \\ &= E\left(u_i|X_i\right)\left(u_j|X_j\right) \\ &= 0 \end{aligned} \tag{15}$$

where i and j are two different observations.

Assumption 6: There is zero covariance between u_i and X_i, or $E(u_i X_i) = 0$, as presented in the following formula:

$$\begin{aligned} cov\left(u_i, X_i\right) &= E\left[u_i - E\left(u_i\right)\right]\left[X_i - E\left(X_i\right)\right] \\ &= E\left[u_i\left(X_i - E\left(X_i\right)\right)\right] \qquad \text{since } E\left(u_i\right) = 0 \end{aligned}$$

71 Var stands for variance.

72 Cov stands for covariance.

$$
\begin{aligned}
&= E(u_i X_i) - E(X_i)\,E(u_i) \qquad \text{since } E(X_i) \text{ is nonstochastic} \\
&= E(u_i X_i) \qquad \text{since } E(u_i) = 0 \\
&= 0 \text{ by assumption}
\end{aligned} \tag{16}
$$

Assumption 7: The number of observations is larger than the number of parameters to be estimated.[73]

Assumption 8: The X values in a given sample are not all the same.

Assumption 9: There is no specification bias or error in the regression model.

Assumption 10: There is no perfect multicollinearity. In other words, there are no perfectly linear relationships between exogenous variables.

Note that the above assumptions may certainly be questioned. However, in any scientific study, assumptions are drawn because they enable the development of the subject matter in measurable steps, not because they inevitably copy reality exactly. Blaug (1992) notes "if simplicity is a desirable criterion of good theory, all good theories idealize and oversimplify outrageously" (Blaug 1992, p. 92).[74]

In the context of an OLS regression, we calculate the following model to investigate the variable *Cost of Debt* in the lending relationships (Hernández-Cánovas and Martínez-Solano 2010):

$$
\begin{gathered}
\textit{Cost of Debt}_i = \beta_0 + \beta_1\, \textit{Loan Characteristics} + \\
\beta_2\, \textit{Relationship Characteristics} + \beta_3\, \textit{Firm Characteristics} + \\
\beta_4\, \textit{Control Variables} + \epsilon_i
\end{gathered} \tag{17}
$$

The dependent variable is defined as the interest rate for the most important credit line in the year 2015. The next section discusses the logit and probit approaches.

3.6.3 The logit model

According to Hoetker (2007), the logit and probit models have become vital tools in management researchers' analytical repertoire.[75] These models are suitable

73 Alternatively, the number of observations must be larger than the number of exogenous variables.

74 See Gujarati (2004) and Maddala (1983) for a more in-depth analysis.

75 This section closely follows Hoetker (2007), Abbott (2014), and Torres-Reyna (2011).

for use whenever two alternatives are possible. The logit model is typically used whenever a variable is binary, meaning it can have two outcomes. At the beginning, the linear probability model (LPM) is presented, which is as follows:

$$P_i = E\left(Y = 1X_i\right) = \beta_1 + \beta_2 X_i \tag{18}$$

where X is, for example, income, and Y=1 means, for example, the family owns a house. Consider the following representation of homeownership:

$$P_i = E\left(Y = 1/X_i\right) = \frac{1}{1 + e^{-(\beta_1 + \beta_2 X_i)}} \tag{19}$$

Formula (19) can also be written as:

$$P_i = \frac{1}{1 + e^{-z_i}} = \frac{e^2}{1 + e^z} \tag{20}$$

and $Z_i = \beta_i + \beta_2 X_i$.

Equation (20) shows what is known as the (cumulative) logistic distribution function.[76] It is easy to verify that, as Z_i ranges from $-\infty$ to $+\infty$, P_i ranges between 0 and 1, and that P_i is non-linearly related to Z_i (i.e., X_i). This fulfills the earlier requirements. Now an estimation problem arises because P_i is non-linear, not only in X, but also in the β's, as presented in formula (19). Thus, the OLS procedure to estimate the parameters cannot be used. Formula (19) can be linearized, however, which is presented below: When P_i, the probability of owning a house, is given by (20), then $(1 - P_i)$, and the probability of not owning a house is:

$$1 - P_i = \frac{1}{1 + e^z i} \tag{21}$$

This formula can be written as:

$$\frac{P_i}{1 - P_i} = \frac{1 + e^{z_i}}{1 + e^{-z_i}} = e^{z_i} \tag{22}$$

Now $P_i/(1-P_i)$ is simply the odds ratio in favor of owning a house: the ratio of the probability that a family will own a house to the probability that it will not own a house. Considering the natural log of (22), we obtain the following formula:

$$\begin{aligned} L_i &= \ln\left(\frac{P_i}{1 - P_i}\right) = Z_i \\ &= \beta_1 + \beta_2 X_i \end{aligned} \tag{23}$$

where L is the log of the odds ratio, which is not only linear in X, but also in the parameters. L is called the logit, and, thus, the name logit model for models such as formula (23).[77]

---

76 See Kramer (1991) and Maddala (1983) for more details of logit and probit models.
77 See Gujarati (2004) and Maddala (1983) for more details.

3.6.4 The probit model

To show the course of a dichotomous dependent variable, we need to apply a cumulative distribution function (CDF). The logit model uses the cumulative logistic function, as shown in (19). However, this is not the only CDF that can be applied. The normal CDF has often been found to be useful. The estimating model that develops from the normal CDF is popularly known as the probit model. This model is presented based on utility theory, or the rational choice perspective on behavior, as shown by McFadden (1973).

To motivate the probit model, we assume that, for example, the decision of the ith family to own a house or not depends on an unobservable utility index I_i (also known as a latent variable). This variable is influenced by one or more explanatory variables, for example, income X_i, so that the greater the value of index I_i, the greater the probability of a family owning a house. Index I_i is presented as follows:

$$l_i = \beta_1 + \beta_2 X_i \tag{24}$$

where X_i is the income of the ith family.

The question then arises how the (unobservable) index is associated with the actual decision to own a house. $Y = 1$ means the family owns a house; $Y = 0$ means the family does not. It is assumed that there is a threshold level of the index, called I_i^*, so that if I_i surpasses I_i^*, the family will own a house, and otherwise it will not. The threshold I_i^*, like I_i, is not observable. However, when it is assumed that it is normally distributed with the same mean and variance, it is possible not only to estimate the parameters of the index given in formula (24), but also to obtain information regarding the unobservable index itself. Considering an assumption of normality, the probability that I_i^* is less than or equal to I_i can be computed from the standardized normal CDF as follows:[78]

$$P_i = P(Y = 1X) = \mathrm{P}(I_i^* \leq I_i) = P(Z_i \leq \beta_1 + \beta_2 X_i) = F(\beta_1 + \beta_2 X_i) \tag{25}$$

where $P(Y = 1\ \mathrm{X})$ is the probability that an incident occurs given the value(s) of X, or explanatory, variable(s), and Z_i is the standard normal variable, i.e., $Z \sim N(0, \sigma^2)$. F stands for the standard normal CDF, which can be shown as:

$$F(I_i) = \frac{1}{\sqrt{2\pi}} \int_{-\infty}^{I_i} e^{-z^2/2} dz \tag{26}$$

78 A normal distribution with zero mean and unit (= 1) variance is called a standard or standardized normal variable (Gujarati 2004).

$$= \frac{1}{\sqrt{2\pi}} \int_{\infty}^{\beta_1+\beta_2 X_i} e^{-z^2/2} dz$$

P shows the probability that an incident will occur, for example, the probability of owning a house. So, it is calculated by the area of the standard normal curve from $-\infty$ to I_i. To obtain information on I_i, the utility index, as well as on β_1 and β_2, the inverse of (25) is calculated to obtain:

$$\begin{aligned} I_i &= F^{-1}(I_i) = F^{-1}(P_i) \\ &= \beta_1 + \beta_2 X_i \end{aligned} \tag{27}$$

where F^{-1} is the inverse of the normal CDF. The question arises whether the logit or probit model is preferable. In most studies, the models are quite similar, the main difference being that the logistic distribution has slightly fatter tails. This means the conditional probability Pi approaches 0 or 1 at a slower rate in logit than in probit models. This can be seen more clearly from Table 3-3.[80]

Table 3-3: Values of cumulative probability functions

This table presents the cumulative normal and logistic distributions.[79]

Z	(28) Cumulative normal $P_1(Z) = \frac{1}{\sqrt{2\pi}} \int_{-\infty}^{z} e^{-s^2/2} ds$	(29) Cumulative logistic $P_2(Z) = \frac{1}{1+e^{-z}}$
−3.0	0.0013	0.0474
−2.0	0.0228	0.1192
−1.5	0.0668	0.1824
−1.0	0.1587	0.2689
−0.5	0.3085	0.3775
0	0.5000	0.5000
0.5	0.6915	0.6225
1.0	0.8413	0.7311
1.5	0.9332	0.8176
2.0	0.9772	0.8808
3.0	0.9987	0.9526

79 The table comes from Gujarati (2004).

80 See Gujarati (2004) and Maddala (1983) for more in-depth analysis.

In this study, we use a probit model to examine the endogenous variables *Collateral Requirements*, *Collateral Type*, and *Credit Availability*. According to Hernández-Cánovas and Martínez-Solano (2010), obtaining data on collateral requirements can be a challenge, because firm owners may be reluctant to provide information on personal assets pledged as collateral.

In line with Hernández-Cánovas and Martínez-Solano (2010), we managed to skirt this issue by asking respondents about the necessity of pledging collateral in order to have their credit lines extended. The categories ranged from 0 % to 100 %. We subsequently defined a dummy variable ranging from 1, meaning collateral or personal guarantees were pledged, to 0, meaning no guarantees were provided. This variable is then used as an endogenous variable in the regression that investigated the effect on the probability of pledging collateral or personal guarantees (Hernández-Cánovas and Martínez-Solano 2010). We define two dummy variables, *Collateral Requirements* and *Personal Guarantees*, that equal 1 when the sample responses exceed the median in the dataset, and 0 otherwise.

$$\begin{aligned} \textit{Collateral Requirements}_i = \beta_0 + \beta_1 \textit{ Loan Characteristics} + \\ \beta_2 \textit{ Relationship Characteristics} + \beta_3 \textit{Firm Characteristics} + \\ \beta_4 \textit{Control Variables} + \epsilon_i \end{aligned} \tag{30}$$

$$\begin{aligned} \textit{Collateral Type (Personal Guarantees)}_i = \beta_0 + \beta_1 \textit{ Loan Characteristics} + \\ \beta_2 \textit{ Relationship Characteristics} + \beta_3 \textit{Firm Characteristics} + \\ \beta_4 \textit{Control Variables} + \epsilon_i \end{aligned} \tag{31}$$

The necessity of pledging collateral is due mainly to the existence of asymmetric information and the risk of moral hazard. General borrower risk may be another important reason. The literature argues that collateral may also be pledged because it provides a key signal to lenders, and, thus, reduces the problem of adverse selection (Besanko and Thakor 1987; Chan and Thakor 1987). The pledged securities typically help lenders distinguish between borrowers with respect to the associated risk they carry. However, some authors, for example, Chan and Kanatas (1985) argue that collateral is used by borrowers to signal quality (Hernández-Cánovas and Martínez-Solano 2010).

The equation includes a range of explanatory variables to reduce the impact of sample heterogeneity (Harhoff and Körting 1998). First, and in line with Petersen and Rajan (1994) and Harhoff and Körting (1998), firm size and age proxy for the company and its degree of information asymmetry. Some studies document that firm age reflects company reputation. Moreover, Berger et al. (2001) find that firm age is an indicator of a company's information opacity. Therefore, it may be easier for a bank to obtain information about an older, more mature, company. As a result, a lender that is large or older should be less likely to pledge securities.

Second, Myers (1977), Smith and Warner (1979a, 1979b), Stulz and Johnson (1985), and Boot, Thakor, and Udell (1991) document that pledging securities decreases the likelihood that the borrower will participate in opportunistic behavior that would raise the risk of default. The problem of moral hazard occurs when companies have incentives to take on high risks during the time of the loan, or when they hide information during the preceding negotiations (Hernández-Cánovas and Martínez-Solano 2010).

Thus, there are at least two lines of argumentation. On the one hand, companies that pledge collateral are the riskier borrowers (Boot et al. 1991; Swary and Udell 1988). The bank demands securities in the event of default, because the bank could have a claim against the company. On the other hand, Bester (1985), Besanko and Thakor (1987), and Chan and Kanatas (1985) find that the safest companies will pledge securities to signal their quality in order to stand out from others. Typically, to assess a company's credit risk, a bank could use a rating agency. However, this is a challenge when studying SMEs, because accurate credit ratings do not exist. In this case, accounting data could be used as an alternative. Therefore, our study asks for the equity ratio as a leverage indicator, and for sales growth to reflect the ability of growth and the ability to generate profits. It is assumed that more indebted and less solvent firms, i.e., riskier companies, are more likely to pledge securities (Hernández-Cánovas and Martínez-Solano 2010).

There are also great challenges when assessing credit availability in the SME sector. According to Hernández-Cánovas and Martínez-Solano (2010), a firm's debt ratio is not an appropriate measurement because it is influenced by two factors, the supply of and demand for financing. Hence, when considering this ratio, it cannot be clearly determined from where the financing stems. In order to assess credit availability appropriately, we would need to evaluate short- and long-term loans.

Long-term loans usually finance one-off needs, so the bank would assess the specific risk of the firm one time. This way of doing business is called transaction-based lending. Short-term loans are typically used to fund firms' production cycles multiple times. During each loan request, the bank can evaluate the state of its relationship with the customer. This way of doing business is called relationship-based lending. Considering these differences, we expect that the existence and strength of relationship lending varies according to the type of loan requested (Hernández-Cánovas and Martínez-Solano 2010).

Therefore, our analysis examines short-term loans, and, more specifically, credit lines. We focus on the ease with which lines of credit are renewed. As we noted earlier, these types of loans tend to be more revealing for our purposes. The survey responses were measured on a five-point Likert scale ranging from 1 (totally disagree) to 5 (totally agree). We define a dummy variable, *Credit Availability*, that equals 1 when the sample responses exceed the median in the dataset, and 0 otherwise. The impact of the lending relationship on credit availability is analyzed as follows:

$$\begin{gathered} \textit{Credit Availability}_i = \beta_0 + \beta_1 \textit{ Loan Characteristics} + \\ \beta_2 \textit{ Relationship Characteristics} + \beta_3 \textit{Firm Characteristics} + \\ \beta_4 \textit{Control Variables} + \epsilon_i \end{gathered} \quad (32)$$

The next section will discuss the robustness of the dataset while briefly presenting different approaches to checking the robustness of the data.

3.7 Robustness tests of data

Before the statistical analysis, we conduct some preliminary tests to ensure the validity of the data used in the multivariate analyses. First, independent variables are tested on their multicollinearity. In general, a certain degree of multicollinearity is typical for regression analyses. However, a high degree is problematic, because the estimates of the regression parameters may not be reliable.

A correlation matrix of the independent variables provides a first indication of the presence of multicollinearity. We use various correlation coefficients depending on the scale level of the variables. The Pearson correlation coefficient is for metrically scaled and normally distributed variables; Spearman and Kendall's tau do not assume a normal distribution and, therefore, these correlation coefficients are appropriate for dichotomous and ordinally scaled variables. Because the independent variables have different scale levels, the correlation coefficients according to Spearman, Pearson and Kendall's tau are calculated (Bonett and Wright 2000; Spearman 1904a, 1904b). Correlation coefficients close to 1 indicate strong multicollinearity, which does not apply to our dataset. All three correlation coefficients show similar results.[81] However, because the correlation matrix only captures pairwise dependencies, further tests are needed.

---

81 See Appendix Table A - 1, Table A - 2, Table A - 3 for correlation tables.

As part of the multivariate analyses, we also evaluate the Variance Inflation Factors (VIF). The rapidity with which variances and covariances increase can be studied by using VIFs, because they show multicollinearity in a regression analysis. Multicollinearity is present when there is a correlation between independent variables in a model, which would impact the regression results.

VIFs can estimate how much the variance of a regression coefficient is inflated due to multicollinearity. How large the VIF can be before it causes a problem is an open question, although it is agreed that the more the VIF increases, the less reliable the regression results will be (Gujarati 2004; O'Brien 2007). The calculation of the VIFs showed no signs of multicollinearity.

Outlier diagnostics are another important preliminary test. We calculate boxplots for this purpose, which show only a few extreme values in the dataset. For example, the variable *Credit Line Volume* showed some extreme values because there are some large firms in the dataset compared to the median firm, and they carry a higher credit line volume than the smaller firms. In this case, the natural logarithm of the variable is applicable. We calculate the logarithm of this variable, and we are able to overcome the outlier problem without any further transformation of the data.

In order to further test the robustness of the regression results, we next modify the dataset to test whether the multivariate regression analyses deliver the same results. Thus, for example, we exclude the variable *Counterpart*, which investigates whether a survey participant is the SME's contact person for the most important bank. We find that, in thirty-one cases, the participant was not the firm's counterpart for the business relationship. However, the multivariate regression analyses delivered the same results and, consequently, we can assume the results remain robust.[82]

82 See Appendix Table A - 4, Table A - 5, Table A - 6 for the multivariate regression analysis.

4 Empirical evaluation

Chapter 4 presents our descriptive statistics, the results of our regression analyses, and offers a comprehensive interpretation of the empirical findings. In this section, we provide an overview of the dataset, as well as an evaluation of the housebank variables. We also put the results of the descriptive statistics into the context of the housebank definition discussed in section 2.4.2. Moreover, by means of the descriptive statistics, we can generate important insights into the structure of the dataset before conducting the multivariate analyses. Subsequently, we evaluate the endogenous variables. In this context, the effects of the relationship characteristics, loan characteristics, firm characteristics, and control variables on the *Collateral Requirements*, *Collateral Type*, *Cost of Debt*, and *Credit Availability* variables are presented.

4.1 Descriptive statistics

At the beginning of the questionnaire, survey participants were asked which position they hold in the company. Respondents were permitted to give multiple answers because one participant can simultaneously be a shareholder and an executive, which is often the case in SMEs. However, most participants were the owner or, respectively, the shareholder of the company, and were also on the executive board.

Participants were also asked how many years of job experience they have in their positions. 269 (46.7 %) said they have more than twenty years of job experience, 190 (32.99 %) had ten or more but less than twenty years, 72 (12.5 %) had five or more years of experience but less than ten years, and 41 (7.12 %) had one or more years but less than five years. Only 4 (0.69 %) participants indicated they had less than one year of job experience in their position.

Next, we inquired whether the participant is the contact person in the firm for banks. 549 (95.31 %) said they are the contact person; only 27 (4.69 %) were not. We used the variable *Relevance* to investigate the importance of the bank in the corporate finance. The variable was inquired on a five-point Likert-type scale. The mean and median values showed common consent. Thus, the results emphasized that on average respondents perceive this bank important for the corporate finance functions of the firm.

Additionally, we asked whether participants have a designated loan officer at their most important bank. According to Höwer (2016), banks use different

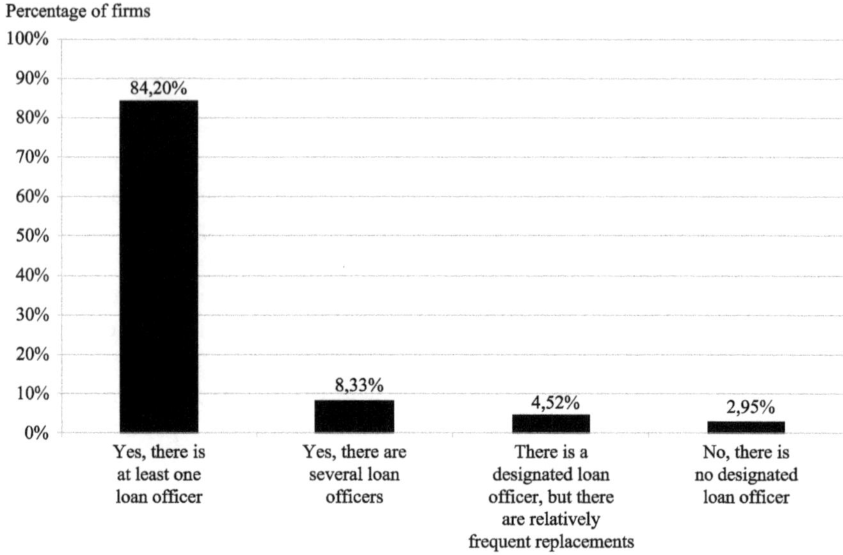

Figure 4-1: Loan officer

This figure shows whether a designated *Loan Officer* is in place for the sample of 576 firms. The figure illustrates the percentage of surveyed firms and is divided into four categories for whether there is one loan officer, several loan officers, frequent replacements of loan officers, or no designated officer.

forms of information when it comes to financing or to renegotiating contracts (Berger, Klapper, and Udell 2001; Jiménez et al. 2009). As described in the literature review, research typically distinguishes between hard and soft information. Hard information can be confirmed by financial data or ratings; soft information relies more on, e.g., degrees of trust. Soft information is generated by the loan officer and cannot be directly verified by others. This form of information turns out to be particularly valuable once a firm is in financial distress and must reorganize its debt (Höwer 2016; Stein 2002). Figure 4-1 illustrates participants' answers about designated loan officers.

485 (84.20 %) respondents said that there is at least one loan officer in-charge of their firm, while only 17 (2.95 %) participants said there is no designated loan officer assigned to their company. Uchida et al. (2012) find that a greater amount of soft information is produced by loan officers who are frequently in contact with the firm and work at small banks. Thus, loan officers are crucial in the production of soft information and are a critical component

of a lending relationship. However, so far there is no clear evidence why loan officers at large banks do not produce as much soft information as loan officers at small banks. Uchida et al. (2012) document that loan officers at small and large banks generally appear to have the same potential to engage in soft information production.

The following section presents the firm characteristics. Data on observable firm characteristics are used to reduce the impact of the heterogeneity of firms in the dataset and to convey an understanding of the composition of the sample (Harhoff and Körting 1998).

Table 4-1 summarizes the key firm characteristics. On average, the firms in the dataset are 49 years old and employ a median of 55 employees. The majority of the firms are corporations and most of these firms have a revenue of EUR 2 million up to EUR 10 million, while the firms show on average an annual sales growth of 7.60 % and an equity ratio of 40.50 %. Most of the companies in the sample have not been in financial distress. With respect to the equity ratio, it is expected that companies with a relatively stable equity ratio have a good starting position in loan negotiations and re-negotiations. In addition, the indication of a high sales growth reflects the growth potential of a company and may influence banks to be more willing to invest in these companies. On top of that, a firm in financial distress may be worth supporting for a bank in view of the fact that they add economic value to society, particularly, if the bank is a savings bank.

Most of the participants said that they consider their firm a family business. 408 companies are also family firms according to the definition used in this study. Of those 408 companies, most are managed by the second generation. Le Breton-Miller and Miller (2006) conclude that family companies undertake higher investments in durable relations with stakeholders, which may lead to superior stakeholder retention and stable partners and, thus, may be better in relationship management.

The companies in the dataset use short- and long-term bank debt and credit lines frequently. To obtain a credit line, companies typically pledge collateral on the firm's assets. In addition, the results show an average credit interest rate for the credit line of around 3.81 % as presented in section 4.1.3. Moreover, in median respondents generally agree with the statement that short-term bank debt is automatically renewed on maturity when required from the bank. Overall, there seems to be a high use of short-term bank debt by the firms in the dataset translating into a frequent evaluation and reevaluation of the relationship by the bank.

Table 4-1: Summary of firm, loan, and relationship characteristics

This table presents the number of firms, the mean, median, standard deviation (SD), minimum (min), and maximum (max) of the key firm characteristics for the sample of 576 companies.[83] Participants were asked for a metric input when answering the firm age, size, sales growth, and equity ratio; the other variables: legal form, revenue, and financial distress were inquired on a nominal and dichotomous scale. Regarding the legal form: sole proprietorships were assigned to one, partnerships (GbR, OHG, KG) were assigned to two, GmbH & Co. KG were assigned to three, corporations (GmbH, AG, KGaA) were assigned to four, and other legal forms were assigned to five. With respect to the revenue: up to below EUR 1 million was assigned to one, EUR 1 million up to below EUR 2 million was assigned to two, EUR 2 million up to below EUR 10 million was assigned to three, EUR 10 million up to below EUR 50 million was assigned to four, EUR 50 million up to below EUR 500 million was assigned to five, and EUR 500 million and more was assigned to six. Considering the variable financial distress, it was inquired whether firms had been in financial distress in the post financial crisis period starting in 2007, while firm answers of one indicated that these firms had been in financial distress, answers that were assigned to value zero translated into firms that had not been in financial distress. The variables *Legal Form* and *Revenue* are not included in this table. Moreover, this table shows the family firm variables. Participants were inquired to give answers to these variables on a dichotomous scale. An affirmative response was assigned the value one, while a negative answer was assigned the value zero. In addition, participants answered the questions of the generation on a scale ranging from one for first generation to five for fifth and higher generations. The variable *Short-Term Bank Debt* indicates the frequency the firm uses bank financing of < 1 year. The variable *Credit Lines* inquired the frequency the firm finances business operations with lines of credit. *Long-Term Bank Debt* notes the frequency the firm uses bank financing of > 1 year. These three variables were measured on an ordinal five-point Likert-type scale ranging from 1 (never) to 5 (always). *Cost of Debt* measures the interest rate that had to be paid for the most important credit line with the reference day January 1, 2015. For this variable, a metric input in percent was given. *Credit Availability* inquired whether short-term bank debt with the main bank is renewed automatically upon maturity and was measured on an ordinal five-point Likert-type scale ranging from 1 (does not apply at all) to 5 (strongly applies). The variables *Collateral Requirements* and *Collateral Type* are not included in this table as both variables were measured on a nominal scale. The *Number* of banks the firm works with was measured on a nominal scale. *Duration* was measured by the number of years the firm has worked with the most important bank on a metric scale. The variable *Length Comparison* was measured on a five-point Likert-type scale and was measured from 1 (does not apply at all) to 5 (strongly applies). *Finance Share*[84] indicates the percentage of the total volume of all bank loans in 2015 that the bank held in corporate finance and was measured on a metric scale. *Meeting Frequency* shows how often meetings between the firm and the bank are taking place on average per year and was measured on a metric scale. *Information Exchange*

83 The control variables covering the industry variables are not included in this table, as these were all measured on a nominal scale.

84 The variable *Finance Share* is part of the relationship characteristics in the descriptive statistics since this variable is part of the definition of housebank relationships.

Table 4-1: Continued

measures whether more information is exchanged with the most important bank on average compared to the exchange with the other banks. *Scope* notes whether the bank provides most other bank services for the firm besides the debt financing and was as well measured on a five-point Likert-type scale ranging from 1 (does not apply at all) to 5 (strongly applies). *Behavior* specifies whether a respondent thinks that the bank would carry a special responsibility towards the firm when the firm is in financial distress and was measured on the five-point Likert-type scale. With the variable *Trust* respondents express the level of trust between the firm and the bank based on experiences from the past and was measured again on the five-point Likert-type scale. The variables *Loan Officer* and *Bank Type* were not included in this table as these two variables were based on the evaluation of different statements. The control variables *Industry* and *Headquarters* are also not included in this table, as both were measured on a nominal scale.[85]

	N	Mean	Median	SD	Min	Max
Firm characteristics						
Firm Age	576	49	30	44.73	2	350
Firm Size	576	104	55	128.82	1	500
Sales Growth	576	7.60	5	13.99	-25	100
Equity Ratio	576	40.50	35	27.94	-30	100
Financial Distress	576	0.31	0	0.46	0	1
Family Firm Self-assessment	576	0.77	1	0.42	0	1
Family Firm Ownership	576	0.78	1	0.42	0	1
Family Firm Management	576	0.75	1	0.43	0	1
Family Firm Generation	408	2.03	2	1.17	1	5
Loan characteristics						
Short-term Bank Debt	576	4.12	4	1.09	1	5
Credit Lines	576	3.58	4	1.32	1	5
Long-term Bank Debt	576	3.39	3	1.28	1	5
Relationship characteristics						
Number	576	2.84	2	1.68	1	10
Duration	576	29.47	24	22.40	1	161
Length Comparison	477	4.01	5	1.37	1	5
Finance Share	576	46.86	50	39.17	0	100
Meeting Frequency	576	2.77	2	2.76	0	30
Information Exchange	477	3.39	4	1.35	1	5
Scope	576	4.07	4	1.11	1	5
Behavior	576	3.64	4	1.17	1	5
Trust	576	3.97	4	1.04	1	5

85 In addition, the tables show no significant correlations between the variables. This is also discussed in section 3.7, as well as in Tables A-1, A-2, and A-3 in the Appendix.

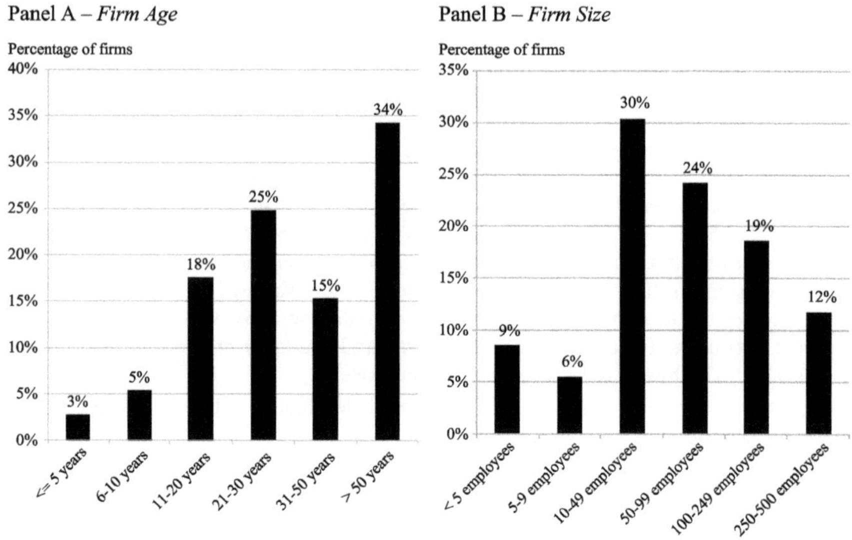

Figure 4-2: Distribution of companies by age and size

Panel A shows the number of years since the founding of the firms (*Firm Age*) and the percentage of surveyed companies for the sample of 576 firms. Panel B shows the number of employees (*Firm Size*) and the percentage of surveyed companies for the sample of 576 firms.

4.1.1 Firm characteristics and control variables

We evaluated firm age for the sample of 576 companies. Participants were asked to indicate the year of the firm's founding. The variable *Firm Age* is a proxy for the availability of public information, and, thus, a measure for the firm's information transparency. In addition, according to Montoriol-Garriga (2006), firm age has a positive effect on credit availability (see also Angelini et al. 1998; Harhoff and Körting 1998). As per the results, the firms are on average 49 years old, while the median value is 30 years. The youngest firm in the dataset was founded in 2014; the oldest company was founded in 1666. Figure 4-2 shows the distribution by firm age and size.

In order to evaluate sample firm size, participants were asked to note the average number of employees in 2015. Guiso (2003) states that credit rationing is often due to a lack of firm size and equity. Dietsch (2003) shows for France that the degree of credit decreased with firm size. Moreover, this variable is also used to proxy for the level of information availability. In the literature review, it is argued that firm size has an increasing effect on the number of bank relationships (Neuberger and Räthke 2009). On average, the sample firms have 104 employees, while the median is 55 employees, suggesting that a skew is present in the dataset. For example, some companies in the dataset have up to 500 employees. The largest group of firms employs 10–49 people, while the smallest group of firms employs 5–9 people.

Participants were also asked whether the company belongs to one of the following forms: sole proprietorship, partnership (GbR, OHG, KG), GmbH & Co. KG, or corporation (GmbH, AG, KGaA). GbR, OHG, KG, and GmbH & Co. KG are unlimited liability companies, while GmbH, AG, and KGaA are limited liability companies. Therefore, the variable *Legal Form* captures whether the company owners have limited or unlimited liability, which is particularly interesting in an SME context, as these companies are often limited liability companies. We also expected to garner more insights by including the legal form, because the publication requirements for GmbH, AG, and KGaA corporations are higher than for sole proprietorships or partnerships. This translates into an indicator for the level of publicly available hard information to the bank (e.g., audited balance sheets and income statements, etc.).

Note that the majority of firms in the dataset are corporations (70 %). The second most common legal form is the GmbH & Co. KG, with 25 %, followed by three categories with 2 % each (sole proprietorship, partnership (GbR, OHG, KG), and other legal forms). In addition, three survey participants stated that their companies were stock-listed.[86] However, none had a significant effect on the regression results. There are no subsidiaries in the dataset.

In order to analyze the financial figures and determine the financial strength and growth potential of the companies, we first requested the revenue figures of the companies according to their 2015 annual results. The results show that, on average, companies had revenues ranging from EUR 2 million to EUR 10 million in 2015. Thus, the largest group (38 %) had revenue in this category, while the smallest group (1 %) had revenues of EUR 500 million or more.

Second, participants were required to indicate their firms' annual sales growth based on 2015 annual results. Montoriol-Garriga (2006) also studies sales growth as an indicator of firm performance, and, as per Hernández-Cánovas and Martínez-Solano (2010), it can be a reflection of the ability to generate profits.

86 The companies were initially filtered with no stock market listing. However, this may be due to the Dafne database not providing the latest information. As stated, there is no significant effect of stock-listed companies on the regression results.

On average, companies had annual sales growth of 7.6 % in 2015, with a median of 5 %. The smallest group of companies (2 %) showed sales growth of greater than 50 % and less than or equal to 100 %, while 7 % had negative sales growth. Most of the companies showed between 0 % and 10 % sales growth in 2015.

Third, participants were asked to express their companies' equity ratios according to the 2015 annual results. The variable *Equity Ratio* measures firm leverage. It is a direct measure of firm riskiness and an important determinant for credit decisions. It is expected that more indebted and less solvent (i.e., riskier) companies are more likely to pledge securities (Hernández-Cánovas and Martínez-Solano 2010). On average, the companies have equity ratios of 40.50 %, with a median of 35 %. The largest group of companies (31 %) has an equity ratio of greater than 25 % to 50 %, while the smallest group (1 %) exhibits a negative equity ratio. This can arise when the debt of a company is greater than its assets. In contrast, thirty-four companies indicated an equity ratio of 100 %. A high equity ratio may translate into greater bargaining power toward banks, for example, during renegotiations, suggesting a better starting position. Figure 4-3 illustrates the sales growth and the equity ratio results for the dataset.

To evaluate companies' general prior financial distress, participants were asked about their companies' financial position following the recent 2007–2009 global financial crisis. Aoki and Dinç (1997) write about financial distress in the context of relationship banking, and state that it is "a type of financing in which the financier is expected to make additional financing in a class of uncontractible states in the expectation of future rents over time" (Aoki and Dinç 1997, p. 5). They emphasize the aspect of funding availability (see also Petersen and Rajan 1994).

Boot (2000) explores the benefits of relationship lending in terms of its contractual features, such as flexibility. Relationship lending is usually less rigid than, for example, a capital market funding deal. Thus, renegotiations tend to be smoother. Lehmann and Neuberger (2001) further support this line of reasoning and show that housebanks make critical services and loans available when a firm becomes financially distressed. A close relationship with a relationship lender can become even more important during times of crisis (Ono et al. 2014). Transactional lenders may increase credit availability for firms during normal times, but they may be hesitant to provide more support during downturns. Therefore, as Elsas (2001) also notes, the relationship bank has a special responsibility to a firm during financial crises.

According to Elsas and Krahnen (2003), a company is considered in financial distress when it is not able to meet current obligations, such as, e.g., bank loans, and needs liquidity on short notice. According to their results, 177 (31 %) firms noted they had been in financial distress, while 399 (69 %) said that they had

Panel A – *Sales Growth*

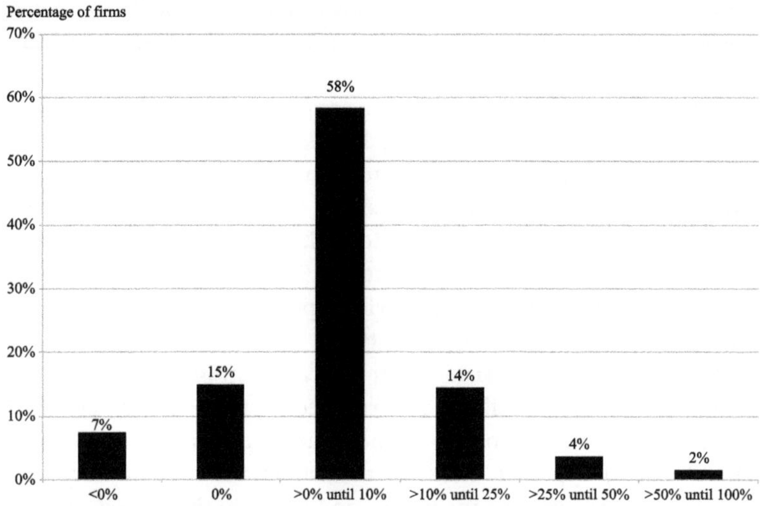

Panel B – *Equity Ratio*

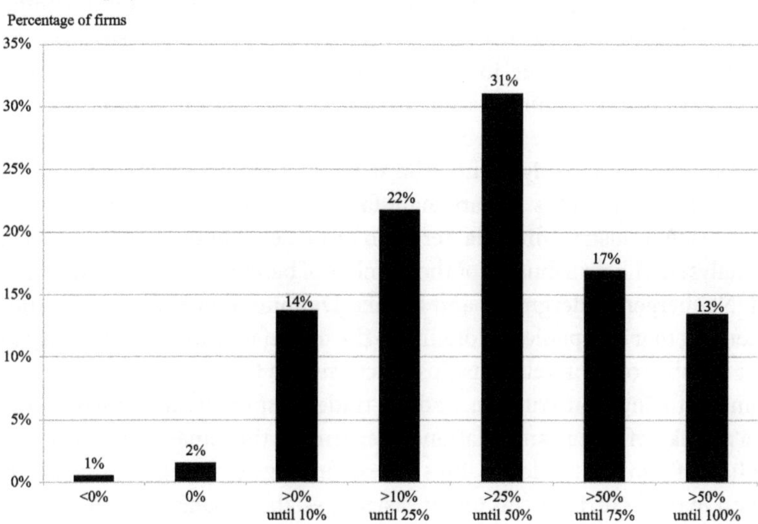

Figure 4-3: Distribution of companies according to the sales growth and equity ratio

Panel A shows the distribution of companies according to *Sales Growth* based on 2015 annual results; panel B shows the *Equity Ratio* based on 2015 annual results for the sample of 576 companies. *Sales Growth* and the *Equity Ratio* are shown in percent.

not experienced that situation since the financial crisis began in 2007. Financial distress may prompt the bank to reassess the firm's credit quality. Consequently, loan parameters may deteriorate, both for price and non-price parameters (Harhoff and Körting 1998).

In contrast, Höwer (2016) finds that, in some circumstances, banks can "lean against the wind" and continue funding distressed but viable companies. Banks, as delegated monitors, have the ability to gather and process soft information. Consequently, if a bank receives a bad signal relating to a firm's private information, this can assist the loan officer to make more efficient decisions about firm restructuring or liquidation (Diamond 1984; Höwer 2016). The effects of financial distress on credit parameters will be presented in more detail when we analyze the multivariate regression results.

We also collect control variables that indicate firm industry and headquarters. The variable *Industry* reflects the firm's sector in the dataset, i.e., the firm's primary activities. We categorize the industries according to the Statistisches Bundesamt (2016) approach. This set of distinct industry dummy variables allows a clear way to organize the various industries in the dataset. In addition, we would expect that the investment risks of the firms vary across industries and financial parameters. The results show that the largest group of companies (37.50 %) belongs to the manufacturing industry, while the smallest groups (2.60 %) belongs to other industries including energy and agriculture, and forestry and fishing. Figure 4-4 illustrates the distribution of industries in our dataset.

As the distribution highlights, the dataset offers comprehensive industrial coverage. The main industries are manufacturing, service, and construction. We evaluate each industry's financial terms in more detail in the multivariate regression analyses. The distribution of the number of bank relationships was also analyzed. Neuberger, Pedergnana, and Räthke-Döppner (2008) show in a study for Switzerland that companies belonging to the manufacturing industry engage in a higher number of bank relationships. According to the results of our study, firms in manufacturing, construction, and the trade, hospitality, and tourism industry have a median of three bank relationships; firms in the remaining industries have a median of two bank relationships. These findings may suggest that construction and manufacturing firms find it easier to establish bank relationships, which could be attributable to the tangibility of their assets. Banks may be more amenable to offer financing when tangible collateral is readily available.

Furthermore, a variable was included asking participants to note whether the company is located in West or East Germany, and whether the firm's headquarters are located in an urban or a rural area. This approach is in line with Lehmann

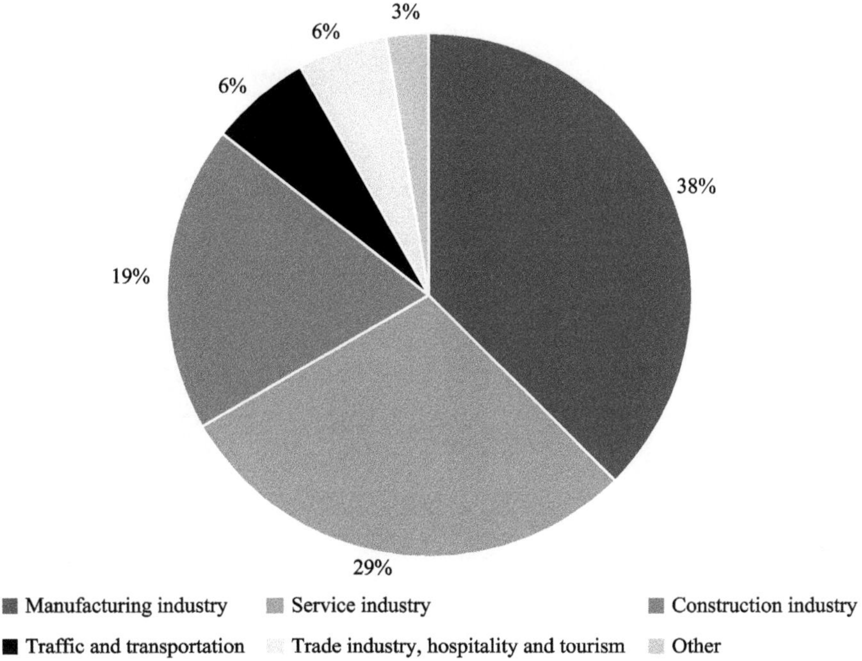

Figure 4-4: Distribution of companies by industry

This figure shows the distribution of companies according to the industry classifications based on the Statistisches Bundesamt (2016) categorization for the sample of 576 firms.

and Neuberger (2001), who also include a dummy variable to determine whether a firm is located in West Germany, and Howorth and Moro (2012), who assess firm region. This variable captures potential geographic effects. The largest share of firms (42 %) are headquartered in West Germany and in an urban area, while the smallest share (10 %) is in East Germany in an urban area.

To gain a more comprehensive understanding of the companies in the sample and of their ownership and management structures, participants also completed a self-assessment. They were asked whether their company would be classified as a family business. Anderson and Reeb (2003) argue that families tend to hold a longer-term perspective for the company compared to other shareholders, which may help promote long-term investment projects. Indeed, Mach's (2007) survey of German family firms finds that their top objective is long-term value orientation.

Mietzner and Tyrell (2012) also expect family firms to exhibit different behavior when engaging with stakeholders than non-family firms. Interactions

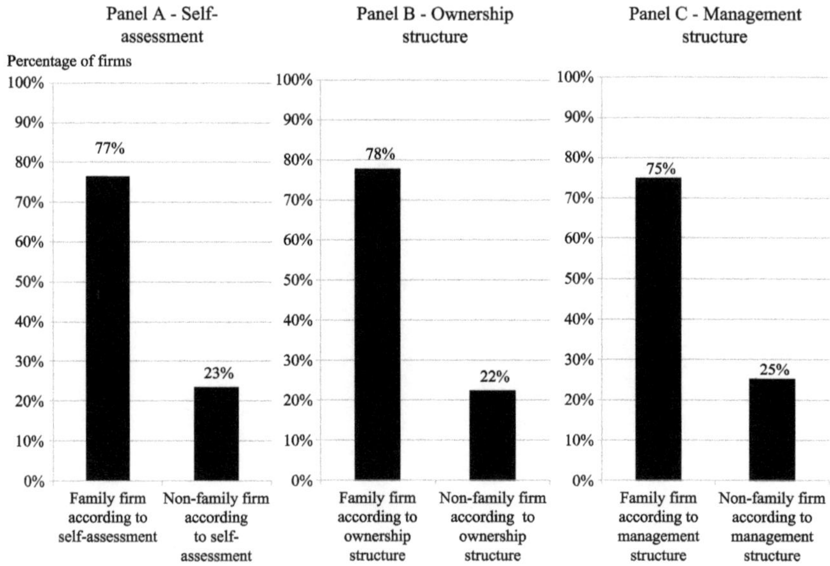

Figure 4-5: Family firm assessment

This figure shows the family firm variables for the sample of 576 companies. Panel A shows the results for the self-assessment, panel B shows the family firm analysis according to ownership structure, and panel C shows the family firm investigation based on management structure.

with financiers, or relationship management, is one of the key aspects to ensuring stable and sustainable funding of the company in promoting its long-term goals (Schraml 2010).

To describe in more detail, companies were first asked a simple, yet revealing, question about whether they consider the company a family firm. This was essential first to grasp the participant's opinion or perception, besides the various definitions. 77 % said they consider their firm a family business; 23 % did not. Participants were also asked whether a family member or multiple family members hold at least 50 % of the shares in the company. 78 % said they did, while 22 % said they do not. Following this question, respondents were then asked whether these family members are part of the management of the company. 75 % had family members active in management, while 25 % did not. We only classify companies as family firms if both conditions were met. Overall, both characteristics are present in the majority of the companies (71 %). Figure 4-5 illustrates these results.

Participants who stated that family members hold at least 50 % of shares and are also active in management were then asked to provide what generation is currently managing the firm. Founders or buyers of the company were considered first generation. 408 companies were examined. The largest group of companies (44 %) is managed by the first generation, 25 % are managed by the second generation, 19 % are managed by the third generation, and 7 % are managed by the fourth generation. The smallest group of companies (5 %) is managed by the fifth or higher generation.

4.1.2 Loan characteristics

The loan characteristics are evaluated by means of short- and long-term bank debt and credit lines. We also examine the amount of collateralization needed to obtain the credit line, the type of collateral, the cost of the debt, and credit availability.

Participants were asked how frequently they require short-term bank debt, defined as debt with a maturity of less than one year. The variable is measured on a scale from 1 (never) to 5 (always). According to Berger and Udell (1995a), short-term debt allows for a particularly efficient investigation of the firm-bank relationship, because it resolves information asymmetries well, especially for smaller firms. When a firm applies for additional funds to realize a project, the bank can evaluate its specific risk each time before making the credit decision. Because this type of loan is typically required multiple times, the bank is able to continuously reconsider the state of its relationship with the firm.

The results show that, on average, the firms in our dataset often use short-term bank debt. In this context, respondents also revealed the frequency with which they use credit lines to finance business operations. Credit lines, which are also classified as short-term bank financing, are generally used often as well. Overall, we find that 7 % of the companies never use credit lines, but 27 % (the highest percentage) say they always do.

In addition, participants were also asked whether their company is funded with long-term bank debt. Long-term bank debt is defined as bank financing of greater than one year. The results show that, on average, the firms in our dataset only occasionally use long-term bank debt. Figure 4-6 illustrates the frequency the companies finance business operations with short- and long-term bank debt and credit lines.

4.1.3 Endogenous variables

The variable *Collateral Requirements* examines the proportion of collateral and/or guarantees required to obtain the most important credit line. It is measured on a nominal scale. Berger and Udell (1995a) likewise focus their analysis of

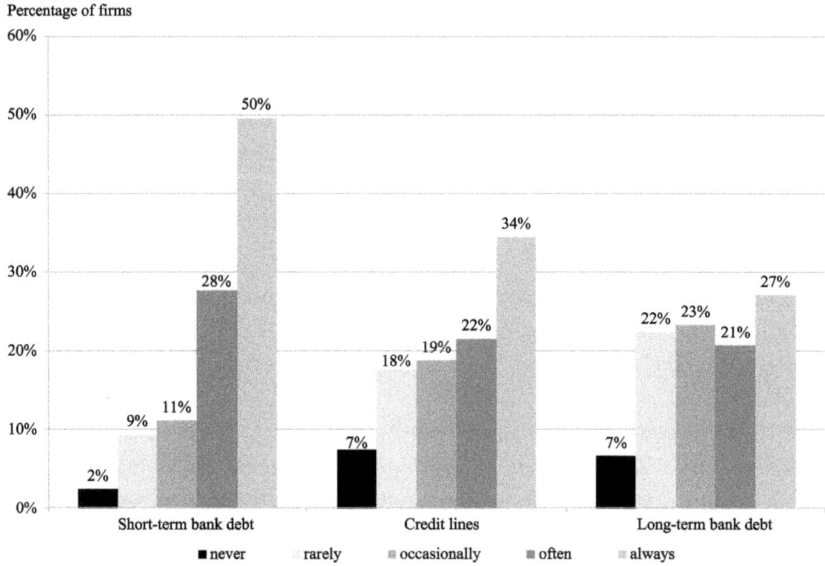

Figure 4-6: Frequency of bank financing

The x-axis shows the distribution of companies that say they use short-term bank debt, credit lines, and long-term bank debt for the sample of 576 firms. The y-axis shows the percentage of firms surveyed.

collateral requirements and interest rates on credit lines. This type of credit can be especially revealing, because relationships are more likely to matter in this context than for other types of loans, for example, mortgages, equipment loans, and spot loans. Credit lines are often one-time loans for non-recurring credit needs. They are thus more transaction-driven and less relationship-driven. Hence, the effect of relationship lending may be somewhat diluted when we analyze these loans in a sample.

According to Berger and Udell (1995a), lines of credit also allow for a precise assessment of the firm-bank relationship because they are an important instrument to resolve information asymmetry between the firm and the bank, particularly for financing of small firms. The results show that the smallest group of companies (5 %) is required to pledge from 25 % to 50 %, while the largest group (43 %) is not required to pledge anything.

The variable *Collateral Type* is used to capture whether the main type of collateral deposited is company assets, personal guarantees of the firm owner's assets, or both. This variable is measured on a nominal scale. The majority of companies

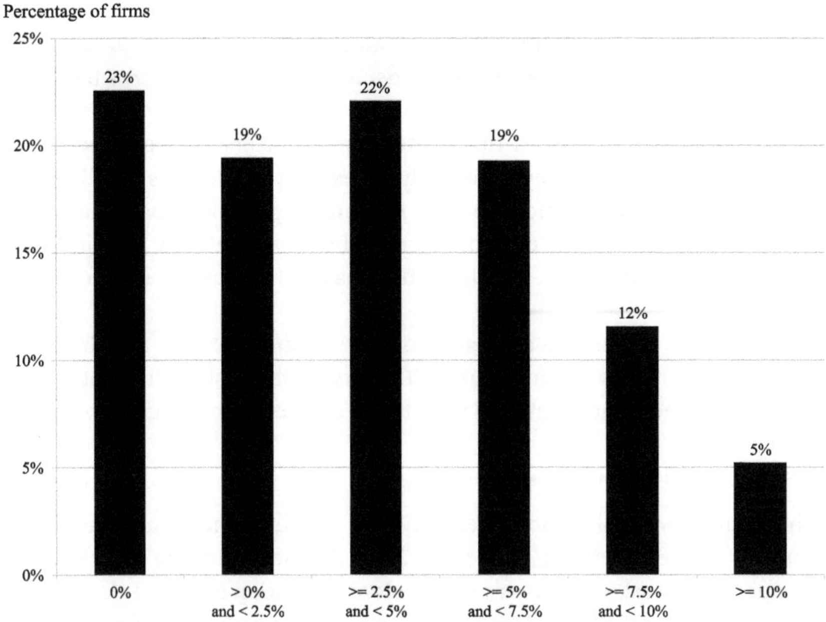

Figure 4-7: Credit interest rate

This figure shows the distribution of companies according to the interest rate they were required to pay for their most important credit line for the sample of 576 companies. The percentage of surveyed firms is also presented.

(53 %) are required to pledge collateral on the firm's assets, while 27 % are required to pledge collateral and personal guarantees. The smallest share of companies (21 %) is required to deposit personal guarantees.

The variable *Cost of Debt* measures the interest rate on the most important credit line using reference day January 1, 2015. Participants were asked to provide a metric input in percentage. On average, companies paid an interest rate of 3.81 % in order to receive a credit line. The smallest share (5 %) paid greater than or equal to 10 %; the largest share (23 %) were not required to pay anything. Figure 4-7 illustrates the distribution of companies according to credit line interest rate.

Participants were then asked whether their short-term bank debt with their main bank is automatically renewed upon maturity. This variable was measured on an ordinal five-point Likert-type scale ranging from 1 (does not apply) to 5 (strongly applies).

As we noted earlier, when a company applies for additional financing to realize a project, the bank most likely reevaluates the specific risk of the potential borrower before making the credit decision. Since short-term bank debt is typically required multiple times, the bank can continuously reconsider its relationship with the firm. In this context, loan officers are expected to play a crucial role, because they ultimately assess the borrower's creditworthiness, and subsequently decide whether to grant or prolong a loan (Kano et al. 2011). Automatic renewal of short-term debt upon maturity implies easier access to short-term credit, which in turn may indicate reduced information asymmetries.

The results show that, on average, short-term bank debt with a main bank is renewed automatically upon maturity. The largest share of participants (38 %) were granted automatic renewal. 6 % were not granted automatic renewal.

4.1.4 Relationship characteristics

In this section, we analyze firms' relationships with their most important banks, according to the definition in section 2.4.2. At the beginning of the survey, participants were asked to answer all questions in relation to this bank. However, if firms have several bank relationships, participants were reminded to answer all questions only in relation to their most important bank. We provided no specific definition to participants of what characterizes the most important bank, because this study aims to determine whether housebank relationships exist, by using several variables.

As described in section 2.4.2, relationship lending is defined as long-term in nature, and is characterized by a competitive advantage of the bank over its rivals in terms of the firm's information. The relationship is also defined by the bank holding a major, often dominant, proportion of the credit financing of the firm relative to other banks and carrying out most other financial services for the firm. Moreover, the relationship is characterized by a certain level of trust and the bank holding special responsibility for the firm during financial distress.

Note that the terms relationship lending, relationship banking, and housebank are used interchangeably throughout this thesis. This section evaluates whether these points apply to the bank relationships explored in this survey by means of the descriptive analyses. Thus, the housebank relationship is measured by the *Number* of bank relationships, the *Duration* of the relationship, and the *Finance Share*. This section also analyzes the variable *Bank Type*, indicated by survey participants as the most important bank, the level of interaction, measured by *Meeting Frequency*, *Information Exchange*, and *Scope*. We also measure level of

Trust based on past experience, and the expected *Behavior* of the bank during times of distress.

Participants were asked the number of bank relationships they maintain. As described in the literature review, examining the number of bank relationships and its effect on lending have yielded mixed results. Since Petersen and Rajan (1994), the duration of a lending relationship (length) and the number of bank relationships (concentration) have turned out to be the most commonly used proxies for measuring relationship lending in applied empirical work for SMEs (Hernández-Cánovas and Martínez-Solano 2010).

For example, Castelli et al. (2006) find a negative link between engaging in multiple bank relationships and firm performance. We argue here that, overall, the number of bank relationships may have two contradictory implications. On the one hand, it may signal banking relationship quality: financially stable firms may have long-term relationships with just a few banks, financially unstable firms may have in short-term relationships with multiple banks, because they face difficulties obtaining needed credit. On the other hand, it may simply signal convenience: financially stable firms may have long-term relationships with multiple banks because it is easier for them to establish relationships. They may also have greater capital needs. The variables *Duration* and *Number* are used in the multivariate regression analyses to measure this effect.

On average, the companies in our dataset maintain three bank relationships, with a median of two. The largest share (34 %) maintains two bank relationships; the smallest share (1 %) have seven or eight. 17 % maintain just one bank relationship.

Firms generally seem to prefer to concentrate their borrowing with one or two banks. As we noted earlier, Harhoff and Körting (1998) were among the first to highlight that smaller companies tend to concentrate their borrowing with only one bank. They found that concentrated debt financing is beneficial to firms, while a growing number of bank relationships decreases credit availability.

These descriptive results are also in line with Neuberger and Räthke (2009), who document that companies engage in two bank relationships on average. They determine that firm size and age tend to increase the number of bank relationships. The number may also increase when the firm requires a higher loan amount (Neuberger and Räthke 2009). Table 4-2 illustrates those results.

The results show that the number of bank relationships seems to increase with the number of employees, but that it decreases slightly at six bank relationships. Subsequently, seven or more bank relationships again correlate with increasing firm size. The number also rises as the firm ages, until it hits six bank relationships. Then, seven or more relationships again seem more characteristic of slightly younger companies.

Table 4-2: Number of banks according to average firm size, age, and finance share

This table shows the average number of employees (*Firm Size*), average number of years a firm is in business (*Firm Age*), average finance share a firm carries on its balance sheet from the housebank (*Finance Share*), and the number of observations measured by the *Number* of bank relationships (N).

	N	1 Bank	N	2 Banks	N	3 Banks	N	4 Banks	N	5 Banks
Firm Size	99	38	196	72	148	113	59	170	33	208
Firm Age	99	29	196	39	148	56	59	57	33	79
Finance Share	99	41	196	48	148	50	59	53	33	47
	N	6 Banks	N	7 Banks	N	8 Banks	N	9 Banks	N	10 Banks
Firm Size	21	265	6	233	5	402	0	0	9	412
Firm Age	21	100	6	40	5	67	0	0	9	76
Finance Share	21	40	6	34	5	26	0	0	9	22

We also find that the number of bank relationships decreases with the loan amount provided by the housebank. Thus, our results do not follow those of Neuberger and Räthke (2009). With respect to firm size and age, the results do confirm Neuberger and Räthke (2009).

Tirri (2007) emphasizes that firms may engage in multiple bank relationships as they try to reduce the hold-up problem and the probability of being credit rationed. In contrast, engaging in a smaller number of bank relationships typically decreases information asymmetries and agency issues. These positive effects may compensate for potential hold-up problems.

Hainz and Wiegand (2013) argue that maintaining a second bank relationship helps to resolve the hold-up problem. In this context, the question arises whether a housebank relationship can exist despite another relatively primary bank relationship being in place. In this context, Elsas and Krahnen (1998) find, however, that the existence of housebanks is clear. Thus, there is no need for exclusivity in a bank-firm relationship. Firms with a housebank and normal bank relationships may even be better at controlling potential hold-up problems in the housebank relationship.

In addition, it was argued in the literature review that the number of bank relationships is a crucial factor in determining whether a company can withstand financial distress. Thus, it may be proof that relationship lending helps mitigate information asymmetries. Angelini et al. (1998) state that a limited number of bank relationships has a positive effect on credit availability, while Cotugno et al. (2013a) and Cotugno et al. (2013b) also find that companies with exclusive or few bank relationships tended to experience less credit constraints between 2007 and 2009 than companies with multiple bank relationships.

In contrast, Shikimi (2013) concludes that financially distressed companies engage in multiple bank relationships to improve access to finance. Höwer (2016) also finds that companies with multiple bank relationships can better weather financial distress and have a lower probability of experiencing distress in general.

Nevertheless, coordination problems and free-riding issues may occur and make it difficult for banks to help restructure distressed companies. Banks may not have access to sufficient private information to properly evaluate negative indicators from a new customer. Consequently, companies that recently changed their main bank may exhibit higher potential for getting into financial distress and even entering into bankruptcy proceedings.

The results of this study show that firms in financial distress during the past financial crisis, as well as those that were not, generally maintain the same number of bank relationships. 177 (31 %) distressed firms had on average three bank relationships (M = 2.66), with a median of two. 399 (69 %) non-distressed firms also maintained on average three bank relationships (M = 2.91), with a median of two. These results slightly suggest that financially stable firms may find it easier to maintain bank relationships while simultaneously building new ones if they so desire.

To measure *Duration*, participants were asked to indicate the length in years of the company's main banking relationship. Classification of the categories followed the classification of the variable *Firm Age*. On average, the companies in the dataset had bank relationships of 28.47 years. The largest share (24 %) had a relationship duration of 11 to 20 years with their housebanks, and the smallest share (9 %) had a relationship of less than or equal to five years. In contrast, 14 % had relationships of 51 to 70 years. Whether length is an indicator of quality has been a somewhat controversial topic in the literature. Harhoff and Körting (1998) have argued that time allows banks to better assess overall firm quality.

In addition, and to put the *Duration* results into context, the participants also stated whether the relationship to the most important bank is in general longer than that with other banks. The majority of participants (57 %) strongly agree that the housebank relationship tends to be longer. Only 9 % said length did not signal quality.

From a relationship lending context, there are frequent references to close banking relationships. For example, Petersen and Rajan (1994) illustrate relationship banking by writing "through close and continued interaction, a firm may provide a lender with sufficient information about, and a voice in, the firm's affairs so as to lower the cost and increase the availability of credit" (Petersen and Rajan 1994, p. 5). According to the authors, relationship banking is defined by long-term relationships.

Ogawa et al. (2010) document for Japan that the duration of the main bank relationship has an increasing effect on the number of lending relationships. The authors interpret this finding as either the influence of a reputation effect of borrowers, or of companies' counterbalance actions against the monopoly power of the housebank. However, our results do not show that the number of bank relationships increases relative to the duration of the bank relationship. Figure 4-8 illustrates these results and shows that there are younger and older banks demonstrating the same number of bank relationships.

Ongena and Smith (2001) show for Norway that companies exhibit a greater probability of ending a banking relationship as it matures. They posit this is to avoid a "lock-in" effect. According to Ongena and Smith (2001), companies with multiple bank relationships tend to have the shortest relationships, and to end relationships more often. However, these companies also typically end younger relationships and retain longer-term relationships. In this context, Ongena and Smith (2001) show that companies end bank relationships as they grow, and the specific bank perhaps is not able to continue to fulfill their needs. Consequently, companies shift from small banks to large banks, and engage in durable relationships with Norway's two largest banks.

In this survey, participants were asked to specify the share of financing from their balance sheets that is provided by the housebank. Evaluation of this variable shows that companies have on average 46.86 % of credit volume on their balance sheet financed by the most important bank. The largest share of companies (34 %) has more than or equal to 75 % to 100 % of credit volume provided by this bank in their balance sheet, while the smallest share (6 %) has only 1 % to less than 25 %.

D'Auria et al. (1999) likewise measure closeness by a bank's share of firm debt. Gambacorta and Mistrulli (2014) additionally include duration when studying closeness. They study the UniCredit Group and find that this banking group showed a greater likelihood to center its support on firms with more intense informational closeness.[87] However, Bartoli et al. (2012) note that, when we include rating, the importance of informational closeness decreases.[88]

---

87 Gambacorta and Mistrulli (2014) measure the closeness of the bank-borrower relationship using different indicators: "the functional distance between the bank and the borrower, the concentration of lenders, the length of borrowers' credit history, and the event that, during the period under investigation, a new lending relationship was established or a preexisting one terminated" (Gambacorta and Mistrulli 2014, p. 755).

88 Bartoli et al. (2012) define rating as the log of the firm's rating, a discrete variable that equals 1 for borrowers with the highest probability of default, and 14 for those with the lowest probability of default.

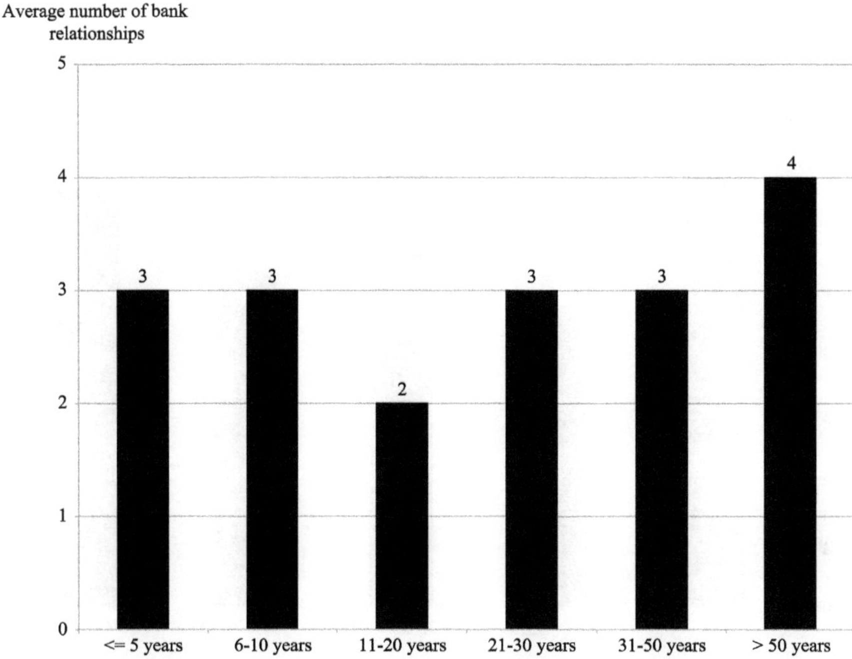

Figure 4-8: Duration measured by average number of bank relationships

This figure shows the distribution of companies according to the *Duration* of their most important bank relationship, as well as the average *Number* of bank relationships for each firm in the survey for the sample of 576 firms.

Harhoff and Körting (1998) also find that one bank tends to provide at least two-thirds of total firm credit volume. According to Cole (1998), for a firm that is specifically seeking to improve its access to financing and reduce its lending costs, the housebank should contribute a large share of its overall financing. As Elsas (2001) also puts it, a relationship bank exists to provide a (relative to peer banks) large, often dominant, share of the credit financing of a firm, and to perform most other critical firm financial services. Figure 4-9 illustrates the *Finance Share* according to *Sales Growth*.

Weinstein and Yafeh (1998) point out, however, that the main bank as a large debtholder may restrict firm growth. Our study investigates this finding by also asking participants to provide sales growth numbers in relation to financing share for the surveyed companies. Our findings do not confirm Weinstein and Yafeh's (1998) notion for our sample, as firm growth measured by means of sales

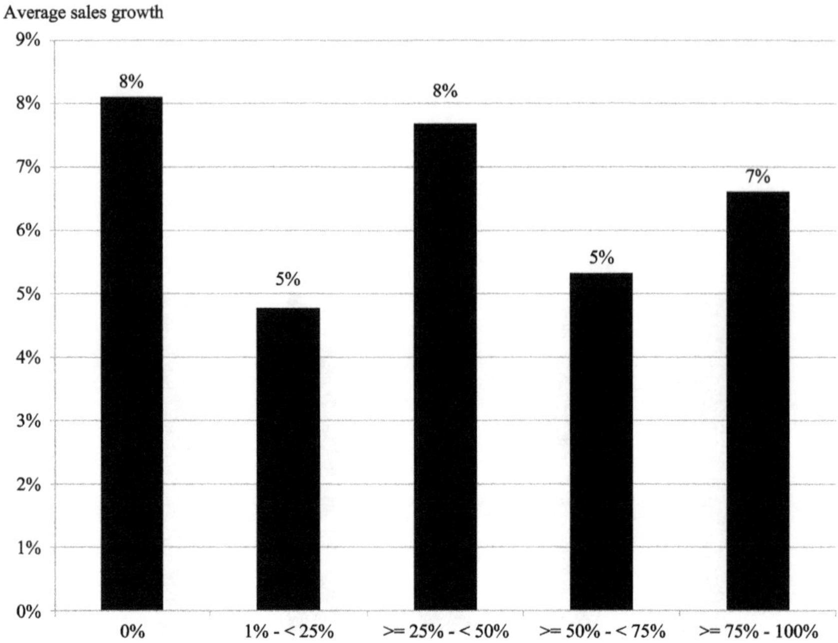

Figure 4-9: Finance share according to sales growth

This figure shows the percentage of average *Sales Growth* in 2015 for the 576 sample companies by the *Finance Share* on their balance sheets from their housebanks.

growth is evenly distributed over financing share. Companies with zero debt provided by their most important bank showed an average sales growth of 8 %. Companies with between 75 % and 100 % of debt on their balance sheet provided by the housebank showed an average sales growth of 7 %.

Participants also denoted the type of the most important bank, differentiating among savings, state, cooperative, and private banks. Stein (2002) argues that banks are not alike in their ability to process crucial soft information. According to the results, 41 % of firms attested that their most important bank is a savings bank, followed by 30 % with a private bank. Figure 4-10 illustrates the distribution of the variable *Bank Type* according to the participants' answers throughout the dataset. It also provides a more detailed analysis of the private banking sector by differentiating among the largest private banks in Germany.

Commerzbank was the most common private bank, with 46 %, followed by Deutsche Bank (29 %). In this context, Alessandrini et al. (2008, 2009) find that

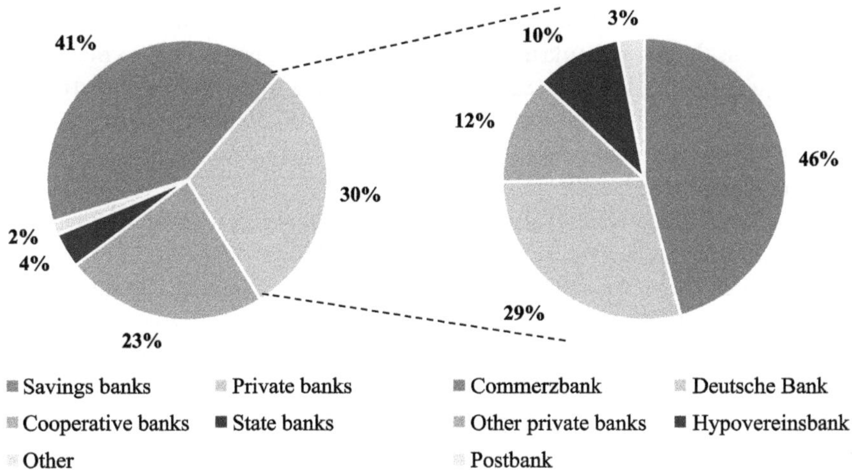

Figure 4-10: Bank types and private banks

The left-hand side of the figure shows in percent the distribution of companies according to the variable *Bank Type* that survey participants denote as their most important bank for the sample of 576 firms. The right-hand side breaks down the private banking sector in more detail for firms that consider their most important bank to be a private bank for the sample of 170 companies.

banking consolidation has made access for informationally opaque companies in regional banking markets more difficult. They thus observe a persistent importance of regional banking markets for small companies and for the regional economy. Jiménez et al. (2009) document for Spain that younger and smaller companies tend to begin a lending relationship with a local bank, while older and larger companies usually begin a relationship with a more geographically distant bank.

Figure 4-10 analyzes whether the companies in our dataset also follow this pattern. We find that companies that consider their most important bank a state bank are on average fifty-seven years old, while companies that are using private banks are on average forty-five years old. Companies that maintain a relationship with a savings bank or a cooperative bank are likewise older. Thus, regarding the descriptive results, there appears to be a similar pattern in our dataset.

In the context of the discussion about private and public banks and financial distress, Höwer (2016) emphasizes that public banks have a responsibility to support distressed but viable firms, while private banks may have incentives to make tough liquidation choices in order to attract low-risk customers. The author finds that savings banks and cooperative banks have lower shares of distressed firms that enter bankruptcy proceedings. These banks tend to make efficient liquidation decisions because they also have a higher share of distressed firms with improved ratings. Yet, a firm's likelihood of closing after financial distress is higher for customers of savings banks and cooperative banks than for customers of private banks.

Petersen and Rajan (1994) also emphasize the information aspect between the bank and the firm. They note that relationship banking is defined by information supply, which is a vital factor (*"sufficient information"*). Following this line of reasoning, information supply appears to play a key role, as long-term relationships between banks and firms counteract information asymmetries. To capture this variable, we asked participants to note how many times on average per year the firm meets with their most important bank, whether in person or otherwise. The majority of respondents (56 %) stated they hold one to two meetings per year with the bank; the smallest share (4 %) hold no meetings. In contrast, 32 % of firms engage in three to five meetings per year. The average number of meetings is 2.77. The impact of this interaction variable will be analyzed further in our multivariate analysis.

Because small firms are often considered informationally opaque, relationship banking may be of significant value as a means to mitigate information asymmetries between borrowers and lenders (Harhoff and Körting 1998; Hernández-Cánovas and Martínez-Solano 2010). As Boot (2000) notes, access to information is by nature intertwined with the concept of relationship lending. And, according to Elsas (2001), the relationship bank likely has an information advantage over its competitors. With respect to the assessment of the level of information, Elsas and Krahnen (2003) find that housebanks establish an informationally strong relationship with companies. Our results appear to confirm this finding.

A bank's timely liquidity provision is often based on the amount of information provided by the firm, and the amount of information gathered by the bank in the past (Fischer 2000). Relationship banks show a lower probability of requiring more information from a firm during times of distress (Hainz and Wiegand 2013). In addition, bank relationships characterized by low asymmetric information tend to have longer maturities.

Kirschenmann and Norden (2012) find that small companies can use the advantage of reduced asymmetric information and their improved bargaining power to obtain better credit terms. This point will also be analyzed in the context of the multivariate analyses in section 4.2. The descriptive analysis tests whether firms perceive they engage in more information exchange on average with their housebanks than with other banks.[89] The largest share of respondents (29 %) strongly agree that more information is exchanged with this bank; the smallest share (11 %) did not agree.

Boot (2000) finds that relationship banking includes funding activities, as well as other financial services, such as transaction, cash management, and pension plans. This notion is shared by Degryse and Van Cayseele (2000). This note that one source of information is related to the scope of a firm-bank relationship, which in turn relates to the breadth of a relationship or the amount of services a firm obtains from a bank. Hence, the supply of other financial services should be of great value in lending relationships. We therefore asked participants to specify whether their housebank provides most of their other banking services besides loan financing (e.g., payments and cash management). The largest share (48 %) strongly agreed that their primary bank provides most of their other banking services; only 4 % disagreed.

Ongena and Smith (2000a, 2000b) posit that a greater scope of financial services may hold advantages for both the customer and the bank, while Santikian (2014) finds that a more intense relationship (i.e., more financial services) is associated with higher credit availability at more favorable terms. We investigate this idea in the multivariate analyses in section 4.2. Cole (1998) finds that pre-existing relationships, where firms have purchased other financial services from a bank, are more important than length in increasing the likelihood that credit volume will be extended. When banks can learn more about the payment behavior of their customers, information asymmetries are reduced, and, consequently, the bank will be better at adapting contracts to meet its customers' financial needs.

Participants were also asked whether they believe their housebanks would fully support them during times of distress, and whether they thus carry an implicit responsibility to the company in a liquidity squeeze. This support may be reflected in, e.g., the suspension of loan repayments for a defined period. We found that 62 % of respondents perceive their bank as a support system and agree that they would expect the bank to take on a special responsibility during distress. Only 19 % believe their bank would partially support them in a liquidity squeeze, while 6 % indicated the statement would not apply at all. The answers offer important insights, because, during the last financial crisis, headlines repeatedly stated that SMEs needed alternative sources of funding because banks were not willing to extend credit (Padevit 2014).

---

89 The variable *Information Exchange* was only tested for companies that indicated they have more than one bank relationship.

Aoki and Dinç (1997) find that mutual expectations are central to the customer-bank relationship. For example, entrepreneurs expect assistance during temporary financial difficulties. Banks, in turn, expect future earnings and follow-up financing. These expectations can be traced to the commitment inherent in the definition of relationship lending, which helps maintain these expectations over time.

Harhoff and Körting (1998) examine the mutual trust concept between the firm and the bank and find that the relationship is characterized by high levels of trust. Hernández-Cánovas and Martínez-Solano (2010) find similar results for their sample of Spanish firms, and Ongena and Smith (2000a, 2000b) document further that the relationship between a customer and its housebank tends to extend beyond the execution of simple, anonymous financial transactions. According to Elsas (2001), relationship banks are not only long-term in nature, but also involve a higher level of trust.

The variable, *Trust,* therefore, measures whether participants believe that the relationship is characterized by high levels of trust. We measure it by asking respondents for their opinion on the following statement: "In my opinion there is great trust between our company and this bank." The largest share of respondents (74 %) agrees there is great trust between the firm and the most important bank, while only 3 % did not agree.

Hernández-Cánovas and Martínez-Solano (2010) state that banks are more likely to renew financing for firms with which they have a relationship based on trust.[90] And Howorth and Moro (2012) show for Italy that the level of trust, rather than the duration of the relationship, influences the lending decision. Thus, the level of trust has a decreasing effect on interest rates. Guiso (2003) also documents a positive effect on credit availability. Hence, the regression analysis will investigate the effect of trust on the credit parameters and aims to determine whether these empirical findings can be confirmed or dismissed.

Overall, a clear picture emerges as to how the firms in our dataset perceive the relationship with their most important bank. Most of the companies have a designated *Loan Officer* in place that is their primary point of contact. With regard to the *Number* of bank relationships and the median value, the companies have two bank relationships. For the *Duration* of the relationship, the average is almost

---

90 In addition, companies were asked to indicate whether they planned to change their most important bank soon. Only 7 % stated they planned to change their banks, while 93 % are not. Of those planning to change, 5 % stated that the reason was overly high collateral and/or guarantee requirements. 18 % felt that credit availability was too low, and 31 % said the costs for loans were too high. 46 % noted other reasons.

Table 4-3: Overview of variables of family firms versus non-family firms

This table shows the variables *Number, Trust, Scope,* and *Equity Ratio* of family firms and non-family firms from the empirical evaluation.

	Family firms			Non-family firms		
Variables	**N**	**Mean**	**Median**	**N**	**Mean**	**Median**
Number	408	2.85	3	168	2.82	2
Trust	408	4.07	4	168	4.06	4
Scope	408	4.04	4	168	4.07	5
Equity Ratio	408	41.03	35	168	39.21	33

thirty years. Firms appear to maintain longer relationships with their most important banks than with other banks. Moreover, firms have on average 47 % of *Finance Share* from their most important bank on their balance sheets. And, according to the results, in most cases, a savings bank is the most important bank type.

With respect to the interaction process, the results show that *Meeting Frequency* is on average two to three times per year. In this context, participants confirmed that the *Information Exchange* is greater with this one bank than with other banks. Furthermore, the number of banking services provided by the most important bank for the firm, called the *Scope* of the relationship, is higher than with any other bank. This bank is also perceived by survey participants as carrying an implicit responsibility toward the firm for the case the firm experiences distress. The relationship is also characterized strongly by *Trust*.

Overall, we classify a firm-bank relationship as a housebank relationship if it follows the definition in section 2.4.2. The relationship must be long-term in nature, involve great mutual trust, offer an information advantage, and imply a special responsibility during times of financial distress. Our descriptive findings confirm the empirical findings in the literature review.

4.1.5 Family firms versus non-family firms

Family firms as well as non-family firms expressed that they have at least one designated loan officer. In addition, savings banks were expressed as main bank by most of the participants. Family firms tend to have one more bank relationship with respect to the median value than non-family firms. Family firms and non-family firms expressed that there is trust in the firm-bank relationship. In addition, the firms in both samples indicated that the housebank provides most of the other bank services for the firm besides debt financing. Moreover, the

Table 4-4: Differences between family firms and non-family firms

This table shows the mean, median, and differences between the mean and the median for the variables *Meeting Frequency, Duration*, and *Finance Share* for the sample of 408 family firms and 168 non-family firms. We test the differences using the two-sample *t*-test and the two-sample Wilcoxon rank-sum test (Mann-Whitney). Significance is measured at the 10 % (*), 5 % (**), and 1 % (***) levels. The significance of the two-sample *t*-test is shown next to the mean, while the significance of the two-sample Wilcoxon rank-sum test (Mann-Whitney) is next to the median.[91]

	Family firms			**Non-family firms**			**Differences**	
Variables	**N**	**Mean**	**Median**	**N**	**Mean**	**Median**	**Mean**	**Median**
Meeting Frequency	408	2.71	2	168	2.90	2	-0,19	0
Duration	408	31.17	25	168	25.35	22	5.82***	3***
Finance Share	408	51.07	53	168	36.64	20	14.43***	32.5***

equity ratio showed to be slightly higher in the family firm sample. Table 4-3 presents the results of the descriptive statistics of family and non-family firms.

Hypotheses 4 through 6 investigate differences in family firms versus non-family firms. In order to provide some descriptive details with respect to these differences, we test how the following three variables for differences manifest themselves: *Meeting Frequency, Duration*, and *Finance Share.* The variable *Meeting Frequency* tests the fourth hypothesis, which argues that family firms have more contact with their housebanks than non-family firms. This is based on the assumption that family firms generally exhibit different behavior when engaging with stakeholders than non-family firms. The variable *Duration* tests the fifth hypothesis, which assumes that family firms maintain a longer relationship with their housebanks than non-family firms. This is because family firms often have longer-term planning horizon.

The variable *Finance Share* tests the sixth hypothesis, which assumes that family firms obtain the dominant share of their debt financing from their housebank, compared to non-family firms that prefer to spread their credit needs. Table 4-4 illustrates the mean, median, and difference between *Family Firms* and *Non-Family Firms* for the variables *Meeting Frequency, Duration*, and *Finance Share.*

91 The dataset is comprised of 408 family firms and 168 non-family firms. Therefore, there may be a bias toward family firms. However, the findings were carefully considered, as also shown in sections 4.2.5, 4.2.6, and 4.2.7.

Family firms are attractive relationship partners and are usually in a good position to develop and nurture social capital. Thus, their interactions with financiers represent a key factor in maintaining stable and sustainable funding for the company, and in the company's relationship management (Schraml 2010).

This study attempts to detect this presumed relationship by studying *Meeting Frequency* of family versus non-family firms in our sample. We find that *Family Firms* do not appear to have more meetings with their housebanks than *Non-Family Firms* because the test results are not significant and the null hypothesis cannot be rejected. *Family Firms* and *Non-Family Firms* hold on average two to three meetings per year. On the one hand, having more contact with a housebank may signal good relationship management with one of a firm's most important stakeholders: banks. However, on the other side, firms may be required to have more meetings because of, for example, financial struggles. However, in light of the relatively high equity ratio, the latter reason appears unlikely.

Mach (2007) finds evidence that the top objective of German family firms is long-term value orientation. Family enterprises are developing long-term goals and are thereby ensuring the survival of the company (Koeberle-Schmid et al. 2012; Mach 2007). At the same time, long-term orientation plays an important role in building sustainable relationships with stakeholders. It is also important for the development of a positive reputation (Le Breton-Miller and Miller 2006).

Table 4-4 exemplifies the evaluation of relationship duration between family and non-family firms. With respect to the Wilcoxon rank-sum test, the *Family Firms* in the sample seem to maintain longer bank relationships than *Non-Family Firms* because the test results are significant and the null hypothesis is rejected. *Family Firms* show on average a relationship duration of 31.17 years, while *Non-Family Firms* show an average of 25.35 years. Regarding housebank design, relationship duration appears to be a significant aspect, because it means repeated interactions between the firm and a bank. This longevity provides the basis for a stronger development of trust.

Le Breton-Miller and Miller (2006) argue that family companies undertake more investments in durable relations with stakeholders, which may lead to superior stakeholder retention and stable partners. Therefore, in the context of the literature review, we expect that family firms will obtain the dominant portion of their debt financing from their housebanks in order to build and maintain a close relationship with this important stakeholder.

Table 4-4 illustrates the breakdown of bank financing share between family and non-family firms. In our sample, *Family Firms* obtain more debt financing from their housebanks than *Non-Family Firms* because the test results are significant and the null hypothesis can be rejected. *Family Firms* show on average a

51.07 % share of debt financing on their balance sheets from their housebanks, while *Non-Family Firms* show a 36.64 % average.

Sirmon and Hitt (2003) argue that the social capital of the family increases when effective relationships with stakeholders are in place (e.g., housebanks). Social capital is defined as the "sum of the actual and potential resources embedded within, available through, and derived from the network" (Nahapiet and Ghoshal 1998, p. 243). Ultimately, according to Le Breton-Miller and Miller (2006), long-term relationships are more easily formed in family businesses where CEOs are influential and have a longer tenure.

4.2 Multivariate analyses

We present the results of our multivariate regression analyses in the following sections. We first divide the explanatory variables into groups, introduced consecutively to observe potential effects in detail. Model (1) includes the loan characteristics: Finance Share, Lines of Credit, Short-term Bank Debt, and Long-term Bank Debt. Model (2) encompasses the relationship characteristics, which include the variables: *Number* of bank relationships from which the firm borrows, *Duration* of the bank relationship, *Trust* based on experience, *Meeting Frequency*, *Scope* of the banking services, *Loan Officer*, and *Bank Type*. Model (3) introduces the firm characteristics: *Firm Age, Firm Size, Limited Liability Company, Equity Ratio, Sales Growth*, and *Financial Distress*, as well as control variables composed of different industries: *Construction, Trade, Hospitality, Tourism, Traffic, Transportation*, and *Service Industry*. Model (4) then presents the loan characteristics, firm characteristics, and control variables. Finally, Model (5) includes all the endogenous variables. Sections 4.2.1 to 4.2.4 present a detailed discussion of the multivariate regression results for the full sample, while sections 4.2.5 to 4.2.7 discuss the results for the sample of family versus non-family firms.

4.2.1 Full sample - Collateral requirements

The value of lending relationships can be measured via collateral requirements. This is because collateral is key to managing moral hazard, although it puts a (deadweight) repossession cost on the bank (Boot et al. 1991), as explained in section 2.2.1. To minimize risk arising from a company's operations, a bank may request the firm to deposit collateral and/or guarantees. The variable *Collateral Requirements* indicates the secured share of the volume of the most important credit line. The collateral may include business collateral and/or personal guarantees. Collateral in loan agreements demonstrates incentive and signaling

Table 4-5: Probit regression – Full sample – Collateral requirements

This table shows the regression results for the dependent variable *Collateral Requirements* for the sample of 576 firms. This variable documents the proportion of collateral and guarantees that were required to obtain the most important credit line, and then, for the purpose of the multivariate analysis, defines a dummy variable that equals 1 when the response exceeds the median sample responses, and 0 otherwise. The loan characteristics are measured by the variable *Finance Share*, which indicates the overall share of total debt financing of the firm that is financed by the most important bank. It is measured with a metric input in %. The variable *Lines of Credit* indicates the frequency with which a firm finances its business with lines of credit. The variable *Short-term Bank Debt* indicates the frequency with which the firm uses bank financing of less than one year, and the variable *Long-term Bank Debt* indicates that for more than one year. Variables are measured on an ordinal five-point Likert-type scale ranging from 1 (never) to 5 (always). The variable *Number* of banks the firm works with is measured with a metric input with integer numbers. The variable *Duration* shows the number of years the firm has worked with the most important bank and is measured with a metric input in years. The variable *Trust* indicates whether trust exists between the firm and the bank and is measured on an ordinal five-point Likert-type scale ranging from 1 (does not apply at all) to 5 (strongly applies). The variable *Meeting Frequency* indicates how often on average physical or non-physical meetings between the firm and the bank occur per year and is measured with a metric input. The variable *Scope* shows whether the bank provides most of the other bank services for the firm besides debt financing and is measured on an ordinal five-point Likert scale ranging from 1 (does not apply at all) to 5 (strongly applies). The variable *Loan Officer* indicates whether the firm has a permanent relationship manager at the bank and is measured on a dichotomous scale. The variable *Bank Type* indicates whether the bank is savings, co-operative, or private bank, and is measured on a dichotomous scale that equals 1 for *Savings Banks*, and 0 otherwise. The variable *Firm Age* indicates the number of years since the firm's founding, as recorded in the survey, and is measured on a metric input. The variable *Firm Size* is measured by the average number of employees in the year 2015 and is measured with a metric input. The variable *Legal Form* indicates whether the firm is a limited liability company (GmbH, AG, KGaA, GmbH & Co. KG) or an unlimited liability company (KG, OHG, or GbR), and is measured on a dichotomous scale that equals 1 for *Limited Liability Company*, and 0 otherwise. The variable *Equity Ratio* indicates the solvency of the firm as measured by the firm's equity ratio in the year 2015 according to the annual results and is measured with a metric input in %. The variable *Sales Growth* indicates the firm's sales growth in the year 2015 according to the annual results and is measured with a metric input in %. The variable *Financial Distress* is a dichotomous variable indicates whether the firm had been in financial distress since 2007. The variable *Industry* is a set of industry variables indicating to which industry the firm belongs, which is measured on a nominal scale, and is represented by the *Construction Industry*, the *Trade, Hospitality, Tourism Industry*, the *Traffic and Transportation Industry*, and the *Service Industry*. Standard errors are corrected for heteroskedasticity and given in parentheses. *, **, and *** denote statistical significance at the 10 %, 5 %, and 1 % levels, respectively.

Table 4-5: Continued

Variables	(1)	(2)	(3)	(4)	(5)
Loan characteristics					
Finance Share	0.014***				0.014***
	(0.002)				(0.002)
Lines of Credit	0.945***				0.935***
	(0.148)				(0.156)
Short-term Bank Debt	0.049				0.046
	(0.166)				(0.172)
Long-term Bank Debt	0.482***				0.487***
	(0.150)				(0.162)
Relationship characteristics					
Number		0.217**		0.134**	0.041**
		(0.106)		(0.125)	(0.145)
Duration		-0.074		-0.054	-0.004
		(0.069)		(0.089)	(0.102)
Trust		-0.130*		-0.118*	-0.016*
		(0.130)		(0.134)	(0.153)
Meeting Frequency		0.436***		0.379***	0.037***
		(0.112)		(0.119)	(0.135)
Scope		0.072		0.058	0.080
		(0.117)		(0.121)	(0.139)
Loan Officer		0.056		0.041	-0.107
		(0.149)		(0.156)	(0.183)
Bank Type - Savings Bank		0.194**		0.182**	0.162**
		(0.111)		(0.115)	(0.130)
Firm characteristics					
Firm Age			-0.056**	-0.043**	-0.097**
			(0.082)	(0.096)	(0.111)
Firm Size			-0.058**	-0.024**	-0.074**
			(0.042)	(0.048)	(0.054)
Legal Form (Limited Liability Company)			-0.144**	-0.137**	-0.105**
			(0.125)	(0.126)	(0.146)
Equity Ratio			-0.007***	-0.007***	-0.001***
			(0.002)	(0.002)	(0.002)
Sales Growth			0.001	-0.001	-0.001
			(0.004)	(0.004)	(0.005)
Financial Distress			0.640***	0.591***	0.316**

Table 4-5: Continued

Variables	**(1)**	**(2)**	**(3)**	**(4)**	**(5)**
			(0.126)	(0.129)	(0.151)
Control variables					
Construction Industry			0.423***	0.425**	0.487***
			(0.163)	(0.165)	(0.186)
Trade, Hospitality, and Tourism Industry			0.268	0.231	0.464
			(0.271)	(0.274)	(0.321)
Traffic and Transportation Industry			0.180	0.113	0.549*
			(0.260)	(0.265)	(0.308)
Service Industry			-0.068	-0.046	0.034
			(0.137)	(0.139)	(0.156)
Observations	576	576	576	576	576
Log-likelihood	-276.935	-379.842	-361.657	-352.847	-267.361
Pseudo R2	0.298	0.036	0.092	0.115	0.330
LR chi2	234.579	28.765	72.861	90.468	260.364

effects, which serve to clarify moral hazard and adverse selection problems under asymmetric information. If a loan is secured, the borrower's incentive to take on a riskier plan after obtaining it is thus discouraged.

Additionally, collateralization may encourage a borrower to disclose hidden risks (Besanko and Thakor 1987; Lehmann and Neuberger 2001). We measured the responses for this dependent variable on a five-point Likert-type scale, ranging from 5 = "does not apply at all" to 1 = "strongly applies." Then, for the purposes of the multivariate analysis, we define a dummy variable that equals 1 when the response exceeds the median sample responses, and 0 otherwise.

Collateral is pledged in approximately 57 % of the cases, as described in the descriptive statistics in section 4.1.3. The results of the probit models are in Table 4-5, as mentioned earlier, and the exogenous variables are added gradually.

The probit regression evaluates the full sample of 576 firms in each model. Model (5), which includes all explanatory variables, gives the best estimation, with a pseudo R2 of 0.33, a log-likelihood of -267.361, and a LR chi2 of 260.364. Model (1) has slightly lower explanatory power than Model (5). However, it is not surprising that loan characteristics have the second greatest influence, as these variables are determined by the bank itself. Model (2) also contains some critical explanatory content.

In the following sections, we present and interpret the regression coefficients for each probit regression. The predicted probability of admission can be measured by means of these coefficients. However, interpretation is not as straightforward as it would be for coefficients in linear or logit regressions. In a probit regression, the increase in probability attributed to a one-unit increase in a given predictor depends on both the values of the other predictors and the beginning value of the given predictors. A positive coefficient implies that an increase in the predictor will lead to an increase in predicted probability, while a negative coefficient implies it will lead to a decrease in predicted probability (UCLA Statistical Consulting Group 2006a).

Model (1) presents the loan characteristics. Note that the coefficient of the variable *Finance Share* carries a positive coefficient that is significant at the 1 % level. *Finance Share* captures the share of total debt financing of the firm that is financed by the most important bank. De Bodt et al. (2005) and Elsas (2005) also study the bank's share of a borrower's total debt financing. They find that housebank status is systematically related to debt financing share. The bank's crucial lending position may create access to distinct sources of information and may decrease competitive pressure from other banks. This result is in line with the result in Table 2-6, which illustrates the overall effects regarding the costs and benefits of the housebank relationship (see also Jiménez, Salas, and Saurina 2006).

The variable *Lines of Credit*, expressing the frequency with which the firm finances its business with lines of credit, also shows a positive coefficient significant at the 1 % level. Moreover, the variable *Long-term Bank Debt*, meaning the frequency with which the firm uses bank financing of greater than one year, also has a positive and highly significant effect on the dependent variable. Only the variable *Short-term Bank Debt* lacks significance.

It appears as if long-term loans have a greater probability of a collateral requirement, while the companies that finance themselves with short-term debt show no significant coefficients. This result suggests there is a difference in the use of guarantees depending on the type of loan. If the company obtains more long-term loans from the bank, the bank may, therefore, be exposed to more severe moral hazard issues. For shorter-term loans, there is less risk of opportunistic behavior on the part of the company, and, thus, they have no significant effect on collateral requirements. This result suggests that banks take moral hazard issues into account when determining collateral requirements (Hernández-Cánovas and Martínez-Solano 2010).

Model (2) illustrates the relationship characteristics. The variable *Number* shows a positive coefficient that is significant at the 5 % level, suggesting that having multiple bank relationships increases the amount of collateral needed for the most important line of credit. Accordingly, companies that maintain more bank relationships tend to be subject to higher collateral requirements. This may be attributable to the fact that each bank (even the most important one) has less access to the company's non-collateralized assets in the case of bankruptcy. As a result, collateral requirements rise. Hence, the number of banks has a positive sign and highlights that collateral is demanded by banks more often when the company borrows from multiple banks.[92]

This finding follows Boot and Thakor (1994), who find that a bank is more likely to demand collateral to secure its own position because of the possibility that the company will do business with multiple banks (see also Harhoff and Körting 1998; Niskanen and Niskanen 2000; and Jiménez et al. 2009). With respect to the literature review, our results confirm this evaluation for bank-based financial systems. However, the finding is in contrast to Ziane (2003), Pozzolo (2004), Menkhoff et al. (2006), Jiménez et al. (2006), Wen and Tseng (2006), and Hübler et al. (2008). Three of these studies focus on bank-based systems in Spain, Italy, and France. Thus, Jiménez et al. (2006) find that their results provide direct evidence of a negative correlation between collateral and borrower risk. In addition, Pozzolo (2004) states that the share of secured loans decreases with the number of bank relationships, possibly because multi-banking decreases the incentives to monitor borrowers' behavior or to require collateral of companies in financial distress (see also Rajan and Winton 1995).

The variable *Duration* carries negative coefficients in the model specifications, but they are insignificant. This result is in contrast to the literature evaluation in Table 2-6, which indicates that length of the lending relationship increases the amount of securities that must be pledged in bank-based financial systems.

With respect to exclusivity and duration, Hernández-Cánovas and Martínez-Solano (2006) document that banks exploit their monopoly power over a firm to increase profits. They find that the duration of a bank relationship contributes to the likelihood of pledging guarantees, which is in accordance with results from Italy and Japan (see also Jiménez et al. 2006). Berger et al. (2011) find for Bolivia that collateral pledging due to ex ante information asymmetries is associated

92 Sometimes banks also rank second or third in security pledging. However, this was not part of the survey, as the pretest showed that the majority of respondents could not distinguish between ranks, so the answers would likely have been too unspecific.

with companies that have relatively short relationships, and which are not well known to the lender. In contrast, Degryse and Van Cayseele (2000) show for Belgium that collateral requirements marginally decrease with the duration of the lending relationship, which contrasts with Ono et al. (2012), Ono and Uesugi (2009), and Kano et al. (2011). However, our study finds no effect of *Duration* on collateral requirements.

The variable *Trust* shows a negative coefficient that is significant at the 10 % level, suggesting that level of trust tends to decrease the amount of securities required with the most important line of credit. In contrast, the few studies in Table 2-6 that study *Trust* found a positive relationship. For example, Hernández-Cánovas and Martínez-Solano (2010) document a positive sign on trust, which demonstrates that companies actually need to pledge more collateral to banks with which they have a relationship of trust.

The variable *Meeting Frequency* describes how often physical or non-physical meetings between the firm and the bank occur on average per year. The variable carries a positive coefficient and is significant at the 1 % level. Entrepreneurs usually possess all the necessary information about their future investment projects. But banks generally do not have as complete an information set about firms' projects. Housebanks, as a firm's first financier, tend to have an informational advantage, which enables them to secure their loans with better collateral and/or guarantees (see also Lehmann and Neuberger 2001; Machauer and Weber 1998; and Van Damme 1994).

Hernández-Cánovas and Martínez-Solano (2010) find that, due to the problem of adverse selection, collateral is being used to reduce issues triggered by information asymmetries. The results of this variable point in a different direction. They suggest that a more contact increases the amount of securities required, and, hence, an informational advantage may allow the relationship lender to protect their loans with better collateral and/or guarantees. The bank may also be better at assessing the quality of collateral, and a lender would typically try to secure its loans with the highest quality collateral.

The variables *Scope* and *Loan Officer* do not display significant coefficients. With respect to the scope of the lending relationship, this result is in contrast to, for example, Degryse and Van Cayseele (2000), Jiménez et al. (2006), and Ziane (2003). These authors document that collateral requirements increase with the scope of products a firm purchases from its bank. This result also differs from the overall evaluation of bank-based financial systems in Table 2-6.

The variable *Bank Type* is included to assess the behavior of the three types: private banks, cooperative banks, and savings banks. Since including all banks would have led to multicollinearity, *Savings Banks* are included in this regression. The coefficient of the variable shows a positive coefficient that is significant at the 5 % level, suggesting that borrowers pledge more collateral at savings banks. This finding is in line with Jiménez et al. (2009), who document that the likelihood of collateralized loans is higher with local banks (those with headquarters and decision-making power physically closer to the borrower) than with more distant banks.

According to Jiménez et al. (2009), the likelihood of collateral for loans increases as bank-firm organizational proximity increases (the inverse of distance), which is consistent with Inderst and Mueller (2007). They note that, in an imperfectly competitive loan market, a local relationship lender has an information advantage over more distant transaction lenders. "Competitive pressure from the transaction lenders prevents the local lender from extracting the full surplus from projects, so that she inefficiently rejects marginally profitable projects" (Inderst and Mueller 2007, p. 1). The authors also find, "that borrowers for whom local lenders have a relatively smaller information advantage face higher collateral requirements [...]" (Inderst and Mueller 2007, p. 1).

Our results show that the variable *Meeting Frequency* appears to demonstrate a particular increase in the incidence of pledging collateral. This finding is consistent with the theory that explains collateral as a solution to moral hazard problems. In other words, the relationship lender will try to secure its position by requiring the borrower to pledge collateral. In addition, Jiménez et al. (2009) state that distant banks rely on hard data in their lending decisions and lend to borrowers of observed high credit quality. Thus, the likelihood of collateral being required for loans granted by distant lenders is lower than for loans granted by local lenders.

Model (3) shows that firm characteristics, especially *Firm Age* and *Firm Size*, offer proxies for firm-bank asymmetry problems. Firm age reflects the reputation that the company conveys to the market (Harhoff and Körting 1998; Petersen and Rajan 1994). Firm size reflects the proportion of information opacity (Berger et al. 2001). Accordingly, it would be less costly for a bank to obtain information about large companies or those with long histories.

Firm Age shows a negative coefficient that is significant at the 5 % level. This means that older companies tend to pledge less collateral. *Firm Size* exhibits a negative coefficient that is also significant at the 5 % level. According to these results, a lender that is larger and older is less likely to secure its loans. Firm size effects may also have explanatory power for bargaining power, and age effects may influence and reflect the quality of firms (Harhoff and Körting 1998). It is reasonable to assume that larger companies with greater negotiating power are better at mitigating collateral requirements than smaller companies (Harhoff and Körting 1998).

Therefore, the results document that larger firms are likely to pledge less collateral, probably due to the smaller information asymmetries for larger than smaller companies (Niskanen and Niskanen 2000), while smaller companies are more likely to pledge collateral and/or personal guarantees (Hernández-Cánovas and Martínez-Solano 2010). However, the relation among firm age, size, and collateral may be reversed when the company uses collateral to display its quality. Hernández-Cánovas and Martínez-Solano (2010) document that the collateralization of a loan decreases the probability that the firm will engage in opportunistic actions that increase the risk of default.

Moreover, we include the variable *Limited Liability Company* in the probit regression analysis. In the case of corporations, owners have a limitation of liability to the assets of the company, that is, they are not liable to private assets. In contrast to corporations, partners at an OHG or partnership are personally liable without limitation. This includes all partners at the OHG and the general partners at the KG (possibly "bypassed" by the GmbH & Co. KG). Consequently, limited liability companies are expected to pledge business collateral instead of personal guarantees more often. Partnerships cannot separate these liabilities, and, thus, are more likely to have to deposit personal guarantees as securities (Avery, Bostic, and Samolyk 1998).

Section 4.2.2 will break out personal from business collateral, and will explore in more detail whether there is an influence of the legal form on the amount of business collateral and personal guarantees required. In Model (3), the variable *Limited Liability Company* exhibits a negative coefficient that is significant at the 5 % level. Therefore, the incidences of collateral decrease when corporations are compared to unlimited liability companies (the omitted category). This result is broadly consistent with evidence that collateral is pledged more often by opaque firms which often carry the legal form of unlimited liability (Berger et al. 2011).

In addition, Model (3) introduces two balance sheet indicators. A firm's bargaining power in the bank relationship is strongly associated with its financial performance (Fredriksson and Moro 2014). Credit quality is the main factor banks consider when deciding on collateral requirements (Jiménez et al. 2006). The variable *Equity Ratio* reflects the solvency of the firm in the year 2015 according to the annual results, and it carries a negative effect that is significant at the 1 % level. Collateral is likely to be a response to adverse selection. Because credit markets under perfect information are hypothetical, collateral requirements are assumed to be a response to imperfect information. Collateral helps reveal information about the default risk of loan applicants (Bester 1985).

Bester (1985) argues further that banks require collateral in order to categorize borrowers' risk levels efficiently. Thus, the role of collateral is to provide an incentive for the borrower to try to operate the business as a going concern (Chan and Kanatas 1985). Hence, low-risk firms tend to pledge a sufficient amount of collateral to distinguish themselves from high-risk firms.

Besanko and Thakor (1987) document the same results. They find that low-risk borrowers tend to pledge more collateral than high-risk borrowers. However, our findings show that collateral requirements decrease as the equity ratio increases. Of course, a better or higher equity ratio also indicates higher bargaining power, especially in renegotiations.

These results are in line with Howorth and Moro (2012), who document that companies that do not pledge collateral are likely to be considered low risk. The variable *Sales Growth* carries no significant coefficient.

The variable *Financial Distress* shows a positive coefficient at the 1 % level. The distress variable has significant explanatory influence. Firms that were in financial distress prior to the questionnaire and subsequent to the 2007-2009 financial crisis show a greater probability of collateral requirements for a credit line. The distress variable has positive coefficients because the bank is more likely to require collateral if the company has been in financial distress. Thus, it highlights that collateral requirements were initially tightened in the post-crisis period of a company.

Model (3) also introduces dummy industry variables that control for various industry affiliations. The coefficient of the *Construction Industry* variable has a positive and significant effect at the 1 % level on the dependent variable. Collateral requirements appear considerably more likely in the construction industry than in other industries. This finding highlights that firms in this industry are more likely to provide fixed assets, such as vehicles and machinery, as collateral. The other industries do not carry a significant coefficient except *Traffic, Transportation*, which carries a positive coefficient at the 10 % level but only in Model (5). Hence, this finding is excluded.

Model (4) shows the relationship and firm characteristics as well as the control variables, and Model (5) presents all the endogenous variables and confirms the significances. Section 4.2.2 investigates whether private assets or business assets were provided as security for the credit line.

4.2.2 Full sample - Collateral type

When studying the variable *Collateral Requirements* in the field of small business finance, analyzing the separation between personal and firm wealth is also instructive (see also Avery et al. 1998; De Bodt et al. 2005). A further distinction can be made between business collateral (assets of the borrowing firm) and personal guarantees (assets outside the firm belonging to the owner of the firm).[93]

The theoretical models in the literature generally focus on business collateral. Unfortunately, data limitations prevent a clean distinction between the two, as studies typically focus on the type of asset pledged rather than its ownership (Berger and Udell 1995a). This study examines the *Collateral Type* pledged to obtain the credit line, and it therefore differentiates between: 1) collateral on the assets of the owner's wealth (*Personal Guarantees*), and 2) collateral on the assets of the company (*Business Collateral*). We explore the frequency of personal guarantees versus business collateral and use the variable *Personal Guarantees* as dependent variable in the regression analysis.

Business Collateral includes business assets such as company equipment and machinery. *Personal Guarantees* include an authorization for the bank to liquidate any or all personal assets to repay the debt if the company is unable to pay. Such assets may include, for example, cash accounts and the owner's personal property.

Academic literature on the relationship between personal guarantees and business collateral in small business finance has been limited thus far. This is because only certain datasets capture the information necessary to allow for a complete differentiation by collateral type. Therefore, little is known about the impact of using different forms of collateral. But a fuller analysis of this topic is crucial, because companies whose owners lack the resources to pledge credible personal commitments may be shut out of the small business loan market.

Ang, Lin, and Tyler (1995), Avery et al. (1998), Berger and Udell (1995a), De Bodt et al. (2005), and Hernández-Cánovas and Martínez-Solano (2010) are among the empirical studies that have investigated the meaning of personal guarantees in loan financing, particularly for small firms. In this context, Berger and Udell (1995a) distinguish between firm assets pledged as collateral and owner assets provided as personal guarantees.

De Bodt et al. (2005) also examine the main types of collateral pledged for financial debts, while Hernández-Cánovas and Martínez-Solano (2010) analyze collateral type for loans and credit. Moreover, Avery et al. (1998) study lines of credit by using the 1993 NSSBF loan-based sample. The authors document that personal guarantees and assets are potentially important credit enhancements

93 These two forms of collateral are sometimes referred to as "inside" and "outside" collateral (Berger and Udell 1995a).

for small companies seeking credit. They may even be suitable as substitutes for firm collateral, at least for lines of credit.

Financial intermediaries may have more difficulty in determining the riskiness of loan arrangements with smaller companies. If true creditworthiness is not fully understood by the bank, it can face serious adverse selection risk. A pledge of personal guarantees, which Avery et al. (1998) term personal commitments, is regarded as a credit enhancement that can limit the risk of not receiving lending. According to Avery et al. (1998), company owners deciding to pledge personal commitments should either be granted credit they would otherwise not be qualified for or be able to negotiate better credit terms.

Bester (1985) studies potential adverse selection issues where borrowers have better information than bank. He argues that creditworthy borrowers can use personal commitments as a signal of their quality. Furthermore, regarding the risk of moral hazard, personal commitments may mitigate incentives for wrongdoing, because borrowers' personal wealth is at stake. Therefore, an understanding of the relationships among company risk, personal commitments, moral hazard, and adverse selection is vital (Avery et al. 1998). Table 4-6 presents the results of the multivariate regression analysis for the endogenous variable *Personal Guarantees.*

The probit regression evaluates 576 firms in the model. Model (5) includes all explanatory variables and shows the best estimation with a pseudo R2 of 0.129, a log-likelihood of -194.066, and a LR chi2 of 57.441. Model (1) presents the loan characteristics. The variables *Finance Share* and *Lines of Credit* carry positive coefficients. But while *Finance Share* is insignificant, *Lines of Credit* has a significance at the 5 % level. This means that the level of personal guarantees rises with the use of the credit line. Furthermore, the variable *Short-term Bank Debt* demonstrates a positive influence at the 10 % level, but there is no significant impact of *Long-term Bank Debt.*

Model (2) shows the relationship characteristics. The variable *Number* carries a negative coefficient on the dependent variable *Personal Guarantees* that is significant at the 1 % level. The variable *Duration* also documents a negative coefficient that is significant at the 5 % level. This variable has a decreasing effect on the dependent variable *Personal Guarantees.* Thus, the number and duration of bank relationships have a decreasing effect on personal guarantees. Over the course of the relationship, the capacities and character of the entrepreneur become clearer. The lender then seems to ease the requirement that personal assets be pledged as collateral.

The variable *Trust* carries a negative coefficient that is significant at the 5 % level, and it therefore, has a decreasing effect on the dependent variable *Personal*

Table 4-6: Probit regression – Full sample – Personal guarantees

This table shows the regression results for the dependent variable *Personal Guarantees* for the sample of 576 firms. This variable documents whether the main type of collateral pledged to obtain the most important credit line was personal guarantees on the firm owner's assets. The loan characteristics are measured by the variable *Finance Share*, which indicates the overall share of total debt financing of the firm that is financed by the most important bank. It is measured with a metric input in %. The variable *Lines of Credit* indicates the frequency with which a firm finances its business with lines of credit. The variable *Short-term Bank Debt* indicates the frequency with which the firm uses bank financing of less than one year, and the variable *Long-term Bank Debt* indicates that for more than one year. Variables are measured on an ordinal five-point Likert-type scale ranging from 1 (never) to 5 (always). The variable *Number* of banks the firm works with is measured with a metric input with integer numbers. The variable *Duration* shows the number of years the firm has worked with the most important bank and is measured with a metric input in years. The variable *Trust* indicates whether trust exists between the firm and the bank and is measured on an ordinal five-point Likert-type scale ranging from 1 (does not apply at all) to 5 (strongly applies). The variable *Meeting Frequency* indicates how often on average physical or non-physical meetings between the firm and the bank occur per year and is measured with a metric input. The variable *Scope* shows whether the bank provides most of the other bank services for the firm besides debt financing and is measured on an ordinal five-point Likert scale ranging from 1 (does not apply at all) to 5 (strongly applies). The variable *Loan Officer* indicates whether the firm has a permanent relationship manager at the bank and is measured on a dichotomous scale. The variable *Bank Type* indicates whether the bank is savings, co-operative, or private bank, and is measured on a dichotomous scale that equals 1 for *Savings Banks*, and 0 otherwise. The variable *Firm Age* indicates the number of years since the firm's founding, as recorded in the survey, and is measured on a metric input. The variable *Firm Size* is measured by the average number of employees in the year 2015 and is measured with a metric input. The variable *Legal Form* indicates whether the firm is a limited liability company (GmbH, AG, KGaA, GmbH & Co. KG) or an unlimited liability company (KG, OHG, or GbR), and is measured on a dichotomous scale that equals 1 for *Limited Liability Company*, and 0 otherwise. The variable *Equity Ratio* indicates the solvency of the firm as measured by the firm's equity ratio in the year 2015 according to the annual results and is measured with a metric input in %. The variable *Sales Growth* indicates the firm's sales growth in the year 2015 according to the annual results and is measured with a metric input in %. The variable *Financial Distress* is a dichotomous variable that indicates whether the firm had been in financial distress since 2007. The variable *Industry* is a set of industry variables indicating to which industry the firm belongs, which is measured on a nominal scale, and is represented by the *Construction Industry*, the *Trade, Hospitality, Tourism Industry*, the *Traffic and Transportation Industry*, and the *Service Industry*. Standard errors are corrected for heteroskedasticity and given in parentheses. *, **, and *** denote statistical significance at the 10 %, 5 %, and 1 % levels, respectively.

Table 4-6: Continued

Variables	(1)	(2)	(3)	(4)	(5)
Loan characteristics					
Finance Share	0.002				0.003
	(0.002)				(0.002)
Lines of Credit	0.337**				0.410**
	(0.165)				(0.182)
Short-term Bank Debt	0.050*				0.065*
	(0.173)				(0.187)
Long-term Bank Debt	0.191				0.183
	(0.160)				(0.189)
Relationship characteristics					
Number		-0.365***		-0.260***	-0.266***
		(0.138)		(0.163)	(0.169)
Duration		-0.177**		-0.101**	-0.105**
		(0.088)		(0.112)	(0.114)
Trust		-0.132**		-0.068**	-0.133**
		(0.168)		(0.175)	(0.181)
Meeting Frequency		0.089		0.115	0.065
		(0.141)		(0.153)	(0.161)
Scope		-0.081		-0.155	-0.170
		(0.148)		(0.158)	(0.162)
Loan Officer		-0.033*		-0.013*	-0.026*
		(0.185)		(0.193)	(0.198)
Bank Type - Savings Bank		0.262*		0.218*	0.209*
		(0.141)		(0.147)	(0.149)
Firm characteristics					
Firm Age			-0.020	-0.029*	-0.026*
			(0.106)	(0.121)	(0.124)
Firm Size			-0.146***	-0.118*	-0.126*
			(0.056)	(0.063)	(0.065)
Legal Form (Limited Liability Company)			-0.329*	-0.340*	-0.426**
			(0.172)	(0.175)	(0.182)
Equity Ratio			-0.000*	-0.000*	0.001
			(0.003)	(0.003)	(0.003)
Sales Growth			-0.012*	-0.013*	-0.011*
			(0.007)	(0.007)	(0.007)

(*continued on next page*)

Table 4-6: Continued

Financial Distress			0.386***	0.355**	0.290*
			(0.148)	(0.152)	(0.159)
Control variables					
Construction Industry			0.397**	0.432**	0.429**
			(0.200)	(0.203)	(0.205)
Trade, Hospitality, and Tourism Industry			-0.242	-0.269	-0.228
			(0.392)	(0.406)	(0.401)
Traffic and Transportation Industry			0.798	0.782	0.917
			(0.283)	(0.289)	(0.296)
Service Industry			0.380**	0.356**	0.395**
			(0.171)	(0.173)	(0.178)
Observations	576	576	576	576	576
Log-likelihood	-218.886	-214.439	-202.102	-199.072	-194.066
Pseudo R2	0.018	0.037	0.093	0.106	0.129
LR chi2	7.802	16.696	41.370	47.430	57.441

Guarantees. If the bank trusts the company, it does not need personal guarantees. This may be the first signs that a strategy built on trust could exist when considering lending relationships, even after the financial crisis. The variable *Meeting Frequency* carries a positive coefficient, but it is not significant, so there is no observable effect on the dependent variable *Personal Guarantees*. There is no significant effect of the variable *Scope* on collateral requirements.

The variable *Loan Officer* carries a negative coefficient that is significant at the 10 % level, suggesting that the relationship with the loan officer contributes to a decreasing effect on *Personal Guarantees*. This result shows how the variable may also be related to variables such as trust. Trust may be used somewhat to compensate loan officers for information asymmetries and may help determine a company's creditworthiness. Therefore, a trusting relationship can help banks and SMEs by giving the loan officer access to more soft information (Moro and Fink 2013). The variable *Bank Type* carries a positive coefficient that is significant at the 10 % level on *Personal Guarantees*. Thus, there is a slight indication that savings banks are more likely to require personal commitments.

Model (3) outlines the firm characteristics. *Firm Age* carries a negative coefficient which is, however, not significant in Model (3) but significant at the 10 %

level in Models (4) and (5). *Firm Size* shows a negative coefficient at the 1 % level in Model (3) and is significant at the 10 % level in Models (4) and (5). Accordingly, it decreases the requirement to pledge *Personal Guarantees*. As expected, larger companies are proxies for better information availability, as banks are better able to assess their creditworthiness.

Firm size does not present a significant effect on firm collateral. It may not be necessary to obtain personal guarantees because enough tangible assets are available to satisfy the lender. Larger companies generally own more assets than smaller companies, so firm assets may be adequate security for banks. Moreover, larger companies, similar to older companies, are likely to be better known by the bank. In this context, the costs associated with screening, contracting, monitoring, and servicing loans may lead to economies of scale, which would suggest that banks are leaning more toward larger borrowers in providing credit. Consequently, we expect that larger companies are required to pledge personal collateral less often than smaller companies (Avery et al. 1998; Lehmann and Neuberger 2001; Lehmann et al. 2004; Ogawa et al. 2010). Accordingly, older firms tend to pledge more business collateral than younger firms, again because older firms tend to have more tangible assets.

Firm age is generally considered a proxy for the availability of public information and, therefore, a measure of a firm's information transparency (Degryse and Van Cayseele 2000). Due to longer more established relationships with banks, these borrowers are typically better known, and, hence, banks can better assess their business and their creditworthiness. Consequently, loan terms such as collateral requirements are assumed to be more favorable for older than younger companies (Avery et al. 1998; Degryse and Van Cayseele 2000; Hernández-Cánovas and Martínez-Solano 2006).

The results of the descriptive statistics show that companies with personal guarantee pledges have a median age of twenty-six and have thirty-five employees, while companies with business collateral have a median age of forty-seven and have seventy employees.

As the bank-borrower relationship progresses, banks use the information they obtain to adjust the contract terms. The ability to engage in monitoring during the course of the relationship produces information about overall firm performance and the value of the collateral (Berger and Udell 1995a).[94]

94 Theoretical models of collateral demonstrate that it is associated with safer borrowers and loans (Besanko and Thakor 1987; Bester 1985; Chan and Kanatas 1985). In contrast, Boot et al. (1991) find evidence that riskier borrowers may also pledge collateral more often.

Examination of the legal form will also offer more insight. We expect that companies such as corporations, that carry a limited liability legal form, will be required to provide more information to lenders than, for example, sole proprietorships.

The variable *Limited Liability Company* has a negative coefficient that is significant at the 10 % level in Models (3) and (4), and at the 5 % level in Model (5). This means that companies with the legal forms GmbH, AG, and KGaA tend to pledge fewer personal guarantees, again because they possess more tangible assets that lenders will accept as security (Avery et al. 1998). Furthermore, the variable *Sales Growth*, as a proxy for the development potential of a company, and the variable *Equity Ratio* have a negative effect on the pledging of *Personal Guarantees*. However, *Equity Ratio* does not have a significant impact in Model (5).

Bester (1985) notes that creditworthy borrowers do not seem to be required to pledge personal guarantees as a signal of their quality. According to Jiménez et al. (2006), riskier companies face a greater likelihood of needing personal guarantees (Alem 2004; Peltoniemi 2007), which is in line with our results here.

The variable *Financial Distress* carries a positive coefficient that is significant at the 1 % level in Model (3), and at the 5 % and 10 % levels, respectively, in Models (4) and (5). This finding signifies a key effect on the pledging of *Personal Guarantees*. It is also in line with expectations, because it seems reasonable to conclude that a bank will try to secure its position by obtaining personal guarantees in the event of financial distress. When companies become distressed, personal guarantees may ultimately enforce better behavior, as borrowers realize that their personal wealth is at stake. In the context of this study, when a bank provides money to a firm to protect it from temporary liquidity restraints, the bank is said to be acting as the lender of last resort. From a firm perspective, the company would prefer to pledge personal guarantees to obtain the necessary financing. Firms are most likely to receive this type of support from their housebanks.

Additionally, with respect to the industry dummies in Model (4), we expect it will be more difficult for companies with fewer tangible business assets (such as professional services companies) to pledge business collateral. The results in Table 4-6 appear to confirm this assumption. Hernández-Cánovas and Martínez-Solano (2010) find further that industrial sector firms show a lower probability of providing personal guarantees than firms in the construction and service industry. Our study also confirms this result, because firms in the *Construction Industry* show a greater likelihood of pledging personal guarantees. Companies that have fewer tangible business assets (such as the *Service Industry*) may be required to provide personal securities (Avery et al. 1998; Hernández-Cánovas and Martínez-Solano 2010). Model (5) includes all the variables and confirms the significant effects on the variable *Personal Guarantees*.

4.2.3 Full sample - Cost of debt

The variable *Cost of Debt* is defined as the interest rate on the most important credit line for the year 2015. It is a metric variable, and the focus is again on lines of credit. This approach follows prior studies that use short-term interest rates to analyze the benefits of relationship banking (Hernández-Cánovas and Martínez-Solano 2010; Kano et al. 2011). If relationship lending is of benefit to SMEs, we posit that the set of relationship variables should cause a reduction in *Cost of Debt*. For the sake of robustness, we again include a set of controlling variables. Table 4-7 shows the results.[95]

The OLS regression evaluates the full sample of 576 firms in each model. In the following sections, we present and interpret the regression coefficients for each regression. The coefficients are the values for the regression equation for predicting the dependent from the independent variable. The coefficients reveal the relationship between the independent variables and the dependent variable. They thus give the amount of increase in the dependent variable that would be predicted by a one-unit increase in the independent variables (UCLA Statistical Consulting Group 2006b). The VIFs show no multicollinearity. The average VIF values are rather low and the maximum mean VIF is 1.38, so all values are well below the critical value of 5 (Kutner, Nachtsheim, and Neter 2005).

Model (1) introduces the loan characteristics. Note particularly that the variable *Finance Share* carries a positive coefficient that is significant at the 1 % level. The effect of the variable *Finance Share* confirms the literature evaluation in Table 2-6. It may also suggest a potential lock-in effect. In such a situation, the relationship lender may be willing to exploit its higher hold-up power by threatening to cut credit, raise costs, or extract rents, as borrowers are locked in to the relationship (the "hold-up problem"). This result also seems to suggest that SMEs involved in lending relationships are subject to the information monopoly of the lender. The variable *Lines of Credit* also shows a positive effect on *Cost of Debt*.

De Bodt et al. (2005) conclude that there is no single number of bank relationships that is right for all SMEs. The authors conclude that two aspects

95 The data are cross-sectional, so a pooled regression could not be performed because panel data would have been required.

Table 4-7: Ordinary least squares – Full sample – Cost of debt

This table shows an analysis of the dependent variable *Cost of Debt* for the sample of 576 firms. This variable documents the interest rate on the most important credit line with the reference day January 1, 2015. The loan characteristics are measured by the variable *Finance Share*, which indicates the overall share of total debt financing of the firm that is financed by the most important bank. It is measured with a metric input in %. The variable *Lines of Credit* indicates the frequency with which a firm finances its business with lines of credit. The variable *Short-term Bank Debt* indicates the frequency with which the firm uses bank financing of less than one year, and the variable *Long-term Bank Debt* indicates that for more than one year. Variables are measured on an ordinal five-point Likert-type scale ranging from 1 (never) to 5 (always). The variable *Number* of banks the firm works with is measured with a metric input with integer numbers. The variable *Duration* shows the number of years the firm has worked with the most important bank and is measured with a metric input in years. The variable *Trust* indicates whether trust exists between the firm and the bank and is measured on an ordinal five-point Likert-type scale ranging from 1 (does not apply at all) to 5 (strongly applies). The variable *Meeting Frequency* indicates how often on average physical or non-physical meetings between the firm and the bank occur per year and is measured with a metric input. The variable *Scope* shows whether the bank provides most of the other bank services for the firm besides debt financing and is measured on an ordinal five-point Likert scale ranging from 1 (does not apply at all) to 5 (strongly applies). The variable *Loan Officer* indicates whether the firm has a permanent relationship manager at the bank and is measured on a dichotomous scale. The variable *Bank Type* indicates whether the bank is savings, co-operative, or private bank, and is measured on a dichotomous scale that equals 1 for *Savings Banks*, and 0 otherwise. The variable *Firm Age* indicates the number of years since the firm's founding, as recorded in the survey, and is measured on a metric input. The variable *Firm Size* is measured by the average number of employees in the year 2015 and is measured with a metric input. The variable *Legal Form* indicates whether the firm is a limited liability company (GmbH, AG, KGaA, GmbH & Co. KG) or an unlimited liability company (KG, OHG, or GbR), and is measured on a dichotomous scale that equals 1 for *Limited Liability Company*, and 0 otherwise. The variable *Equity Ratio* indicates the solvency of the firm as measured by the firm's equity ratio in the year 2015 according to the annual results and is measured with a metric input in %. The variable *Sales Growth* indicates the firm's sales growth in the year 2015 according to the annual results and is measured with a metric input in %. The variable *Financial Distress* is a dichotomous variable indicates whether the firm had been in financial distress since 2007. The variable *Industry* is a set of industry variables indicating to which industry the firm belongs, which is measured on a nominal scale, and is represented by the *Construction Industry*, the *Trade, Hospitality, Tourism Industry*, the *Traffic and Transportation Industry*, and the *Service Industry*. Standard errors are corrected for heteroskedasticity and given in parentheses. *, **, and *** denote statistical significance at the 10 %, 5 %, and 1 % levels, respectively.

Table 4-7: Continued

Variables	**(1)**	**(2)**	**(3)**	**(4)**	**(5)**
Loan characteristics					
Finance Share	0.015***				0.015***
	(3.781)				(3.760)
Lines of Credit	0.833***				0.733***
	(6.626)				(6.152)
Short-term Bank Debt	-0.379				-0.382
	(-1.168)				(-1.280)
Long-term Bank Debt	-0.168				-0.136
	(-0.581)				(-0.473)
Relationship characteristics					
Number		-0.131**		-0.052**	-0.033**
		(-1.738)		(0.566)	(0.361)
Duration		-0.484**		-0.152	-0.092
		(-2.679)		(-0.743)	(-0.464)
Trust		-0.075***		-0.102***	-0.273***
		(-0.237)		(-0.345)	(-0.982)
Meeting Frequency		-0.441		-0.353	-0.078
		(1.575)		(1.344)	(-0.295)
Scope		-0.089*		-0.162	-0.142
		(-0.290)		(-0.573)	(-0.534)
Loan Officer		-0.691**		-0.496**	-0.664**
		(-1.648)		(-1.192)	(-1.738)
Bank Type - Savings Bank		0.872***		0.745***	0.642**
		(3.033)		(2.763)	(2.537)
Firm characteristics					
Firm Age			-0.212***	-0.203***	-0.023***
			(1.057)	(0.894)	(0.099)
Firm Size			-0.486***	-0.502***	-0.479***
			(-4.682)	(-4.125)	(-4.246)
Legal Form (Limited Liability Company)			0.254**	0.247**	0.522**
			(0.940)	(0.897)	(2.020)
Equity Ratio			-0.017***	-0.017***	-0.005***
			(-3.083)	(-3.042)	(-0.894)
Sales Growth			-0.012*	-0.013*	-0.012*
			(-1.317)	(-1.363)	(-1.316)

(continued on next page)

Table 4-7: Continued

Financial Distress			1.805***	1.723***	1.125***
			(6.132)	(5.769)	(3.778)
Control variables					
Construction Industry			0.343	0.383	0.369
			(0.947)	(1.063)	(1.038)
Trade, Hospitality, Tourism Industry			-1.328**	-1.340**	-1.173**
			(-2.235)	(-2.212)	(-2.171)
Traffic, Transportation Industry			1.000	0.999	1.341**
			(1.559)	(1.530)	(2.009)
Service Industry			-0.350	-0.319	-0.106
			(-1.043)	(-0.950)	(-0.338)
Observations	576	576	576	576	576
Adjusted R-squared	0.148	0.027	0.148	0.156	0.250
F-value	27.483	3.056	10.608	7.496	12.743
Mean VIF	1.38	1.09	1.18	1.27	1.34

are most crucial when making banking decisions: 1) the main bank type the firm does business with, and 2) the degree of opacity that defines the firm.

A decrease in the variable *Cost of Debt* for firms that interact with more banks is assessed in Model (2). The variable *Number* carries a negative coefficient that is significant at the 5 % level. This variable increases with firm size and with firm age. This result is in line with previous findings (De Bodt et al. 2005). However, it appears that an increasing number of bank relationships, and, therefore, a more diversified bank portfolio, have a negative and statistically significant effect at the 5 % level. This implies that bank relationships do not weaken lending relationships.

In contrast, Hernández-Cánovas and Martínez-Solano (2006, 2010) find that firms that engage in only two bank relationships experience the lowest cost of debt, while firms that engage in more than two face the highest cost of debt. Hernández-Cánovas and Martínez-Solano (2006) present for Spain that riskier firms that engage in fewer bank relationships tend to obtain bank debt at a lower cost. This may suggest that concentrated bank relationships decrease uncertainty about a firm. These results are also in accordance with prior results (Montoriol-Garriga 2006; Streb et al. 2002). The empirical findings in Table 2-6 also show a positive effect for the variable *Number* on lending costs.

The variable *Duration* carries a negative coefficient but does not significantly influence the cost of lending with respect to Models (4) and (5). This may be attributable to the fact that repeated and close interactions with the main bank appear to be more important than the sole aspect of relationship length. A long-lasting relationship does not in itself imply that confidential information exchanged between the firm and the bank leads to a decrease in price, although the probability is higher than it would be for a younger relationship. At the same time, we assume that length ensures a certain amount of trust.

In contrast, Stein (2014) finds that relationship strength, as measured by the share of bank debt, decreases costs, while relationship duration increases them. Stein (2014) also assesses relationship lending by strength and duration. According to Degryse and Van Cayseele (2000) for Belgium, a longer duration leads to a higher loan rate. This suggests the possibility of an intertemporal shifting of rents by banks. This effect was also noted in the literature evaluation in Table 2-6.[96]

However, for Germany, we find no influencing effect of relationship length on the cost of debt, even decades later. This result may be attributable to frequent changes in loan officers and in bank structures due to regulatory changes, given that hard factors are becoming more important than soft factors.

The results further indicate that a higher assessment of trustworthiness by the main bank reduces financing costs, meaning that a higher indication on the five-point Likert scale leads to a potentially lower interest rate. The variable *Trust* carries a negative coefficient that is significant at the 1 % level. This supports the assumption that trust plays an important role in establishing a strong and close relationship that is expected to benefit lenders by reducing information asymmetries and, therefore, lowering *Cost of Debt*.

Fisman and Khanna (1999) find a positive relationship between trust and information flows. They show that this relationship is especially strong in more urban countries. For our purposes, it is even more important that they note that many different aspects influence trust besides the flow of information.

Tang et al. (2017) use survey data from China to examine firm managers' trust in their loan managers. They find that trust has a negative effect on the likelihood that the firm manager will be pessimistic about a loan application. A strategy built on trust seems to come into play more strongly when considering the interest rate. Thus, a relationship built on trust is reflected more in the price aspect than in the collateral requirements. In addition, the variable *Cost of*

96 See also Dietsch (2003), Degryse and Ongena (2005), and Hernández-Cánovas and Martínez-Solano (2006, 2010).

Debt appears to be influenced by the variable *Loan Officer*, which carries a negative coefficient at the 5 % level.

The finding for *Loan Officer* provides an interesting insight, as this variable has gone somewhat unnoticed by scholars, as the overall investigation of the empirical findings in Table 2-6 show. Hence, the degree of soft information and a well-established relationship with the loan officer decrease prices. It seems that *Trust* affects the interest rate because a rising trust indicator in the lending relationship can lead to the lowering of costs. Therefore, lenders appear to consider not only collateral classes and recovery rates, but also the level of trust.

Overall, our findings show that a firm's degree of trust in its main bank is an important factor in determining the cost of debt, thereby complementing the understanding of banking relationships with insights from trust literature. This finding is important in light of the recent financial crisis, during which time trust in banks declined dramatically in response to the effects of the crisis. However, trust in banks and banking relationships relates to bank reputation and confidence. While a better bank reputation can induce firms to, e.g., purchase more services, a deterioration in trust and reputation can increase the number of bank relationships and a firm's propensity to maintain or terminate a bank relationship (Ongena et al. 2011). Thus, the negative coefficients in Table 4-7 suggest that lower lending costs result also from reduced financial risk.

The variable *Savings Banks* shows a positive effect and is significant at the 1 % level in Models (2) and (4) and significant at the 5 % level in Model (5). Höwer (2016) analyzes bank types and finds that savings and cooperative banks make up a lower percent of distressed firms that close. However, the author also documents that a firm's likelihood of closing during a time of distress is higher for corporate customers of savings and cooperative banks. This result is in contrast to customers of private banks. Therefore, it appears that savings banks require higher interest rates in order to maintain a certain amount of immunity from distressed firms.

This finding may also indicate that savings banks are worse at evaluating risk, and thus require a risk premium. In this case, trust may help to reduce the information asymmetries between the lender and the borrower and, consequently, may help the lender to better assess the borrower's risks.

Model (3) illustrates the firm characteristics. The variable *Firm Age* carries a negative coefficient that is significant at the 1 % level, similarly to the variable *Firm Size*, which is also negatively related to the dependent variable *Cost of Debt*. This result is in line with prior research and suggests that firm size is negative correlated with opacity and riskiness.

Degryse and Van Cayseele (2000) find that greater availability of public information, as measured by firm age, results in lower loan interest rates. However, the overall effect from the literature evaluation in Table 2-6 demonstrates no significant effect of firm age on the costs of lending. The variable *Limited Liability Company* carries a positive coefficient that is significant at the 5 % level. As a result, large corporations appear to be charged higher prices. With regard to *Equity Ratio*, a decrease in the variable *Cost of Debt* is documented. Lower-leveraged firms are less risky, and, hence, face less credit rationing (Kirschenmann 2016). The variable *Sales Growth* has a negative coefficient and is significant at the 10 % level.

The variable *Financial Distress* is positive and highly statistically significant at the 1 % level. Firms in financial distress appear to pay higher interest rates on lines of credit. Information asymmetries are more obvious as soon as a firm faces financial distress, because the bank then has less security about the firm's future.

Rosenfeld (2014) studies U.S. publicly traded firms in order to determine how banking relationships impact the future of firms in financial distress. He demonstrates that firms that were able to obtain a relationship-based loan six months prior to the distress show a significantly greater likelihood of recovering. Nevertheless, this likelihood decreases when the degree of severity of the distress increases.

In contrast, Weinstein and Yafeh (1998) find that banks may make loans available for firms in financial distress, but they are likely to impose, for example, higher interest rates. This in turn can hinder the firm's chance of succeeding and can destroy the value of the lending relationship. The analysis of the variable *Credit Availability* in section 4.2.4 sheds more light on this.

In addition, Model (3) introduces the control variables. The *Trade, Hospitality, and Tourism Industry* shows a negative coefficient that is significant at the 5 % level. The other industries lack significance, although the *Traffic, Transportation Industry* shows a positive coefficient that is significant at the 5 % level in Model (5). Model (4) shows the relationship and firm characteristics as well as the control variables, and Model (5) presents all the endogenous variables and confirms the significances.

4.2.4 Full sample - Credit availability

An automatic renewal of short-term debt upon maturity implies that a firm can renew its access to short-term credit easily, which in turn implies lower credit constraints. We obtain the dependent variable *Credit Availability* from the survey by asking participants that question. We use a five-point Likert-type scale that ranges from 1 (does not apply) to 5 (strongly applies), and transform the responses into a dummy variable that equals 1 when the response exceeds the median of the sample responses, and 0 otherwise. Whenever a strong, interactive firm-bank relationship reduces informational asymmetries in lending to opaque SMEs, we should observe better access to capital for more transparent firms. Because the strength of a relationship also depends on an assessment of trustworthiness by each party, we expect to find a positive association between trust variables and credit availability. The results of the probit model are in Table 4-8.

The probit regression in each model evaluates the full sample of 576 firms. Model (5), which includes all explanatory variables, shows the best estimation, with a pseudo R2 of 0.104, a log-likelihood of -342.773, and a LR chi2 of 79.574. Note that Model (1) has lower explanatory power than Model (5). In Model (1), the loan characteristics are illustrated.

The variable *Finance Share* shows a positive coefficient that is significant at the 1 % level. *Lines of Credit* is significant and positive, indicating that firms that frequently use short-term credit to finance their operations are less financially constrained. Firms commonly use lines of credit or overdraft agreements to provide continuous liquidity for seasonal working capital needs. However, lines of credit are reviewed frequently (e.g., annually) by loan officers, who request hard information to continually assess a client's creditworthiness and decide whether to renew a contract. Frequent use of lines of credits, therefore, creates a steady firm-bank interaction, increases monitoring, and makes firms less opaque. Furthermore, with respect to the variables *Short-term* and *Long-term Bank Debt*, the coefficients are not significant, and, thus, have no effect on the dependent variable.

Model (2) presents the relationship characteristics. The results of our study show that the variable *Number* carries a positive coefficient, which is significant at the 1 % level. In this context, Hernández-Cánovas and Martínez-Solano (2006) document that banks exploit their monopoly power over a firm to increase profits. Small companies that engage in just one bank relationship (with a maximum of two) face higher monopoly issues and more credit rationing.

In contrast, Cotugno et al. (2013a) and Cotugno et al. (2013b) find that companies with exclusive, single bank relationships, or only a few bank relationships, were less exposed to credit rationing. And De Bodt et al. (2005) find that having multiple bank relationships increased the probability of facing financial rationing (see also Streb et al. 2002).

Alem (2004) documents for Argentina that the probability of a company's default rises when the company engages in debt financing with multiple banks (Jiménez et al. 2009). In addition, Höwer (2016) finds that the strength of the

Table 4-8: Probit regression – Full sample – Credit availability

This table shows the analysis of the dependent variable *Credit Availability* for the sample of 576 firms. This variable asks participants to express whether short-term debt with their main bank is renewed automatically upon maturity. The responses were measured on a five-point Likert-type scale ranging from 5 = "does not apply at all" to 1 = "strongly applies." For the purpose of the multivariate analysis, a dummy variable is then defined that equals 1 when the response exceeds the median sample responses, and 0 otherwise. The loan characteristics are measured by the variable *Finance Share*, which indicates the overall share of total debt financing of the firm that is financed by the most important bank. It is measured with a metric input in %. The variable *Lines of Credit* indicates the frequency with which a firm finances its business with lines of credit. The variable *Short-term Bank Debt* indicates the frequency with which the firm uses bank financing of less than one year, and the variable *Long-term Bank Debt* indicates that for more than one year. Variables are measured on an ordinal five-point Likert-type scale ranging from 1 (never) to 5 (always). The variable *Number* of banks the firm works with is measured with a metric input with integer numbers. The variable *Duration* shows the number of years the firm has worked with the most important bank and is measured with a metric input in years. The variable *Trust* indicates whether trust exists between the firm and the bank and is measured on an ordinal five-point Likert-type scale ranging from 1 (does not apply at all) to 5 (strongly applies). The variable *Meeting Frequency* indicates how often on average physical or non-physical meetings between the firm and the bank occur per year and is measured with a metric input. The variable *Scope* shows whether the bank provides most of the other bank services for the firm besides debt financing and is measured on an ordinal five-point Likert scale ranging from 1 (does not apply at all) to 5 (strongly applies). The variable *Loan Officer* indicates whether the firm has a permanent relationship manager at the bank and is measured on a dichotomous scale. The variable *Bank Type* indicates whether the bank is savings, co-operative, or private bank, and is measured on a dichotomous scale that equals 1 for *Savings Banks*, and 0 otherwise. The variable *Firm Age* indicates the number of years since the firm's founding, as recorded in the survey, and is measured on a metric input. The variable *Firm Size* is measured by the average number of employees in the year 2015 and is measured with a metric input. The variable *Legal Form* indicates whether the firm is a limited liability company (GmbH, AG, KGaA, GmbH & Co. KG) or an unlimited liability company (KG, OHG, or GbR), and is measured on a dichotomous scale that equals 1 for *Limited Liability Company*, and 0 otherwise. The variable *Equity Ratio* indicates the solvency of the firm as measured by the firm's equity ratio in the year 2015 according to the annual results and is measured with a metric input in %. The variable *Sales Growth* indicates the firm's sales growth in the year 2015 according to the annual results and is measured with a metric input in %. The variable *Financial Distress* is a dichotomous variable indicates whether the firm had been in financial distress since 2007. The variable *Industry* is a set of industry variables indicating to which industry the firm belongs, which is measured on a nominal scale, and is represented by the *Construction Industry*, the *Trade, Hospitality, Tourism Industry*, the *Traffic and Transportation Industry*, and the *Service Industry*. Standard errors are corrected for heteroskedasticity and given in parentheses. *, **, and *** denote statistical significance at the 10 %, 5 %, and 1 % levels, respectively.

(*continued on next page*)

Table 4-8: Continued

Variables	**(1)**	**(2)**	**(3)**	**(4)**	**(5)**
Loan characteristics					
Finance Share	0.005***				0.005***
	(0.001)				(0.001)
Lines of Credit	0.256***				0.261***
	(0.048)				(0.051)
Short-term Bank Debt	-0.177				-0.191
	(0.127)				(0.130)
Long-term Bank Debt	0.098				0.063
	(0.117)				(0.125)
Relationship characteristics					
Number		0.078***		0.018***	0.007***
		(0.030)		(0.034)	(0.035)
Duration		0.151*		0.015*	0.003*
		(0.060)		(0.076)	(0.077)
Trust		0.358***		0.384***	0.349***
		(0.114)		(0.116)	(0.117)
Meeting Frequency		0.288***		0.242***	0.092***
		(0.097)		(0.100)	(0.104)
Scope		0.018**		0.000**	0.003**
		(0.100)		(0.102)	(0.104)
Loan Officer		0.175**		0.132**	0.095**
		(0.129)		(0.132)	(0.134)
Bank Type - Savings Bank		0.093		0.084	0.041
		(0.097)		(0.098)	(0.099)
Firm characteristics					
Firm Age			0.228***	0.221***	0.179**
			(0.070)	(0.081)	(0.083)
Firm Size			0.110***	0.086**	0.096**
			(0.037)	(0.042)	(0.042)
Legal Form (Limited Liability Company)			0.046	0.063	0.174
			(0.107)	(0.108)	(0.111)
Equity Ratio			0.004**	0.003**	0.001**
			(0.002)	(0.002)	(0.002)
Sales Growth			0.003**	0.005**	0.005**
			(0.003)	(0.004)	(0.004)
Financial Distress			0.150	0.123	-0.097

Table 4-8: Continued

			(0.104)	(0.106)	(0.112)
Control variables					
Construction Industry			0.256**	0.268**	0.270**
			(0.139)	(0.140)	(0.141)
Trade, Hospitality, Tourism Industry			0.404*	0.423*	0.547**
			(0.228)	(0.231)	(0.238)
Traffic, Transportation Industry			0.017	-0.016	0.084
			(0.214)	(0.217)	(0.221)
Service Industry			-0.065	-0.047	0.028
			(0.117)	(0.118)	(0.120)
Observations	576	576	576	576	576
Log-likelihood	-370.759	-364.141	-362.896	351.647	-342.773
Pseudo R2	0.031	0.048	0.051	0.081	0.104
LR chi2	23.601	36.837	39.328	61.826	79.574

most important bank relationship has significant effects because companies with multiple bank relationships show a greater ability to absorb financial shocks. Those firms also show a lower probability of slipping into financial distress. However, coordination difficulties and free-riding issues can make it problematic for banks to restructure a company. This is because, one bank may not have enough private information to process negative signals from companies (especially new customers). Companies that recently changed their main bank have a greater likelihood of not only slipping into financial distress, but also of closing subsequently (Höwer 2016).

In addition, the variable *Duration* demonstrates a positive effect on credit availability and is significant, but only at the 10 % level. Several scholars have documented that firms that maintain longer bank relationships experience better credit availability (see, e.g., Degryse and Van Cayseele 2000; Dietsch 2003; Degryse and Ongena 2005; Hernández-Cánovas and Martínez-Solano 2006, 2010). Kirschenmann (2016) shows for Bulgaria that opaque companies and companies that recently entered a new bank relationship are more often affected by credit rationing. The author demonstrates that decreasing information asymmetries over the relationship duration can contribute to a reduction in credit rationing, because banks are eager to fulfill firms' growing demands for financing. In addition, the literature review in Table 2-6 also demonstrated a positive effect of duration on credit availability.

But the variable *Trust* is more important and highly significant, which is in line with the argumentation that relationship length can facilitate the development of trust. The coefficient for *Trust* is positive and highly statistically significant at the 1 % level, indicating that a firm's access to short-term credit increases with a higher assessment of trustworthiness of their business counterparties (see also Hernández-Cánovas and Martínez-Solano 2010). This finding gives rise to the notion that trust plays a pivotal role in modern lending relationships.

In this context, Ongena and Smith (2000a) argue that bankers perceive the creation of strong customer relationships as a core element when offering financial services. At the same time, a loyal customer is more likely to purchase other financial services from the bank when there is a trusting relationship (Boot 2000; Ongena et al. 2011). According to Ongena and Smith (2000a), the benefits of such a relationship may be the transmission of confidential information on the part of firms, and the implicit commitment on the part of banks to continue doing business with the firm through financially difficult times. Mayer (1988) and Edwards and Fischer (1994) likewise stress that banks in Germany bear a special responsibility to their clients during times of distress.

In addition, the variable *Meeting Frequency* carries a positive coefficient and is significant at the 1 % level. This variable highlights that frequent and recurring contact, whether in person or not, creates benefits for both lenders and borrowers. Firms become more transparent to banks, and experience real non-pricing benefits.

The production of soft information in the relationship was investigated via *Meeting Frequency*, and the analysis shows an impact on the probability that a firm will be credit rationed. We find that soft information lowers the probability that SMEs may be credit rationed. This finding is in line with Bartoli et al. (2012), who also study soft information by defining a dummy variable (through a survey on Italian manufacturing companies). They find that, during the crisis, a large bank in their dataset (UniCredit) deployed soft information to move its loan supply toward companies with lower ex ante information asymmetries.

The variables *Scope* and *Loan Officer* have a positive effect on credit availability and are significant at the 5 % level. The finding for *Scope* is in line with (Dietsch 2003). The result for *Loan Officer* is interesting, because the evaluation of the literature review in section 2.7.4 offered no final statements.

However, Hainz and Wiegand (2013) conducted a survey in 2011 based on a written questionnaire sent to the CFOs of German manufacturing companies. In total, 1,139 companies participated, including small companies (less than 50 employees), medium companies (50–249 employees) and large companies (more than 249 employees). Hainz and Wiegand (2013) document no effect on credit availability of relationship banking. They posit that this is because banks use hard rather than soft information in the credit risk models on which they base their decisions about granting a loan. In contrast, our findings here indicate a different direction, particularly with regard to the variable *Trust*. Overall, it seems as if banks make credit more readily available to firms when they have acquired superior information.

Focusing on firm characteristics in Model (3), *Firm Age* is positively related to the variable *Credit Availability*. This result in line with prior research demonstrating that firms become less opaque and, therefore, less risky as they age (Degryse and Van Cayseele 2000). Montoriol-Garriga (2006) also finds that firm age has a positive effect on the availability of bank financing.

Note further that the coefficient on the variable *Firm Size* is significantly positive at the 1 % level, which suggests that variable has an influence on the availability of credit. The variable *Limited Liability Company* does not appear to impact the probability of obtaining financing, which follows Dorfleitner et al. (2016). The two balance sheet indicators, the *Equity Ratio* and the *Sales Growth*, carry a positive coefficient that is significant at the 5 % level. These companies are of course less likely to slip into financial distress.

The coefficient of the variable *Financial Distress* is not significant, suggesting that a temporary relaxation of loan terms can be obtained through relationship lending. For companies in financial distress, multiple bank relationships can be ambiguous for two reasons. First, there is a free-rider problem in monitoring, which leads to inefficiencies in renegotiation (Diamond and Dybvig 1983; Höwer 2016). Hoshi, Kashyap, and Scharfstein (1990) document that Japanese companies with close relationships tend to recover better after financial distress. They find that renegotiation is less costly for companies because free-riding issues and information asymmetries are less severe. And Rajan (1992) states that a rise in the number of bank relationships reduces the likelihood that a firm is able to renegotiate with a single lender. As a result, renegotiation costs tend to rise.

Second, there is a risk of coordination failure, which rises with the number of lenders (Thakor 1996). Coordination is even more difficult when lenders are less concentrated (Bris and Welch 2005). Brunner and Krahnen (2008) document for distressed companies in Germany that the likelihood of coordination problems rises with multiple bank relationships. The authors also find that the duration of a workout plan increases, and the prospect of a turnaround declines.

We find no significant difference here with respect to the number of bank relationships for firms that indicated they were or were not in financial distress. There are two possible explanations. On the one hand, it may be that companies have learned from past situations that there is no advantage to engaging in multiple bank relationships during financial downturns, because of potential coordination problems. On the other hand, it may be that firms would like to engage in multiple bank relationships, but have trouble establishing solid relationships due to a weak credit history or low ratings (Höwer 2016).

In addition, in Model (3), the *Construction Industry* and the *Trade, Hospitality, and Tourism Industry* demonstrate a positive effect on the dependent variable. Model (5) then highlights the overall significances of the variables. In summary, the central findings show that *Number* has a positive effect on *Collateral Requirement* and *Credit Availability*, and a negative effect on *Cost of Debt*. However, *Duration* of the bank-borrower relationship, which is a commonly used proxy for relationship lending in the literature, is not associated with housebank status. Based on our sample, where the average duration of bank-borrower relationships is rather high, there is no continuous significant influence on credit conditions. Duration alone does not improve credit conditions, but trust can significantly improve credit terms. *Trust* is a quality indicator of business-to-business relationships, and is a major factor influencing credit conditions. There is a negative effect on *Cost of Debt*, and a positive effect on *Credit Availability*.

Meeting Frequency shows positive effects on *Collateral Requirements* and *Credit Availability*. *Scope* (number of banking services) has a positive effect on *Credit Availability*, while the variable *Loan Officer* also influences credit parameters. The variable *Bank Type*, represented by savings banks, has a positive effect on *Collateral Requirements* and on *Cost of Debt*.

Another firm characteristic that could influence the endogenous variables is the difference between family and non-family firms. Agency models predict that agency costs emerge with fractional ownership, a situation found less frequently in family firms (Voordeckers and Steijvers 2006). It is expected that family firms show measurable special effects due to relationship management, as better dealing with their stakeholders is expected. This effect is reflected in the credit conditions. Therefore, rather than including a dummy variable in the previous multivariate regression analyses, we created two separate samples to study and better highlight the possible different effects of family and non-family firms. A firm is defined as a family firm when more than 50 % of its shares are owned by persons related to each other, and when these persons are active in firm management. Hence, a family management aspect is also included.[97]

97 It is common to include a family versus non-family firm classification. See, e.g., Voordeckers and Steijvers (2006), who include a family firm variable that is defined as a company in which the family owns the majority of the shares.

The next sections examine which variables have a greater impact on the study of family versus non-family firms. In this context, we outline certain structural differences, because the family firm sample compared to the non-family firm sample is much larger and, hence, may dominate the results. Therefore, the three following tables present the analyses of the endogenous variables: *Collateral Requirements*, *Cost of Debt*, and *Credit Availability* for family firms and non-family firms.

4.2.5 Family versus non-family firms - Collateral requirements

The central question in this chapter is the effect of family ownership and management structure on collateral requirements, the cost of debt, and access to financing through the housebank. Family firms provide a clean and powerful test of whether firm ownership and management influence price and non-price terms and conditions. Because these shareholders typically have undiversified portfolios, are concerned with firm and family reputation, and often desire to pass the firm onto their descendants, they represent a unique class of shareholders that potentially affect these dependent variables (Anderson, Mansi, and Reeb 2003). To this end, we address one specific question: Do family firms enjoy lower collateral requirements, lower costs of debt financing, and better access to finance than non-family firms?

Relationships that signal mutual trust may be beneficial to both borrowers and banks, because they may lead to better credit terms for borrowers, and to a reliable portfolio of customers for banks (Lehmann and Neuberger 2001). This could indicate a kind of relationship management, in which the aspiration is to capture the stakeholder for the long-term. Creating good relationships requires consistent action, meaning that such relationships must be built and purposefully strengthened. If the effort to find a stable partner only occurs when it is needed, it may be too late, because there may not be sufficient time to build a good relationship. This would point to a stable relationship among all those borrowers who have also recognized this link. It is expected that relationship building and its impact on price and non-price conditions can be better detected at family than at non-family firms.

Relationship building is closely linked with the idea of sustaining social capital. According to Sirmon and Hitt (2003), social capital encompasses three dimensions: the structural, the cognitive, and the relational. The structural dimension is based on network connections, the cognitive dimension on a common language and narratives, and the relational dimension on trust, norms, and duties. Each dimension is embedded within the family unit and links the relationships the family business has with its stakeholders. In line with Sirmon and Hitt (2003), the social capital of the family increases when there are effective relationships with stakeholders (e.g., housebanks) in place. This allows family businesses to generate resources from their networks (e.g., knowledge, finance capital).

In this context, we analyze the three dependent variables *Collateral Requirements*, *Cost of Debt*, and *Credit Availability* by dividing the sample into family and non-family firms. For these two samples, the multivariate regression analysis on the variable *Collateral Type* was not repeated because the sample size was too small after the division. Table 4-9 shows the split sample for the dependent variable *Collateral Requirements*.

The probit regression evaluates the 408 family firms and the 168 non-family firms. The family firm model shows a pseudo R2 of 0.288, a log-likelihood of -193.286, and a LR chi2 of 156.234, while the non-family firm model carries a pseudo R2 of 0.466, a log-likelihood of -61.532, and a LR chi2 of 107.448. Thus, the non-family firm sample has slightly greater explanatory power. With respect to the loan characteristics, the variables *Finance Share* and *Lines of Credit* carry a positive coefficient that is significant at the 1 % level. Moreover, the variable *Long-term Bank Debt* also has a positive effect on the dependent variable in the family firm sample. These findings confirm the empirical findings in section 4.2.1 thus far. Loan characteristics play a determining role from the beginning when it comes to collateral requirements.

In addition, the variable *Number* carries a positive coefficient and is significant at the 5 % level in the family firm and the non-family firm sample. The variable *Duration* turns out to be insignificant, and, thus, has no influence on *Collateral Requirements*. These results confirm the findings of the multivariate regression analysis in section 4.2.1. The variable *Trust* carries a negative coefficient that is significant at the 5 % level in the family firm sample. The variable *Meeting Frequency* shows a positive coefficient in both samples. It is significant at the 1 % level in the family firm sample, and at a 10 % level in the non-family firm sample. The communication of important company decisions creates a particular basis of trust between the family business and the housebank, which enables the dismantling of information asymmetries.

In addition, the results reflect how family businesses engage in relationship management. They tend to be very careful in handling confidential information, not only as it applies to finances, but also key business decision-making behavior. Thus, the circle of confidants is very select. There is of course certain information that the company must convey to the bank. Nevertheless, in view of the generally high equity ratio of family businesses, we assume they can enjoy a high degree

Table 4-9: Probit regression – Family firm versus non-family firm sample – Collateral requirements

This table shows the analysis of the dependent variable *Collateral Requirements* for the split sample of 408 family firms and 168 non-family firms. This dependent variable documents whether the main type of collateral pledged to obtain the most important credit line was a personal guarantee on the firm owner's assets, or collateral on the company's assets. The loan characteristics are measured by the variable *Finance Share*, which indicates the overall share of total debt financing of the firm that is financed by the most important bank. It is measured with a metric input in %. The variable *Lines of Credit* indicates the frequency with which a firm finances its business with lines of credit. The variable *Short-term Bank Debt* indicates the frequency with which the firm uses bank financing of less than one year, and the variable *Long-term Bank Debt* indicates that for more than one year. Variables are measured on an ordinal five-point Likert-type scale ranging from 1 (never) to 5 (always). The variable *Number* of banks the firm works with is measured with a metric input with integer numbers. The variable *Duration* shows the number of years the firm has worked with the most important bank and is measured with a metric input in years. The variable *Trust* indicates whether trust exists between the firm and the bank and is measured on an ordinal five-point Likert-type scale ranging from 1 (does not apply at all) to 5 (strongly applies). The variable *Meeting Frequency* indicates how often on average physical or non-physical meetings between the firm and the bank occur per year and is measured with a metric input. The variable *Scope* shows whether the bank provides most of the other bank services for the firm besides debt financing and is measured on an ordinal five-point Likert scale ranging from 1 (does not apply at all) to 5 (strongly applies). The variable *Loan Officer* indicates whether the firm has a permanent relationship manager at the bank and is measured on a dichotomous scale. The variable *Bank Type* indicates whether the bank is savings, co-operative, or private bank, and is measured on a dichotomous scale that equals 1 for *Savings Banks*, and 0 otherwise. The variable *Firm Age* indicates the number of years since the firm's founding, as recorded in the survey, and is measured on a metric input. The variable *Firm Size* is measured by the average number of employees in the year 2015 and is measured with a metric input. The variable *Legal Form* indicates whether the firm is a limited liability company (GmbH, AG, KGaA, GmbH & Co. KG) or an unlimited liability company (KG, OHG, or GbR), and is measured on a dichotomous scale that equals 1 for *Limited Liability Company*, and 0 otherwise. The variable *Equity Ratio* indicates the solvency of the firm as measured by the firm's equity ratio in the year 2015 according to the annual results and is measured with a metric input in %. The variable *Sales Growth* indicates the firm's sales growth in the year 2015 according to the annual results and is measured with a metric input in %. The variable *Financial Distress* is a dichotomous variable indicates whether the firm had been in financial distress since 2007. The variable *Industry* is a set of industry variables indicating to which industry the firm belongs, which is measured on a nominal scale, and is represented by the *Construction Industry*, the *Trade, Hospitality, Tourism Industry*, the *Traffic and Transportation Industry*, and the *Service Industry*. Standard errors are corrected for heteroskedasticity and given in parentheses. *, **, and *** denote statistical significance at the 10 %, 5 %, and 1 % levels, respectively.

(continued on next page)

Table 4-9: Continued

Variables	Family firms	Non-family firms
Loan characteristics		
Finance Share	0.012***	0.019***
	(0.002)	(0.004)
Lines of Credit	0.842***	1.056***
	(0.184)	(0.335)
Short-term Bank Debt	0.034	0.301
	(0.203)	(0.379)
Long-term Bank Debt	0.470**	0.465
	(0.195)	(0.349)
Relationship characteristics		
Number	0.108**	0.134**
	(0.175)	(0.312)
Duration	-0.094	0.283
	(0.124)	(0.238)
Trust	-0.143**	0.218
	(0.179)	(0.343)
Meeting Frequency	0.053***	0.426*
	(0.158)	(0.319)
Scope	-0.011	0.721**
	(0.163)	(0.337)
Loan Officer	-0.165	-0.258
	(0.226)	(0.387)
Bank Type - Savings Bank	0.251**	0.046**
	(0.154)	(0.282)
Firm characteristics		
Firm Age	-0.086**	-0.186**
	(0.136)	(0.248)
Firm Size	-0.155**	-0.057**
	(0.070)	(0.112)
Legal Form (Limited Liability Company)	-0.141**	-0.009
	(0.175)	(0.318)
Equity Ratio	-0.000*	-0.002***
	(0.003)	(0.005)
Sales Growth	-0.003	-0.009
	(0.006)	(0.009)
Financial Distress	0.354***	0.034
	(0.180)	(0.332)

Table 4-9: Continued

Control variables		
Construction Industry	0.387**	0.529*
	(0.212)	(0.485)
Trade, Hospitality, Tourism Industry	0.375	0.244
	(0.348)	(0.977)
Traffic, Transportation Industry	0.375	1.303
	(0.346)	(0.801)
Service Industry	-0.031	0.353
	(0.195)	(0.306)
Observations	408	168
Log-likelihood	-193.286	-61.532
Pseudo R2	0.288	0.466
LR chi2	156.234	107.448

of independence from banks. As a result, not all developments in the company would have to be communicated directly to the principal bank.

However, the family businesses we examine here seem to be communicating fully, so their housebank relationships appear consolidated and the relationships of trust seem strong. The variable *Scope* shows only a positive effect in the non-family firm sample, while there is no effect in the family firm sample. The variable *Loan Officer* shows no effect in either sample.

The variable *Savings Banks* carries a positive coefficient that is significant at the 5 % level for both samples. Moreover, the variables *Firm Age* and *Firm Size* show negative coefficients that are significant at the 5 % level. Hence, these variables show no differences between the family and non-family firm sample. However, the variable *Limited Liability Company* shows a negative coefficient. It is only significant at the 5 % level in the family firm sample, which highlights that the legal form only has an influence in the family firm sample.

The variable *Equity Ratio* carries a negative coefficient that is significant at the 10 % level in the family firm sample, and at the 1 % level in the non-family firm sample. We posit that equity ratio may have a lower impact in family firms because they are more likely to have a personally liable partner. But a healthy equity ratio reflects the higher bargaining power of companies with the bank. The housebank may not wish to damage the company by imposing high collateral requirements, because, in view of the high level of debt financing, these companies are important customers.

With respect to the firm's ownership structure, Voordeckers and Steijvers (2006) show for Belgium that family firms have a greater likelihood of pledging collateral, which is in line with Kano et al. (2011). However, we cannot confirm these findings for Germany. With regard to the industry variables, the variable *Construction Industry* carries a positive coefficient in both samples, which emphasizes that companies from the construction industry usually pledge more collateral. This is probably because they have more tangible assets than, for example service industry firms.

4.2.6 Family firms versus non-family firms - Cost of debt

This section investigates the impact of the family firm on the cost of debt. Table 4-10 shows the analysis of the dependent variable *Cost of Debt* which measures the interest rate on the most important credit line.

The OLS regression evaluates 408 family firms and 168 non-family firms. The VIFs exhibit no multicollinearity, as the average values for both samples are rather low, at 1.37 and 1.49. Thus, all values are well below the critical value of 5 (Kutner et al. 2005). Regarding the loan characteristics, the variable *Finance Share* carries a positive coefficient that is significant at the 5 % level in both samples. Again, it appears that, if a company obtains a larger financing share from one bank, they are more likely to face hold-up problems. And this seems to apply to family and non-family firms alike.

In this context, the variable *Lines of Credit* also shows a positive coefficient, which is significant at the 1 % level in the family firm sample, and at the 5 % level in the non-family firm sample. Furthermore, the variable *Number* carries a negative coefficient that is significant at the 5 % level, while *Duration* shows no effect on the dependent variable. The results for the variable *Number* highlight that it may be advantageous to have more than one bank relationship, as hold-up problems may be more manageable. Hence, multiple relationships may counteract somewhat the problems that can arise through the dependence shown by *Finance Share* and *Lines of Credit*. Receiving a higher amount of financing from one bank also means that the offer becomes more expensive, so the presence of many banks can rectify that. This result is in line with Elsas 2001, 2005 and Elsas and Krahnen 1998, 2002, 2003, who state that the mere duration of a relationship should not be a decisive factor in determining credit parameters.

The variable *Trust* shows a negative coefficient that is significant at the 1 % level in the family firm sample, but at the 10 % level in the non-family firm sample. Since the variable is more impactful in the family firm sample, this may hint at family firms building more trusting relationships with their banks. The

Table 4-10: Ordinary least squares – Family firm versus non-family firm sample – Cost of debt

This table shows the analysis of the dependent variable *Cost of Debt* for the split sample of 408 family firms and 168 non-family firms. This variable documents the interest rate on the most important credit line with the reference day January 1, 2015. The loan characteristics are measured by the variable *Finance Share*, which indicates the overall share of total debt financing of the firm that is financed by the most important bank. It is measured with a metric input in %. The variable *Lines of Credit* indicates the frequency with which a firm finances its business with lines of credit. The variable *Short-term Bank Debt* indicates the frequency with which the firm uses bank financing of less than one year, and the variable *Long-term Bank Debt* indicates that for more than one year. Variables are measured on an ordinal five-point Likert-type scale ranging from 1 (never) to 5 (always). The variable *Number* of banks the firm works with is measured with a metric input with integer numbers. The variable *Duration* shows the number of years the firm has worked with the most important bank and is measured with a metric input in years. The variable *Trust* indicates whether trust exists between the firm and the bank and is measured on an ordinal five-point Likert-type scale ranging from 1 (does not apply at all) to 5 (strongly applies). The variable *Meeting Frequency* indicates how often on average physical or non-physical meetings between the firm and the bank occur per year and is measured with a metric input. The variable *Scope* shows whether the bank provides most of the other bank services for the firm besides debt financing and is measured on an ordinal five-point Likert scale ranging from 1 (does not apply at all) to 5 (strongly applies). The variable *Loan Officer* indicates whether the firm has a permanent relationship manager at the bank and is measured on a dichotomous scale. The variable *Bank Type* indicates whether the bank is savings, co-operative, or private bank, and is measured on a dichotomous scale that equals 1 for *Savings Banks*, and 0 otherwise. The variable *Firm Age* indicates the number of years since the firm's founding, as recorded in the survey, and is measured on a metric input. The variable *Firm Size* is measured by the average number of employees in the year 2015 and is measured with a metric input. The variable *Legal Form* indicates whether the firm is a limited liability company (GmbH, AG, KGaA, GmbH & Co. KG) or an unlimited liability company (KG, OHG, or GbR), and is measured on a dichotomous scale that equals 1 for *Limited Liability Company*, and 0 otherwise. The variable *Equity Ratio* indicates the solvency of the firm as measured by the firm's equity ratio in the year 2015 according to the annual results and is measured with a metric input in %. The variable *Sales Growth* indicates the firm's sales growth in the year 2015 according to the annual results and is measured with a metric input in %. The variable *Financial Distress* is a dichotomous variable indicates whether the firm had been in financial distress since 2007. The variable *Industry* is a set of industry variables indicating to which industry the firm belongs, which is measured on a nominal scale, and is represented by the *Construction Industry*, the *Trade, Hospitality, Tourism Industry*, the *Traffic and Transportation Industry*, and the *Service Industry*. Standard errors are corrected for heteroskedasticity and given in parentheses. *, **, and *** denote statistical significance at the 10 %, 5 %, and 1 % levels, respectively.

(*continued on next page*)

Table 4-10: Continued

Variables	Family firms	Non-family firms
Loan characteristics		
Finance Share	0.012**	0.019**
	(2.398)	(2.370)
Lines of Credit	0.707***	0.645**
	(5.253)	(2.173)
Short-term Bank Debt	-0.123	-0.819
	(-0.358)	(-1.071)
Long-term Bank Debt	-0.304	-0.064
	(-0.868)	(-0.097)
Relationship characteristics		
Number	-0.020**	-0.085**
	(0.184)	(-0.478)
Duration	-0.268	0.411
	(-1.087)	(0.935)
Trust	-0.150***	-0.529*
	(-0.444)	(-1.015)
Meeting Frequency	-0.185**	-0.688*
	(-0.622)	(0.959)
Scope	-0.134	-0.354
	(-0.413)	(-0.649)
Loan Officer	-0.904**	-0.363
	(-1.883)	(-0.519)
Bank Type - Savings Bank	0.613***	0.676*
	(2.014)	(1.200)
Firm characteristics		
Firm Age	-0.235**	-0.527***
	(0.859)	(-1.056)
Firm Size	-0.468***	-0.332**
	(-3.356)	(-1.584)
Legal Form (Limited Liability Company)	0.813***	-0.187
	(2.639)	(-0.335)
Equity Ratio	-0.010***	-0.001**
	(-1.384)	(0.050)
Sales Growth	-0.006*	-0.022*
	(-0.408)	(-1.599)
Financial Distress	1.126***	0.949
	(3.145)	(1.535)

Table 4-10: Continued

Control variables		
Construction Industry	0.138	1.147
	(0.326)	(1.603)
Trade, Hospitality, Tourism Industry	-1.041**	-2.390
	(-1.710)	(-1.480)
Traffic, Transportation Industry	0.960	2.033
	(1.396)	(0.990)
Service Industry	-0.032	-0.321
	(-0.080)	(-0.554)
Observations	408	168
Adjusted R-squared	0.287	0.300
F-value	9.864	3.878
Mean VIF	1.37	1.49

variable *Meeting Frequency* also carries a negative coefficient and is again slightly more significant at the 5 % level in the family firm sample. This compares to a 10 % significance in the non-family firm sample.

Trust and information sharing play an important role in reducing agency problems such as moral hazard and adverse selection. This is an interesting point, because it is frequently argued in the literature that family businesses tend to disclose less information. Here it seems to be beneficial for them to do so. Therefore, the benefits of higher levels of trust include lower monitoring costs, which seem to result in a negative effect on the cost of debt, particularly for family firms. Trust affects the reliability of the information provided for the lending decision and potential moral hazard.

In addition, more meetings overall seem to reduce the opaqueness of the borrower for the bank. In this context, Howorth and Moro (2006) show that intense monitoring is perceived to signal a lack of trust in a borrower and may lead to a lower demand for finance by small companies. Harhoff and Körting (1998) argue that trust captures information not contained in other explanatory variables, such as company age. In addition, trust is expected to increase with more frequent communication and closer relationships (Lewicki and Bunker 1996). Because small companies are usually more informationally opaque, trust represents an important factor in the lending decision.

The outcome of the variable *Loan Officer* is also interesting. A good relationship is expected to be reflected primarily in the relationship with the bank's loan officer. The variable *Loan Officer* shows an influence only in the family firm sample on *Cost of Debt*, with a significance at the 5 % level. In general, family businesses are very reserved in disclosing information, yet they seem to recognize the benefit here, and thus it makes economic sense to share information. They know relationship management is important and provides credibility that non-family businesses may not have. The banking world overall is changing, so it is wise to have a partner for the future. Relationship building can help nurture this important relationship.

The variable *Savings Banks* carries a positive coefficient that is significant at the 1 % level in the family firm sample, and at the 10 % level in the non-family firm sample. Moreover, the variables *Firm Age* and *Firm Size* show negative coefficients that are significant at the 1 % and 5 % levels, respectively. Hence, these variables show no differences between the two samples, which confirms the results of the multivariate regression analysis in section 4.2.3. The variable *Limited Liability Company* shows a positive coefficient, but it is significant at the 1 % level only in the family firm sample. Hence, this variable emphasizes that *Legal Form* exhibits a greater effect in the family firm sample.

The variable *Equity Ratio* carries a negative coefficient that is significant at the 1 % level in the family firm sample and at the 5 % level in the non-family firm sample. Family firms have a mean equity ratio of 41.03 % and a median of 35 %, while non-family firms have a mean of 39.21 % and a median of 33 %. Because family firms have higher equity ratios, this is also reflected in the influence on the pricing of credit. A healthy equity ratio reflects the bargaining power of companies toward the bank. Given their higher levels of debt financing, these companies are important customers at their housebanks.

Note that the variable *Financial Distress* seems to affect the family firm sample more, as it shows a positive effect on the dependent variable and is significant at the 1 % level. Family firms often maintain the structure of their company, especially with regard to management. They may not show flexibility, while non-family firms do. Overall, they are more willing to replace management if a change in leadership is needed to bring the company back on course. Thus, family businesses tend to be more rigid, which seems to be reflected in the greater impact on them of financial distress.

4.2.7 Family firms versus non-family firms - Credit availability

Table 4-11 presents the results of the dependent variable *Credit Availability* in both the family and non-family firm samples.

The probit regression evaluates the 408 family firms and 168 non-family firms. The family firm model shows a pseudo R2 of 0.067, a log-likelihood of

Table 4-11: Probit regression – Family firm versus non-family firm sample – Credit availability

This table shows the analysis of the dependent variable *Credit Availability* for the split sample of 408 family firms and 168 non-family firms. This variable asks participants to express whether short-term debt with the main bank is renewed automatically upon maturity. The responses were measured on a five-point Likert-type scale ranging from 5 = "does not apply at all" to 1 = "strongly applies." For the purpose of the multivariate analysis, a dummy variable was then defined that equals 1 when the response exceeds the median sample responses, and 0 otherwise. The loan characteristics are measured by the variable *Finance Share*, which indicates the overall share of total debt financing of the firm that is financed by the most important bank. It is measured with a metric input in %. The variable *Lines of Credit* indicates the frequency with which a firm finances its business with lines of credit. The variable *Short-term Bank Debt* indicates the frequency with which the firm uses bank financing of less than one year, and the variable *Long-term Bank Debt* indicates that for more than one year. Variables are measured on an ordinal five-point Likert-type scale ranging from 1 (never) to 5 (always). The variable *Number* of banks the firm works with is measured with a metric input with integer numbers. The variable *Duration* shows the number of years the firm has worked with the most important bank and is measured with a metric input in years. The variable *Trust* indicates whether trust exists between the firm and the bank and is measured on an ordinal five-point Likert-type scale ranging from 1 (does not apply at all) to 5 (strongly applies). The variable *Meeting Frequency* indicates how often on average physical or non-physical meetings between the firm and the bank occur per year and is measured with a metric input. The variable *Scope* shows whether the bank provides most of the other bank services for the firm besides debt financing and is measured on an ordinal five-point Likert scale ranging from 1 (does not apply at all) to 5 (strongly applies). The variable *Loan Officer* indicates whether the firm has a permanent relationship manager at the bank and is measured on a dichotomous scale. The variable *Bank Type* indicates whether the bank is savings, co-operative, or private bank, and is measured on a dichotomous scale that equals 1 for *Savings Banks*, and 0 otherwise. The variable *Firm Age* indicates the number of years since the firm's founding, as recorded in the survey, and is measured on a metric input. The variable *Firm Size* is measured by the average number of employees in the year 2015 and is measured with a metric input. The variable *Legal Form* indicates whether the firm is a limited liability company (GmbH, AG, KGaA, GmbH & Co. KG) or an unlimited liability company (KG, OHG, or GbR), and is measured on a dichotomous scale that equals 1 for *Limited Liability Company*, and 0 otherwise. The variable *Equity Ratio* indicates the solvency of the firm as measured by the firm's equity ratio in the year 2015 according to the annual results and is measured with a metric input in %. The variable *Sales Growth* indicates the firm's sales growth in the year 2015 according to the annual results and is measured with a metric input in %. The variable *Financial Distress* is a dichotomous variable indicates whether the firm had been in financial distress since 2007. The variable *Industry* is a set of industry variables indicating to which industry the firm belongs, which is measured on a nominal scale, and is represented by the *Construction Industry*, the *Trade, Hospitality, Tourism Industry*, the *Traffic and Transportation Industry*, and the *Service Industry*. Standard errors are corrected for heteroskedasticity and given in parentheses. *, **, and *** denote statistical significance at the 10 %, 5 %, and 1 % levels, respectively.

Variables	**Family firms**	**Non-family firms**
Loan characteristics		
Finance Share	0.002**	0.009***
	(0.002)	(0.003)

(*continued on next page*)

Table 4-11: Continued

Lines of Credit	0.251***	0.344***
	(0.060)	(0.107)
Short-term Bank Debt	-0.171	-0.254
	(0.150)	(0.284)
Long-term Bank Debt	-0.111	0.468*
	(0.151)	(0.259)
Relationship characteristics		
Number	0.025***	0.086**
	(0.044)	(0.072)
Duration	0.078*	0.008
	(0.092)	(0.164)
Trust	0.210***	0.914*
	(0.138)	(0.248)
Meeting Frequency	0.218***	0.328*
	(0.123)	(0.235)
Scope	0.215*	0.608***
	(0.123)	(0.227)
Loan Officer	0.027**	0.370*
	(0.164)	(0.270)
Bank Type - Savings Bank	0.028	0.281
	(0.118)	(0.200)
Firm characteristics		
Firm Age	0.144**	0.216**
	(0.099)	(0.175)
Firm Size	0.144*	0.173**
	(0.055)	(0.084)
Legal Form (Limited Liability Company)	0.088	0.400**
	(0.133)	(0.228)
Equity Ratio	0.001**	0.006**
	(0.002)	(0.004)
Sales Growth	0.004*	0.003*
	(0.005)	(0.006)
Financial Distress	-0.138	0.183
	(0.134)	(0.231)
Control variables		
Construction Industry	0.132	0.886***
	(0.158)	(0.344)

Table 4-11: Continued

Trade, Hospitality, Tourism Industry	0.428*	1.761**
	(0.251)	(0.842)
Traffic, Transportation Industry	0.022	0.156
	(0.256)	(0.493)
Service Industry	0.098	-0.137
	(0.152)	(0.215)
Observations	408	168
Log-likelihood	-550.972	-189.763
Pseudo R2	0.067	0.196
LR chi2	78.714	92.273

-550.972, and a LR chi2 of 78.714, while the non-family firm model carries a pseudo R2 of 0.196, a log-likelihood of -189.763, and a LR chi2 of 92.273. Thus, the non-family firm sample exhibits slightly higher explanatory power. In terms of the loan characteristics, the variables *Finance Share* and *Lines of Credit* carry a positive coefficient in the family firm sample. While the variable *Finance Share* is significant at the 5 % level, the variable *Lines of Credit* is significant at the 1 % level. These variables also carry positive coefficients in the non-family firm sample that are significant at the 1 % level. Additionally, the variable *Long-term Bank Debt* also has a positive effect on the dependent variable in the non-family firm sample, which is slightly significant at the 10 % level. These findings so far confirm the empirical findings in section 4.2.1. Therefore, loan characteristics play a critical role when considering access to bank financing.

The variable *Number* has a positive coefficient that is significant at the 1 % level in the family firm sample and at the 5 % level in the non-family firm sample. The variable *Duration* carries a positive coefficient in the family firm sample that is significant at the 10 % level. Long-term orientation is often seen as a competitive advantage of family businesses over non-family businesses. James (1999) explores the extended planning horizon of family firms, and attributes it to the fundamental desire of the family to pass on the company to future generations.

According to Le Breton-Miller and Miller (2006), long-term orientation plays an important role in building sustainable relationships with stakeholders. Ultimately, firms want strong, stable partners at their side. We expect that family businesses experience more beneficial credit availability than non-family firms because they are better at nurturing firm-bank relationships. Robust relationship building is likely reflected in more trusting relationships, since trust plays such a pivotal role.

The variable *Trust* carries a positive coefficient that is highly significant at the 1 % level in the family firm sample, while it is only significant at the 10 % level in the non-family firm sample. The same results are found for the variable *Meeting Frequency*.

As a possible consequence of relationship management, and of the fact that family businesses provide their banks with more information, they can expect strong support from their banks during times of distress. In addition, the variable *Scope* carries a positive coefficient that is significant at the 10 % level in the family firm sample, and at the 1 % level in the non-family firm sample.

Loan Officer also shows a positive coefficient in both samples. It is significant at the 5 % level in the family firm sample, and only at the 10 % level in the non-family firm sample. As we noted earlier, companies build solid relationships with their loan officers, and family businesses have realized how that can positively impact availability. Loan officers can gain access to inside information, conveyed through repeated interactions between the loan officer and the entrepreneur (Diamond 1989; Fama 1985; Petersen and Rajan 1994). Such information assists the officer's subjective assessment of the firm's creditworthiness and loan decisions and is generally considered soft information (Berger and Udell 2002; Petersen 2004).

Soft information is a critical determinant of corporate lending, particularly to SMEs (Garcia-Appendini 2011). The results show that soft information can mitigate the repercussions of credit contractions (De Mitri, Gobbi, and Sette 2010a; Jiangli et al. 2008). According to D'Aurizio et al. (2015), "The reason is that hard information, such as past performance and standardized risk measures, are less reliable in predicting firm risk profiles during a crisis. Soft information about a firm's current results and future plans, which is continuously updated and better targeted to the characteristics of the borrower, can reduce such uncertainty" (D'Aurizio et al. 2015, p. 280).

The variables *Firm Age* and *Firm Size* show positive coefficients that are significant at the 5 % level; *Firm Size* in the family firm sample is only significant at the 10 % level. Regarding firm size, family firms have a median of fifty-two employees, while non-family firms have a median of sixty-eight. These findings confirm the results of the multivariate regression analysis in section 4.2.4.

The variable *Limited Liability Company* shows a positive effect at the 5 % level in the non-family firm sample. The results of the descriptive statistics show that a larger percent of limited liability companies fall in the non-family firm sample. Thus, the effect is stronger here. The advantage of limited liability companies over sole proprietorships and partnerships is that information is more readily available for the bank.

The variable *Equity Ratio* carries a positive coefficient in the family and non-family firm sample that is significant at the 5 % level. In addition, we added *Sales Growth*, which exhibits a positive coefficient that is significant at the 10 % level in both samples. However, note that the variable *Financial Distress* is not significant in either sample, which emphasizes that times of distress do not seem to significantly affect access to finance in a housebank relationship.

For the most part, family businesses do not appear to have been affected by credit rationing since the financial crisis of 2007–2009. On the one hand, family businesses tend to exhibit fundamentally healthy equity ratios, so their bargaining power toward their banks is probably higher. On the other hand, this could be the result of good relationship management. If the company and the housebank maintain solid long-term contact, characterized by an extensive information flow, the housebank would be expected to support the firm even during times of extreme financial difficulties. For example, Elsas and Krahnen (1998) find that housebanks provide a form of liquidity insurance during any unexpected deterioration in a borrower's financial situation.

Hypothesis 7 stated that family firms may receive better pricing and non-pricing terms from their relationship lenders than non-family firms. Examining the relationship characteristics results, we find that family firms exhibit higher significance. Particularly, the variables *Trust*, *Meeting Frequency*, and *Loan Officer* are more significant in the family firm sample, and, as a result, the hypothesis can be supported.

In addition to the firm's equity position, it seems there are other, less easily observable, characteristics that bankers perceive in the firms analyzed here. That is, family ownership may be perceived as a proxy for firm characteristics that bankers favor, such as the firm's long-term viewpoint, the cohesiveness of its management structure, its concern for reputation, its ability to self-regulate, and possibly the personal contacts among the owners, banks, and the community at large. These factors may be part of what the literature refers to as "character," and may influence a loan decision. While it is not possible to measure the relative influence of each of these characteristics or variables, it appears likely that together they represent a more conservative approach to investments, a factor that could reduce moral hazard problems for banks. This translates to a greater availability of loans to family firms. Overall, in relative terms, the negative aspects also linked with family businesses do not seem to discourage lenders (see also Bopaiah 1998).

5 Concluding remarks

5.1 Summary and discussion of the main results

This study began by raising the following questions: 1) how relationship banking is defined today and 2) how it affects pricing and non-pricing loan terms, in particular collateral requirements, the cost of debt, and credit availability. We aimed to identify the effect of banking relationships on these variables because these loan terms are determined by unobservable relationship characteristics, in addition to firm characteristics (see also Shikimi 2013). Furthermore, in the literature review we analyzed 177 studies in depth to contrast market- and bank-based financial systems.

Relationship banking is based on the concept of financial intermediation. Financial intermediaries play an important role in facilitating the circulation of loanable funds between investors and borrowers (Freixas and Rochet 1997). The vision behind this theory is to derive the existence of financial intermediaries from an asymmetric information perspective in the principal-agent relationship between investors and borrowers. Diamond (1984) states that banks as financial intermediaries have a comparative advantage in monitoring borrowers because a bank can realize economies of scale. Based on this theory, in bank-based financial systems financial intermediaries act as delegated monitors by decreasing the costs of collecting and processing information about firms and management, thereby decreasing agency costs and, to some extent, resolving agency problems (see also Chakraborty and Ray 2006; Holmström and Tirole 1997).

Agency theory posits that improved information flows will be associated with better assessment of risk, greater availability of credit, and more accurate pricing (Howorth and Moro 2012). A primary mechanism for this information processing is thought to be the bank-borrower relationship, which provides lenders with an opportunity to gather private firm information that can be used in developing loan contract terms (see, e.g., Boot and Thakor 1994).

However, after the worldwide financial crisis starting in 2007 and the widespread rise of new information technologies credit risk models became popular and information processing changed significantly. New market entrants reinforced these changes which manifest themselves in banking regulation that places greater emphasis on the use of hard over soft information. Therefore, the basic concept of relationship banking has become somewhat outdated (see also Hainz and Wiegand 2013).

Presbitero and Zazzaro (2011) point out that government interventions and bank mergers and acquisitions have reinforced the changes in the structure of the financial system. Developments in information technology have made financial markets more competitive. Hence, firms experiencing lending difficulties with their most important bank during times of distress may want to consider the many new alternative methods of financing.

Ultimately, the bank financing environment has changed dramatically, but the empirical evidence on this point is mixed. Sapienza and Zingales (2012) write that "Something important was destroyed in the last few months of 2008. It is an asset crucial to production, even if it is not made of bricks and mortar. [...] This asset is trust" (Sapienza and Zingales 2012, p. 123). They go on to note that trust is often understood as "the expectation that another person (or institution) will perform actions that are beneficial, or at least not detrimental, to us regardless of our capacity to monitor those actions. When we say we trust someone, we imply that we think that he will engage in beneficial, non-detrimental action so that we will consider cooperating with him" (Sapienza and Zingales 2012, p. 124).[98] The empirical findings of this study indicate that it is the outcome of longer relationships, e.g., increased trust, rather than solely their duration that is associated with lending decisions (Howorth and Moro 2012).

Our contribution to relationship banking is based on the results of a survey conducted among German SMEs. The idea was to analyze whether more favorable situations for collateral, improved lending rates, and better access to finance arise from an increasing intensity of the housebank relationship. Moreover, we aimed to determine how family businesses perform, and where the characteristics in the individual items differ from those of non-family businesses. We are then able to provide more insight as to whether family businesses have a closer, more intense relationship with their housebanks because of heightened relationship management and whether this effect should be measurable in the relationship characteristics.

Bank lending is by far the most important type of debt for both family and non-family firms. For our purposes, family firms represent an interesting subject of investigation because they are expected to have a positive impact on decreasing agency conflicts in the lender relationship. We examined whether this would translate into more favorable credit conditions. This question is closely related to differences between the incentive structures of family and non-family companies and, thus, to banks' potential risk-shifting problems (Jensen and Meckling

98 See also Lins et al. (2017) and Gambetta (2000).

1976). Family firms appear to value the identification of the family with the firm and often wish to pass the company on to descendants. This desire translates into higher attachment (Anderson et al. 2003). Therefore, family firms may be perceived as more creditworthy because they have less incentive to default in the future (D'Aurizio et al. 2015).

Altruism in family firms, however, may have a downside (Schulze, Lubatkin, and Dino 2003). It can cause "free riding" by family members as well as entrenchment of ineffective managers (Chrisman et al. 2004). Schulze et al. (2003) write that parents' altruism can lead them to be generous to their children even in the face of free riding and even if the children lack the competence or intentions to sustain the wealth of the company (Voordeckers and Steijvers 2006). Overall, we expected to find measurable effects when analyzing family versus non-family firms.

To gain perspective on these firms, we analyzed 576 companies, 408 family firms and 168 non-family firms. With the help of a survey, we collected vital data on loan contract and borrower characteristics from SMEs in Germany. The study used industry survey data rather than an evaluation of different databases as it allowed to focus on information that is directly related to firms' decisions about their bank relationships. Hence, this methodology provided a direct measure of the value of the bank relationship as perceived by the firm. This last point is critical because, without this direct measure, it would be impossible to focus our analysis on the factors that influence the value of bank relationships at the firm level.

The literature provides six factors to assess housebank status: 1) whether the housebank has a (relative to peer banks) large, often dominant share of the debt financing of the company, 2) whether the relationship is long-term in nature, 3) whether a special relationship of trust exists between the borrower and the bank, 4) whether the bank has an information advantage over competitive banks, 5) whether the bank performs most of the firm's other financial services, and 6) whether the bank carries a special responsibility to the firm during times of financial distress. When these factors are in place, there is a higher probability of observing a housebank relationship (see also Elsas 2001; Elsas and Krahnen 1998). The analysis showed that these determining factors are present in the sample, and, thus, relationship lending to this day remains characterized by these factors. Therefore, we conclude that housebank relationships still exist.

Overall, the analyzed SMEs carry on average 46.86 % of the debt financing of the firms, while the median value is even higher at 50 %. Collateral required to obtain the principal credit line ranges from 25 % to less than 50 % with a median value of 0 %. In 53 % of cases, when firm assets are pledged, 21 % provide personal guarantees, while 27 % provide a mix of firm assets and personal guarantees. The lending rate on the main credit line in 2015 averaged 3.81 % with a 3 % median. Credit availability (whether current account overdrafts at the main bank are automatically extended when due) was measured on a scale of 1 (does not apply at all) to 5 (fully applies) with an average of 3 and a median of 4. This means, there was a high level of approval on this question since relationship banking is primarily influenced by relationship variables. The empirical analysis focused on these variables.

Based on theory and prior empirical evidence, we derived hypotheses to examine the firm-bank lending relationship. Table 5-1 gives an overview. Four of the seven hypotheses were confirmed and three were rejected because the significance of the effects was low.

The hypotheses make an important contribution to the profound understanding of the value of relationship lending between firms and banks today. They are particularly important for the research framework and to assess the value of bank relationships after the worldwide financial crisis. In addition, the empirical analysis offers an essential extension to the literature, particularly when we draw correlations that have been somewhat controversial in the literature. The main hypothesis we examine here is based on the idea that a strong bank-borrower relationship may have a positive effect on credit availability. Table 5-2 presents the relationship variables that influence the credit conditions.

Overall, the number of bank relationships is related to housebank status, the cost of debt, and credit availability. However, the duration of the firm-bank relationship, which is a commonly used proxy variable for relationship lending in the literature, is not associated with housebank status. Based on our sample where the average duration is rather high, we find no continuous significant influence on credit conditions.

The mere duration of a bank relationship does not improve credit conditions, but trust in the relationship can lead to an improvement in credit terms. Likewise, duration alone does not characterize the intensity of the relationship. However, duration is a vital condition for a lending relationship because repeated transactions between firms and their main banks create interactions, information, and trust. A strong and resilient lending relationship is characterized by breadth, intimacy, and trust (see, e.g., Elsas and Krahnen 1998; Harhoff and Körting 1998; Elsas 2001; Hernández-Cánovas and Martínez-Solano 2010). Trust is a quality indicator of a business-to-business relationship and is a major factor influencing credit conditions. It can be influenced by the following: the quantity of information provided to the most important bank and periodic reviews (more than two meetings per year), the amount of banking services

Table 5-1: Overview of confirmed and rejected hypotheses

This table shows an overview of the hypotheses analyzed. Four were confirmed; three were rejected.

		Confirmed	**Rejected**
Hypothesis 1:	*Firms with more bank relationships receive better credit terms from their most important banks than firms with fewer bank relationships.*	✓	
Hypothesis 2:	*Firms in long-term relationships with their most important banks experience increased credit availability and reduced lending costs.*		X
Hypothesis 3:	*Credit availability and pricing are better for firms that have a trusting relationship with their most important banks.*	✓	
Hypothesis 4:	*Family firms have more contact with their housebanks than non-family firms.*	✓	
Hypothesis 5:	*Family firms maintain longer relationships with their housebanks than non-family firms.*		X
Hypothesis 6:	*Family firms obtain the largest share of their external capital demands from their housebanks compared to non-family firms.*		X
Hypothesis 7:	*Family firms receive better pricing and non-pricing terms from their housebanks than non-family firms.*	✓	

Table 5-2: Matrix - Variables for bank lending terms and conditions

This table summarizes the relationship variables in the relationship between the company and the housebank and shows their effect on loan terms and conditions. + means positive effect and – means negative effect, in other words, significance at the 5 % level or higher in at least two variables. 0 means no effect, in other words, significance at the 5 % level or lower or non-significant.

Exogenous variables	*Collateral Requirements*	*Cost of Debt*	*Credit Availability*
Number	+	–	+
Duration	0	0	0
Trust	0	–	+
Meeting Frequency	+	0	+
Scope	0	0	+
Loan Officer	0	–	+
Bank Type	+	+	0

(product portfolio size) provided by the main bank, and the presence of a designated loan officer at the bank.

Compared to the empirical findings in the literature review in Table 2-6, our results confirm the *Number* of bank relationships and how they influence collateral requirements. The effect on pricing in terms of the interest rate and credit availability was not confirmed. But the coefficients are significant and have a negative effect on the cost of debt and a positive effect on credit availability. Moreover, the influence of the variable *Duration* does not confirm the results of the literature review. However, with regard to *Trust* we show that its effect on pricing and on access to finance is confirmed even after the crisis. In addition, the effect of *Scope* on access to finance from the literature review was confirmed.

We find several variables, largely neglected in the literature so far that show effects as well. The variable *Meeting Frequency* significantly increases access to bank financing, while *Loan Officer* has a negative effect on credit pricing and a positive effect on credit access. Even with respect to the German three-pillar system, two effects were determined: corporate customers at savings banks appear to pledge more collateral and to pay higher interest rates. In addition, the current transformation of the German banking system as presented in section 2.5.1, which discussed the reduction in branch network over the past years, has led and will further lead to a growing distance between the bank and the customer and this distance then creates higher information asymmetries amplifying unfavorable financing parameters.

According to Hainz and Wiegand (2013), firms should make sure to nurture their bank relationships. The inclusion of the variable *Financial Distress* in the multivariate regression analysis of the dependent variable *Credit Availability* shows that the effect of the independent variable *Trust* is highly significant, while *Financial Distress* carries no significant coefficients. Bolton et al. (2016) also show that relationship lending is an important mitigating factor during the crises (see also Malafronte et al. 2014). The authors go even further by noting that if more companies could be encouraged to pursue a long-term bank relationship and if relationship banks could be encouraged to hold larger equity capital buffers prior to a financial shock, the effects of financial disasters on corporate investment and the economy would be smaller.

One could conclude that it is advisable to cultivate several bank relationships at a very early stage of a company's lifetime and to nurture those relationships closely over the years. The findings show that having more than one bank relationship contributes to higher credit availability. In this context, the question arises as to whether firms with multiple bank relationships have a better chance of absorbing shocks and obtaining better credit conditions. Bank-dependent borrowers (in Germany, these are typically small firms) face significant hold-up risk from their relationship banks. Therefore, closer bank relationships may also be a source of rents for the banks.

We also explore whether relationship banks impose higher loan rates. They may be competing fiercely for new borrowers and may impose above-market rates (Degryse et al. 2009). Our empirical findings show that bank-dependent borrowers benefit to a greater degree than non-bank dependent borrowers from favorable non-price conditions.

Note that the effect of the variable *Number* is negative on *Collateral Requirements* and *Cost of Debt*, but positive on *Credit Availability*. Thus, it has a positive outcome on these dependent variables when more than one bank relationship is in place. We conclude that rent shifting is not occurring, which may be the result of measurably increased transparency in the financial system.

Regarding the variable *Trust*, it was primarily important to determine potential effects after the financial crisis. We show that, first and foremost, this variable exhibits a highly significant effect on *Cost of Debt* and *Credit Availability*. The effect is even stronger when we consider only family firms.

Family businesses tend to value longer-term and familiar financing relationships. Financing a family business with a long-term bank loan enables close cooperation with the bank. Graham and Harvey (2001) find that far-sighted companies choose long-term bank loans in order to limit the risk of refinancing during bad times. To maintain a strong relationship, the behavior of the family business toward the bank, as well as that of the bank toward the borrower, is critical. Only when both sides invest in this relationship and can credibly commit to enhancing the relationship, the variables will be strong enough to influence the lending relationship.

For the family firm sample, the exogenous variables *Trust, Loan Officer, Meeting Frequency, and Number* show a measurable effect on the endogenous variables. The observed differences between family and non-family firms in the change in credit granted could also stem from differences in the ability to provide hard and verifiable information. Also, the cost of borrowing and credit availability were analyzed to check for differences in the change in the net interest rate charged to family and non-family firms. The variables *Trust* and *Loan Officer* appeared to have significant effects on the endogenous variables.

Family firms value the identification of the family with the firm and often desire to pass the company on to their descendants. This desire translates into higher attachment (Anderson et al. 2003). Therefore, family firms may be perceived as more creditworthy because they have less incentive to default in the future (D'Aurizio et al. 2015). Family firms seem better able to develop personal and well-informed relationships with lenders, which suggests that the family's presence allows these relationships to build over successive generations. Given these realities, the quality of the family's reputation is more likely to create long-lasting consequences for the firm relative to that of non-family firms (Niskanen, Karjalainen, and Niskanen 2010). The effects on credit conditions were likewise measurable.

These results are important in two ways. First, family firms are common all over the world among SMEs. So their access to financial markets is a significant factor in the performance of the economy. Financially constrained firms tend to lower investment and employment levels (Campello, Graham, and Harvey 2010) while aggravating the potential impact of credit supply shocks (D'Aurizio et al. 2015).

Contrary to the transaction-oriented design of banking relationships, our results tend to favor a relationship-oriented approach. Thus, although some companies have a comparatively strong bargaining position with regard to the equity ratio, business allocation is not based primarily on the price of banking services. Companies prioritize on the basis of other qualitative criteria which in addition to maintaining an independent relationship with a single bank include long-term reliability and personal experience with a loan officer. The changes so far have not yet led to the replacement of the long-term planning bank-oriented financial system with a short-term, cost-oriented one.

5.2 Limitations and avenues for future research

Note that our study has some shortcomings. First, to evaluate traditional relationship banking, only a one-year window for analysis was available (see also Ono et al. 2014). Therefore, only a cross-sectional regression analysis was possible and, thus, we consider only one point in time. Moreover, the method of online surveys holds various advantages and disadvantages. But online surveys comprise one of the primary databases.

Primary databases allow researchers to align their vision along specific goals and purposes cutting down on wasted resources. The researcher can modify the course of study when desired. Primary research may be more expensive than secondary research, however. In addition, this collection method is often more time-consuming and may require other assets besides monetary ones. An online survey is typically less expensive because it offers low cost implementation and rapid data collection compared to, for example, large-scale personal interviews. Nevertheless, the outcome of primary data collection methods may not always turn out as expected. Additionally, this method is at risk of a lack of representativeness due to selection bias.

A selection bias can emerge when the data selection occurs in such a way that appropriate randomization is not obtained. As a result, the sample collected lacks representativeness. The distribution of the characteristics in the sample no longer corresponds to the true distribution in the population. In our study, sample bias may occur because there may be too many small or large companies. Moreover, family firms may be underrepresented, as the literature review showed that approximately 95 % of all companies in Germany are family-owned (Bundesverband der Deutschen Industrie e.V. 2015). Factors, for instance, participant motivation and identity with the topic, can also distort the results.

Thus, our aim should be that the survey data reflect the real economy as much as possible. The data may not be fully representative, which would impact the empirical findings, so we must assess the selection bias appropriately to derive suitable concluding remarks.

Despite these drawbacks, especially in recent years, surveys have gained in increasing importance (Bieber and Bytzek 2012).[99] Therefore, we analyzed a unique and comprehensive new dataset using industry survey data to focus on information directly related to firms' financial decision-making processes. There was no access to the participants' identities because strict confidentiality during the survey was enforced. Moreover, the sample was limited mostly to smaller borrowers who are most likely to rely on banks for external financing.

Furthermore, the sample may not reflect the real economy because the companies that participated are likely to be those that identified most strongly with the topic. This does not necessarily ensure a good cross-section of the corporate landscape. So, for example, the economy might contain more small companies than are represented by our dataset. The same applies to the distribution of family businesses.

---

99 As discussed in section 3.1, using secondary databases also holds certain disadvantages. Secondary data can include information that someone has already researched, prepared, and analyzed. This data collection method is usually quite cost-effective, offers readily usable observations, and requires less time for gathering information (Ghauri and Grønhaug 2005). It also usually provides statistically reliable data, and, therefore, less expertise from researchers is needed. In contrast, however, the information provided may be inappropriate for the research question, and the data may lack the necessary details. Or, it may provide a vast amount of information (Denscombe 2014) that would need to be customized and examined exhaustively to judge its validity. Researchers may also be confronted with a lack of control over data quality. Government and other official institutions usually guarantee quality data, but other institutions may not (Bryman and Bell 2015). Selection bias in a weakened form is also a risk.

Thus, to address possible distortions in the dataset, we conducted some preliminary tests to ensure the validity of the data used in the multivariate analyses. First, we tested independent variables for multicollinearity. In general, there is always a certain degree present in regression analyses. A correlation matrix of the independent variables provided a first indication. Correlation coefficients close to the value of 1 indicate a strong multicollinearity, which did not apply to the dataset. In addition, as part of the multivariate analyses, we evaluated the Variance Inflation Factors (VIF), which showed no signs of multicollinearity. Outlier diagnostics are another important preliminary test. We calculated boxplots to test for outliers. The boxplots showed only a few extreme values in our dataset. In this case, the natural logarithm of the variable is applicable.

In order to further test the robustness of the regression results, we modified the dataset to check whether we obtained the same results. Our results were unchanged, which provided evidence of the robustness of the multivariate results. Furthermore, we addressed endogeneity problems. For example, a bank may be more willing to grant loans to firms that have already pledged collateral (D'Aurizio et al. 2015). This problem was addressed by creating subsamples of firms that provided collateral and those that did not. We find that this problem is not prevalent in our dataset.

Since the development of the OLS regression, this has been one of the most widely used and important methods in statistics. In principle, however, the weaknesses of the methodology must also be taken into account. First, note that OLS regressions lead to information compression, without which it would be difficult to transform the wealth of possible variables into coherent, practical concepts. But the information compression reduces the complexity, and a disadvantage is the resulting loss of information. Another recurrent problem with the practice of OLS analysis is deciding how many factors to include. Too few or too many can have severe consequences for interpretation, so choosing the optimal number of variables is an important decision.

Furthermore, the size of the sample must be taken into account. Again, there are differences of opinion about the optimal sample size of an OLS regression relative to the number of variables included. In this context, the sensitivity of the results must be noted. Smaller samples run the risk of being volatile as soon as a variable is changed. This can lead to misinterpretations. Therefore, future studies should consider collecting a larger sample over a longer period of time. Finally, with regard to the composition of the sample only German firms were observed. Scholars need to handle any cross-country applications carefully (see also Ono et al. 2014).

It is also necessary to evaluate more deeply whether the enhanced bargaining power of the borrower is due to a hold-up problem or to a strategy to mitigate the soft budget constraint, which would increase the availability of credit to SMEs. Thus, it is important to control in-depth for market conditions, such as the number of competitors and the regulatory system. These issues should be addressed in future studies.

When developing multivariate models, it is essential to verify their validity. In light of some of our limitations, future investigations could carry out a more comprehensive data collection in order to increase the validity and reliability of the housebank relationship. In this context, it would be advisable to perform the multivariate regression analysis with an even larger sample size. Accordingly, the issues of collateral in the housebank relationship, the loan interest rates, and the access to finance could be examined more closely. It would also be interesting to explore the exact nature of the information being exchanged and communicated within the housebank relationship. It would be instructive to determine how the information shared with the housebank differs from that shared in transactional bank relationships.

In conclusion, despite the advantages and disadvantages of the survey tool and the methodology the subject matter of housebanks seems to arouse great interest. This is likely because SMEs remain largely reliant on bank-related lending (e.g., credit lines and banks loans) to finance their business operations. The EBA report documents that other sources of financing, for example, equity finance, capital market debt, and securitization, are not as widely used by SMEs (European Banking Authority 2016). Lending conditions have also been noticeably impacted by the financial crisis with a substantial credit contraction observed since 2008.

According to the European Central Bank (2017a), 25 % of SMEs consider the ability to obtain credit in the future as their most important concern. 20 % consider credit rating as the most important concern, followed by the risk of financial distress (16 %). The interest rate on new debt was the most critical factor for 13 %.

In contrast, large companies generally exhibit better financial situations than SMEs. Approximately 39 % of large companies applied for a bank loan and 86 % of those received it. In fact, the rejection rate was only 1 %, while, for SMEs, the success rate was 74 % and the rejection rate 6 %. The average interest rate on credit lines for large companies is approximately 180 basis points lower than that for SMEs.

These findings show that large companies profit from easier access to finance and they progress more smoothly with their external financing terms and conditions. Overall, access to financing in recent years has been of much greater concern to SMEs than to large companies. The findings show that about 16 % of SMEs indicated some issues with bank loan financing (e.g., they were discouraged from applying, they were rejected, the costs were too high, or they received only part of what they applied for). For large companies, that number was 10 %. Financing difficulties differ by firm size, with micro and small companies most affected (European Banking Authority 2016).

According to the KfW results, in 2016 two-thirds of all SMEs used bank credit to finance an investment. Overall, bank loans remain the second most important financing source, and, thus, SMEs continue to rely primarily on their own funds for investment financing (Schwartz 2017). We offer some recommendations for action for different stakeholders next.

The popularity of collateralized loans has decreased in recent years. Dorfleitner et al. (2016) also point to the market penetration of FinTechs. Against this background and with regard to the value proposition of banks, firms may want to consider investing in their housebank relationships even more to secure their positions. Our recommendations for political, economic, and further research action are derived from this notion.

Interactions between banks and businesses are essential as they are the very foundation of the economic engine and its stability. Developments in information technology and digitization should enable banks and industry to work together more easily. Future work may want to develop the legal framework so that banks can cooperate, for example, with FinTechs without having to operate on uncertain terrain. In addition, the efforts of the banks themselves are important because the developments and the pressure will continue. It is vital for the business model of banks to maintain frequent dialogue with their customers and to evaluate their needs.

We noted earlier that most SMEs are family businesses. About 95 % of all companies in Germany are family-owned. Hence, these firms traditionally rely very strongly on bank lending and loans with different maturities. In fact, credit lines and leasing contracts represent their most important sources of funding after internal financing (Zimmermann 2017). Zimmermann (2017) posits that bank loans will remain an important source of financing because 55 % of companies conducted credit negotiations in 2016 and long-term loans were most in demand, followed by medium- and short-term loans. In light of the fast-changing banking environment, it is important for SMEs and, thus, for family firms to constantly reassess their financing sources.

Of course, all of this change will lead to further shifts in the position of banks. Our study has shown that banks are one of the most important pillars of the financial system. Therefore, researchers should continue to study developments in detail as this is the only way for industry and policymakers to respond sustainably and proactively. For researchers, further efforts should be made to interview entrepreneurs, despite the difficulty and time required. Today, companies have a larger repertoire of financing options available to them besides the more traditional banking and finance methods. Continued globalization and open markets have reinforced competition in the financial system. Future research should investigate the new developments and continue to provide important empirical findings. In this context, exploring the determinants of banks' strategies further represents an interesting topic (Ono et al. 2014). It would also be interesting to study which companies are obtaining financing from FinTechs because it may not be the companies with the most stable lending relationships.

As the Deutsche Bundesbank (2018b) reports, during the financial crisis and the European debt crisis companies in the euro area began substituting bank loans with other debt instruments and equity. Thus, future research should explore the ramifications and burden for SMEs as well as recommendations for action by policymakers.

An EU-wide capital discount factor was proposed by the EBA in January 2014 (European Banking Authority 2016). Article 501(1) of the CRR introduced the SME SF, under which capital requirements for credit risk on exposures to SMEs are multiplied by a factor of 0.7619 (Amtsblatt der Europäischen Union 2013). The SME SF allows banks to decrease capital requirements for credit risk on exposures to firms with annual turnovers of less than EUR 50 million. As detailed in the EBA (2016) report, the intention of this deduction was to promote increased lending to SMEs following the crisis and to ease regulatory changes that could have a disproportionate effect on SME lending, thus, ensuring the adequate flow of credit (European Banking Authority 2016; Mayordomo and Rodríguez-Moreno 2016). At the same time, German policymakers should also continue their efforts to support a good financial environment for SMEs because they are such an important driver of the German economy.

6 References

Abbott, M. G. (2014). *Marginal effects in probit models: Interpretation and testing.* Retrieved from http://econ.queensu.ca/faculty/abbott/econ452/452note15.pdf.

Acharya, V., Almeida, H., Ippolito, F., & Perez, A. (2014). Credit lines as monitored liquidity insurance: Theory and evidence. *Journal of Financial Economics*, 112, 287–319.

Adam, T. R., & Streitz, D. (2016). Hold-up and the use of performance-sensitive debt. *Journal of Financial Intermediation*, 26, 47–67.

Agarwal, R., & Elston, J. A. (2001). Bank–firm relationships, financing and firm performance in Germany. *Economics Letters*, 72, 225–232.

Agarwal, S., & Hauswald, R. (2008). The choice between arm's-length and relationship debt: Evidence from eLoans. *Working Paper*.

Agarwal, S., & Hauswald, R. (2010). Distance and Private Information in Lending. *The Review of Financial Studies*, 23(7), 2757–2788.

Agrawal, A., & Jayaraman, N. (1994). The dividend policies of all-equity firms: A direct test of the free cash flow theory. *Managerial and Decision Economics*, 15(2), 139–148.

Aguilera, R. V., & Crespi-Cladera, R. (2016). Global corporate governance: On the relevance of firms' ownership structure. *Journal of World Business*, 51(1), 50–57.

Aguilera, R. V., & Jackson, G. (2003). The cross-national diversity of corporate governance: Dimensions and determinants. *Academy of management Review*, 28(3), 447–465.

Aguilera, R. V., & Jackson, G. (2010). Comparative and international corporate governance. *The Academy of Management Annals*, 4(1), 485–556.

Akerlof, G. A. (1970). The market for "lemons": Quality uncertainty and the market mechanism. *Quarterly Journal of Economics*, 84(3), 488–500.

Albareto, G., Benvenuti, M., Mocetti, S., Pagnini, M., & Rossi, P. (2008). Lending organizational structure and the use of credit scoring: Evidence from a survey on Italian banks. *Bank of Italy Occasional Paper* (12), 1–43.

Albertazzi, U., & Bottero, M. (2014). Foreign bank lending: Evidence from the global financial crisis. *Journal of International Economics*, 92, S22–S35.

Albertazzi, U., & Marchetti, D. J. (2010). Credit supply, flight to quality and evergreening: an analysis of bank-firm relationships after Lehman. *Working Paper* (756).

Alchian, A. A., & Woodward, S. (1988). The firm is dead; long live the firm a review of Oliver E. Williamson's the economic institutions of capitalism. *Journal of economic literature*, 26(1), 65–79.

Alem, M. (2004). Insurance motives in banking relationships: Evidence from Argentina. *Working Paper*.

Alessandrini, P., Presbitero, A. F., & Zazzaro, A. (2008). Banks, distances and firms' financing constraints. *Review of Finance*, 13(2), 261–307.

Alessandrini, P., Presbitero, A. F., & Zazzaro, A. (2009). Global banking and local markets: a national perspective. *Cambridge Journal of Regions, Economy and Society*, 2(2), 173–192.

Allen, F., & Gale, D. (1999). Diversity of opinion and financing of new technologies. *Journal of Financial Intermediation*, 8(1–2), 68–89.

Allen, F., & Gale, D. (2000). *Comparing financial systems*. Massachusetts: MIT Press.

Allen, L., DeLong, G., & Saunders, A. (2004). Issues in the credit risk modeling of retail markets. *Journal of Banking & Finance*, 28(4), 727–752.

Alparslan, A. (2007). *Strukturalistische Prinzipal-Agent-Theorie: Eine Reformulierung der Hidden-Action-Modelle aus der Perspektive des Strukturalismus*. Wiesbaden: Springer-Verlag.

Alsos, G. A., Isaksen, E. J., & Ljunggren, E. (2006). New Venture Financing and Subsequent Business Growth in Men–and Women–Led Businesses. *Entrepreneurship Theory and Practice*, 30(5), 667–686.

Amit, R., & Villalonga, B. (2014). Financial performance of family firms. In L. Melin, M. Nordqvist, & P. Sharma (Eds.), *The Sage handbook of family business* (pp. 157–178). London: Sage.

Ampenberger, M., Schmid, T., Achleitner, A.-K., & Kaserer, C. (2013). Capital structure decisions in family firms: Empirical evidence from a bank-based economy. *Review of Managerial Science*, 7(3), 247–275.

Amtsblatt der Europäischen Union. (2013). *Verordnung (EU) Nr. 575/2013 des Europäischen Parlaments und des Rates vom 26. Juni 2013 über Aufsichtsanforderungen an Kreditinstitute und Wertpapierfirmen und zur Änderung der Verordnung (EU) Nr. 646/2012 Text von Bedeutung für den EWR*. Retrieved from http://eur-lex.europa.eu/legal-content/DE/TXT/?uri=celex%3A32013R0575.

Anderson, R. C., Mansi, S. A., & Reeb, D. M. (2003). Founding family ownership and the agency cost of debt. *Journal of Financial Economics*, 68(2), 263–285.

Anderson, R. C., & Reeb, D. M. (2003). Founding-family ownership and firm performance: Evidence from the S&P 500. *The Journal of Finance*, 58(3), 1301–1328.

Ang, J. S., Lin, J. W., & Tyler, F. (1995). Evidence on the lack of separation between business and personal risks among small businesses. *The Journal of Entrepreneurial Finance*, 4(2), 197–210.

Angelini, P., Di Salvo, R., & Ferri, G. (1998). Availability and cost of credit for small businesses: Customer relationships and credit cooperatives. *Journal of Banking & Finance*, 22(6–8), 925–954.

Angelkort, A., & Stuwe, A. (2011). *Basel III and SME financing*. Bonn: Friedrich-Ebert-Stiftung, Zentrale Aufgaben.

Antoniou, A., Guney, Y., & Paudyal, K. (2008). The determinants of capital structure: Capital market-oriented versus bank-oriented institutions. *Journal of Financial and Quantitative Analysis*, 43(1), 59–92.

Aoki, M., & Dinç, S. (1997). Relational financing as an institution and its viability under competition. *Working Paper*, Stanford University.

Arbeitskreis Finanzierung. (1988). Ansätze zur Gestaltung des Netzes von Bankverbindungen durch eine Unternehmung. *Zeitschrift für betriebswirtschaftliche Forschung*, 40, 739–767.

Arrow, K. J. (1984). The economics of agency. *Stanford University Technical Report* (451), 1–33.

Arrow, K. J. (1985). Informational structure of the firm. *The American Economic Review*, 75(2), 303–307.

Attar, A., & Campioni, E. (2003). Costly state verification and debt contracts: A critical resume. *Research in Economics*, 57(4), 315–343.

Audretsch, D. B., Hülsbeck, M., & Lehmann, E. E. (2013). Families as active monitors of firm performance. *Journal of Family Business Strategy*, 4(2), 118–130.

Avery, R. B., Bostic, R. W., & Samolyk, K. A. (1998). The role of personal wealth in small business finance. *Journal of Banking & Finance*, 22(6–8), 1019–1061.

Ayadi, R., Arbak, E., & Pieter De Groen, W. (2012). *Regulation of European banks and business models: Towards a new paradigm?* Brussels: Centre for European Policy Studies.

Azariadis, C. (1975). Implicit contracts and underemployment equilibria. *Journal of political Economy*, 83(6), 1183–1202.

Azariadis, C., & Stiglitz, J. E. (1983). Implicit contracts and fixed price equilibria. *The Quarterly Journal of Economics*, 98, 1–22.

Baker, G. P., & Wruck, K. H. (1989). Organizational changes and value creation in leveraged buyouts: The case of the OM Scott & Sons Company. *Journal of Financial Economics*, 25(2), 163–190.

Balderston, T. (1991). German banking between the wars: The crisis of the credit banks. *Business History Review*, 65(3), 554–605.

Bank for International Settlements. (2014). *Basel Committee on Banking Supervision - Basel III leverage ratio framework and disclosure requirements.* Retrieved from https://www.bis.org/publ/bcbs270.pdf.

Bannier, C. (2005). Vertragstheorie–Eine Einführung mit finanzökonomischen Beispielen und Anwendungen, 1. *Aufl.*, Heidelberg.

Barca, F. (1995). On corporate governance in Italy: Issues, facts and agenda. *Working Paper.*

Barontini, R., & Caprio, L. (2006). The effect of family control on firm value and performance: Evidence from continental Europe. *European Financial Management*, 12(5), 689–723.

Bartoli, F., Ferri, G., Murro, P., & Rotondi, Z. (2012). Soft information and loan supply in the crisis: Evidence from the credit files of a large bank. *Working Paper.*

Bartoli, F., Ferri, G., Murro, P., & Rotondi, Z. (2014). Bank support and export: Evidence from small Italian firms. *Small Business Economics*, 42(2), 245–264.

Basler Ausschuss für Bankenaufsicht. (2004). Internationale Konvergenz der Eigenkapitalmessung und der Eigenkapitalanforderungen. *Überarbeitete Rahmenvereinbarung. Bank für Internationalen Zahlungsausgleich, Basel.*

Becchetti, L., & Garcia, M. M. (2011). Informal collateral and default risk: Do 'Grameen-like'banks work in high-income countries? *Applied Financial Economics*, 21(13), 931–947.

Beck, T., Degryse, H., De Haas, R., & Van Horen, N. (2017). When arm's length is too far. Relationship banking over the business cycle. *Finance and Insurance.*

Beck, T., Demirgüç-Kunt, A., & Pería, M. S. M. (2011). Bank financing for SMEs: Evidence across countries and bank ownership types. *Journal of Financial Services Research*, 39(1–2), 35–54.

Behr, P., & Schmidt, R. H. (2015). The German banking system: Characteristics and challenges. *White Paper Series* (32).

Bencivenga, V. R., & Smith, B. D. (1991). Financial intermediation and endogenous growth. *The Review of Economic Studies*, 58(2), 195–209.

Bennedsen, M., Nielsen, K. M., Pérez-González, F., & Wolfenzon, D. (2007). Inside the family firm: The role of families in succession decisions and performance. *The Quarterly Journal of Economics*, 122(2), 647–691.

Berg, G., & Schrader, J. (2009). Relationship lending in times of crises: What about default and interest rates. *Working Paper.*

Berger, A. N., Frame, W. S., & Ioannidou, V. (2011). Tests of ex ante versus ex post theories of collateral using private and public information. *Journal of Financial Economics*, 100(1), 85–97.

Berger, A. N., Goulding, W., & Rice, T. (2014). Do small businesses still prefer community banks? *Journal of Banking & Finance*, 44, 264–278.

Berger, A. N., Klapper, L. F., & Udell, G. F. (2001). The ability of banks to lend to informationally opaque small businesses. *Journal of Banking & Finance*, 25(12), 2127–2167.

Berger, A. N., Miller, N. H., Petersen, M. A., Rajan, R. G., & Stein, J. C. (2005). Does function follow organizational form? Evidence from the lending practices of large and small banks. *Journal of Financial Economics*, 76(2), 237–269.

Berger, A. N., Rosen, R. J., & Udell, G. F. (2007). Does market size structure affect competition? The case of small business lending. *Journal of Banking & Finance*, 31, 11–33.

Berger, A. N., & Udell, G. F. (1995a). Relationship lending and lines of credit in small firm finance. *The Journal of Business*, 68(3), 351–381.

Berger, A. N., & Udell, G. F. (1995b). Universal banking and the future of small business lending. *Working Paper.*

Berger, A. N., & Udell, G. F. (2002). Small business credit availability and relationship lending: The importance of bank organisational structure. *The economic journal*, 112(477), 32–53.

Berglöf, E., & Perotti, E. (1994). The governance structure of the Japanese financial keiretsu. *Journal of Financial Economics*, 36(2), 259–284.

Berle, A., & Means, G. (1932). *Private property and the modern corporation.* New York: Harcourt, Brace & World.

Bernanke, B. S., & Mihov, I. (1998). Measuring monetary policy. *The Quarterly Journal of Economics*, 113(3), 869–902.

Besanko, D., & Thakor, A. V. (1987). Competitive equilibrium in the credit market under asymmetric information. *Journal of Economic Theory*, 42(1), 167–182.

Bester, H. (1985). Screening vs. rationing in credit markets with imperfect information. *American Economic Review*, 75(4), 850–855.

Bharath, S., Dahiya, S., Saunders, A., & Srinivasan, A. (2007). So what do I get? The bank's view of lending relationships. *Journal of Financial Economics*, 85, 368–419.

Bharath, S. T., Dahiya, S., Saunders, A., & Srinivasan, A. (2009). Lending relationships and loan contract terms. *The Review of Financial Studies*, 24(4), 1141–1203.

Bharath, S., Dahiya, S., Saunders, A., & Srinivasan, A. (2011). Lending relationships and loan contract terms. *The Review of Financial Studies*, 24(4).

Bhattacharya, S., & Thakor, A. V. (1993). Contemporary banking theory. *Journal of Financial Intermediation*, 3(1), 2–50.

Bhide, A. (1993). The hidden costs of stock market liquidity. *Journal of Financial Economics*, 34(1), 31–51.

Bieber, I. E., & Bytzek, E. (2012). Online-Umfragen: Eine geeignete Erhebungsmethode für die Wahlforschung? *Methoden – Daten – Analysen*, 6(2), 185–211.

Binks, M. R., & Ennew, C. T. (1997). Smaller businesses and relationship banking: The impact of participative behavior. *Entrepreneurship Theory and Practice*, 21(4), 83–92.

Blackwell, D. W., & Winters, D. B. (1997). Banking relationships and the effect of monitoring on loan pricing. *The Journal of Financial Research*, 20(2), 275–289.

Blaug, M. (1992). *The methodology of economics: Or, how economists explain* (2 ed.). Cambridge: Cambridge University Press.

Block, J. H. (2012). R&D investments in family and founder firms: An agency perspective. *Journal of Business Venturing*, 27(2), 248–265.

Bloom, N., & Van Reenen, J. (2007). Measuring and explaining management practices across firms and countries. *Quarterly Journal of Economics*, 122(4), 1351–1408.

Board, T. F. R. (2008). *Survey of Small Business Finances*. Retrieved from https://www.federalreserve.gov/pubs/oss/oss3/nssbftoc.htm.

Bodenhorn, H. (2003). Short-term loans and long-term relationships: Relationship lending in early America. *Journal of Money, Credit and Banking*, 35(4), 485–505.

Bodenhorn, H. (2007). Usury ceilings and bank lending behavior: Evidence from nineteenth century New York. *Explorations in Economic History*, 44, 179–202.

Bolton, P., Freixas, X., Gambacorta, L., & Mistrulli, P. E. (2016). Relationship and transaction lending in a crisis. *The Review of Financial Studies*, 29(10), 2643–2676.

Bolton, P., & Scharfstein, D. S. (1996). Optimal debt structure and the number of creditors. *Journal of political Economy*, 104(1), 1–25.

Bonett, D. G., & Wright, T. A. (2000). Sample size requirements for estimating Pearson, Kendall and Spearman correlations. *Psychometrika*, 65(1), 23–28.

Bongini, P., Battista, M. L. D., & Nieri, L. (2015). Relationship lending through the cycle: What can we learn from three decades of research? *Working Paper*.

Boot, A. W. A. (2000). Relationship banking: What do we know? *Journal of Financial Intermediation*, 9, 7–25.

Boot, A. W. A., Greenbaum, S., & Thakor, A. V. (1993). Reputation and discretion in financial contracting. *American Economic Review*, 83(5), 1165–1183.

Boot, A. W. A., & Thakor, A. V. (1994). Moral hazard and secured lending in an infinitely repeated credit market game. *International Economic Review*, 35(4), 899–920.

Boot, A. W. A., & Thakor, A. V. (1997). Financial system architecture. *The Review of Financial Studies*, 10(3), 693–733.

Boot, A. W. A., Thakor, A. V., & Udell, G. F. (1991). Secured Lending and Default Risk: Equilibrium Analysis, Policy Implications and Empirical Results. *The Economic Journal*, 101(406), 458–472.

Bopaiah, C. (1998). Availability of credit to family businesses. *Small Business Economics*, 11(1998), 75–86.

Bourdieu, P. (1986). The forms of capital. In J. G. Richardson (Ed.), *Handbook of theory and research for the sociology of education* (pp. 241–258). New York: Greenwood Press.

Boyd, J. H., & Prescott, E. C. (1986). Financial intermediary-coalitions. *Journal of Economic Theory*, 38(2), 211–232.

Brackschulze, K., Mayer-Fiedrich, M. D., & Müller, S. (2011). *Finanzierung mittelständischer Unternehmen nach Basel III* (2 ed.). München: Verlag Franz Vahlen.

Bradley, M., Jarrell, G. A., & Kim, E. H. (1984). On the existence of an optimal capital structure: Theory and evidence. *The Journal of Finance*, 39(3), 857–878.

Brancati, E. (2015). Innovation financing and the role of relationship lending for SMEs. *Small Business Economics*, 44(2), 449–473.

Brealey, R., Leland, H. E., & Pyle, D. H. (1977). Informational asymmetries, financial structure, and financial intermediation. *The Journal of Finance*, 32(2), 371–387.

Breid, V. (1995). Aussagefähigkeit agencytheoretischer Ansätze im Hinblick auf die Verhaltenssteuerung von Entscheidungsträgern. *Zeitschrift für betriebswirtschaftliche Forschung*, 47(9), 821–854.

Brick, I. E., & Palia, D. (2007). Evidence of jointness in the terms of relationship lending. *Journal of Financial Intermediation*, 16, 452–476.

Bridges, S., & Guariglia, A. (2008). Financial constraints, global engagement, and firm survival in the United Kingdom: Evidence from micro data. *Scottish Journal of Political Economy*, 55(4), 444–464.

Bris, A., & Welch, I. (2005). The optimal concentration of creditors. *The Journal of Finance*, 60(5), 2193–2212.

Bromiley, P., & Harris, J. (2006). Trust, transaction cost economics, and mechanisms. In R. Bachmann & A. Zaheer (Eds.), *Handbook of trust research* (pp. 124–143). Cheltenham: Edward Elgar Publishing.

Brunner, A., & Krahnen, J. P. (2008). Multiple lenders and corporate distress: Evidence on debt restructuring. *The Review of Economic Studies*, 75(2), 415–442.

Bryman, A., & Bell, E. (2015). *Business research methods* (4 ed.). Oxford: Oxford University Press.

Bundesanstalt für Finanzdienstleistungsaufsicht. (2004). *Basel II: Internationale Konvergenz der Eigenkapitalmessung und Eigenkapitalanforderungen - das überarbeitete Rahmenwerk*. Retrieved from https://www.bafin.de/SharedDocs/Veroeffentlichungen/DE/Anschreiben/ sc_040626_basel2.html.

Bundesanstalt für Finanzdienstleistungsaufsicht. (2016). *MaRisk-Novelle*. Retrieved from https://www.bafin.de/DE/PublikationenDaten/Jahresbericht/Jahresbericht2016/Kapitel3/Kapitel3_1/Kapitel3_1_3/kapitel3_1_3_artikel.html.

Bundesanstalt für Finanzdienstleistungsaufsicht. (2017). *Rundschreiben 09/2017 (BA) - Mindestanforderungen an das Risikomanagement - MaRisk*. Retrieved from https://www.bafin.de/SharedDocs/Veroeffentlichungen/DE/Rundschreiben/2017/rs_1709_marisk_ba.html?nn=9450904.

Bundesministerium der Finanzen. (2013). *Basel III – ein Meilenstein im Bankenaufsichtsrecht*. Retrieved from http://www.bundesfinanzministerium.de/Content/DE/Monatsberichte/ 2013/10/Inhalte/Kapitel-3-Analysen/3-1-meilenstein-im-bankenaufsichtsrecht.html.

Bundesministerium der Finanzen. (2017). *Fragen und Antworten zu Basel III*. Retrieved from http://www.bundesfinanzministerium.de/Content/DE/FAQ/2012-10-18-basel-drei-faq.html.

Bundesverband der Deutschen Industrie e.V. (2015). Faktencheck - Mittelstand und Familienunternehmen. *Industrie-Förderung GmbH*, 1–22.

Burghof, H.-P. (1998). *Eigenkapitalnormen in der Theorie der Finanzintermediation*: Duncker & Humblot.

Burt, R. S. (2003). *Structural Holes - The Social Structure of Competition*. Cambridge: Harvard University Press.

Calcagnini, G., Farabullini, F., & Giombini, G. (2012). The impact of the recent financial crisis on bank loan interest rates and guarantees. *Working Paper*.

Calomiris, C. W., & Kahn, C. M. (1991). The role of demandable debt in structuring optimal banking arrangements. *American Economic Review*, 81(3), 497–513.

Calomiris, C. W., & Pornrojnangkool, T. (2009). Relationship banking and the pricing of financial services. *Journal of Financial Services Research*, 35, 189–224.

Campbell, D. E., & Kelly, J. S. (1994). Trade-off theory. *American Economic Review*, 84(2), 422–426.

Campello, M., Graham, J. R., & Harvey, C. R. (2010). The real effects of financial constraints: Evidence from a financial crisis. *Journal of Financial Economics*, 97(3), 470–487.

Casson, M. (1999). The economics of the family firm. *Scandinavian Economic History Review*, 47(1), 10–23.

Castelli, A., Dwyer, G. P., & Hasan, I. (2006). Bank relationships and small firms' financial performance. *Working Paper, Federal Reserve Bank of Atlanta* (2006–2005).

Cenni, S., Monferrà, S., Salotti, V., Sangiorgi, M., & Torluccio, G. (2015). Credit rationing and relationship lending. Does firm size matter? *Journal of Banking & Finance*, 53, 249–265.

Cerasi, V., & Daltung, S. (1994). The optimal size of a bank: Costs and benefits of diversification. *European Economic Review*, 44, 1701–1726.

Cerqueiro, G., Degryse, H., & Ongena, S. (2011). Rules versus discretion in loan rate setting. *Journal of Financial Intermediation*, 20, 503–529.

Chakraborty, A., Fernando, C., & Mallick, R. (2010). The importance of being known: relationship banking and credit limits. *Quarterly Journal of Finance and Accounting*, 49(2).

Chakraborty, A., & Hu, C. X. (2006). Lending relationships in line-of-credit and nonline-of-credit loans: Evidence from collateral use in small business. *Journal of Financial Intermediation*, 15(1), 86–107.

Chakraborty, A., & Mallick, R. (2012). Credit gap in small businesses: some new evidence. *International Journal of Business*, 17(1), 66–80.

Chakraborty, S., & Ray, T. (2006). Bank-based versus market-based financial systems: A growth-theoretic analysis. *Journal of Monetary Economics*, 53(2), 329–350.

Chan, Y.-S., & Kanatas, G. (1985). Asymmetric valuations and the role of collateral in loan agreements. *Journal of Money, Credit and Banking*, 17(1), 84–95.

Chan, Y. S., & Thakor, A. V. (1987). Collateral and competitive equilibria with moral hazard and private information. *The Journal of Finance*, 42(2), 345–363.

Chandler, G. N., & Hanks, S. H. (1998). An examination of the substitutability of founders human and financial capital in emerging business ventures. *Journal of Business Venturing*, 13(5), 353–369.

Chrisman, J. J., Chua, J. H., Le Breton-Miller, I., Miller, D., & Steier, L. P. (2018). Governance mechanisms and family firms. *Entrepreneurship Theory and Practice*, 42(2), 171–186.

Chrisman, J. J., Chua, J. H., & Litz, R. A. (2004). Comparing the agency costs of family and non–family firms: Conceptual issues and exploratory evidence. *Entrepreneurship Theory and Practice*, 28(4), 335–354.

Chrisman, J. J., Sharma, P., Steier, L. P., & Chua, J. H. (2013). The influence of family goals, governance, and resources on firm outcomes. *Entrepreneurship Theory and Practice*, 37(6), 1249–1261.

Chua, J. H., Chrisman, J. J., Kellermanns, F., & Wu, Z. (2011). Family involvement and new venture debt financing. *Journal of Business Venturing*, 26(4), 472–488.

Chua, J. H., Chrisman, J. J., & Sharma, P. (1999). Defining the family business by behavior. *Entrepreneurship Theory and Practice*, 23(4), 19–39.

Claessens, S., Djankov, S., Fan, J. P., & Lang, L. H. (2002). Disentangling the incentive and entrenchment effects of large shareholdings. *The Journal of Finance*, 57(6), 2741–2771.

Clarke, G. R., Cull, R., & Kisunko, G. (2012). External finance and firm survival in the aftermath of the crisis: Evidence from Eastern Europe and Central Asia. *Journal of Comparative Economics*, 40(3), 372–392.

Coase, R. H. (1937). The nature of the firm. *Economica*, 4(16), 386–405.

Cole, R. A. (1998). The importance of relationships to the availability of credit. *Journal of Banking & Finance*, 22, 959–977.

Cole, R. A., Goldberg, L. G., & White, L. J. (2004). Cookie cutter vs. character: the micro structure of small business lending by large and small banks. *Journal of Financial and Quantitative Analysis*, 39(2).

Coleman, A. D. F., Esho, N., & Sharpe, I. G. (2006). Does bank monitoring influence loan contract terms? *Journal of Financial Services Research*, 30, 177–198.

Coleman, J. S. (2000). Social capital in the creation of human capital. *American Journal of Sociology*, 94, 95–120.

Conigliani, C., Ferri, G., & Generale, A. (1997). The impact of bank-firm relations on the propagation of monetary policy squeezes. *Moneta e Credito*.

Connelly, B. L., Tihanyi, L., Certo, S. T., & Hitt, M. A. (2010). Marching to the beat of different drummers: The influence of institutional owners on competitive actions. *Academy of Management Journal*, 53(4), 723–742.

Cooper, A. C., Gimeno-Gascon, F. J., & Woo, C. Y. (1994). Initial human and financial capital as predictors of new venture performance. *Journal of Business Venturing*, 9(5), 371–395.

Corbett, J., & Jenkinson, T. (1996). The financing of industry, 1970–1989: An international comparison. *Journal of the Japanese and international economies*, 10(1), 71–96.

Cosci, S., & Meliciani, V. (2002). Multiple banking relationships: Evidence from the Italian experience. *The Manchester School Supplement*, 70, 37–54.

Cotugno, M., Monferrà, S., & Sampagnaro, G. (2013a). Relationship lending, hierarchical distance and credit tightening: Evidence from the financial crisis. *Journal of Banking & Finance*, 37(5), 1372–1385.

Cotugno, M., Stefanelli, V., & Torluccio, G. (2013b). Relationship lending, default rate and loan portfolio quality. *Applied Financial Economics*, 23(7), 573–587.

Cowling, M. (1999). The incidence of loan collateralization in small business lending contracts: evidence from the UK. *Applied Economics Letters*, 6, 291–293.

Cowling, M. (2010). The role of loan guarantee schemes in alleviating credit rationing in the UK. *Journal of Financial Stability*, 6, 36–44.

Cressy, R. (1996). Commitment lending under asymmetric information: theory and tests on U.K. startup data. *Small Business Economics*, 8, 397–408.

Cressy, R., & Toivanen, O. (2001). Is there adverse selection in the credit market? *Venture Capital*, 3, 215–238.

Daily, C. M., & Dollinger, M. J. (1992). An empirical examination of ownership structure in family and professionally managed firms. *Family Business Review*, 5(2), 117–136.

Danes, S. M., Stafford, K., Haynes, G., & Amarapurkar, S. S. (2009). Family capital of family firms: Bridging human, social, and financial capital. *Family Business Review*, 22(3), 199–215.

D'Auria, C., Foglia, A., & Reedtz, P. M. (1999). Bank interest rates and credit relationships in Italy. *Journal of Banking & Finance*, 23(7), 1067–1093.

D'Aurizio, L., Oliviero, T., & Romano, L. (2015). Family firms, soft information and bank lending in a financial crisis. *Journal of Corporate Finance*, 33, 279–292.

Davidson, R., & MacKinnon, J. G. (1993). *Estimation and Inference in Econometrics*. Oxford: Oxford University Press.

Davis, E. P. (1994). Banking, corporate finance, and monetary policy: An empirical perspective. *Oxford Review of Economic Policy*, 10(4), 49–67.

Davis, E. P., & Stone, M. R. (2004). Corporate financial structure and financial stability. *Journal of Financial Stability*, 1(1), 65–91.

De Bodt, E., Lobez, F., & Statnik, J.-C. (2005). Credit rationing, customer relationship and the number of banks: An empirical analysis. *European Financial Management*, 11(2), 195–228.

De Mitri, S., Gobbi, G., & Sette, E. (2010a). Relationship lending in a financial turmoil. *Bank of Italy's Working Papers* (772).

De Mitri, S., Gobbi, G., & Sette, E. (2010b). Relationship lending in a financial turmoil. *Bank of Italy Working Paper*(772), 1–50.

Deeg, R. (1999). *Finance capitalism unveiled: Banks and the German political economy*. Michigan: University of Michigan Press.

Degryse, H., Kim, M., & Ongena, S. (2009). *Microeconometrics of banking: Methods, applications and results*. Oxford: Oxford University Press.

Degryse, H., & Ongena, S. (2005). Distance, lending relationships, and competition. *The Journal of Finance*, 60(1), 231–266.

Degryse, H., & Ongena, S. (2008). Competition and regulation in the banking sector: A review of the empirical evidence on the sources of bank rents. In A. Thakor & A. Boot (Eds.), *Handbook of Financial Intermediation and Banking* (pp. 483–554). Amsterdam: Elsevier.

Degryse, H., & Van Cayseele, P. (2000). Relationship lending within a bank-based system: Evidence from European small business data. *Journal of Financial Intermediation*, 9, 90–109.

Demirgüç-Kunt, A., & Detragiache, E. (2009). Basel core principles and bank soundness: Does compliance matter? *The World Bank Policy Research Working Paper*.

Demirgüç-Kunt, A., & Levine, R. (1999). Bank-based and market-based financial systems: Cross-country comparisons. *Thee World Bank Policy Research Working Paper*, 1(1), 1–70.

Denscombe, M. (2014). *The good research guide: For small-scale social research projects* (5 ed.). London: McGraw-Hill Education.

Desender, K. A., Aguilera, R. V., Crespi, R., & García-Cestona, M. (2013). When does ownership matter? Board characteristics and behavior. *Strategic Management Journal*, 34(7), 823–842.

Desender, K. A., Aguilera, R. V., Lópezpuertas-Lamy, M., & Crespi, R. (2016). A clash of governance logics: Foreign ownership and board monitoring. *Strategic Management Journal*, 37(2), 349–369.

Destatis - Statistisches Bundesamt. (2017). *Bevölkerung in Deutschland voraussichtlich auf 82,8 Millionen gestiegen*. Retrieved from https://www.destatis.de/DE/PresseService/Presse/Pressemitteilungen/2017/01/PD17_033_12411pdf.pdf?__blob=publicationFile.

Detragiache, E., Garella, P., & Guiso, L. (2000). Multiple versus single banking relationships: Theory and evidence. *The Journal of Finance*, 55(3), 1133–1161.

Detzer, D., Dodig, N., Evans, T., Hein, E., Herr, H., & Prante, F. J. (2017). *The German Financial System and the Financial and Economic Crisis* (Vol. 45). Cham: Springer.

Deutsche Bundesbank. (2009). *Deutsche Bundesbank Monthly Report January 2009*. Frankfurt am Main: Deutsche Bundesbank.

Deutsche Bundesbank. (2011). *Deutsche Bundesbank Monthly Report September 2011*. Frankfurt am Main: Deutsche Bundesbank.

Deutsche Bundesbank. (2012). *Deutsche Bundesbank Monthly Report January 2012*. Frankfurt am Main: Deutsche Bundesbank.

Deutsche Bundesbank. (2014). *Deutsche Bundesbank Monthly Report December 2014*. Frankfurt am Main: Deutsche Bundesbank.

Deutsche Bundesbank. (2015). *Deutsche Bundesbank Monthly Report December 2015*. Frankfurt am Main: Deutsche Bundesbank.

Deutsche Bundesbank. (2016). *Deutsche Bundesbank Monthly Report December 2016*. Frankfurt am Main: Deutsche Bundesbank.

Deutsche Bundesbank. (2017a). *Bankstellenbericht 2016 - Entwicklung des Bankstellennetzes im Jahr 2016*. Retrieved from https://www.bundesbank.de/Redaktion/DE/Downloads/Aufgaben/Bankenaufsicht/Bankstellenstatistik/bankstellenbericht_2016.html.

Deutsche Bundesbank. (2017b). *Die Banken in Deutschland*. Retrieved from https://www.bundesbank.de/de/service/schule-und-bildung/schuelerbuch-geld-und-geldpolitik-digital/die-banken-in-deutschland-613922.

Deutsche Bundesbank. (2017c). *Deutsche Bundesbank Monthly Report December 2017*. Frankfurt am Main: Deutsche Bundesbank.

Deutsche Bundesbank. (2018a). *Deutsche Bundesbank Monthly Report January 2018*. Frankfurt am Main: Deutsche Bundesbank.

Deutsche Bundesbank. (2018b). *Deutsche Bundesbank Monthly Report March 2018*. Frankfurt am Main: Deutsche Bundesbank.

Dewally, M., & Shao, Y. (2014). Liquidity crisis, relationship lending and corporate finance. *Journal of Banking & Finance*, 39, 223–239.

Di Giuli, A., Caselli, S., & Gatti, S. (2011). Are small family firms financially sophisticated? *Journal of Banking & Finance*, 35(11), 2931–2944.

Diamond, D. W. (1984). Financial intermediation and delegated monitoring. *The Review of Economic Studies*, 51(3), 393–414.

Diamond, D. W. (1989). Reputation acquisition in debt markets. *Journal of political Economy*, 97(4), 828–862.

Diamond, D. W. (1991). Monitoring and reputation: The choice between bank loans and directly placed debt. *Journal of political Economy*, 99(4), 689–721.

Diamond, D. W., & Dybvig, P. H. (1983). Bank runs, deposit insurance, and liquidity. *Journal of political Economy*, 91(3), 401–419.

Dietsch, M. (2003). Financing small businesses in France. *European Investment Bank (EIB) papers*, 8(2), 93–119.

Dismuke, C., & Lindrooth, R. (2006). Ordinary least squares. *Methods and Designs for Outcomes Research*, 93, 93–104.

Dorfleitner, G., & Hornuf, L. (2016). *FinTech- Markt in Deutschland*: Bundesministerium der Finanzen.

Dorfleitner, G., Hornuf, L., Schmitt, M., & Weber, M. (2016). FinTech-Markt in Deutschland.

Dreux, D. R. (1990). Financing family business: Alternatives to selling out or going public. *Family Business Review*, 3(3), 225–243.

Du, J., Guariglia, A., & Newman, A. (2015). Do social capital building strategies influence the financing behavior of chinese private small and medium-sized enterprises? *Entrepreneurship Theory and Practice*, 39(3), 601–631.

Duarte, F. D., & Gama, D. A. P. M. (2011). The role of collateral and relationship lending in loan pricing: evidence from United Kingdom SMEs. *Working Paper.*

Dunkelberg, W. C., Leeds, M. A., & Scott, J. A. (2004). Loan search and banking relationships. *Working Paper.*

Edwards, J., & Fischer, K. (1994). *Banks, Finance and Investment in Germany.* Cambridge: Cambridge University Press.

Ehrhardt, O., Nowak, E., & Weber, F.-M. (2006). Running in the family—the evolution of ownership, control, and performance in German family-owned firms 1903–2003. *Swiss Finance Institute Research Paper* (06-13).

Eisenhardt, K. M. (1989). Agency theory: An assessment and review. *Academy of management Review*, 14(1), 57–74.

Ellul, A. (2008). Control motivations and capital structure decision. *Working Paper.*

Elsas, R. (2001). *Die Bedeutung der Hausbank – Eine ökonomische Analyse.* Wiesbaden: Deutscher Universitäts-Verlag.

Elsas, R. (2005). Empirical determinants of relationship lending. *Journal of Financial Intermediation*, 14, 32–57.

Elsas, R., & Krahnen, J. P. (1998). Is relationship lending special? Evidence from credit-file data in Germany. *Journal of Banking & Finance*, 22, 1283–1316.

Elsas, R., & Krahnen, J. P. (2002). Collateral, relationship lending and financial distress: An empirical study on financial contracting. *CFS Working Paper*, 17.

Elsas, R., & Krahnen, J. P. (2003). Universal banks and relationships with firms. *CFS Working Paper*, 20.

Elyasiani, E., & Goldberg, L. G. (2004). Relationship lending: A survey of the literature. *Journal of Economics and Business*, 56(4), 315–330.

Ergungor, O. E. (2005). The profitability of bank–borrower relationships. *Journal of Financial Intermediation*, 14(4), 485–512.

European Banking Authority. (2016). *EBA report on SMEs and SME supporting factor*. Retrieved from https://www.eba.europa.eu/documents/10180/1359456/EBA-Op-2016-04++Report+ on+SMEs+and+SME+supporting+factor.pdf.

European Central Bank. (2017a). Survey on the access to finance of enterprises in the euro area - October 2016 to March 2017. *European Central Bank Publication*, 1–40.

European Central Bank. (2017b). The euro area bank lending survey - First quarter of 2017. *European Central Bank Publictaion*, 1–49.

European Commission. (2015). User guide to the SME definition. *Publications Office of the European Union*.

Ewert, R., Schenk, G., & Szczesny, A. (2000). Determinants of bank lending performance in Germany - Evidence from credit File Data. *Schmalenbach Business Review*, 52, 344–362.

Faccio, M., & Lang, L. (2002). The ultimate ownership of Western European corporations. *Journal of Financial Economics*, 65(3), 365–395.

Fama, E. F. (1985). What's different about banks? *Journal of Monetary Economics*, 15(1), 29–39.

Fama, E. F., & Jensen, M. C. (1983). Separation of ownership and control. *Journal of Law and Economics*, 26(2), 301–325.

Farinha, L. A., & Santos, J. A. C. (2002). Switching from single to multiple bank lending relationships: Determinants and implications. *Journal of Financial Intermediation*, 11, 124–151.

Fattoum-Guedri, A., Guedri, Z., & Delmar, F. (2018). Multiple blockholder structures and family firm performance. *Entrepreneurship Theory and Practice*, 42(2), 231–251.

Feldenkirchen, W. (1991). Banking and economic growth: Banks and industry in the nineteenth century and their changing relationship during industrialisation. In R. Lee (Ed.), *German industry and German industrialisation*. London: Routledge.

Feldman, R. J. (1997). Small business loans, small banks and big change in technology called credit scoring. *The Region, Federal Reserve Bank of Minneapolis*, 19–25.

Ferri, G., & Messori, M. (2000). Bank–firm relationships and allocative efficiency in Northeastern and Central Italy and in the South. *Journal of Banking & Finance*, 24(6), 1067–1095.

Ferri, G., Murro, P., & Rotondi, Z. (2014). Bank lending technologies and SME credit rationing in Europe in the 2009 crisis. *Working Paper*.

Fink, M., & Kessler, A. (2010). Cooperation, trust and performance - Empirical results from three countries. *British Journal of Management*, 21(2), 469–483.

Fiordelisi, F., Monferrà, S., & Sampagnaro, G. (2014). Relationship lending and credit quality. *Journal of Financial Services Research*, 46(3), 295–315.

Fischer, K.-H. (2000). Acquisition of information in loan markets and bank market power - An empirical investigation. *Working Paper.*

Fisman, R., & Khanna, T. (1999). Is trust a historical residue? Information flows and trust levels. *Journal of Economic Behavior & Organization*, 38, 79–92.

Florin, J., Lubatkin, M., & Schulze, W. (2003). A social capital model of high-growth ventures. *Academy of Management Journal*, 46(3), 374–384.

Fohlin, C. (2007). *Finance capitalism and Germany's rise to industrial power.* Cambridge: Cambridge University Press.

Fohlin, C. (2016). Financial systems. In D. C. & H. M. (Eds.), *Handbook of Cliometrics.* Berlin, Heidelberg: Springer.

Fraser, D. R., Rhee, S. G., & Shin, G. H. (2012). The impact of capital market competition on relationship banking: Evidence from the Japanese experience. *Journal of Empirical Finance*, 19(4), 411–426.

Fredriksson, A., & Moro, A. (2014). Bank–SMEs relationships and banks' risk-adjusted profitability. *Journal of Banking & Finance*, 41, 67–77.

Freixas, X., & Rochet, J.-C. (1997). *Microeconomics of banking.* Cambridge: MIT Press.

Freixas, X., & Rochet, J.-C. (2008). *Microeconomics of banking* (2 ed.). Cambridge: MIT Press.

Galai, D., & Masulis, R. W. (1976). The option pricing model and the risk factor of stock. *Journal of Financial Economics*, 3(1–2), 53–81.

Gale, D. (1992). *Information capacity and financial collapse.* Cambridge: Cambridge University Press.

Gale, D., & Hellwig, M. (1985). Incentive-compatible debt contracts: The one-period problem. *The Review of Economic Studies*, 52(4), 647–663.

Gallo, M. Á., Tàpies, J., & Cappuyns, K. (2004). Comparison of family and nonfamily business: Financial logic and personal preferences. *Family Business Review*, 17(4), 303–318.

Gama, D. A. P. M., & Duarte, F. D. (2015). Collateral and relationship lending in loan pricing: evidence from UK SMEs. *WSEAS Transactions on Business and Economics*, 12, 21–35.

Gambacorta, L., & Mistrulli, P. E. (2014). Bank heterogeneity and interest rate setting: What lessons have we learned since Lehman Brothers? *Journal of Money, Credit and Banking*, 46(4), 753–778.

Gambetta, D. (2000). Can we trust trust? In D. Gambetta (Ed.), *Trust: Making and breaking cooperative relations* (pp. 213–237). University of Oxford: Department of Sociology.

Gan, J. (2007). The real effects of asset market bubbles: Loan-and firm-level evidence of a lending channel. *The Review of Financial Studies*, 20(6), 1941–1973.

Garcia-Appendini, E. (2011). Lending to small businesses: The value of soft information. *Working Paper*.

Gerschenkron, A. (1962). *Economic backwardness in historical perspective: A book of essays*. Cambridge: Belknap Press of Harvard University Press.

Ghauri, P. N., & Grønhaug, K. (2005). *Research methods in business studies: A practical guide* (3 ed.). Harlow: Pearson Education.

Gibb Dyer, W. (2006). Examining the "family effect" on firm performance. *Family Business Review*, 19(4), 253–273.

Gloy, B. A., Gunderson, M. A., & Ladue, E. L. (2005). The costs and returns of agricultural credit delivery. *American Agricultural Economics Association*, 87(3), 703–716.

Goldberg, V. P. (1980). Relational exchange: Economics and complex contracts. *American Behavioral Scientist*, 23(3), 337–352.

Gomez-Mejia, L. R., Cruz, C., Berrone, P., & De Castro, J. (2011). The bind that ties: Socioemotional wealth preservation in family firms. *Academy of Management Annals*, 5(1), 653–707.

Gomez-Mejia, L. R., Larraza-Kintana, M., Moyano-Fuentes, J., & Firfiray, S. (2018). Managerial family ties and employee risk bearing in family firms: Evidence from Spanish car dealers. *Human Resource Management*, 57(5), 993–1007.

Gopalan, R., Udell, G. F., & Yerramilli, V. (2007). Why do firms switch banks? *Working Paper*.

Gordon, R. J. (1999). Has the 'New Economy' rendered the productivity slowdown obsolete? *Northwestern University and NBER Working Paper*.

Gorton, G., & Schmid, F. A. (2000). Universal banking and the performance of German firms. *Journal of Financial Economics*, 58(1–2), 29–80.

Graham, J. R., & Harvey, C. R. (2001). The theory and practice of corporate finance: Evidence from the field. *Journal of Financial Economics*, 60(2–3), 187–243.

Greenbaum, S. I., Kanatas, G., & Venezia, I. (1989). Equilibrium loan pricing under the bank-client relationship. *Journal of Banking & Finance*, 13(2), 221–235.

Greenbaum, S. I., Thakor, A. V., & Boot, A. (2015). *Contemporary financial intermediation*. London: Academic Press.

Guiso, L. (2003). Small business finance in Italy. *EIB papers*, 8(2), 121–149.

Gujarati, D. (2004). *Basic Econometrics 4th Edition*. New York: Tata McGraw-Hill.

Hackbarth, D., Hennessy, C. A., & Leland, H. E. (2007). Can the trade-off theory explain debt structure? *The Review of Financial Studies*, 20(5), 1389–1428.

Hainz, C., & Wiegand, M. (2013). How does relationship banking influence credit financing? Evidence from the financial crisis. *Ifo Working Paper*.

Hanley, A. (2002). Do binary collateral outcome variables proxy collateral levels? The case of collateral from start-ups and existing SMEs. *Small Business Economics*, 18, 317–331.

Hanley, A., & Crook, J. (2005). The role of private knowledge in reducing the information wedge: a research note. *Journal of Business Finance & Accounting*, 32, 1 & 2.

Hao, L. (2004). Bank Effects and the Determinants of Loan Yield Spreads. *Working Paper*.

Harhoff, D., & Körting, T. (1998). Lending relationships in Germany – Empirical evidence from survey data. *Journal of Banking & Finance*, 22(10–11), 1317–1353.

Harhoff, D., Stahl, K. O., & Woywode, M. (1995). Growth and exit of West German firms: An empirical investigation on the impact of liability statutes. *ZEW Discussion Paper* (95–19).

Haubrich, J. G. (1989). Financial intermediation: Delegated monitoring and long-term relationships. *Journal of Banking & Finance*, 13(1), 9–20.

Hauswald, R., & Marquez, R. (2006). Competition and strategic information acquisition in credit markets. *The Review of Financial Studies*, 19(3), 967–1000.

Haynes, G. W., Walker, R., Rowe, B. R., & Hong, G.-S. (1999). The intermingling of business and family finances in family-owned businesses. *Family Business Review*, 12(3), 225–239.

Hellwig, M. (1991). Banking, financial intermediation and corporate finance. In A. Giovannini & C. Mayer (Eds.), *European financial integration* (pp. 63). Cambridge: Cambrige University Press.

Henke, S. (2002). *Anreizprobleme beim Transfer der Kreditrisiken aus Buchkrediten*. Berlin: Duncker & Humblot.

Hernández-Cánovas, G., & Martínez-Solano, P. (2006). Banking relationships: Effects on debt terms for small Spanish firms. *Journal of Small Business Management*, 44(3), 315–333.

Hernández-Cánovas, G., & Martínez-Solano, P. (2010). Relationship lending and SME financing in the continental European bank-based system. *Small Business Economics*, 34, 465–482.

Hess, W. (2008). Familienunternehmen–Hoffnungsträger einer soliden Wirtschaftsentwicklung. *Allianz Dresdner Economic Research Working Paper*.

Hilferding, R. (1910). *Das Finanzkapital*. Frankfurt: Europäische Verlagsanstalt.

Hirschman, A. O. (1982). Rival interpretations of market society: Civilizing, destructive, or feeble? *Journal of Economic Literature*, 20(4), 1463–1484.

Hite, J. M. (2005). Evolutionary processes and paths of relationally embedded network ties in emerging entrepreneurial firms. *Entrepreneurship Theory and Practice*, 29(1), 113–144.

Hochfellner, D., Montes, J., Schmalz, M., & Sosyura, D. (2015). Winners and Losers of Financial Crises: Evidence from Individuals and Firms. *Working Paper*.

Hoetker, G. (2007). The use of logit and probit models in strategic management research: Critical issues. *Strategic Management Journal*, 28(4), 331–343.

Holmström, B. (1979). Moral hazard and observability. *The Bell Journal of economics*, 10(1), 74–91.

Holmström, B., & Tirole, J. (1993). Market liquidity and performance monitoring. *Journal of political Economy*, 101(4), 678–709.

Holmström, B., & Tirole, J. (1997). Financial intermediation, loanable funds, and the real sector. *Quarterly Journal of Economics*, 112(3), 663–691.

Hommel, U., & Schneider, H. (2003). Financing the German Mittelstand. *European Investment Bank Papers*, 8(2), 53–90.

Horiuchi, A., Packer, F., & Fukuda, S. i. (1988). What role has the "main bank" played in Japan? *Journal of the Japanese and international economies*, 2(2), 159–180.

Hoshi, T., Kashyap, A., & Scharfstein, D. (1990). The role of banks in reducing the costs of financial distress in Japan. *National Bureau of Economic Research Working Paper*.

Houston, J., & James, C. (1996). Bank Information Monopolies and the Mix of Private and Public Debt Claims. *The Journal of Finance*, 51(5), 1863–1889.

Höwer, D. (2016). The role of bank relationships when firms are financially distressed. *Journal of Banking & Finance*, 65, 59–75.

Howorth, C., & Moro, A. (2006). Trust within entrepreneur bank relationships: Insights from Italy. *Entrepreneurship Theory and Practice*, 30(4), 495–517.

Howorth, C., & Moro, A. (2012). Trustworthiness and interest rates: An empirical study of Italian SMEs. *Small Business Economics*, 39, 161–177.

Hübler, O., Menkhoff, L., & Suwanaporn, C. (2008). Financial liberalisation in emerging markets: How does bank lending change? *World Economy*, 31(3), 393–415.

Hutcheson, G. D. (2011). Ordinary Least-Squares Regression. In L. Moutinho & G. D. Hutcheson (Eds.), *The SAGE Dictionary of Quantitative Management Research*. Thousand Oaks: SAGE Publications.

Hutchinson, R. W. (1995). The capital structure and investment decisions of the small owner-managed firm: Some exploratory issues. *Small Business Economics*, 7(3), 231–239.

Huynh, K. P., Petrunia, R. J., & Voia, M. (2010). The impact of initial financial state on firm duration across entry cohorts. *The Journal of Industrial Economics*, 58(3), 661–689.

IfM Bonn. (2016). *Familienunternehmen-Definition des IfM Bonn*. Retrieved from http://www.ifm-bonn.org/definitionen/familienunternehmen-definition/.

IfM Bonn. (2017). *KMU-Definition des IfM Bonn*. Retrieved from https://www.ifm-bonn.org/definitionen/kmu-definition-des-ifm-bonn/.

Inderst, R., & Mueller, H. M. (2007). A lender-based theory of collateral. *Journal of Financial Economics*, 84(3), 826–859.

James, C. (1987). Some evidence on the uniqueness of bank loans. *Journal of Financial Economics*, 19, 217–235.

James, H. S. (1999). Owner as manager, extended horizons and the family firm. *International Journal of the Economics of Business*, 6(1), 41–55.

Janney, J. J., & Folta, T. B. (2006). Moderating effects of investor experience on the signaling value of private equity placements. *Journal of Business Venturing*, 21(1), 27–44.

Jensen, M. C. (1986). Agency costs of free cash flow, corporate finance, and takeovers. *American Economic Review*, 76(2), 323–329.

Jensen, M. C., & Meckling, W. H. (1976). Theory of the firm: Managerial behavior, agency costs and ownership structure. *Journal of Financial Economics*, 3(3), 305–360.

Jensen, M. C., & Murphy, K. J. (1990). Performance pay and top-management incentives. *Journal of political Economy*, 98(2), 225–264.

Jiangli, W., Unal, H., & Yom, C. (2008). Relationship lending, accounting disclosure, and credit availability during the Asian financial crisis. *Journal of Money, Credit and Banking*, 40(1), 25–55.

Jiménez, G., Salas, V., & Saurina, J. (2006). Determinants of collateral. *Journal of Financial Economics*, 81(2), 255–281.

Jiménez, G., Salas, V., & Saurina, J. (2009). Organizational distance and use of collateral for business loans. *Journal of Banking & Finance*, 33, 234–243.

Jost, P.-J. (2001). *Die Prinzipal-Agenten-Theorie in der Betriebswirtschaftslehre*. Stuttgart: Schäffer-Poeschel.

Kadan, O., Reny, P. J., & Swinkels, J. M. (2017). Existence of optimal mechanisms in principal-agent problems. *Econometrica*, 85(3), 769–823.

Kano, M., Uchida, H., Udell, G. F., & Watanabe, W. (2011). Information verifiability, bank organization, bank competition and bank–borrower relationships. *Journal of Banking & Finance*, 35(4), 935–954.

Karolyi, S. A. (2018). Personal lending relationships. *The Journal of Finance*, 73(1), 5–49.

Kets de Vries, M. F. (1993). The dynamics of family controlled firms: The good and the bad news. *Organizational dynamics*, 21(3), 59–71.

Kiener, S. (2013). *Die Principal-Agent-Theorie aus informationsökonomischer Sicht*. Heidelberg: Springer-Verlag.

Kirschenmann, K. (2016). Credit rationing in small firm-bank relationships. *Journal of Financial Intermediation*, 26, 68–99.

Kirschenmann, K., & Norden, L. (2012). The relationship between borrower risk and loan maturity in small business lending. *Journal of Business Finance & Accounting*, 39((5) (6)), 730–757.

Klein, B., Crawford, R. G., & Alchian, A. A. (1978). Vertical integration, appropriable rents, and the competitive contracting process. *The Journal of Law and Economics*, 21(2), 297–326.

Klein, S. B., Astrachan, J. H., & Smyrnios, K. X. (2005). The F-PEC scale of family influence: Construction, validation, and further implication for theory. *Entrepreneurship Theory and Practice*, 29(3), 321–339.

Klement, J. (2007). *Kreditrisikohandel, Basel II und interne Märkte in Banken*. Wiesbaden: Deutscher Universitäts-Verlag.

Kocka, J. (1980). The rise of the modern industrial enterprise in Germany. In A. D. Chandler & H. Daems (Eds.), *Managerial hierarchies: Comparative perspectives on the rise of the modern industrial enterprise*. Cambridge: Harvard University Press.

Koeberle-Schmid, A., Fahrion, H.-J., & Witt, P. (2012). *Family Business Governance – Als Erfolgsfaktor von Familienunternehmen*. Berlin: Erich Schmidt Verlag.

Köhler-Ulbrich, P., Hempell, H. S., & Scopel, S. (2016). The euro area bank lending survey: Role, development and use in monetary policy preparation. *European Central Bank - Occasional Paper Series* (179).

Kramer, J. (1991). *The Logit Model for Economists*. London: Edward Arnold.

Kraus, A., & Litzenberger, R. H. (1973). A state-preference model of optimal financial leverage. *The Journal of Finance*, 28(4), 911–922.

Krempel, K., & Von Weizsäcker, R. (2006). *Familienunternehmen: Auf lange Sicht erfolgreich?* Retrieved from https://www.vwl.wi.tum.de/fileadmin/w00bpu/www/publikationen/familien unternehmenauflangesichterfolgreich.pdf.

Küpper, H.-U. (2013). *Controlling: Konzeption, Aufgaben und Instrumente* (6 ed.). Stuttgart: Schäffer-Poeschel.

Küpper, H.-U., Friedl, G., Hofmann, C., Hofmann, Y., & Pedell, B. (2013). *Controlling: Konzeption, Aufgaben, Instrumente* (6 ed.). Stuttgart: Schäffer-Poeschel.

Kutner, M. H., Nachtsheim, C. J., & Neter, J. (2005). *Applied Linear Statistical Models* (5 ed.). New York: McGraw-Hill.

Kysucky, V., & Norden, L. (2016). The benefits of relationship lending in a cross-country context: A meta-analysis. *Management Science*, 62(1), 90–110.

La Porta, R., Lopez-De-Silanes, F., & Shleifer, A. (1999). Corporate ownership around the world. *Journal of Finance*, 54(2), 471–517.

La Porta, R., Lopez-De-Silanes, F., Shleifer, A., & Vishny, R. W. (1996). Trust in large organizations. *NBER Working Paper Series* (5864).

La Porta, R., Lopez-de-Silanes, F., Shleifer, A., & Vishny, R. W. (1997). Legal determinants of external finance. *The Journal of Finance*, 52(3), 1131–1150.

La Porta, R., Lopez-de-Silanes, F., Shleifer, A., & Vishny, R. W. (1998). Law and finance. *Journal of Political Economy*, 106(6), 1113–1155.

La Porta, R., Lopez-de-Silanes, F., Shleifer, A., & Vishny, R. W. (2000). Agency problems and dividend policies around the world. *The Journal of Finance*, 55(1), 1–33.

Lansberg, I., Perrow, E. L., & Rogolsky, S. (1988). Family business as an emerging field. *Family Business Review*, 1(1), 1–8.

Le Breton-Miller, I., & Miller, D. (2006). Why Do Some Family Businesses Out-Compete? Governance, Long-Term Orientations, and Sustainable Capability. *Entrepreneurship Theory and Practice*, 30(6), 731–746.

Le Breton-Miller, I., Miller, D., & Lester, R. H. (2011). Stewardship or agency? A social embeddedness reconciliation of conduct and performance in public family businesses. *Organization Science*, 22(3), 704–721.

Lehmann, E., & Neuberger, D. (2001). Do lending relationships matter? Evidence from bank survey data in Germany. *Journal of Economic Behavior & Organization*, 45, 339–359.

Lehmann, E., Neuberger, D., & Räthke, S. (2004). Lending to small and medium-sized firms: is there an East-West gap in Germany? *Small Business Economics*, 23, 23–39.

Leiner, D. J. (2014). *SoSci Survey (Programm-Version 2.6.00-i) [Computer software]*. Retrieved from https://www.soscisurvey.de.

Leland, H. E. (1998). Agency costs, risk management, and capital structure. *The Journal of Finance*, 53(4), 1213–1243.

Levin, R. I., & Travis, V. R. (1987). Small company finance - what the books don't say. *Harvard Business Review*, 65(6), 30–32.

Levine, R. (1991). Stock markets, growth, and tax policy. *The Journal of Finance*, 46(4), 1445–1465.

Levine, R. (2002). Bank-based or market-based financial systems: Which is better? *Journal of Financial Intermediation*, 11(4), 398–428.

Levine, R. (2005). Finance and growth: Theory and evidence. In P. Aghion & S. N. Durlauf (Eds.), *Handbook of economic growth* (Vol. 1, pp. 865–934). Amsterdam: Elsevier.

Lewicki, R. J., & Bunker, B. B. (1996). Developing and maintaining trust in work relationships. *Trust in organizations: Frontiers of theory and research*, 114, 139.

Lewicki, R. J., McAllister, D. J., & Bies, R. J. (1998). Trust and distrust: New relationships and realities. *Academy of management Review*, 23(3), 438–458.

Li, Y. (2016). The Rise of Intangible Capital and Financial Fragility. *Working Paper*.

Li, Y., Spigt, R., & Swinkels, L. (2017). The impact of FinTech start-ups on incumbent retail banks' share prices. *Financial Innovation*, 3(1), 26.

Li, Y., & Srinivasan, A. (2011). Relationship bank behavior during borrower distress and bankruptcy. *Working Paper*.

Liberti, J. M., & Mian, A. R. (2009). Estimating the effect of hierarchies on information use. *The Review of Financial Studies*, 22(10), 4057–4090.

Liberti, J. M., & Petersen, M. A. (2018). Information: Hard and soft. *NBER Working Paper* (25075).

Likert, R. (1932). *A technique for the measurement of attitudes*. New York: The Science Press.

Lins, K. V., Servaes, H., & Tamayo, A. (2017). Social capital, trust, and firm performance: The value of corporate social responsibility during the financial crisis. *The Journal of Finance*, 72(4), 1785–1824.

Longenecker, J. G., Moore, C. W., & Petty, J. W. (1997). *Credit scoring and the small business: A review and the need for research.* Paper presented at the Paper presented at the USASBE 1997 National Conference, San Francisco.

Lummer, S. L., & McConnell, J. J. (1989). Further evidence on the bank lending process and the capital-market response to bank loan agreements. *Journal of Financial Economics*, 25(1), 99–122.

Ma, X., Yiu, D. W., & Zhou, N. (2014). Facing global economic crisis: Foreign sales, ownership groups, and corporate value. *Journal of World Business*, 49(1), 87–100.

Mach, A. E. (2007). Die Unternehmenskultur im Familienunternehmen – was trägt sie, was prägt sie, was bedeutet sie für den Unternehmenserfolg? *Alphazirkel*, 1–33.

Machauer, A., & Weber, M. (1998). Bank behavior based on internal credit ratings of borrowers. *Journal of Banking & Finance*, 22, 1355–1383.

Maddala, G. S. (1983). *Limited-dependent and qualitative variables in econometrics*. Cambridge: Cambridge University Press.

Mahrt-Smith, J. (2006). Should banks own equity stakes in their borrowers? A contractual solution to hold-up problems. *Journal of Banking & Finance*, 30(10), 2911–2929.

Malafronte, I., Monferrà, S., Porzio, C., & Sampagnaro, G. (2014). Competition, specialization and bank–firm interaction: What happens in credit crunch periods? *Applied Financial Economics*, 24(8), 557–571.

Mauer, D. C., & Sarkar, S. (2005). Real options, agency conflicts, and optimal capital structure. *Journal of Banking & Finance*, 29(6), 1405–1428.

Mayer, C. (1988). New issues in corporate finance. *European Economic Review*, 32, 1167–1189.

Mayer, C. (1994). The assessment: Money and banking: Theory and evidence. *Oxford Review of Economic Policy*, 10(4), 1–13.

Mayordomo, S., & Rodríguez-Moreno, M. (2016). "Support is appreciated": On the effectiveness of the SME supporting factor. *Working Paper*.

McConaughy, D. L., Walker, M. C., Henderson, G. V., & Mishra, C. S. (1998). Founding family controlled firms: Efficiency and value. *Review of Financial economics*, 7(1), 1–19.

McFadden, D. (1973). *Conditional logit analysis of qualitative choice behavior*. New York: Wiley.

Means, G. (1991). *The Modern Corporation and Private Property*. New York: Routledge.

Menkhoff, L., Neuberger, D., & Suwanaporn, C. (2006). Collateral-based lending in emerging markets: Evidence from Thailand. *Journal of Banking & Finance*, 30(1), 1–21.

Metten, M. (2010). *Corporate Governance: Eine aktienrechtliche und institutionenökonomische Analyse der Leitungsmaxime von Aktiengesellschaften*. Wiesbaden: Gabler Verlag.

Miarka, T. (2000). *Financial intermediation and deregulation*. Heidelberg: Physica.

Mietzner, M., Schweizer, D., & Proelss, J. (2018). Hidden champions or black sheep? The role of underpricing in the German mini-bond market. *Small Business Economics*, 50(2), 375–395.

Mietzner, M., & Tyrell, M. (2012). Das Verhalten von Familienunternehmen gegenüber ihren Stakeholdern. *Familienunternehmen und Stiftungen*, 3(Fall), 108–113.

Milani, C. (2014). Borrower–lender distance and loan defaultrates: Macro evidence from the Italian local markets. *Journal of Economics and Business*, 71, 1–21.

Miller, D., & Le Breton-Miller, I. (2005). *Managing for the long run: Lessons in competitive advantage from great family businesses*. Boston: Harvard Business Press.

Miller, D., Le Breton-Miller, I. & Lester, R. H. (2013). Family firm governance, strategic conformity, and performance: Institutional vs. strategic perspectives. *Organization Science*, 24(1), 189–209.

Miller, D., Le Breton-Miller, I., Lester, R. H., & Cannella, A. A. (2007). Are family firms really superior performers? *Journal of Corporate Finance*, 13(5), 829–858.

Mirrlees, J. A. (1999). The theory of moral hazard and unobservable behaviour: Part I. *The Review of Economic Studies*, 66(1), 3–21.

Mishra, C. S., & McConaughy, D. L. (1999). Founding family control and capital structure: The risk of loss of control and the aversion to debt. *Entrepreneurship Theory and Practice*, 23(4), 53–64.

Mitchell, K., & Pearce, D. K. (2011). Lending technologies, lending specialization, and minority access to small-business loans. *Small Business Economics*, 37, 277–304.

Montoriol-Garriga, J. (2006). Relationship lending and small business finance: Empirical analysis of cost of capital, credit rationing, and firm performance. *Doctoral dissertation, Tesis Doctoral. Barcelona: Universitat Pompeu Fabra.*

Morck, R., & Nakamura, M. (1999). Banks and corporate control in Japan. *The Journal of Finance*, 54(1), 319–339.

Moro, A., & Fink, M. (2013). Loan manager trust and credit access for SMEs. *Journal of Banking & Finance*, 37, 927–936.

Muñoz-Bullón, F., & Sánchez-Bueno, M. J. (2012). Do family ties shape the performance consequences of diversification? Evidence from the European Union. *Journal of World Business*, 47(3), 469–477.

Myers, S. C. (1977). Determinants of corporate borrowing. *Journal of Financial Economics*, 5(2), 147–175.

Myers, S. C. (1984). The capital structure puzzle. *The Journal of Finance*, 39(3), 574–592.

Myers, S. C., & Majluf, N. S. (1984). Corporate financing and investment decisions when firms have information that investors do not have. *Journal of Financial Economics*, 13, 187–221.

Nahapiet, J., & Ghoshal, S. (1998). Social capital, intellectual capital, and the organizational advantage. *Academy of management Review*, 23(2), 242–266.

Nassr, I. K., & Wehinger, G. (2015). Unlocking SME finance through market-based debt. *OECD Journal: Financial Market Trends*, 2014(2), 89–190.

Neuberger, D. (2005). What's Common to Relationship Banking and Relationship Investing? Reflections within the Contractual Theory of the Firm. *Working Paper.*

Neuberger, D., Pedergnana, M., & Räthke-Döppner, S. (2008). Concentration of banking relationships in Switzerland: The result of firm structure or banking market structure? *Journal of Financial Services Research*, 33(2), 101–126.

Neuberger, D., & Räthke, S. (2009). Microenterprises and multiple bank relationships: The case of professionals. *Small Business Economics*, 32, 207–229.

Niskanen, M., Karjalainen, J., & Niskanen, J. (2010). The role of auditing in small, private family firms: is it about quality and credibility? *Family Business Review*, 23(3), 230–245.

Niskanen, J., & Niskanen, M. (2000). Does relationship banking have value for small firms? *The Finnish Journal of Business Economics*, 2, 245–262.

Nooteboom, B. (2002). *Trust: Forms, foundations, functions, failures and figures.* Cheltenham: Edward Elgar Publishing.

Nooteboom, B., Berger, H., & Noorderhaven, N. G. (1997). Effects of trust and governance on relational risk. *Academy of Management Journal*, 40(2), 308–338.

Norden, L., & Weber, M. (2010). Credit line usage, checking account activity, and default risk of bank borrowers. *The Review of Financial Studies*, 23(10), 3665–3699.

Norton, E. (1991). Capital structure and small public firms. *Journal of Business Venturing*, 6(4), 287–303.

O'Boyle, E. H., Pollack, J. M., & Rutherford, M. W. (2012). Exploring the relation between family involvement and firms' financial performance: A meta-analysis of main and moderator effects. *Journal of Business Venturing*, 27, 1–18.

O'Brien, R. M. (2007). A caution regarding rules of thumb for variance inflation factors. *Quality & quantity*, 41(5), 673–690.

Obstfeld, M. (1994). Evaluating risky consumption paths: The role of intertemporal substitutability. *European Economic Review*, 38(7), 1471–1486.

OECD. (1999). *OECD Principles of Corporate Governance.* Retrieved from https://www.oecd.org/officialdocuments/publicdisplaydocumentpdf/?cote=C/MIN(99)6&docLanguage=En.

OECD. (2004). *OECD Principles of Corporate Governance.* Retrieved from https://www.oecd.org/corporate/ca/corporategovernanceprinciples/31557724.pdf.

OECD. (2015). *G20/OECD Principles of Corporate Governance.* Retrieved from https://www.oecd.org/daf/ca/Corporate-Governance-Principles-ENG.pdf.

OECD. (2018). *G20/OECD Principles of Corporate Governance.* Retrieved from https://www.oecd.org/corporate/principles-corporate-governance.htm.

Ogawa, K., Sterken, E., & Tokutsu, I. (2010). Multiple bank relationships and the main bank system: Evidence from a matched sample of Japanese small firms and main banks. In C. G. & S. E. (Eds.), *The Economics of Imperfect Markets - Contributions to Economics* (pp. 73–90). Heidelberg: Physica-Verlag.

Ogura, Y. (2010). Interbank competition and information production: evidence from the interest rate difference. *Journal of Financial Intermediation*, 19, 279–304.

Ongena, S., & Smith, D. C. (2000a). Bank relationships: A review. In S. A. Zenios & P. T. Harker (Eds.), *Performance of financial institutions - Efficiency, innovation, regulation* (pp. 221–258). Cambridge: Cambridge University Press.

Ongena, S., & Smith, D. C. (2000b). What determines the number of bank relationships? Cross-country evidence. *Journal of Financial Intermediation*, 9(1), 26–56.

Ongena, S., & Smith, D. C. (2001). The duration of bank relationships. *Journal of Financial Economics*, 61, 449–475

Ongena, S., Tümer-Alkan, G., & Vermeer, B. (2011). Corporate choice of banks: Decision factors, decision maker, and decision process - First evidence. *Journal of Corporate Finance*, 17, 326–351

Ono, A., Hasumi, R., & Hirata, H. (2014). Differentiated use of small business credit scoring by relationship lenders and transactional lenders: Evidence from firm–bank matched data in Japan. *Journal of Banking & Finance*, 42, 371–380

Ono, A., Sakai, K., & Uesugi, I. (2012). The effects of collateral on firm performance. *Journal of the Japanese and international economies*, 26(1), 84–109.

Ono, A., & Uesugi, I. (2009). Role of collateral and personal guarantees in relationship lending: Evidence from Japan's SME loan market. *Journal of Money, Credit and Banking*, 41(5), 935–960.

Ono, A., Uesugi, I., & Yasuda, Y. (2013). Are lending relationships beneficial or harmful for public credit guarantees? Evidence from Japan's emergency credit guarantee program. *Journal of Financial Stability*, 9(2), 151–167.

Ortiz-Molina, H., & Penas, M. F. (2008). Lending to small businesses: the role of loan maturity in addressing information problems. *Small Business Economics*, 30, 361–383.

Padevit, C. (2014). Banken kehren KMU den Rücken. *Finanz und Wirtschaft*, 22.

Park, Y. (2008). Parsimonious lenders: bank concentration and credit availability to small businesses. *Munich Personal RePEc Archive* (9266).

Peltoniemi, J. (2007). The benefits of relationship banking: Evidence from small business financing in Finland. *Journal of Financial Services Research*, 31(2–3), 153–171.

Pérez-González, F. (2006). Inherited control and firm performance. *American Economic Review*, 96(5), 1559–1588.

Petersen, M. A. (1999). Banks and the role of lending relationships: Evidence from the US experience. *Rassegna Economica*, 63(1), 37–61.

Petersen, M. A. (2004). Information: Hard and soft. *Working Paper*.

Petersen, M. A., & Rajan, R. G. (1994). The benefits of lending relationships: Evidence from small business data. *The Journal of Finance*, 49(1), 3–37.

Petersen, M. A., & Rajan, R. G. (1995). The Effect of Credit Market Competition on Lending Relationships. *The Quarterly Journal of Economics*, 110(2), 407–443.

Petersen, M. A., & Rajan, R. G. (2002). Does distance still matter? The information revolution in small business lending. *The Journal of Finance*, 58(6), 2533–2570.

Petersen, T. (1989). *Optimale Anreizsysteme: Betriebswirtschaftliche Implikationen der Prinzipal-Agent-Theorie*. Wiesbaden: Gabler Verlag.

Philippon, T. (2016). The FinTech opportunity. *Working Paper Stern School of Business*, New York University.

Picot, A. (1991). Ökonomische Theorien der Organisation. In D. Ordelheide, B. Rudolph, & E. Bußmann (Eds.), *Betriebswirtschaftslehre und Ökonomische Theorie* (pp. 143–172). Stuttgart: C.E. Poeschel Verlag.

Picot, A., & Dietl, H. (1993). Neue Institutionenökonomie und Recht. In C. Ott & H.-B. Schäfer (Eds.), *Ökonomische Analyse des Unternehmensrechts* (pp. 306–330). Heidelberg: Physica-Verlag.

Picot, A., Dietl, H., & Franck, E. (2008). *Organisation: Eine ökonomische Perspektive* (Vol. 4). Stuttgart: Schäffer-Poeschel.

Plankensteiner, D., & Zimmermann, V. (2009). Unternehmensbefragung 2009 - Unternehmensfinanzierung – deutliche Spuren der Krise: Keine Kreditklemme, aber massive Finanzierungsschwierigkeiten - Auswertung zu den Themen Finanzierungsbedingungen und Investitionen. *KfW Bankengruppe*, 1–59.

Polanyi, M. (1958). *Personal Knowledge Towards a Post-critical Philosophy*. London: Routledge.

Poutziouris, P. Z. (2001). The views of family companies on venture capital: Empirical evidence from the UK small to medium-size enterprising economy. *Family Business Review*, 14(3), 277–291.

Pozzolo, A. F. (2004). The role of guarantees in bank lending. *EFMA 2004 Basel Meetings Paper*.

Presbitero, A. F., & Zazzaro, A. (2011). Competition and relationship lending: Friends or foes? *Journal of Financial Intermediation*, 20, 387–413.

Prowse, S. D. (1992). The structure of corporate ownership in Japan. *The Journal of Finance*, 47(3), 1121–1140.

Putnam, R. D. (2001). *Bowling alone: The collapse and revival of American community*. New York: Simon and Schuster Paperbacks.

Qian, J., & Strahan, P. E. (2007). How laws and institutions shape financial contracts: The case of bank loans. *The Journal of Finance*, 62(6), 2803–2834.

Rajan, R. G. (1992). Insiders and outsiders: The choice between relationshipand arm's length debt. *Journal of Finance*, 47, 1367–1400.

Rajan, R. G., & Winton, A. (1995). Covenants and collateral as incentives to monitor. *The Journal of Finance*, 50(4), 1113–1146.

Rajan, R. G., & Zingales, L. (1998). Which capitalism? Lessons form the East Asian crisis. *Journal of Applied Corporate Finance*, 11(3), 40–48.

Rajan, R. G., & Zingales, L. (2001). Financial systems, industrial structure, and growth. *Oxford Review of Economic Policy*, 17(4), 467–482.

Ramakrishnan, R. T., & Thakor, A. V. (1984). Information reliability and a theory of financial intermediation. *The Review of Economic Studies*, 51(3), 415–432.

Redlefsen, M., & Eiben, J. (2006). Finanzierung von Familienunternehmen. *INTES Zentrum für Familienunternehmen.*

Reize, F., & Lo, V. (2008). Mittelstand - auch kleine Unternehmen - erfolgreich im Ausland! *KfW-Mittelstandspanel 2008*, 1–101.

Richter, R., & Furubotn, E. (2010). *Neue Institutionenökonomik: Eine Einführung und kritische Würdigung* (4 ed.). Tübingen: Mohr Siebeck.

Rosenfeld, C. M. (2014). The effect of banking relationships on the future of financially distressed firms. *Journal of Corporate Finance*, 25, 403–418.

Rubach, M. J., & Sebora, T. C. (1998). Comparative corporate governance: Competitive implications of an emerging convergence. *Journal of World Business*, 33(2), 167–184.

Sachverständigenrat zur Begutachtung der Gesamtwirtschaftlichen Entwicklung. (2005). *Die Chance nutzen - Reformen mutig voranbringen. Jahresgutachten 2005/06, Jahresgutachten*. Wiesbaden: Statistisches Bundesamt.

Santikian, L. (2014). The ties that bind: Bank relationships and small business lending. *Journal of Financial Intermediation*, 23, 177–213.

Saparito, P. A., Chen, C. C., & Sapienza, H. J. (2004). The role of relational trust in bank-small firm relationships. *Academy of Management Journal*, 47(3), 400–410.

Sapienza, P., & Zingales, L. (2012). A trust crisis. *International Review of Finance*, 12(2), 123–131.

Sauter, K. (2014). Die DREI Dimensionen der Hausbank-Skala - Eine empirische Analyse über die Ausgestaltung der Hausbankbeziehung bei Familienunternehmen. *unpublished.*

Scharfstein, D. (1988). The disciplinary role of takeovers. *The Review of Economic Studies*, 55(2), 185–199.

Schenone, C. (2010). Lending relationships and information rents: Do banks exploit their information advantages? *Review of Financial Studies*, 23, 1149–1199.

Schindele, A., & Szczesny, A. (2016). The impact of Basel II on the debt costs of German SMEs. *Journal of Business Economics*, 86(3), 197–227.

Schmidt, C. (2016). *Steigerung der Objektivität Interner Revisoren: Rotation als ein effektives Instrument*. Wiesbaden: Springer-Verlag.

Schraml, S. C. (2010). *Finanzierung von Familienunternehmen: Eine Analyse spezifischer Determinanten des Entscheidungsverhaltens*. Wiesbaden: Gabler Verlag.

Schulze, W. S., & Gedajlovic, E. R. (2010). Whither family business? *Journal of Management Studies*, 47(2), 191–204.

Schulze, W. S., Lubatkin, M. H., & Dino, R. N. (2003). Exploring the agency consequences of ownership dispersion among the directors of private family firms. *Academy of Management Journal*, 46(2), 179–194.

Schumpeter, J. (1934). Capitalism, socialism, and democracy: New York: Harper & Row.

Schwartz, M. (2016). KfW-Mittelstandspanel 2016 - Mittelstand nutzt sein finanzielles Polster – Investitionsaufschwung bleibt trotzdem aus. *KfW Bankengruppe - KfW Research*, 1–25.

Schwartz, M. (2017). KfW-Mittelstandspanel 2017 - Rekordjagd im Inland geht ungebremst weiter – neue Herausforderungen durch sektoralen Wandel. *KfW Bankengruppe - KfW Research*, 1–24.

Scott, J. A. (2004). Small business and the value of community financial *Journal of Financial Services Research*, 25(2/3), 207–230.

Scott, J. A. (2006). Loan officer turnover and credit availability for small firms. *Journal of Small Business Management*, 44(4), 544–562.

Scott, J. A., & Dunkelberg, W. C. (1999). *Bank consolidation and small business lending: A small firm perspective*. Paper presented at the Federal Reserve Bank of Chicago Proceedings.

Scott, J. A., & Dunkelberg, W. C. (2003). Bank Mergers and Small Firm Financing. *Journal of Money, Credit and Banking*, 35(6), 999–1017.

Sette, E., & Gobbi, G. (2015). Relationship lending during a financial crisis. *Journal of the European Economic Association*, 13(3), 453–481.

Sharpe, S. A. (1990). Asymmetric information, bank lending and implicit contracts: A stylized model of customer relationships. *The Journal of Finance*, 45(4), 1069–1087.

Shikimi, M. (2013). Do firms benefit from multiple banking relationships? Evidence from small and medium-sized firms in Japan. *International Economics and Economic Policy*, 10(1), 127–157.

Shin, G. H., Fraser, D. R., & Kolari, J. W. (2003). How does banking industry consolidation affect bank–firm relationships? Evidence from a large Japanese bank merger. *Pacific-Basin Finance Journal*, 11(3), 285–304.

Shleifer, A., & Vishny, R. W. (1986). Large shareholders and corporate control. *Journal of political Economy*, 94(3, Part 1), 461–488.

Shleifer, A., & Vishny, R. W. (1997). A survey of corporate governance. *The Journal of Finance*, 52(2), 737–783.

Sirmon, D. G., & Hitt, M. A. (2003). Managing resources: Linking unique resources, management, and wealth creation in family firms. *Entrepreneurship Theory and Practice*, 27(4), 339–358.

Sirri, E., & Tufano, P. (1995). The economics of pooling. In Z. Bodie, D. B. Crane, K. Froot, Mason, M. Scott, R. C., & A. F. Perold (Eds.), *The Global Financial System: A Functional Perspective*: Harvard Business School Press.

Sisli-Ciamarra, E. (2012). Monitoring by affiliated bankers on board of directors: evidence from corporate financing outcomes. *Financial Management*, 665–702.

Sjögren, H. (1994). Long-term financial contracts in the bank-orientated financial system. *Scandinavian Journal of Management*, 10(3), 315–330.

Smith, C. W., & Warner, J. B. (1979a). Bankruptcy, secured debt, and optimal capital structure: Comment. *The Journal of Finance*, 34(1), 247–251.

Smith, C. W., & Warner, J. B. (1979b). On financial contracting: An analysis of bond covenants. *Journal of Financial Economics*, 7(2), 117–161.

Spearman, C. (1904a). "General Intelligence," objectively determined and measured. *The American Journal of Psychology*, 15(2), 201–292.

Spearman, C. (1904b). The proof and measurement of association between two things. *The American Journal of Psychology*, 15(1), 72–101.

Sraer, D., & Thesmar, D. (2007). Performance and behavior of family firms: Evidence from the French stock market. *Journal of the European Economic Association*, 5(4), 709–751.

Statista. (2018). *Top-100 der deutschen Banken nach der Bilanzsumme in den Geschäftsjahren 2015 und 2016*. Retrieved from https://de.statista.com/statistik/daten/studie/157580/ umfrage/bilanzsumme-der-groessten-banken-in-deutschland/.

Statistisches Bundesamt. (2016). *Wirtschaftsbereiche*. Retrieved from https://www.destatis.de/ DE/ZahlenFakten/Wirtschaftsbereiche/Wirtschaftsbereiche.html.

Steijvers, T., Voordeckers, W., & Vanhoof, K. (2010). Collateral, relationship lending and family firms. *Small Business Economics*, 34(3), 243–259.

Stein, I. (2014). The price impact of lending relationships. *German Economic Review*, 16(3), 367–389.

Stein, J. C. (2002). Information production and capital allocation: Decentralized versus hierarchical firms. *The Journal of Finance*, 57(5), 1891–1921.

Sterken, E., & Tokutsu, I. (2003). What are the determinants of the number of bank relations of Japanese firms? *Working Paper*.

Stiglitz, J. E. (1985). Credit markets and the control of capital. *Journal of Money, Credit and Banking*, 17(2), 133–152.

Stiglitz, J. E. (2000). The contributions of the economics of information to twentieth century economics. *The Quarterly Journal of Economics*, 115(4), 1441–1478.

Stiglitz, J. E., & Weiss, A. (1981). Credit rationing in markets with imperfect information. *American Economic Review*, 71(3), 393–410.

Stone, M., & Brooks, R. J. (1990). Continuum regression: Cross-validated sequentially constructed prediction embracing ordinary least squares, partial least squares and principal components regression. *Journal of the Royal Statistical Society. Series B (Methodological)*, 52(2), 237–269.

Streb, J. M., Bolzico, J., Druck, P. F., Henke, A., Rutman, J., & Sosa-Escudero, W. (2002). Bank relationships: Effect on the availability and marginal cost of credit for firms in Argentina. *Working Paper*.

Stulz, R. (1990). Managerial discretion and optimal financing policies. *Journal of Financial Economics*, 26(1), 3–27.

Stulz, R., & Johnson, H. (1985). An analysis of secured debt. *Journal of Financial Economics*, 14(4), 501–521.

Swary, I., & Udell, G. F. (1988). Information production and the secured line of credit. *Working Paper*.

Tang, Y., Deng, C., & Moro, A. (2017). Firm-bank trusting relationship and discouraged borrowers. *Review of Managerial Science*, 11(3), 519–541.

Tauber, A. (2017). *Die tickende Zeitbombe in der Euro-Zone*. Retrieved from https://www.welt.de/wirtschaft/article163557326/Die-tickende-Zeitbombe-in-der-Euro-Zone.html.

Terberger, E. (2003). The German financial system: Great institutional change and little effect? *Journal of Institutional and Theoretical Economics (JITE)/ Zeitschrift für die gesamte Staatswissenschaft*, 159(4), 707–716.

Thakor, A. V. (1995). Financial intermediation and the market for credit. In R. A. Jarrow, V. Maksimovic, & W. T. Ziemba (Eds.), *Handbooks in Operations Research and Management Science* (Vol. 9, pp. 1073–1103).

Thakor, A. V. (1996). Capital requirements, monetary policy, and aggregate bank lending: Theory and empirical evidence. *The Journal of Finance*, 51(1), 279–324.

Thakor, A. V., & Wilson, P. F. (1995). Capital requirements, loan renegotiation and the borrower's choice of financing source. *Journal of Banking & Finance*, 19, 693–711.

The Economist Group Limited. (2015). *Family companies - To have and to hold.* Retrieved from https://www.economist.com/special-report/2015/04/18/to-have-and-to-hold.

Theilacker, B. (2010). Covenants - Fluch oder Segen? *Zeitschrift fur das Gesamte Kreditwesen-Ausgabe N*, 63(10), 503.

Tilly, C. (1996). *European Revolutions: 1492–1992 (Making of Europe)*. New York: Wiley.

Tilly, R. H. (1989). Banking institutions in historical and comparative perspective: Germany, Great Britain and the United States in the nineteenth and early twentieth century. *Journal of Institutional and Theoretical Economics*, 145(1), 189–209.

Tirri, V. (2007). Multiple banking relationships and credit market competition: What benefits the firm? *Working Paper*.

Torres-Reyna, O. (2011). *Getting started in logit and ordered logit regression*. Retrieved from http://dss.princeton.edu/training/.

Tucker, P., Hall, S., & Pattani, A. (2013). Macroprudential policy at the Bank of England. *Bank of England Quarterly Bulletin*, 3, 192–200.

Uchida, H., Udell, G. F., & Watanabe, W. (2008). Bank size and lending relationships in Japan. *Journal of the Japanese and international economies*, 22(2), 242–267.

Uchida, H., Udell, G. F., & Yamori, N. (2012). Loan officers and relationship lending to SMEs. *Journal of Financial Intermediation*, 21(1), 97–122.

UCLA Statistical Consulting Group. (2006a). *Introduction to SAS - Probit Regression | Stata Annotated Output*. Retrieved from https://stats.idre.ucla.edu/stata/output/probit-regression/.

UCLA Statistical Consulting Group. (2006b). *Introduction to SAS - Regression Analysis | Stata Annotated Output*. Retrieved from https://stats.idre.ucla.edu/stata/output/regression-analysis/.

Uzzi, B. (1999). Embeddedness in the making of financial capital: How social relations and networks benefit firms seeking financing. *American Sociological Review*, 64(4), 481–505.

Van Damme, E. (1994). Banking: A survey of recent microeconomic theory. *Oxford Review of Economic Policy*, 10(4), 14–33.

Villalonga, B., & Amit, R. (2006). How do family ownership, control and management affect firm value? *Journal of Financial Economics*, 80(2), 385–417.

Vitols, S. (2005). Changes in Germany's bank-based financial system: Implications for corporate governance. *Corporate Governance: An International Review*, 13(3), 386–396.

Von Thadden, E.-L. (2004). Asymmetric information, bank lending and implicit contracts: The winner's curse. *Finance Research Letters*, 1(1), 11–23.

Voordeckers, W., & Steijvers, T. (2006). Business collateral and personal commitments in SME lending. *Journal of Banking & Finance*, 30(11), 3067–3086.

Wagner, D., Block, J. H., Miller, D., Schwens, C., & Xi, G. (2015). A meta-analysis of the financial performance of family firms: Another attempt. *Journal of Family Business Strategy*, 6(1), 3–13.

Ward, J. L. (1997). Growing the Family Business: Special Challenges and Best Practice. *Family Business Review*, 10(4), 323–338.

Weinstein, D. E., & Yafeh, Y. (1998). On the costs of a bank-centered financial system: Evidence from the changing main bank relations in Japan. *The Journal of Finance*, 53(2), 635–672.

Wen, S.-Y., & Tseng, C.-Y. (2006). Collateral, relationship banking, and corporate credit risk. *Proceedings of the 11th Annual Conference of Asia Pacific Decision Sciences Institute.*

Wenger, E., & Terberger, E. (1988). Die Beziehung zwischen Agent und Prinzipal als Baustein einer ökonomischen Theorie der Organisation. *Wirtschaftswissenschaftliches Studium*, 17(10), 506–514.

Wiemann, D. (2011). Prüfungsqualität des Abschlussprüfers: Einfluss der Mandatsdauer auf die Bilanzpolitik beim Mandanten. Wiesbaden: Gabler Verlag.

Williamson, S. D. (1986). Costly monitoring, financial intermediation, and equilibrium credit rationing. *Journal of Monetary Economics*, 18(2), 159–179.

Wilson, P. F. (1993). The pricing of loans in a bank-borrower relationship. *Working Paper.*

Wu, Z., Chua, J. H., & Chrisman, J. J. (2007). Effects of family ownership and management on small business equity financing. *Journal of Business Venturing*, 22(6), 875–895.

Yao, J., & Ouyang, H. (2007). Dark-side evidence on bank–firm relationship in Japan. *Japan and the World Economy*, 19(2), 198–213.

Young, M. N., Peng, M. W., Ahlstrom, D., Bruton, G. D., & Jiang, Y. (2008). Corporate governance in emerging economies: A review of the principal–principal perspective. *Journal of Management Studies*, 45(1), 196–220.

Zeckhauser, R. J., & Pratt, J. W. (1991). *Principals and agents: The structure of business.* Boston: Harvard Business School Press.

Zellweger, T. M., & Nason, R. S. (2008). A stakeholder perspective on family firm performance. *Family Business Review*, 21(3), 203–216.

Ziane, Y. (2003). Number of banks and credit relationships: Empirical results from French small business data. *European Review of Economics and Finance*, 2(3), 32–48.

Zimmermann, V. (2017). Kreditzugang bestenfalls stabil - Erste Anzeichen einer Trendwende? - Unternehmensbefragung. *KfW Bankengruppe*, 1–27.

Zineldin, M. (1995). Bank-company interactions and relationships: Some empirical evidence. *International Journal of Bank Marketing*, 13(2), 30–40.

Zuiker, V. S., Lee, Y. G., Olson, P. D., Danes, S. M., Van Guilder Dik, A., & Katras, M. J. (2002). Business, family, and resource intermingling characteristics as predictors of cashflow problems in family-owned businesses. *Financial Counseling and Planning*, 13(2), 65–81.

Appendix

Sehr geehrte Damen und Herren,

im Rahmen des Forschungsprojekts **„Die Bankbeziehung aus Sicht des Firmenkunden“** führen Herr Prof. Dr. Mark Mietzner und ich, Katharina Sauter, am Lehrstuhl für Finanzierung der Zeppelin Universität in Friedrichshafen eine Befragung zu diesem Thema durch. In dem Forschungsprojekt möchten wir die **Ausgestaltung** der Bankbeziehungen aus Unternehmenssicht untersuchen und dabei mögliche **Wettbewerbsvorteile** für Ihr Unternehmen identifizieren.

Wir möchten Sie ganz herzlich zur Teilnahme an dieser Befragung einladen und würden uns sehr freuen, wenn Sie die Befragung ausfüllen bzw. von **derjenigen Person in Ihrem Unternehmen ausfüllen lassen, die für die Geschäftsbeziehungen mit den Banken zuständig ist**.

Wir würden Ihnen gerne eine **Zusammenfassung der Ergebnisse** nach Abschluss der Studie zusenden. Bei Interesse können Sie am Ende der Befragung Ihre E-Mail-Adresse hinterlassen. Zudem verlosen wir unter allen E-Mail-Adressen als Dankeschön für Ihre Unterstützung **drei Gutscheine von Amazon** im Wert von 1. Platz: 150,00 €, 2. Platz: 100,00 € und 3. Platz: 75,00 €.*

Selbstverständlich erfolgt die Befragung nach den **geltenden Datenschutzrichtlinien in anonymisierter Weise**. Die Daten werden nur für wissenschaftliche Forschungszwecke ausgewertet und verwendet. Das Ausfüllen der Befragung wird etwa **15 Minuten** Ihrer Zeit in Anspruch nehmen. Die **Vollständigkeit** Ihrer Antworten ist für den Erfolg der Studie von größter Bedeutung.

Zur Onlinebefragung gelangen Sie **hier**.

Bitte beachten Sie, dass eine Teilnahme nur bis **31. Mai 2016** möglich ist. Sollten Schwierigkeiten beim Ausfüllen auftreten oder sollten Sie Fragen zum Forschungsprojekt haben, können Sie sich gerne telefonisch (+49 7541 6009-1201) oder per E-Mail (mark.mietzner@zu.de, katharina.sauter@zu.de) an uns wenden. Mehr Informationen zu unseren Personen und zur Forschung am Lehrstuhl für Finanzierung am Friedrichshafener Institut für Familienunternehmen finden Sie unter folgendem Link: https://www.zu.de/lehrstuehle/finanz-fif/index.php.

Für Ihre Teilnahme bedanken wir uns im Voraus ganz herzlich bei Ihnen.

Mit freundlichen Grüßen

Figure A-1: Cover letter

Katharina Sauter

Zeppelin Universität
zwischen
Wirtschaft Kultur Politik

M.A. **Katharina Sauter**
Doktorandin
Lehrstuhl für Finanzierung
Friedrichshafener Institut für Familienunternehmen | FIF

Am Seemooser Horn 20
88045 Friedrichshafen | Bodensee

Tel.: +49 7541 6009-1201
Fax: +49 7541 6009-1299
E-Mail: katharina.sauter@zu.de
Homepage: www.zu.de

Zeppelin Universität gemeinnützige GmbH
Sitz der Gesellschaft Friedrichshafen | Bodensee
Amtsgericht Ulm HRB 632002
Geschäftsführung Prof. Dr. Insa Sjurts (Sprecherin) | Matthias Schmolz

Prof. Dr. Mark Mietzner

Zeppelin Universität
zwischen
Wirtschaft Kultur Politik

Prof. Dr. **Mark Mietzner**
Professor für Finanzierung
Friedrichshafener Institut für Familienunternehmen | FIF

Am Seemooser Horn 20
88045 Friedrichshafen | Bodensee

Tel.: +49 7541 6009-1232
Fax: +49 7541 6009-1299
E-Mail: mark.mietzner@zu.de
Homepage: www.zu.de

Zeppelin Universität gemeinnützige GmbH
Sitz der Gesellschaft Friedrichshafen | Bodensee
Amtsgericht Ulm HRB 632002
Geschäftsführung Prof. Dr. Insa Sjurts (Sprecherin) | Matthias Schmolz

* Nach Abschluss dieser Befragung ziehen wir die Gewinner und versenden die Gutscheine per E-Mail.

Eine Auszahlung in bar ist nicht möglich. Der Rechtsweg ist ausgeschlossen.

Sehr geehrte Damen und Herren,

herzlichen Dank für Ihre Bereitschaft, an diesem Forschungsprojekt teilzunehmen.
Die folgende Befragung beschäftigt sich mit dem Thema **„Die Bankbeziehung aus Sicht des Firmenkunden"** und wird an der Zeppelin Universität durchgeführt.

Wir freuen uns sehr, wenn Sie die Befragung ausfüllen bzw. von **derjenigen Person in Ihrem Unternehmen ausfüllen lassen, die für die Geschäftsbeziehungen mit den Banken zuständig ist**.

Im ersten Teil der Befragung werden wir Ihnen Fragen zu **Ihrem Unternehmen** stellen und im zweiten Teil geht es um die Geschäftsbeziehung mit der aus Ihrer Sicht für Ihr Unternehmen **wichtigsten Bank**.

Falls Sie Geschäftsbeziehungen zu mehreren Banken pflegen, bitten wir Sie, alle Fragen auf die aus Ihrer Sicht für Ihr Unternehmen **wichtigsten Bank** zu beantworten.

Die **Vollständigkeit** Ihrer Antworten ist für den Erfolg der Studie von größter Bedeutung. Die Bearbeitung wird **nur etwa 15 Minuten** Ihrer Zeit in Anspruch nehmen. Wir bitten Sie darum, auch dann die Studie bis zum Ende auszufüllen, wenn zu einer Frage Informationen nicht vollumfänglich verfügbar sein sollten. In diesem Fall würden wir Sie bitten, eine **Schätzung** bei der Beantwortung der Frage abzugeben.

Bitte beachten Sie, dass eine Teilnahme nur bis **31. Mai 2016** möglich ist.

Herzlichen Dank für Ihre Unterstützung.

Mit freundlichen Grüßen

Figure A-2: Questionnaire of the study

M.A.

Katharina Sauter

Doktorandin
Lehrstuhl für Finanzierung
Friedrichshafener Institut für
Familienunternehmen | FIF

Am Seemooser Horn 20
88045 Friedrichshafen

Tel.: +49 7541 6009-1201

Fax.: +49 7541 6009-1299

E-Mail: katharina.sauter@zu.de

Homepage: www.zu.de

Prof. Dr.

Mark Mietzner

Professor für Finanzierung

Friedrichshafener Institut für
Familienunternehmen | FIF

Am Seemooser Horn 20
88045 Friedrichshafen

Tel.: +49 7541 6009-1232

Fax.: +49 7541 6009-1299

E-Mail: mark.mietzner@zu.de

Homepage: www.zu.de

zeppelin universität

zwischen
Wirtschaft Kultur Politik

Zu Beginn ein paar Fragen zu Ihrer Person:

Bei der Bezeichnung von Personengruppen ist sowohl die weibliche als auch die männliche Form gemeint (z. B. Ansprechpartner und Ansprechpartnerin).

Welche Position üben Sie im Unternehmen aus?
Mehrfachantworten möglich

- ☐ Eigentümer, Gesellschafter
- ☐ Vorstand/Geschäftsführung
- ☐ Aufsichtsratsmitglied
- ☐ Beiratsmitglied
- ☐ Mittleres Management (z. B. Abteilungsleiter)
- ☐ Andere (z. B. Projektleiter)

Wie viele Jahre Berufserfahrung haben Sie insgesamt etwa in dieser oder einer vergleichbaren Position?

- ☐ Unter 1 Jahr
- ☐ 1 Jahr bis unter 5 Jahre
- ☐ 5 Jahre bis unter 10 Jahre
- ☐ 10 Jahre bis unter 20 Jahre
- ☐ 20 Jahre und mehr
- ☐ Keine Angabe

Sind Sie der Ansprechpartner für die Geschäftsbeziehungen mit den Banken?

- ☐ Ja
- ☐ Nein

(*continued on next page*)

zeppelin universität

zwischen
Wirtschaft Kultur Politik

Im ersten Teil folgen nun Fragen zu Ihrem Unternehmen:

„Ihr Unternehmen" meint dabei das Unternehmen, in dem Sie arbeiten.

In welchem Jahr wurde Ihr Unternehmen gegründet?

Jahreszahl (4-stellig: jjjj): ☐

Welche Rechtsform hat Ihr Unternehmen?

☐ Einzelunternehmen

☐ Personengesellschaft (GbR, OHG, KG)

☐ GmbH & Co. KG

☐ Kapitalgesellschaft (GmbH, AG, KGaA)

☐ Andere

Ist Ihr Unternehmen börsennotiert?

☐ Ja

☐ Nein

zeppelin universität

zwischen
Wirtschaft Kultur Politik

In welcher Branche ist Ihr Unternehmen tätig (wichtigste Produktgruppe oder Dienstleistung im Unternehmen)?

- ☐ Industrie, Verarbeitendes Gewerbe
- ☐ Bauen
- ☐ Binnenhandel, Gastgewerbe, Tourismus
- ☐ Transport & Verkehr
- ☐ Dienstleistungen
- ☐ Energie
- ☐ Land- & Forstwirtschaft, Fischerei
- ☐ Sonstige

Wie viele Mitarbeiter hat Ihr Unternehmen im Jahr 2015 durchschnittlich beschäftigt?
Wir bitten Sie, hier lediglich eine Schätzung abzugeben.

[ ] Mitarbeiter

Wo befindet sich der Hauptsitz Ihres Unternehmens?

- ☐ Alte Bundesländer, Stadtgebiet
- ☐ Alte Bundesländer, ländlicher Raum
- ☐ Neue Bundesländer, Stadtgebiet
- ☐ Neue Bundesländer, ländlicher Raum

(*continued on next page*)

zeppelin universität

zwischen
Wirtschaft Kultur Politik

Ist Ihr Unternehmen ein Tochterunternehmen eines anderen Unternehmens?

Tochterunternehmen = ein anderes Unternehmen hält 50% oder mehr der Anteile an Ihrem Unternehmen

- ☐ Ja
- ☐ Nein

Wie viele Personen gehören der Geschäftsführung Ihres Unternehmens an?

- ☐ 1
- ☐ 2
- ☐ 3
- ☐ 4
- ☐ 5 und mehr

Würden Sie Ihr Unternehmen als Familienunternehmen bezeichnen?

- ☐ Ja
- ☐ Nein

zeppelin universität

zwischen
Wirtschaft Kultur Politik

Treffen die folgenden Aussagen für Ihr Unternehmen zu:

	Ja	Nein
Ein Familienmitglied/mehrere Familienmitglieder hält/halten mindestens 50% der Anteile am Unternehmen.	☐	☐
Dieses Familienmitglied/diese Familienmitglieder ist/sind in der Geschäftsführung des Unternehmens tätig.	☐	☐

Wenn Sie auf <u>beide Fragen mit „Ja“</u> geantwortet haben, dann gehen Sie bitte zur nächsten Frage, ansonsten gehen Sie bitte zur darauffolgenden Frage des Fragebogens.

(*continued on next page*)

zeppelin universität

zwischen
Wirtschaft Kultur Politik

In welcher Generation wird Ihr Unternehmen geführt (Gründer oder Käufer des Unternehmens gilt als erste Generation)?

- ☐ 1. Generation
- ☐ 2. Generation
- ☐ 3. Generation
- ☐ 4. Generation
- ☐ > 4. Generation

	nie aus Bank-krediten	selten	gelgent-lich	oft	immer aus Bank-krediten
Wie häufig wird Ihr Unternehmen mit Bankkrediten mit einer Laufzeit **<u>unter einem Jahr</u>** finanziert? (z. B. Ersatzinvestitionen, neue Projekte, Anschaffungen)	☐	☐	☐	☐	☐
Wie häufig wird Ihr Unternehmen mit Bankkrediten mit einer Laufzeit **<u>ab einem Jahr</u>** finanziert? (z. B. Ersatzinvestitionen, neue Projekte, Anschaffungen)	☐	☐	☐	☐	☐

zeppelin universität

zwischen
Wirtschaft Kultur Politik

Wie hoch etwa war der Umsatz Ihres Unternehmens gemäß dem Jahresergebnis 2015?

Wir bitten Sie, hier lediglich eine Schätzung abzugeben.

- ☐ Bis unter 1 Mio. EUR
- ☐ 1 Mio. EUR bis unter 2 Mio. EUR
- ☐ 2 Mio. EUR bis unter 10 Mio. EUR
- ☐ 10 Mio. EUR bis unter 50 Mio. EUR
- ☐ 50 Mio. EUR bis unter 500 Mio. EUR
- ☐ 500 Mio. EUR und mehr

Wie hoch etwa war das Umsatzwachstum Ihres Unternehmens im Jahr 2015?

Wir bitten Sie, hier lediglich eine Schätzung abzugeben. (Dezimalzahl)

☐ %

Wie hoch etwa war die Eigenkapitalquote Ihres Unternehmens gemäß dem Jahresergebnis 2015?

Wir bitten Sie, hier lediglich eine Schätzung abzugeben. (Dezimalzahl)

☐ %

(*continued on next page*)

zeppelin universität

zwischen
Wirtschaft Kultur Politik

Befand sich Ihr Unternehmen seit 2007 einmal in einem Liquiditätsengpass?

Ein Unternehmen befindet sich in solch einer Situation, wenn es kurzfristig Liquidität benötigt und aktuelle Verpflichtungen nicht umgehend bedienen kann. Diese Verpflichtungen können sowohl Bankkredite als auch andere Verpflichtungen umfassen.

☐ Ja

☐ Nein

☐ Keine Angabe

Mit wie vielen Banken arbeitet Ihr Unternehmen zusammen?

☐ 1

☐ 2

☐ 3

☐ 4

☐ 5

☐ 6

☐ 7

☐ 8

☐ 9

☐ 10

☐ mehr als 10

zeppelin universität

zwischen
Wirtschaft Kultur Politik

Im zweiten Teil folgen jetzt Fragen und Aussagen zu der aus Ihrer Sicht für Ihr Unternehmen **wichtigsten Bank**.

Es ist wichtig, dass Sie ab jetzt alle Fragen und Aussagen **nur auf diese Bank** beziehen.

Welchem Kreditinstitut ist diese Bank zuzuordnen?

- ☐ Sparkasse
- ☐ Landesbank
- ☐ Genossenschaftsbank (Volksbank/Raiffeisenbank)
- ☐ Deutsche Bank
- ☐ Commerzbank
- ☐ Hypovereinsbank
- ☐ Postbank
- ☐ Andere private Geschäftsbank
- ☐ Sonstiges

(*continued on next page*)

zeppelin universität

zwischen
Wirtschaft Kultur Politik

Inwieweit treffen die folgenden Aussagen auf diese Bank zu:

	trifft gar nicht zu	trifft eher nicht zu	teils, teils	trifft eher zu	trifft voll zu
Unser Unternehmen unterhält zu dieser Bank eine längere Beziehung als zu den übrigen Banken.	☐	☐	☐	☐	☐
Diese Bank würde eine besondere Verantwortung gegenüber unserem Unternehmen zeigen, wenn sich unser Unternehmen einmal in einem Liquiditätsengpass befindet (indem etwa Tilgungen ausgesetzt werden).	☐	☐	☐	☐	☐
Diese Bank führt neben der Kreditfinanzierung die meisten sonstigen Bankdienstleistungen für unser Unternehmen durch (wie Zahlungsverkehr, Cash Management etc.).	☐	☐	☐	☐	☐
Unser Unternehmen tauscht mit dieser Bank mehr Informationen aus als mit den übrigen Banken.	☐	☐	☐	☐	☐
Aus meiner Sicht besteht großes Vertrauen zwischen unserem Unternehmen und dieser Bank.	☐	☐	☐	☐	☐

zeppelin universität

zwischen
Wirtschaft Kultur Politik

Wie häufig finden Treffen zwischen Ihrem Unternehmen und dieser Bank im Jahr durchschnittlich statt?

Wir bitten Sie, hier lediglich eine Schätzung abzugeben. (Ganze Zahl)

☐ Mal pro Jahr

Seit wann besteht die Beziehung zwischen Ihrem Unternehmen und dieser Bank?

Wir bitten Sie, hier lediglich eine Schätzung abzugeben.

Jahreszahl (4-stellig: jjjj): ☐

Wird Ihr Unternehmen von einem festen Firmenkundenbetreuer dieser Bank persönlich betreut?

☐ Ja, es gibt mindestens einen festen Firmenkundenbetreuer

☐ Ja, es gibt mehrere feste Firmenkundenbetreuer

☐ Teils, teils; es gibt einen festen Firmenkundenbetreuer, aber dieser wird relativ häufig ausgetauscht

☐ Nein, es gibt keinen festen Firmenkundenbetreuer

Verfügt diese Bank über einen Sitz/Sitze im Aufsichtsrat Ihres Unternehmens?

☐ Ja

☐ Nein

☐ Kein Aufsichtsrat vorhanden

Verfügt diese Bank über einen Sitz/Sitze im Beirat Ihres Unternehmens?

☐ Ja

☐ Nein

☐ Kein Beirat vorhanden

(*continued on next page*)

zeppelin universität

zwischen
Wirtschaft Kultur Politik

Hält diese Bank Anteile an Ihrem Unternehmen?

☐ Ja, diese Bank hält Anteile von < 25%

☐ Ja, diese Bank hält Anteile von >= 25%

☐ Ja, diese Bank hält Anteile von >= 50%

☐ Ja, diese Bank hält Anteile von > 50%

☐ Nein, diese Bank hält keine Anteile

☐ Keine Angabe

Wie hoch etwa war der <u>prozentuale Anteil</u> dieser Bank am Gesamtvolumen aller Bankkredite Ihres Unternehmens im Jahr 2015?

Bitte geben Sie eine ganze Zahl (ohne Nachkommastellen) ein.

Wir bitten Sie, hier lediglich eine Schätzung abzugeben.

☐ %

	nie über Kredit-linien	selten	gelgent-lich	oft	immer über Kredit-linien
Wie häufig wird Ihr Unternehmen durch die Nutzung von Kreditlinien bei dieser Bank finanziert?	☐	☐	☐	☐	☐

zeppelin universität

zwischen
Wirtschaft Kultur Politik

Wie groß etwa war das in Anspruch genommene Volumen der wichtigsten Kreditlinie Ihres Unternehmens bei dieser Bank im Jahr 2015?

Bitte geben Sie eine ganze Zahl (ohne Nachkommastellen) ein.

Wir bitten Sie, hier lediglich eine Schätzung abzugeben.

☐ €

Wie hoch etwa war der besicherte Anteil am Volumen dieser Kreditlinie?

- ☐ 0%
- ☐ mehr als 0% bis unter 25%
- ☐ 25% bis unter 50%
- ☐ 50% bis unter 75%
- ☐ 75% bis unter 100%
- ☐ 100%

Was waren die wichtigsten Sicherheiten bzw. Garantien, die Ihr Unternehmen oder Gesellschafter/Dritte für den Erhalt dieser Kreditlinie bei dieser Bank hinterlegen mussten?

- ☐ Sicherheiten auf das Vermögen des Unternehmens wurden hinterlegt
- ☐ Persönliche Garantien wurden hinterlegt
- ☐ Beides wurde hinterlegt
- ☐ Keine Sicherheiten und Garantien wurden hinterlegt

Wie hoch etwa war der Zinssatz für diese Kreditlinie bei dieser Bank im Jahr 2015?

Wir bitten Sie, hier lediglich eine Schätzung abzugeben. (Dezimalzahl)

☐ %

(*continued on next page*)

zeppelin universität

zwischen
Wirtschaft Kultur Politik

Inwieweit trifft die folgende Aussage zu:

	trifft gar nicht zu	Trifft eher nicht zu	teils, teils	trifft eher zu	trifft voll zu
<u>Kontokorrentkredite</u> unseres Unternehmens bei dieser Bank werden bei Fälligkeit automatisch verlängert.	☐	☐	☐	☐	☐

	gar nicht wichtig	weniger wichtig	teils, teils	wichtig	sehr wichtig
Wie wichtig ist diese Bank für die Finanzierung Ihres Unternehmens?	☐	☐	☐	☐	☐

Ist es geplant diese Bank in naher Zukunft zu wechseln?

☐ Ja

☐ Nein

Wenn es <u>geplant ist diese Bank in naher Zukunft zu wechseln</u>, dann gehen Sie bitte zur nächsten Frage, ansonsten gehen Sie bitte zur nächsten Seite des Fragebogens.

Was ist die Hauptursache für den Wechsel dieser Bank?

☐ Kreditkosten zu hoch

☐ Kreditverfügbarkeit zu niedrig

☐ Gestellte Sicherheiten und/oder Garantien zu hoch

☐ Andere

zeppelin universität

zwischen
Wirtschaft Kultur Politik

Unter allen teilnehmenden E-Mail-Adressen verlosen wir als Dankeschön für Ihre Unterstützung drei Gutscheine von Amazon im Wert von 1. Platz: 150,00 €, 2. Platz: 100,00 € und 3. Platz: 75,00 €.

☐ Ich will am **Gewinnspiel** teilnehmen. Ich bin damit einverstanden, dass meine E-Mail-Adresse bis zur Ziehung der Gewinner gespeichert wird. Meine E-Mail-Adresse wird nicht an Dritte weitergegeben.

☐ Ich interessiere mich für die **Ergebnisse dieser Studie** und hätte gerne eine Zusammenfassung per E-Mail.

E-Mail: ____________________

Wir bedanken uns ganz herzlich für Ihre Teilnahme an dieser Befragung. Bei eventuellen Fragen und Anregungen stehen wir Ihnen gerne zur Verfügung.

Mit freundlichen Grüßen

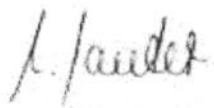

M.A.
Katharina Sauter
Doktorandin
Lehrstuhl für Finanzierung
Friedrichshafener Institut für Familienunternehmen | FIF
Am Seemooser Horn 20
88045 Friedrichshafen
Tel.: +49 7541 6009-1201
Fax.: +49 7541 6009-1299
E-Mail: katharina.sauter@zu.de
Homepage: www.zu.de

Prof. Dr.
Mark Mietzner
Professor für Finanzierung

Friedrichshafener Institut für Familienunternehmen | FIF
Am Seemooser Horn 20
88045 Friedrichshafen
Tel.: +49 7541 6009-1232
Fax.: +49 7541 6009-1299
E-Mail: mark.mietzner@zu.de
Homepage: www.zu.de

(*continued on next page*)

Table A-1: Correlation matrix – Spearman

This table presents the Spearman correlation coefficients between the variables presented in section 3.7.
* denotes statistical significance at the 1 % level.

		1	2	3	4	5	6	7	8	9	10
1	*Collateral Requirements*										
2	*Cost of Debt*	0.4491*									
3	*Credit Availability*	0.2677*	0.2453*								
4	*Finance Share*	0.4810*	0.3439*	0.2672*							
5	*Lines of Credit*	0.4857*	0.3682*	0.2854*	0.3497*						
6	*Short-term Bank Debt*	0.2525*	0.1943*	0.1232*	0.2067*	0.4579*					
7	*Long-term Bank Debt*	0.3280*	0.2004*	0.1846*	0.1763*	0.4290*	0.2251*				
8	*Number*	0.1060	-0.0224	0.1910*	0.0219	0.1831*	0.1608*	0.2442*			
9	*Duration*	0.0073	-0.0866	0.1664*	0.0426	-0.0011	-0.0026	-0.0103	0.2295*		
10	*Trust*	0.0680	0.0052	0.1598*	0.1127*	0.0690	0.0413	-0.0329	-0.0719	0.0819	
11	*Meeting Frequency*	0.1847*	0.0700	0.1632*	0.1832*	0.2141*	0.0868	0.2681*	0.1541*	0.0254	0.1266*
12	*Scope*	0.0235	-0.0052	0.0139	0.0749	-0.0686	-0.0829	-0.0745	-0.2708*	0.0047	0.2838*
13	*Loan Officer*	0.0529	-0.0553	0.0973	0.1196*	0.0285	0.0550	0.0460	0.1012	0.0162	0.1500*
14	*Savings Bank*	0.0682	0.1119*	0.0625	0.0470	0.0229	-0.0305	0.0168	-0.0221	0.1558*	0.0615
15	*Firm Age*	0.0615	-0.0446	0.2262*	0.1098*	0.0810	0.0384	0.1304*	0.3763*	0.6485*	0.0352
16	*Firm Size*	0.0382	-0.1830*	0.1977*	-0.0134	0.0528	0.0486	0.1473*	0.5135*	0.3537*	0.0210
17	*Limited Liability Company*	-0.0771	0.0022	-0.0570	-0.1026	-0.1375*	-0.0212	-0.1489*	-0.1339*	-0.1846*	-0.0142
18	*Equity Ratio*	-0.1784*	-0.2012*	-0.0633	-0.1563*	-0.2741*	-0.1727*	-0.2279*	-0.0093	0.0846	-0.0379
19	*Sales Growth*	-0.0061	-0.0292	-0.0846	0.0112	-0.0919	-0.0691	0.0260	-0.0583	-0.1855*	0.0646
20	*Financial Distress*	0.2264*	0.3136*	0.0364	0.1760*	0.2446*	0.1830*	0.2130*	-0.0551	-0.2022*	0.0051
21	*Family Firm*	0.1625*	0.1272*	0.1281*	0.1648*	0.0984	0.0682	0.1238*	0.0746	0.1325*	0.0004
22	*Construction Industry*	0.1127*	0.0749	0.0830	0.0673	0.0475	0.0298	-0.0191	0.0397	0.0371	-0.0036
23	*Trade, Hospitality, Tourism*	0.0451	-0.0394	0.0754	0.0232	0.0189	-0.0037	0.0031	0.0067	0.0414	-0.0201
24	*Traffic and Transportation*	0.0381	0.0655	0.0053	-0.0718	0.0214	-0.0019	0.1019	0.0015	-0.0167	-0.0022
25	*Service Industry*	-0.0887	-0.0436	-0.1225*	-0.0292	-0.1280*	-0.0552	-0.1104*	-0.2136*	-0.1611*	-0.0045

11	12	13	14	15	16	17	18	19	20	21	22	23	24
0.0085													
0.0907	0.0519												
-0.0104	0.1081*	0.0675											
0.1129*	-0.0986	0.0197	0.0746										
0.1688*	-0.1402*	0.1263*	0.0273	0.4806*									
-0.0690	0.0500	-0.0346	-0.0055	-0.2815*	-0.1319*								
-0.0353	0.0008	-0.0242	0.0266	0.0731	0.0748	0.0598							
0.0590	0.0421	0.0351	-0.0522	-0.1939*	-0.0682	0.0121	0.0327						
0.0947	0.0188	-0.0210	0.0007	-0.1000	-0.1661*	0.0506	-0.2147*	-0.0100					
0.0630	-0.0366	0.0153	0.0097	0.1602*	-0.0897	-0.0371	0.0275	-0.0392	0.0466				
-0.0249	0.0722	0.0403	0.0180	0.0494	-0.0075	-0.0552	-0.0447	0.0682	-0.0349	0.0841			
0.0540	0.0018	-0.0165	0.0005	0.0500	-0.0822	0.0020	-0.0316	-0.0346	0.0481	0.0700	-0.0948		
0.1040	-0.0277	0.0400	-0.0250	-0.0507	0.0530	-0.0619	-0.1436*	0.0186	-0.0088	0.0346	-0.1020	-0.0529	
-0.0911	0.0219	-0.0155	-0.0089	-0.2266*	-0.2256*	0.0785	0.0125	0.0423	0.0005	-0.1440*	-0.2457*	-0.1274*	-0.1371*

Table A-2: Correlation matrix – Pearson

This table presents the Pearson correlation coefficients between the variables presented in section 3.7. * denotes statistical significance at the 1 % level.

		1	2	3	4	5	6	7	8	9	10	11
1	*Collateral Requirements*											
2	*Cost of Debt*	0.3705*										
3	*Credit Availability*	0.2970*	0.2298*									
4	*Finance Share*	0.4795*	0.2718*	0.2974*								
5	*Lines of Credit*	0.4857*	0.2961*	0.3220*	0.3395*							
6	*Short-term Bank Debt*	0.2525*	0.1476*	0.1527*	0.2058*	0.4579*						
7	*Long-term Bank Debt*	0.3280*	0.1525*	0.1891*	0.1741*	0.4290*	0.2251*					
8	*Number*	0.0976	-0.0526	0.1832*	0.0091	0.1815*	0.1632*	0.2425*				
9	*Duration*	-0.0033	-0.1052	0.1492*	0.0323	-0.0068	-0.0053	-0.0172	0.1886*			
10	*Trust*	0.0680	-0.0173	0.1472*	0.1139*	0.0690	0.0413	-0.0329	-0.0777	0.0993		
11	*Meeting Frequency*	0.1847*	0.0414	0.1691*	0.1835*	0.2141*	0.0868	0.2681*	0.1606*	0.0373	0.1266*	
12	*Scope*	0.0235	0.0061	0.0013	0.0786	-0.0686	-0.0829	-0.0745	-0.2731*	0.0378	0.2838*	0.0085
13	*Loan Officer*	0.0529	-0.0674	0.0994	0.1158*	0.0285	0.0550	0.0460	0.0866	0.0043	0.1500*	0.0907
14	*Savings Bank*	0.0682	0.1025	0.0693	0.0558	0.0229	-0.0305	0.0168	-0.0296	0.1776*	0.0615	-0.0104
15	*Firm Age*	0.0639	-0.0759	0.2381*	0.1230*	0.0859	0.0377	0.1463*	0.3695*	0.5901*	0.0364	0.1127*
16	*Firm Size*	0.0620	-0.2099*	0.2131*	0.0038	0.0859	0.0725	0.1507*	0.5360*	0.3424*	0.0220	0.1792*
17	*Limited Liability Company*	-0.0771	0.0404	-0.0556	-0.1075*	-0.1375*	-0.0212	-0.1489*	-0.1164*	-0.1673*	-0.0142	-0.0690
18	*Equity Ratio*	-0.2117*	-0.1957*	-0.1252*	-0.1873*	-0.3034*	-0.1801*	-0.2561*	-0.0750	0.0572	-0.0411	-0.0609
19	*Sales Growth*	-0.0214	-0.0533	-0.1097*	0.0117	-0.0707	-0.0441	-0.0123	-0.0733	-0.2192*	0.0341	0.0646
20	*Financial Distress*	0.2264*	0.3042*	0.0725	0.1770*	0.2446*	0.1830*	0.2130*	-0.0574	-0.1830*	0.0051	0.0947
21	*Family Firm*	0.1625*	0.1053	0.1394*	0.1676*	0.0984	0.0682	0.1238*	0.0542	0.1225*	0.0004	0.0630
22	*Construction Industry*	0.1127*	0.0525	0.0797	0.0731	0.0475	0.0298	-0.0191	0.0389	0.0270	-0.0036	-0.0249
23	*Trade, Hospitality, Tourism*	0.0451	-0.0464	0.0879	0.0241	0.0189	-0.0037	0.0031	-0.0034	0.0451	-0.0201	0.0540
24	*Traffic and Transportation*	0.0381	0.0762	0.0085	-0.0805	0.0214	-0.0019	0.1019	0.0068	-0.0170	-0.0022	0.1040
25	*Service Industry*	-0.0887	-0.0307	-0.1322*	-0.0380	-0.1280*	-0.0552	-0.1104*	-0.1965*	-0.1452*	-0.0045	-0.0911

12	13	14	15	16	17	18	19	20	21	22	23	24
0.0519												
0.1081*	0.0675											
-0.0877	0.0152	0.0939										
-0.1487*	0.1362*	0.0037	0.4864*									
0.0500	-0.0346	-0.0055	-0.2808*	-0.1221*								
0.0221	-0.0439	0.0036	0.0206	-0.0310	0.0615							
0.0052	-0.0221	-0.0804	-0.2759*	-0.1136*	0.0161	0.0506						
0.0188	-0.0210	0.0007	-0.1007	-0.1450*	0.0506	-0.2111*	-0.0148					
-0.0366	0.0153	0.0097	0.1732*	-0.1029	-0.0371	0.0298	-0.0590	0.0466				
0.0722	0.0403	0.0180	0.0401	-0.0184	-0.0552	-0.0492	-0.0065	-0.0349	0.0841			
0.0018	-0.0165	0.0005	0.0536	-0.0747	0.0020	-0.0441	-0.0316	0.0481	0.0700	-0.0948		
-0.0277	0.0400	-0.0250	-0.0630	0.0442	-0.0619	-0.1328*	-0.0031	-0.0088	0.0346	-0.1020	-0.0529	
0.0219	-0.0155	-0.0089	-0.2203*	-0.1925*	0.0785	0.0487	0.0869	0.0005	-0.1440*	-0.2457*	-0.1274*	-0.1371*

Table A-3: Correlation matrix – Kendall's tau

This table presents the Kendall's tau correlation coefficients between the variables presented in section 3.7.
* denotes statistical significance at the 1 % level.

		1	2	3	4	5	6	7	8	9	10	11
1	*Collateral Requirements*	0.4921										
2	*Cost of Debt*	0.2558*	0.9259									
3	*Credit Availability*	0.1472*	0.1547*	0.7385								
4	*Finance Share*	0.2713*	0.2355*	0.1657*	0.8641							
5	*Lines of Credit*	0.2393*	0.2100*	0.1571*	0.1975*	0.4935						
6	*Short-term Bank Debt*	0.1054*	0.0939*	0.0575*	0.0989*	0.1914*	0.3539					
7	*Long-term Bank Debt*	0.1478*	0.1045*	0.0929*	0.0910*	0.1936*	0.0860*	0.4125				
8	*Number*	0.0589	-0.0181	0.1193*	0.0034	0.1018*	0.0757*	0.1241*	0.7745			
9	*Duration*	0.0042	-0.0556	0.1070*	0.0277	-0.0007	-0.0013	-0.0054	0.1485*	0.9729		
10	*Trust*	0.0297	0.0026	0.0780*	0.0564*	0.0302	0.0153	-0.0131	-0.0354	0.0416	0.3875	
11	*Meeting Frequency*	0.0898*	0.0394	0.0887*	0.1021*	0.1043*	0.0358	0.1194*	0.0845*	0.0144	0.0546*	0.4806
12	*Scope*	0.0117	-0.0030	0.0077	0.0426	-0.0341	-0.0349	-0.0338	-0.1514*	0.0027	0.1249*	0.0041
13	*Loan Officer*	0.0191	-0.0232	0.0394	0.0497*	0.0103	0.0169	0.0152	0.0413	0.0068	0.0482*	0.0325
14	*Savings Bank*	0.0333	0.0632*	0.0340	0.0263	0.0112	-0.0126	0.0075	-0.0122	0.0884*	0.0266	-0.0050
15	*Firm Age*	0.0352	-0.0292	0.1459*	0.0708*	0.0465	0.0187	0.0684*	0.2461*	0.5246*	0.0179	0.0639*
16	*Firm Size*	0.0219	-0.1270*	0.1290*	-0.0148	0.0303	0.0236	0.0773*	0.3481*	0.2372*	0.0107	0.0956*
17	*Limited Liability Company*	-0.0351	0.0012	-0.0290	-0.0535	-0.0627*	-0.0082	-0.0621*	-0.0687*	-0.0978*	-0.0057	-0.0310
18	*Equity Ratio*	-0.1022*	-0.1400*	-0.0379	-0.1019*	-0.1572*	-0.0839*	-0.1195*	-0.0053	0.0568	-0.0193	-0.0200
19	*Sales Growth*	-0.0035	-0.0169	-0.0542	0.0067	-0.0525	-0.0334	0.0136	-0.0369	-0.1235*	0.0327	0.0332
20	*Financial Distress*	0.1037*	0.1663*	0.0186	0.0924*	0.1122*	0.0711*	0.0893*	-0.0285	-0.1078*	0.0021	0.0429
21	*Family Firm*	0.0733*	0.0665*	0.0646*	0.0852*	0.0445	0.0261	0.0512*	0.0380	0.0696*	0.0001	0.0281
22	*Construction Industry*	0.0404*	0.0311	0.0333	0.0277	0.0171	0.0091	-0.0063	0.0161	0.0155	-0.0012	-0.0088
23	*Trade, Hospitality, Tourism*	0.0095	-0.0096	0.0177	0.0056	0.0040	-0.0007	0.0006	0.0016	0.0101	-0.0037	0.0112
24	*Traffic and Transportation*	0.0085	0.0170	0.0013	-0.0184	0.0048	-0.0004	0.0209	0.0004	-0.0043	-0.0004	0.0230
25	*Service Industry*	-0.0380	-0.0216	-0.0587*	-0.0144	-0.0550*	-0.0201	-0.0433*	-0.1033*	-0.0805*	-0.0017	-0.0386

12	13	14	15	16	17	18	19	20	21	22	23	24	25
0.4998													
0.0189	0.2665												
0.0532*	0.0242	0.4833											
-0.0570	0.0083	0.0423	0.9860										
-0.0810*	0.0533*	0.0155	0.3350*	0.9855									
0.0229	-0.0116	-0.0025	-0.1492*	-0.0699*	0.4210								
0.0005	-0.0102	0.0151	0.0482	0.0508	0.0317	0.9705							
0.0242	0.0147	-0.0295	-0.1293*	-0.0432	0.0064	0.0221	0.9186						
0.0087	-0.0071	0.0003	-0.0534	-0.0886*	0.0214	-0.1145*	-0.0053	0.4265					
-0.0167	0.0051	0.0043	0.0842*	-0.0471	-0.0155	0.0144	-0.0205	0.0196	0.4139				
0.0261	0.0106	0.0064	0.0206	-0.0032	-0.0183	-0.0187	0.0283	-0.0116	0.0277	0.2617			
0.0004	-0.0026	0.0001	0.0122	-0.0201	0.0004	-0.0077	-0.0084	0.0094	0.0135	-0.0145	0.0895		
-0.0063	0.0066	-0.0055	-0.0132	0.0138	-0.0128	-0.0374*	0.0048	-0.0018	0.0071	-0.0167	-0.0051	0.1020	
0.0095	-0.0049	-0.0038	-0.1132*	-0.1127*	0.0311	0.0062	0.0210	0.0002	-0.0567*	-0.0769*	-0.0233*	-0.0268*	0.3739

Table A-4: Probit regression – Full sample – Collateral requirements with family firm variable

This table shows the regression results for the dependent variable *Collateral Requirements* for the sample of 576 firms. This variable documents the proportion of collateral and guarantees that were required to obtain the most important credit line. For the purpose of the multivariate analysis, a dummy variable is then defined that equals 1 when the response exceeds the median sample responses, and 0 otherwise. The loan characteristics are measured by the variable *Finance Share*, which indicates the overall share of total debt financing of the firm that is financed by the most important bank. It is measured with a metric input in %. The variable *Lines of Credit* indicates the frequency with which a firm finances its business with lines of credit. The variable *Short-term Bank Debt* indicates the frequency with which the firm uses bank financing of less than one year, and the variable *Long-term Bank Debt* indicates that for more than one year. Variables are measured on an ordinal five-point Likert-type scale ranging from 1 (never) to 5 (always). The variable *Number* of banks the firm works with is measured with a metric input with integer numbers. The variable *Duration* shows the number of years the firm has worked with the most important bank and is measured with a metric input in years. The variable *Trust* indicates whether trust exists between the firm and the bank and is measured on an ordinal five-point Likert-type scale ranging from 1 (does not apply at all) to 5 (strongly applies). The variable *Meeting Frequency* indicates how often on average physical or non-physical meetings between the firm and the bank occur per year and is measured with a metric input. The variable *Scope* shows whether the bank provides most of the other bank services for the firm besides debt financing and is measured on an ordinal five-point Likert scale ranging from 1 (does not apply at all) to 5 (strongly applies). The variable *Loan Officer* indicates whether the firm has a permanent relationship manager at the bank and is measured on a dichotomous scale. The variable *Bank Type* indicates whether the bank is savings, co-operative, or private bank, and is measured on a dichotomous scale that equals 1 for *Savings Banks*, and 0 otherwise. The variable *Firm Age* indicates the number of years since the firm's founding, as recorded in the survey, and is measured on a metric input. The variable *Firm Size* is measured by the average number of employees in the year 2015 and is measured with a metric input. The variable *Legal Form* indicates whether the firm is a limited liability company (GmbH, AG, KGaA, GmbH & Co. KG) or an unlimited liability company (KG, OHG, or GbR), and is measured on a dichotomous scale that equals 1 for *Limited Liability Company*, and 0 otherwise. The variable *Equity Ratio* indicates the solvency of the firm as measured by the firm's equity ratio in the year 2015 according to the annual results and is measured with a metric input in %. The variable *Sales Growth* indicates the firm's sales growth in the year 2015 according to the annual results and is measured with a metric input in %. The variable *Financial Distress* is a dichotomous variable indicates whether the firm had been in financial distress since 2007. The variable *Industry* is a set of industry variables indicating to which industry the firm belongs, which is measured on a nominal scale, and is represented by the *Construction Industry*, the *Trade, Hospitality, Tourism Industry*, the *Traffic and Transportation Industry*, and the *Service Industry*. Standard errors are corrected for heteroskedasticity and given in parentheses. *, **, and *** denote statistical significance at the 10 %, 5 %, and 1 % levels, respectively.

Table A-4: Continued

Variables	(1)	(2)	(3)	(4)	(5)
Loan characteristics					
Finance Share	0.014***				0.013***
	(0.002)				(0.002)
Lines of Credit	0.945***				0.936***
	(0.148)				(0.156)
Short-term Bank Debt	0.049				0.048
	(0.166)				(0.173)
Long-term Bank Debt	0.482***				0.466***
	(0.150)				(0.163)
Relationship characteristics					
Number		0.217**		0.105**	0.054**
		(0.106)		(0.125)	(0.145)
Duration		-0.074		-0.074	-0.006
		(0.069)		(0.091)	(0.103)
Trust		-0.130*		-0.117*	-0.019*
		(0.130)		(0.135)	(0.153)
Meeting Frequency		0.436***		0.356***	0.035***
		(0.112)		(0.119)	(0.135)
Scope		0.072		0.078	0.090
		(0.117)		(0.122)	(0.139)
Loan Officer		0.056		0.017	-0.116
		(0.149)		(0.158)	(0.184)
Bank Type - Savings Bank		0.194*		0.191*	0.161*
		(0.111)		(0.116)	(0.130)
Firm characteristics					
Firm Age			-0.013**	-0.009**	-0.120**
			(0.084)	(0.098)	(0.113)
Firm Size			-0.093**	-0.066**	-0.096**
			(0.043)	(0.049)	(0.055)

(continued on next page)

Table A-4: Continued

Legal Form (Limited Liability Company)			-0.154**	-0.151**	0.095**
			(0.125)	(0.127)	(0.146)
Equity Ratio			-0.008***	-0.007***	-0.000***
			(0.002)	(0.002)	(0.002)
Sales Growth			0.001	-0.000	-0.001
			(0.004)	(0.004)	(0.005)
Financial Distress			0.630***	0.576***	0.313**
			(0.127)	(0.130)	(0.151)
Family Firm			0.462*	0.444*	0.250*
			(0.126)	(0.128)	(0.145)
Control variables					
Construction Industry			0.399**	0.399**	0.465**
			(0.164)	(0.166)	(0.187)
Trade, Hospitality, and Tourism Industry			0.242	0.209	0.438
			(0.273)	(0.275)	(0.323)
Traffic and Transportation Industry			0.132	0.072	0.511*
			(0.262)	(0.268)	(0.309)
Service Industry			-0.018	-0.001	0.050
			(0.139)	(0.141)	(0.157)
Observations	576	576	576	576	576
Log-likelihood	-276.935	-379.842	-354.853	-346.811	-265.875
Pseudo R2	0.298	0.036	0.100	0.120	0.326
LR chi2	234.579	28.765	78.743	94.826	256.699

Table A-5: Ordinary least squares – Full sample – Cost of debt with family firm variable

This table shows the analysis of the dependent variable *Cost of Debt* for the sample of 576 firms. This variable documents the interest rate on the most important credit line with the reference day January 1, 2015. The loan characteristics are measured by the variable *Finance Share*, which indicates the overall share of total debt financing of the firm that is financed by the most important bank. It is measured with a metric input in %. The variable *Lines of Credit* indicates the frequency with which a firm finances its business with lines of credit. The variable *Short-term Bank Debt* indicates the frequency with which the firm uses bank financing of less than one year, and the variable *Long-term Bank Debt* indicates that for more than one year. Variables are measured on an ordinal five-point Likert-type scale ranging from 1 (never) to 5 (always). The variable *Number* of banks the firm works with is measured with a metric input with integer numbers. The variable *Duration* shows the number of years the firm has worked with the most important bank and is measured with a metric input in years. The variable *Trust* indicates whether trust exists between the firm and the bank and is measured on an ordinal five-point Likert-type scale ranging from 1 (does not apply at all) to 5 (strongly applies). The variable *Meeting Frequency* indicates how often on average physical or non-physical meetings between the firm and the bank occur per year and is measured with a metric input. The variable *Scope* shows whether the bank provides most of the other bank services for the firm besides debt financing and is measured on an ordinal five-point Likert scale ranging from 1 (does not apply at all) to 5 (strongly applies). The variable *Loan Officer* indicates whether the firm has a permanent relationship manager at the bank and is measured on a dichotomous scale. The variable *Bank Type* indicates whether the bank is savings, co-operative, or private bank, and is measured on a dichotomous scale that equals 1 for *Savings Banks*, and 0 otherwise. The variable *Firm Age* indicates the number of years since the firm's founding, as recorded in the survey, and is measured on a metric input. The variable *Firm Size* is measured by the average number of employees in the year 2015 and is measured with a metric input. The variable *Legal Form* indicates whether the firm is a limited liability company (GmbH, AG, KGaA, GmbH & Co. KG) or an unlimited liability company (KG, OHG, or GbR), and is measured on a dichotomous scale that equals 1 for *Limited Liability Company*, and 0 otherwise. The variable *Equity Ratio* indicates the solvency of the firm as measured by the firm's equity ratio in the year 2015 according to the annual results and is measured with a metric input in %. The variable *Sales Growth* indicates the firm's sales growth in the year 2015 according to the annual results and is measured with a metric input in %. The variable *Financial Distress* is a dichotomous variable indicates whether the firm had been in financial distress since 2007. The variable *Industry* is a set of industry variables indicating to which industry the firm belongs, which is measured on a nominal scale, and is represented by the *Construction Industry*, the *Trade, Hospitality, Tourism Industry*, the *Traffic and Transportation Industry*, and the *Service Industry*. Standard errors are corrected for heteroskedasticity and given in parentheses. *, **, and *** denote statistical significance at the 10 %, 5 %, and 1 % levels, respectively.

(continued on next page)

Table A-5: Continued

Variables	(1)	(2)	(3)	(4)	(5)
Loan characteristics					
Finance Share	0.015***				0.015***
	(3.781)				(3.636)
Lines of Credit	0.833***				0.733***
	(6.626)				(6.134)
Short-term Bank Debt	-0.379				-0.387
	(-1.168)				(-1.294)
Long-term Bank Debt	-0.168				-0.155
	(-0.581)				(-0.536)
Relationship characteristics					
Number		-0.131**		-0.046**	-0.031**
		(-1.738)		(0.507)	(0.341)
Duration		-0.484***		-0.172	-0.101
		(-2.679)		(-0.841)	(-0.505)
Trust		-0.075***		-0.101***	-0.273***
		(-0.237)		(-0.341)	(-0.977)
Meeting Frequency		0.441		0.325	-0.081
		(1.575)		(1.232)	(-0.307)
Scope		-0.089*		-0.137	-0.132
		(-0.290)		(-0.485)	(-0.493)
Loan Officer		-0.691**		-0.524**	-0.671**
		(-1.648)		(-1.266)	(-1.755)
Bank Type - Savings Bank		0.872***		0.754***	0.647**
		(3.033)		(2.800)	(2.553)
Firm characteristics					
Firm Age			-0.140***	-0.141***	-0.002***
			(0.708)	(0.629)	(0.010)
Firm Size			-0.451***	-0.459***	-0.463***
			(-4.296)	(-3.689)	(-4.022)

Table A-5: Continued

Legal Form (Limited Liability Company)			0.244**	0.234**	0.513**
			(0.896)	(0.843)	(1.988)
Equity Ratio			-0.017***	-0.017***	-0.005***
			(-3.131)	(-3.094)	(-0.936)
Sales Growth			-0.012*	-0.013*	-0.012*
			(-1.327)	(-1.365)	(-1.309)
Financial Distress			1.783***	1.699***	1.123***
			(6.062)	(5.712)	(3.769)
Family Firm			0.469	0.476	0.185
			(1.553)	(1.546)	(0.625)
Control variables					
Construction Industry			0.310	0.348	0.356
			(0.853)	(0.961)	(0.999)
Trade, Hospitality, Tourism Industry			-1.359**	-1.365**	-1.185**
			(-2.325)	(-2.285)	(-2.200)
Traffic, Transportation Industry			0.940	0.945	1.316*
			(1.446)	(1.427)	(1.953)
Service Industry			-0.297	-0.268	-0.088
			(-0.878)	(-0.791)	(-0.276)
Observations	576	576	576	576	576
Adjusted R-squared	0.148	0.027	0.151	0.158	0.249
F-value	27.483	3.056	9.770	7.110	12.159
Mean VIF	1.38	1.09	1.19	1.27	1.34

Table A-6: Probit regression – Full sample – Credit availability with family firm variable

This table shows the analysis of the dependent variable *Credit Availability* for the sample of 576 firms. This variable asks participants to express whether short-term debt with the main bank is renewed automatically upon maturity. The responses were measured on a five-point Likert-type scale ranging from 5 = "does not apply at all" to 1 = "strongly applies." For the purpose of the multivariate analysis, a dummy variable is then defined that equals 1 when the response exceeds the median sample responses, and 0 otherwise. The loan characteristics are measured by the variable *Finance Share*, which indicates the overall share of total debt financing of the firm that is financed by the most important bank. It is measured with a metric input in %. The variable *Lines of Credit* indicates the frequency with which a firm finances its business with lines of credit. The variable *Short-term Bank Debt* indicates the frequency with which the firm uses bank financing of less than one year, and the variable *Long-term Bank Debt* indicates that for more than one year. Variables are measured on an ordinal five-point Likert-type scale ranging from 1 (never) to 5 (always). The variable *Number* of banks the firm works with is measured with a metric input with integer numbers. The variable *Duration* shows the number of years the firm has worked with the most important bank and is measured with a metric input in years. The variable *Trust* indicates whether trust exists between the firm and the bank and is measured on an ordinal five-point Likert-type scale ranging from 1 (does not apply at all) to 5 (strongly applies). The variable *Meeting Frequency* indicates how often on average physical or non-physical meetings between the firm and the bank occur per year and is measured with a metric input. The variable *Scope* shows whether the bank provides most of the other bank services for the firm besides debt financing and is measured on an ordinal five-point Likert scale ranging from 1 (does not apply at all) to 5 (strongly applies). The variable *Loan Officer* indicates whether the firm has a permanent relationship manager at the bank and is measured on a dichotomous scale. The variable *Bank Type* indicates whether the bank is savings, co-operative, or private bank, and is measured on a dichotomous scale that equals 1 for *Savings Banks*, and 0 otherwise. The variable *Firm Age* indicates the number of years since the firm's founding, as recorded in the survey, and is measured on a metric input. The variable *Firm Size* is measured by the average number of employees in the year 2015 and is measured with a metric input. The variable *Legal Form* indicates whether the firm is a limited liability company (GmbH, AG, KGaA, GmbH & Co. KG) or an unlimited liability company (KG, OHG, or GbR), and is measured on a dichotomous scale that equals 1 for *Limited Liability Company*, and 0 otherwise. The variable *Equity Ratio* indicates the solvency of the firm as measured by the firm's equity ratio in the year 2015 according to the annual results and is measured with a metric input in %. The variable *Sales Growth* indicates the firm's sales growth in the year 2015 according to the annual results and is measured with a metric input in %. The variable *Financial Distress* is a dichotomous variable indicates whether the firm had been in financial distress since 2007. The variable *Industry* is a set of industry variables indicating to which industry the firm belongs, which is measured on a nominal scale, and is represented by the *Construction Industry*, the *Trade, Hospitality, Tourism Industry*, the *Traffic and Transportation Industry*, and the *Service Industry*. Standard errors are corrected for heteroskedasticity and given in parentheses. *, **, and *** denote statistical significance at the 10 %, 5 %, and 1 % levels, respectively.

Table A-6: Continued

Variables	**(1)**	**(2)**	**(3)**	**(4)**	**(5)**
Loan characteristics					
Finance Share	0.005***				0.005***
	(0.001)				(0.001)
Lines of Credit	0.256***				0.262***
	(0.048)				(0.051)
Short-term Bank Debt	-0.177				-0.197
	(0.127)				(0.130)
Long-term Bank Debt	0.098				0.042
	(0.117)				(0.125)
Relationship characteristics					
Number		0.078***		0.015***	0.005***
		(0.030)		(0.034)	(0.036)
Duration		0.151*		0.028*	0.007*
		(0.060)		(0.076)	(0.077)
Trust		0.358***		0.385***	0.350***
		(0.114)		(0.116)	(0.117)
Meeting Frequency		0.288***		0.230***	0.091***
		(0.097)		(0.100)	(0.104)
Scope		0.018**		0.013**	0.012**
		(0.100)		(0.102)	(0.104)
Loan Officer		0.175**		0.118**	0.088**
		(0.129)		(0.132)	(0.134)
Bank Type - Savings Bank		0.093		0.091	0.048
		(0.097)		(0.098)	(0.099)
Firm characteristics					
Firm Age			0.187***	0.188**	0.160*
			(0.072)	(0.082)	(0.084)
Firm Size			0.131***	0.110***	0.112***
			(0.038)	(0.043)	(0.043)
Legal Form (Limited Liability Company)			0.039	0.055	0.167
			(0.107)	(0.108)	(0.111)
Equity Ratio			0.004**	0.004**	0.000**
			(0.002)	(0.002)	(0.002)

(continued on next page)

Table A-6: Continued

Sales Growth			0.003**	0.005**	0.005*
			(0.003)	(0.004)	(0.004)
Financial Distress			0.133	0.105	-0.102
			(0.104)	(0.107)	(0.113)
Family Firm			0.289*	0.279*	0.193*
			(0.108)	(0.110)	(0.112)
Control variables					
Construction Industry			0.234**	0.245**	0.256**
			(0.139)	(0.140)	(0.141)
Trade, Hospitality, Tourism Industry			0.377*	0.397*	0.524**
			(0.228)	(0.231)	(0.238)
Traffic, Transportation Industry			-0.015	-0.043	0.060
			(0.215)	(0.218)	(0.222)
Service Industry			-0.033	-0.018	0.048
			(0.118)	(0.119)	(0.121)
Observations	576	576	576	576	576
Log-likelihood	-370.759	-364.141	-362.230	351.133	-342.596
Pseudo R2	0.031	0.048	0.053	0.082	0.104
LR chi2	23.601	36.837	40.658	62.854	79.927

www.ingramcontent.com/pod-product-compliance
Ingram Content Group UK Ltd.
Pitfield, Milton Keynes, MK11 3LW, UK
UKHW020834290926
15470UKWH00004B/1335

9 783631 802687